ESTATE PLANNING DESK BOOK

FOURTH EDITION

Revised by WILLIAM H. BEHRENFELD

Adapted from the first three editions
by William J. Casey and
the IBP Research and Editorial Staff.

Institute for Business Planning, Inc.
IBP PLAZA, ENGLEWOOD CLIFFS, N.J. 07632

This publication is designed to provide accurate and authoritative information in regard to the subject matter covered. It is sold with the understanding that the publisher is not engaged in rendering legal, accounting or other professional service. If legal advice or other expert assistance is required, the services of a competent professional person should be sought.

—*From a Declaration of Principles jointly adopted by a Committee of the American Bar Association and a Committee of Publishers and Associations.*

CONTENTS

SECTION III. THE ASSETS OF THE ESTATE   28

SECTION IV. VALUATION OF ESTATE PROPERTY   37

SECTION X. INTRAFAMILY TRANSFERS 123

SECTION XI. CHARITABLE TRANSFERS 140

SECTION XV. TRUST AND ESTATE
ADMINISTRATION   203

*List of tables included appears on pp. 227-28.

NOTE: For a further and more detailed treatment of specific items in which you may be interested, and forms which can be utilized to implement the ideas contained in the desk book, you may wish to refer to the following IBP Services:

Estate Planning
Estate Planning Checklists—Forms
Life Insurance Planning
Pay Planning
Pay Planning Checklists—Forms
Tax Planning

PREFACE

WHAT THIS DESK BOOK WILL DO FOR YOU

The Tax Reform Act of 1976 has made dramatic changes in the estate, gift and income tax laws. In almost all cases, estate plans and legal documents will have to be altered to reflect this new law. In addition, new concepts such as the unified gift and estate credit (which has replaced specific exemptions), the unified rate schedule for estate and gift taxes, the carryover basis in regard to inherited property and other changes will have to be understood by estate planners as they devise plans for their clients in the future. This desk book shows how to do it.

Even though, in smaller estates, the federal estate tax cost will be eliminated, the income tax cost on the sale of property may now exceed the estate tax saving. Executors must furnish carryover basis information to both the treasury and the beneficiaries of a decedent's property under the new law; thus, additional information will now be required in obtaining the inventory of assets of an owner. The original cost or basis will be required on nearly all of the assets, as well as the fair market value on December 31, 1976 for marketable securities owned on that date. The dates of acquisition will be required for all assets.

Due to the carryover basis rules which are brought about by the Tax Reform Act of 1976, new consideration must be given to the use of Flower Bonds, stock redemptions and the choice of the marital deduction provision in the will. The law has also changed the estate tax on certain joint tenancies of spouses with right of survivorship, making an affirmative election necessary when the tenancy is created or the tenancy will be subject to the old "consideration paid test."

Even with the many changes in the law, there are still opportunities for substantial tax savings if the estate planner has a thorough knowledge of the law and has proper information in regard to the individual estate. The reader will find this new fourth edition invaluable in spelling out the complex provisions in the law, as well as in identifying specific areas which need to be closely examined.

This book is both for the professional estate planner and for anyone else interested in putting his or her financial affairs in order. The book explains how to formulate an estate plan which not only makes sense from a tax standpoint, but also takes into consideration the overall impact on the surviving family of the decedent.

I would like to express my appreciation to Jerome A. Manning and Sidney Trachtenberg for their invaluable suggestions on estate planning. I also want to thank Margie Strauss, without whose assistance the fourth edition could not have been done.

Special thanks to my wife, Nancy, for her love, understanding and patience during the preparation of this revision.

William H. Behrenfeld
April, 1977

ABOUT THE AUTHOR

WILLIAM H. BEHRENFELD is a member of the New York Bar and is a Certified Public Accountant (NY). He is a graduate of Boston University with a B.S. degree in Business Administration, Fordham University Law School with a J.D. degree and New York University Graduate Law School with a LL.M. degree in Taxation. He is presently in private practice in Rockland County, New York.

Mr. Behrenfeld is a member of the Estate and Gift Tax Sub-Committee of the American Bar Association and has served on the New York State Society of CPA's Committee on Estate Planning. He is currently serving his second term as President of the New York Association of Attorney-Certified Public Accountants and is the Treasurer and a member of the Board of Directors of the American Association of Attorney-Certified Public Accounts.

He has had articles published in *Estate Planning, The CPA Journal, Taxation for Accountants, The Financial Counselling Study Guide* for the American College of Life Underwriters, and is a contributor to *The Tax Reform Act, a Manual for Tax Practitioners* and *Income Tax, Estate Tax and Fiduciary Accounting Aspects of Estates and Trusts.* Mr. Behrenfeld has spoken on estate planning and related matters before professional development meetings, tax seminars and business associations throughout the United States. He is on the faculty of Manhattanville College in their Paralegal Program, where he teaches courses on Estates, Trusts and Wills, and he is a member of the faculty of the Foundation for Accounting Education.

SECTION I. HOW TO PLAN AN ESTATE

An estate is planned by assembling all pertinent information and data about an individual and his family, analyzing the assets and income and the offsetting liabilities, estimating what will be left after death has cut off his earning power and the maturing liabilities have been discharged and programming a distribution and investment schedule for the remainder that will best meet the family's needs for income and capital.

In the estate planning process, it is necessary to (1) consider how income and assets may be shifted so as to minimize future liabilities, (2) accumulate additional liquid assets so that future liabilities can more readily be met, (3) augment capital (by life insurance or income accumulation, or some other means) so that investment income will more adequately meet family needs in the future and (4) provide for the orderly consumption of capital to meet family needs where it appears that future income will not do the job.

[¶101]   **STEPS IN ESTATE PLANNING**

The series of steps with which the estate planner approaches the planning of an estate will run something like this:

Step 1: Get a complete inventory of the assets, current income and any increments in assets and/or income anticipated by way of inheritance or otherwise. List each asset, setting out its cost, date of acquisition, current value and probable date-of-death value. In the case of insurance, set down cash value as current value and face value as date-of-death value. In sizable estates that show indications of growing rapidly, estimate future values at, let's say, five-year intervals. The valuation of business interests is very intricate, and the estate planner should look behind the owner's estimate to determine whether he is undervaluing or overvaluing a business interest to any substantial degree. The list of assets should embrace those owned by each member of the family and indicate the form of ownership. Make a similar listing of income and its sources. It is very important that the estate owner make a full disclosure of all his assets and liabilities; otherwise, your eventual plan will be incomplete. It may be advisable to hold separate meetings with the husband and wife, in addition to a joint meeting, to achieve this goal of full disclosure.

Step 2: Classify assets into three categories—those that represent cash, those that are to be converted into cash and those that are to be retained if possible. The amount of cash which can be raised with each asset and the problem of converting assets into cash should be analyzed and discussed with the owner, particularly the income tax costs on liquidation of assets. After

1

determining the cash requirements of the estate, it may be necessary to go back and reconsider the classification of assets in order to decide which additional assets should be retained because of their income-producing power or which assets previously classified for retention will have to be sold to meet cash needs or be given away to reduce cash requirements.

Step 3: Estimate the amount of debts and claims which will have to be met out of assets of the estate. This estimate should include current income tax liabilities, debts, funeral and last illness expenses and administration costs.

Step 4: After deducting from the total value of assets at death the estimate of all debts and claims, calculate the estate tax liability which will probably be due (it will be necessary to make some assumptions and to make more than one calculation). You will want to determine the total tax liability which will fall due at the death of the husband and the death of his wife. This is necessary to determine what will be left for the children if both parents should die in a common disaster or within a relatively short period of time. Where estate tax liability is to be minimized by use of the marital deduction, it is necessary to determine how much greater the liability will be if the earlier death of the wife makes the marital deduction no longer available. By adding the total estate taxes and expenses and debts in both estates, the estate owner can be shown a close approximation of the total transfer cost to his children or other ultimate beneficiaries under the current estate asset arrangement.

Step 5: Schedule the liquidation of estate liabilities. Apply cash amounts from the list of cash assets and assets convertible into cash (as determined in Step 2) against the schedules of debts, claims, administration costs (Step 3) and estate tax liability (Step 4) and compute the income tax cost on the liquidation of the assets. Then see whether there is enough cash left to meet the cash needs of the family during the administration of the estate. This comparison of cash available to the estate with liabilities which the estate will have to meet will point up whether it is necessary to arrange for the conversion of additional assets into cash or to add additional liquid resources to the estate picture.

Step 6: Assign the remaining assets to individuals or trusts according to the estate owner's existing will. This will indicate how much is available to satisfy the testamentary wishes of the estate owner and will provide a basis for his re-evaluation of the dispositions he wishes to make in the light of what is likely to be available.

Step 7: Prepare a schedule showing the assets that will be in the hands of each beneficiary after distribution (determining the potential carryover basis of each asset) and show how much annual income these assets will produce. Include the separately owned property of each beneficiary. The annual income available from these sources should be compared with the amount of annual income which the estate owner thinks should be available for the beneficiary.

Step 8: Suggest methods of reducing liabilities. For example, show how lifetime gifts can still reduce estate tax liability by removing future appreciation in value from the donor's estate, and increase assets and income available to family beneficiaries.

Step 9: Show how assets might be increased. For example, inadequacy of liquid assets to meet cash liabilities or of net assets to produce family income may call for additional insurance or additional annual savings to complete an investment program.

Step 10: Show how income might be reorganized to increase liquidity or add to family assets, how the shifting of income-producing properties to other members of the family will save income tax as well as estate tax, how charitable deductions can add to liquidity, how the transfer of income-producing assets to a trust can carry additional insurance, how the shifting of dividend-producing assets to a family corporation can build up liquid assets within the corporation, etc.

Step 11: Make a new and final projection of assets, liabilities, liquid assets available to meet liabilities, net assets available for distribution and annual income produced by these assets after reflecting the steps which have been recommended to increase assets, improve liquidity and reduce estate liabilities.

Step 12: Project the increase and accumulation of estate assets until the owner's retirement age. Take annual savings, assume a conservative rate of investment return, apply a compound interest table to determine what should be accumulated at the age which the owner specifies for his own retirement. Take the cash value of insurance policies at that time and convert that into annual income. Add to this any Social Security and any pension income or profit-sharing assets which may become available at that age. Tabulate total assets and anticipated income for the owner at retirement age. Determine whether or not additional saving or other steps are indicated to provide for the owner's retirement security.

[¶102] **ESTATE PLANNING CHECKLIST**

To help you implement the procedure described above, you'll want to *make a thorough inventory,* covering not only the existing estate but also the potential future estate. This means obtaining full data about all items of property and their valuations; all obligations; the growth element in all investments; the hazard in and speculative character of any investments; the rate at which obligations are being reduced; all insurance, pension and other rights of a contractual nature; all interests in trusts; all possible future bequests. It also means getting a full picture of annual income and expenses.

Beginning on page 9, you'll find forms designed for gathering all the information you need to set up an estate plan. The data should be supplemented by copies of instruments pertinent to the estate plan, including income tax returns, wills, trust instruments, contracts, insurance policies, etc.

[¶102.1]   Formulate Objectives

In this, we must delve into the intangible aspirations of the estate owner as well as into the dollars-and-cents financial requirements of his beneficiaries. We must learn his hopes for his children and what opportunities he would like open to them, his judgment as to his wife's requirements and capacity to manage her affairs, his philosophy on how much ready cash should be made available to children and how early, whether he prefers to give children an opportunity to consume capital or to make them live on income and preserve capital through descent as long as possible. At the outset, we can best crystallize thinking on these matters by asking a series of questions calling for a definition of precise needs.

How much will be needed in liquid funds to clean up his estate? How much income should be provided for the estate owner's wife? How much will be needed to educate his children? What kind of capital position should be developed for his children and at what time? How much should be set aside and protected for grandchildren? What will happen to the family business? What kind of balance between family business and assets which do not require management, and between equity and dollars, should be developed for the estate? Apart from the family business, what assets should be disposed of and liquidated; what assets should be preserved to achieve estate purposes?

[¶102.2]   Valuation of the Estate

This requires placing value on each estate asset. The main problem usually comes in developing a working estimate as to the valuation which may be placed on the family business. In developing values for the purpose of computing estate tax liability and liquidity requirements, we can safely be a little on the high side because the probability is that the estate owner will live for some years and increase the size and value of his holdings. On the other hand, where we are trying to determine the future capital value and income potential of estate assets, we should work on the conservative side so that our plans will hold up under a deflation in values and income.

[¶102.3]   Fix and Minimize Values

The estate inventory may show assets having a highly volatile value. These will consist of such things as a family business, certain untraded stocks, real estate, oil interests, etc. Particularly in the case of a going business and untraded stocks, a grave danger exists that the Treasury will value them for estate purposes by capitalizing earnings to produce a taxable value far in excess of that which could be obtained on the market. Such a valuation may be contested, but the Treasury frequently wins these contests, and it is better to avoid them. We should therefore explore what can be done to minimize and fix the taxable value of assets of this character. Approaches to solving this problem may consist of setting up a binding buy-and-sell agreement with

4

respect to such an asset or recapitalizing a corporate structure to put most of the value into a preferred stock which is subject to more definite standards of value than the more volatile common stock, this being followed up by other steps to move the volatile elements out of the estate, such as gifts or bequests to charity, etc. We may also move to make lifetime gifts of assets of volatile value for the purpose of feeling out the standards of valuation which might be applied to them. While gift tax values will not be binding for estate tax purposes, they do give us some idea of what to expect.

[¶102.4] Estimate and Minimize Estate Tax

Project the estate tax liability as the owner's holdings and testamentary plans stand when the estate planning job begins. Then we will systematically search through and test all possible methods of minimizing that estate tax liability, checking such things as these: (a) best use of the marital deduction; (b) lifetime gifts; (c) trust arrangements; (d) charitable bequests; (e) provision for renunciation; (f) use of powers; (g) rearrangement of insurance; (h) use of annuities; (i) reorganization of business interests to facilitate tax-wise transfers.

[¶102.5] Maximize Estate Values

Explore what can be done, apart from estate tax savings, to increase the value of assets available to the executor and beneficiaries. This will overlap the estate tax saving review, but it will help if we approach the problem from this angle. The transfer of capital into life insurance is one ready method of maximizing estate values. Another is to invest in assets which are of low value now but which the estate owner expects to increase in net value by appreciation, amortization of mortgages, etc.

[¶102.6] Provide Liquidity

Take steps to give the executor and beneficiaries the liquid assets necessary to clear off estate taxes, funeral and administration expenses and other liabilities. It is imperative that we either provide liquidity to effect the transfer of nonliquid assets or make arrangements to convert them to liquid assets without a forced sale and consequent shrinkage in value. We will have to explore what can be done to marshal liquid assets and to provide a market for frozen assets. Our explorations here will cover the desirability of these steps: (a) additional insurance to provide liquidity; (b) arrangement for distribution of cash from family corporations in redemption of stock owned by the estate; (c) arrangement for sale of stock and other nonliquid assets to partners, co-stockholders, employees, other associates, profit-sharing trusts, family trusts and other sources of liquid funds; (d) arrangement for mortgage financing on real estate or other assets if it seems desirable to carry a long-term liability in order to raise cash to meet the short-term liability of death charges.

5

[¶102.7]   **Minimize Income Tax on Future Sale of Estate Assets**

Since the executor, heirs or legatees will use the decedent's basis (with certain adjustments) for assets, a determination should be made as to who may be required to sell the assets and what assets may have to be sold. Thus a determination of carryover basis must be made for each asset, so that assets which are to be sold will have the highest basis.

[¶102.8]   **Reduce Administration Costs**

If we find that the estate has enough liquid assets to meet its probable liabilities, we may arrange for methods of transfer which will take place outside the probate estate and avoid administration costs. These include: (a) passing assets by contract, such as life insurance or government bonds payable to a named beneficiary; (b) placing assets in joint ownership, such as joint tenancy of real estate and joint bank accounts (but we must weigh the savings in administration costs against possible tax disadvantages); (c) transfer of assets to a trust which carries instructions as to ultimate distribution; (d) lifetime gifts, which may save taxes as well as administration costs and may be made in such a way as to preserve necessary control and income interest during life.

[¶102.9]   **Provide Management of Assets**

Consider the arrangement which will best preserve the value and the income-producing capacity of estate assets. Should they be left to the management of the heirs, or should they be placed under professional management? What kind of professional management? What arrangements are necessary to provide for successor management of the family business and what incentives and controls are desirable to improve the chances that successor management will be effective and profitable?

[¶102.10]   **Convert Net Estate Values into Income and Family Security Terms**

Take steps to plan the income of beneficiaries, minimize income tax liability on beneficiary income and divide the net estate capital into that available for consumption and that to be conserved for the production of income. Decide whether to authorize a trustee to invade principal in his discretion and the standards according to which that discretion is to be exercised.

[¶102.11]   **Formulate Plan; Project Results; Evaluate and Test It; Revise and Execute**

Weave all the tentative judgments and decisions arrived at in earlier steps into a comprehensive plan. See how it fits together, test it against the owner's wishes, aspirations, and against all the contingencies we can think of. Revise it as these tests indicate, and then implement the plan finally decided upon by the execution of transfers, trust agreements and wills, the purchase of insurance, the completion of business rearrangements, contracts and all other concrete steps required.

[¶102.12] Periodic Review

No estate plan is ever final. It must be constantly scrutinized and reviewed in light of the owner's changing age and aspirations; his business fortunes; the increases and decreases in his wealth; his income status and that of his beneficiaries; health, accident and death in his family; his experience with and evaluation of his prospective executors and trustees; movements in the value of individual assets and changes in tax and other law.

While every plan should be reviewed at least annually, the estate planner has a duty to call for another look upon any of the following occurrences: death of a member of the family; birth in the family; marriage, divorce or separation; substantial increase or decrease in the value of the estate owner's business; changes in management; a new business venture, sale of the business or merger; retirement; son or son-in-law entering or leaving the business; a marked change in investment portfolios; a marked increase or decrease in the investments values; additional insurance coverage; death of a business associate covered by a buy-and-sell agreement; reduction in insurance; termination of an inter vivos trust; additional gifts; recapitalization of the business; material changes in the health and life expectancy of any member of the family; creation of a family partnership; improved or deteriorated economic condition of any beneficiary; receipt of bequest or expectancy of bequest by any member of the family; changes in income, estate or gift tax law; changes with respect to property, probate or investment law; material changes in economic climate.

[¶103] THE USE OF AN ESTATE PLANNING TEAM

To properly obtain and analyze the estate owner's information and prepare the legal documents necessary to implement the plan requires the skill of more than one individual. It is recommended that an estate planning team work together to achieve the desired goals. Members of the team should be the estate owner's accountant, lawyer, life underwriter, investment counselor and bank trust officer.

[¶103.1] Accountant

He will be familiar with the estate owner's financial affairs and can help in gathering the information as well as determining values of the assets, particularly in valuing a closely held business. He can work up the estate tax and income tax projections.

[¶103.2]   **Lawyer**

The lawyer can determine the legal ownership of the estate owner's property, interpret the tax and probate laws and prepare the legal documents to carry out the plan, such as wills, buy-sell agreements and trusts.

[¶103.3]   **Life Underwriter**

He will review the estate owner's insurance and determine how to best utilize the current insurance and recommend any changes which may be required to meet the needs of the estate owner. The insurance will provide the funding device to pay taxes and administration expenses and the cost of a buy-out agreement.

[¶103.4]   **Investment Counselor**

In addition to reviewing the estate owner's investments, he will make recommendations as to what investments should be changed.

[¶103.5]   **Bank Trust Officer**

By having the trust officer involved in the original planning if the estate owner is going to use a bank as executor or trustee, the trust officer will be in a better position to carry out the precise wishes of the estate owner when the bank is called upon to act in its official capacity.

[¶104]   **THE FACTS YOU NEED**

The first step in estate planning is the process of data gathering. The inventory beginning on the following page is designed to give an accurate and complete picture of a client's assets, previous actions and his objectives. It marshals the facts which permit an informed judgment as to whether his estate plan is sound or whether steps can be developed to utilize the assets and income to realize his financial objectives more effectively. With these facts available, it will be possible to project the probable growth of the estate, determine how tax liabilities against it may be minimized, estimate how much income it can be expected to produce in retirement or for the family after death, measure future needs and propose methods of bridging any gaps between future income and future needs.

PRELIMINARY INVENTORY QUESTIONNAIRE

FAMILY DATA

1. Name

	Name	Date of Birth	Health	Insurable
Husband	Harry M. Jones	9/5/21	good	yes
Wife	Mary P. Jones	11/1/24	good	yes

2. Residence

Home address   80 Gem Place, West Nyack, New York
Business address   100 Main Street, Spring Valley, New York
Present main residence—State   New York
Period of residence in present State   25 years
If less than 10 years, list prior residences:

Any other residence or place which may be considered a residence or domicile, such as apartment or house maintained elsewhere, including summer house, voting address, church membership, club membership, etc., in other state?

3. Citizenship

Husband: USA (x)   Other (   )
Wife: USA (x)   Other (   )

4. Children and grandchildren

	Name	Date of Birth	Married	Number of Children	Occu-pation*	Estim. Assets	Annual Income
children	1. Paul Jones	4/9/47	yes	2	lawyer	$50,000	$25,000
grandchildren	2. Robert Jones	6/14/53	no	none	student	$18,000	3,000
	3. Elizabeth Jones	7/3/67				—0—	—0—
	4. Judith Jones	9/24/70				—0—	—0—

*Source of livelihood of married daughter, occupation of husband.

5. Other dependents

Name	Date of Birth	Relationship

6. Special family problems

Previous marriages and commitments therefrom (copy of decree and settlement papers)

Prospective inheritances

From Harry's mother – estimated $50,000

9

COMPREHENSIVE INVENTORY QUESTIONNAIRE

Schedule A

CASH AND BANK BALANCES

		Average Balance			
		Husband	Wife	Joint	
	Bank			Amount	% from Husband
Cash		$	$	$	
Checking Accounts	Hook Ntl. Bank	25,000			
Savings Accounts	Hook Ntl. Bank			10,000	100%
	1st Ntl. Bank		500		
Total:		$25,000	$500	$10,000	

Schedule B

NOTES, ACCOUNTS RECEIVABLE, MORTGAGES

	Debtor	Nature of Debt	Security	Maturity	Yield	Face Amount	Present Value
1.						$	$
2.							
3.							
Total:						$	$

Schedule C

BOND HOLDINGS

Description of Bonds	Ownership	Number of Units	Face Value	Annual Yield	Cost	Date Acquired	Mkt. Value* 12/31/76	Current Value
New York Tel.	Mary		$10,000	$800	$8,000	10/4/75	$11,750	$12,000
Government Bonds								
Total Bond Value:			$10,000	$800	$8,000			$12,000

Schedule D

STOCKS HELD

Description	Ownership	Number of Shares	Annual Yield	Cost	Date Acquired	Mkt. Value* 12/31/76	Current Value
Dark Corp.	Harry	100	$200	$6,000	7/1/74	$9,000	$10,000
Alpha Ind.	Harry	200	180	9,500	8/1/77		6,000
Total:			$380	$15,500			$16,000

*Market Value 12/31/76 if marketable security or bond.

REAL ESTATE

	Property #1	Property #2	Property #3	Property #4
Description	residence	summer home		
Location	West Nyack	Liberty, NY		
Residence?	yes	no		
Income Producing?	no	no		
Owned in Names of:	Harry & Mary	Harry & Mary		
Form of Ownership	joint	joint		
% of Cost Contributed by Joint Owners	100% by Harry	100% by Harry		
Date of Acquisition	4/1/70	2/1/77		
Year Joint Ownership Created	1970	1977		
If joint ownership created after 1976, did you elect to treat as a taxable gift by filing a gift tax return?	—	yes		
How Acquired (Gift, Purchase, etc.)	purchase	purchase		
Cost Basis	$53,000	$25,000		
Names & Addresses of mortgagees, lienors, etc.	1st Nat. Bank Spring Valley	—		
Encumbrances: Amount	$38,000	—		
Monthly Payments	$553	—		
Annual Income (gross)	—			
Average Annual Interest	—			
Annual Depreciation	—			
Depreciation taken from date of acquisition to 12/31/76				
Annual Costs (Maintenance, etc.)				
Annual Taxes	$2,700	$ 350		
Annual Net Income				
Present Taxable Value	$75,000	$25,000		

Schedule F

LIFE INSURANCE SUMMARY

Insurance on: *Harry Jones*   Owned by: *Harry Jones*

Present Age: *56*   Health: *good*   Present Agent: *Fred Cooper*

Policy	#1	#2	#___	#___	Totals
1. Company	West Ins. Co.	North Ins. Co.			
2. Age at Issue	50	30			
3. Type of Policy	Group	Whole Life			
4. Face Value	$50,000	$60,000			$110,000
5. Dividend Additions or Accumulations	—	—			
6. Terms Riders					
7. Total Death Value	$50,000	$60,000			$110,000
8. Net Premium	—	$1,000			$1,000
9. Cash Value	—	$8,000			$8,000
10. Policy Loans	—	—			
11. Primary Beneficiary	Mary	Mary			
12. Settlement Option	outright	outright			
13. Remainderman	children	children			
14. Secondary Beneficiary	children	children			
15. Settlement Option	annuity	annuity			
16. Remainderman	children	children			
17. Amount Qualified for Marital Deduction	$50,000	$60,000			$110,000
18. Notes:					

Schedule G

EMPLOYEE BENEFITS

Employer's Name and Address *ABC Corp., Spring Valley, New York*

Type of Plan (Obtain copies of Plans)	Check if Applicable	Retirement Benefits	Amount Vested	Death Benefits	Does the plan have the option between lump-sum distribution and installment payments
Pension		$	$	$	
Profit-Sharing	✓		250,000	250,000	yes
Savings					
Deferred Compensation					
Total:		$	$ 250,000	$ 250,000	

	Company	Benefits	Beneficiary	Ownership
Group Insurance	West Ins. Co.	$ 50,000	Mary	Harry
Accident & Health	West Ins. Co.	$250/mo.	Harry	"
Medical	West Ins. Co.	$25,000/illness	Family	"
Surgical	Blue Cross		Family	"
Hospital	Blue Shield		Family	"

Stock Options: Number of shares now (. . . . . . .) later (. . . . . . .) list conditions of additional options becoming exercisable. . . . .

Give: Option price $. . . . . . . ; Current Value $. . . . .

Unrealized Appreciation $_____

Schedule H

MISCELLANEOUS ASSETS

A. Personal Effects

		Current Value
Home furnishings		$15,000
Automobiles		8,000
Jewels & furs		10,000
Collections (art, etc.)		
Miscellaneous personal effects		—

B. Intellectual Property

	Annual Income	Expiration	Current Value
Patents	$.	. . . .	$. . . . . . .
Trade-marks	. . . .	. . . .	. . . .
Copyrights	. . . .	. . . .	. . . .

C. Other Contract Rights: Give details of prospective profits, liabilities and values involved

Total Value of Miscellaneous Assets $33,000

Schedule I

BUSINESS INTERESTS

Co. Name *A B C Corp.* Address *Spring Valley, New York*

Corp. *X* Part. Sole Prop. State Inc. or Law *New York*

Partners or Stockholders Name	Age	Stock P'f'd. Com.	% Partner Int.	Title	Notes
Harry Jones	*56*	*100*		*Pres.*	
Paul Jones	*58*	*100*		*V. P.*	
Peter Jones	*47*	*100*		*Secy.*	

Is There a Business Agreement? (give details or secure copy) *yes*

Is Partner Financially Responsible?

Type: Criss Cross ☐ Date Last Reviewed *7/71*

Partnership Entity ☐ How Funded? *Insurance* Corporate Trustee

Stock Retirement ☒ Amount of Funding $*600,000*

How Is Value Determined? *Agreed Value* Any # 303 IRC Stock Redemption Planned? *no*

Is Life Insurance Carried	Insured	Amount	Owner	Beneficiary
Purpose	*Harry*	*$200,000*	*corp.*	*corp.*
To fund stock retirement plan	*Paul*	*$200,000*	*corp.*	*corp.*
	Peter	*$200,000*	*corp.*	*corp.*

Capitalization:	Par Value	Div. or Interest Rate	Total Authorized	Total Issued	Callable
Common Stock	*$300*		*300*	*300*	
Preferred					
Debentures, etc.					

Owner's estimate of value $*600,000* Liquidation value $*450,000*

Book value as of *7/77*

Is good will included in book value? *no*

Average net earnings (after taxes), last 3 to 5 years $*90,000*

(Secure balance sheets and earning statements)

Checklist of Business Information

(1) List names, ages, and duties of "key men" *Jack Smith, 43, V.P. Sales*

(2) In event of your death, or of any "key man," would there be difficulty in (a) continuing to receive credit? *no* (b) continuing franchise? *no*

(3) In event of your death would it be more desirable to conserve the business or to liquidate the business? *conserve business*
(a) Does your family have the ability to continue it? *yes*

(4) Which associates or employees might like to purchase your interest at your death or retirement (even if they are not in a financial position to do so)?
(a) Are you grooming replacements for yourself and other key men? *no*

(5) Would you like to dispose of your business during your lifetime—e.g., near the retirement age? *no*

(6) Do you have any benefit, security, or incentive plans for your employees? *profit sharing, group term* Have you considered such plans?

(7) Have you a business agreement which governs the disposition of the interest of any associate who dies? *only stockholders*

Schedule J

PERSONAL LIABILITIES

Bills and accounts payable	$..........	Installment contracts	$..........
Loans and Notes	....	Joint notes	....
Bank	..25,000..	Notes endorsed	....
Insurance	....	Accounts guaranteed	....
Brokers	....	Realty taxes	....
To others	....	Personal property taxes	....
Mortgages	....	Disputed or past due taxes	....
Current income tax-estimates	....	Unsettled damage claims	....
Rent on unexpired leases	....	Miscellaneous	....
Total			$..25,000..

Schedule K

INCOME DATA

	Husband	Wife	Others
Income sources	$	$	$
Salary	75,000		
Bonuses	5,000		
Commissions			
Dividends	400		
Interest	1,800	1,100	
Net Rents			
Royalties			
Business profits			
Annuities			
Trusts			
Other			
Total:	$82,000	$1,100	$

For Last 5 Years	1	2	3	4	5
Total family income	$65,000	$70,000	$72,000	$76,000	$83,000
Total tax	25,000	26,000	28,000	32,000	35,000
Living expenses	26,000	28,000	29,000	30,000	33,000
Insurance premiums	1,000	1,000	1,000	1,000	1,000
Available for other savings	13,000	15,000	14,000	13,000	14,000
Top income tax bracket	50%	52%	52%	53%	53%

Notes: 1. Obtain copies of income tax return for 3 years
2. Identify all items of community property income if you live in a community property state.

OBJECTIVES

I. Death or Disability:

a) What are your spouse's minimum income requirements? *$25,000*
b) What income would you want her to have if possible? *$30,000*
c) What is the minimum income required for your family until all the children are no longer dependent? *$25,000*
d) Will any child be dependent after attaining maturity? Give details. *son Robert, age 24, still dependent*
e) To what degree is wife capable of managing financial affairs? *fair*
f) Will wife continue to live in present home? *yes*
g) Should mortgage be paid off? *yes*
h) Social Security status? *none*
i) Should she be protected against: 1—possible senility,   2—possible second husband,   3—her caprices,   4—anything else?   *none*

II. Retirement:

a) At what age do you wish to retire? *65*
b) What is the *minimum* income you need for retirement? *$40,000*
c) What income would you consider *ample* during retirement? *$50,000*
d) Do you want excess of income over your minimum needs to go to your children, or to you? *no*
e) What are your investment objectives? Growth? Income? Safety? *growth*

III. Children:

a) What are your hopes for your children and what are their capabilities? *bright, ambitious*
b) Shall your children be permitted to consume capital or only income? *income only*
c) When and how should capital be distributed? *only for emergencies*
d) Should any special problems be considered and special allowances made, as for example, for physical defects, personality, ability, etc.? *no*
e) What educational and business opportunities do you wish them to be provided for, if possible? *graduate school*

Schedule L

EDUCATIONAL FUNDS

Children	Preparatory		College		Professional	
	Date	Amount	Date	Amount	Date	Amount
Robert		$		$	*1977*	$ *8,000*
Total:		$		$		$ *8,000*

IV. Gifts:

1) Do you have any plans for gifts to your relatives or others during your lifetime? *no* If so, give details.

V. Charity:

1) To which charities do you contribute regularly and how much per annum? *$2,000—church*
2) Which charities would you like to provide for, how much, and in what manner? *$500 — university*

CHECKLIST OF DOCUMENTS AND OTHER INFORMATION NEEDED

			Delivered	Returned
1)	Birth certificate—yours, spouse's, children's	1	10/1/77	
2)	Social Security Card No. 082-29-3410 Marriage certificate	2	10/1/77	
3)	Deeds to realty	3	10/1/77	
4)	Leases on property on which you are the lessor or lessee	4	—	
5)	Partnership agreements	5	—	
6)	Business agreement between yourself and associates	6	10/1/77	
7)	Purchase & sale contracts	7	10/1/77	
8)	Close corporation charters, by-laws & minute books	8	10/1/77	
9)	Balance sheets & profit & loss statements for last 5 years, in all businesses in which you have a proprietary interest	9	10/1/77	
10)	Personal balance sheets and income statements for last 5 years, if any were made	10	10/1/77	
11)	Divorce decrees	11	—	
12)	Property settlements with spouse—antenuptial agreements	12	—	
13)	Trust instruments	13	—	
14)	Your will		10/1/77	
	Spouse's will		10/1/77	
	Will of other members of family, if pertinent	14	10/1/77	
15)	Instruments creating power of appointment of which you are donee or donor	15	—	
16)	Life insurance policies & dividend data	16	10/1/77	
17)	General insurance policies	17	10/1/77	
18)	Copies of employment contracts, pension benefits, etc.	18	10/1/77	
19)	Other legal documents evidencing possible or actual rights and/or liabilities	19	—	
20)	Income tax returns, federal & state, for past five years	20	10/1/77	
21)	Gift tax returns and copies of revenue agent's reports if any	21	10/1/77	
22)	Veterans service records	22	10/1/77	

ADVISORS

Name	Address	Phone No.
Attorney R. C. Smith	500 Main St., Nanuet, N.Y.	352-7000
Accountant Steven Sneed	100 Park Ave., NYC, N.Y.	521-8000
Trust Officer		
Other bank officer		
Life Insurance Underwriter Fred Cooper	200 Shore Dr., Bay, N.Y.	821-8001
Investment Advisor		
Stock Broker utilized by client		
Tax Advisor Steven Sneed	100 Park Ave., NYC, N.Y.	
General Insurance Broker		
Others		

WILLS

Get copies of wills of all family members. Review pertinent data on present and future will plans including the following: Specific Bequests; Specific Devised; Disposition of Residuary Estate; Tax Apportionment; Marital Deduction Provisions; Survivorship Presumptions Created; Trusts; Nomination of Executors, Guardians & Successors; Authority of Executor to Continue Business.

GIFTS

Obtain pertinent data on gifts previously made including the following information: Date; Donated Property; Donee; Value at Time of Gift; Present Value; Donor's Cost Basis; Has a Gift Tax Return Been Filed?; Have Tax Authorities Examined Returns?; Circumstances & Reason for Gift; Has Donor Retained Control?; Remaining Unused Unified Credit Under Federal Law; Are Further Gifts Under Consideration? (Obtain copies of gift tax returns and any Revenue Agent's Reports.)

TRUSTS

For EACH trust, obtain copy and pertinent data including: Trustee; Date Created; Purpose; Revocable or Not (if revocable, how?); Nature of Corpus; Value of Corpus; Corpus Income; Beneficiaries; Gift Over; How are Income & Principal to be Distributed; Term of Trust.

POWER OF APPOINTMENT

If any member of the family group has the right to dispose of property not owned by him or her, be such right during lifetime or by will, details should be given and copies of instruments creating such right should be attached and the approximate value of the property given.

INTEREST IN ESTATE

Obtain copies of any instruments and pertinent data including: Is estate owner beneficiary of outright will? Trust? Does he have a life interest? A contingent interest? Value of interest $........... Estimated income $.......... Disposition if he dies before receipt? Is he a grantee of a power to appoint outside of expected class? Right of withdrawal? Portion of amount? When? Restricted? Value of property subject to right $........? Year grantor decreased? Trust created before 10/21/42?

18

SECTION II.   THE BENEFICIARIES AND THEIR NEEDS

Fitting the estate plan to the people for whom the property owner is concerned and to his evaluation of them is the first and foremost job of the estate planner. Tax saving control over assets and ease of administration, though frequently very important, are secondary to meeting the needs of surviving members of the family and other beneficiaries.

[¶201]   **WHO WILL BE THE BENEFICIARIES?**

The place for the estate planner to start his thinking, therefore, is with the beneficiaries. Individual by individual, he should go down the list, asking himself these questions as he considers each name:

(1) What will this beneficiary's financial position be?

(2) What will he need?

(3) What is his capacity?

(4) Should he get capital—and when?

(5) Can he manage money?

(6) Should he be protected from administrative and investment responsibilities and burdens?

(7) What kind of assets—education, capital, business interests—may he need to best develop his life? To take care of his family?

(8) Does he have any special legal rights? Or liabilities? Or disabilities?

(9) Are any special arrangements—trust funds, guardians, waivers—indicated to deal with these rights, liabilities or disabilities?

[¶202]   **FAMILY INCOME DURING THE PERIOD OF ADMINISTRATION**

When the breadwinner dies, it takes time to get the executor appointed and to inventory the estate. Then the executor may want to defer the creation of any trusts and any significant distributions from the estate until tax liabilities have been ascertained and met. Even after trusts are set up, it takes time for them to accumulate income. Many wills contain a serious oversight in failing to make sure that the widow will have sufficient income for her own support and that of the children during this period. Here are some of the steps that should be considered to relieve this possibly embarrassing situation:

(1) If the widow has sufficient cash and liquid assets in her own name, which, together with insurance proceeds coming to her directly, would cover the cost of living for herself and the family for a one or two-year period, there would be no problem at all. Her joint account securities and bank deposits will also be available for this purpose. In most jurisdictions, the bank account and the transfer of securities will be blocked at the death of one of the joint tenants, but withdrawals and transfers can then be made simply upon presentation of a state death tax waiver and death certificate.

(2) One possibility is the creation of an inter vivos trust which will be in operation immediately upon the husband's death and from which current income and capital can be distributed to aid the family during the period of estate administration.

(3) Most states attempt to solve this difficulty by a statutory provision which gives the widow a forced legacy, payable periodically for a certain period after death, out of the husband's property. These are the widow's awards or allowances. However, sometimes this is inadequate and should be supplemented by providing in the will that the wife is to get a continuing legacy of so many dollars a month commencing with the date of death. The executor will be directed to pay this sum each month until a distribution of a specified size is made from the estate or until a trust created by the will is set in motion to make regular income payments.

(4) Have the will provide that the income of any trust to be established under the will is to accrue from the date of death. The laws of many states provide that income earned by the estate during the period of administration will accrue to residuary legatees and a residuary trust proportionately unless another disposition is made by the will. Where this is the rule either by state law or by explicit direction of the will, the testator might further provide that, until the trusts are set up, the executor is to have the discretion to make, as advance payments of income to the wife from the general estate, such payments as the executor computes to be equal to the income which is currently accruing to the trust that will be set up later for the widow's benefit. He might further provide that additional principal advances may be made to the widow and that any such payments which are made from principal during the period of administration should be added back to trust principal from trust income after the trusts are functioning. This recoupment should be spread over a sufficient period of time so that the widow will not have her cash difficulties simply postponed, not solved. In making advances to the widow before the period for the presentation of claims has expired, the executor must protect himself against the claims of creditors to which he would be responsible to the extent of distributions made to other persons. This may be done by getting some kind of a refunding bond from the widow so that distributions made to her and needed for creditors can be recovered. The same thing is true of any advance payments made to the widow from principal which are to be recouped later from income which becomes distributable to the widow.

[¶203]   **THE WIFE AS BENEFICIARY**

A wife is ordinarily not only the prime beneficiary of the estate but also the prime asset of the family. Her death before the husband's will not only deprive the family of the guidance and services she provides but may also increase its annual income tax cost and sharply increase the cash needed to meet the cost of the husband's death. This asset status of a wife may call for insurance on her life to cover the increased cash liabilities which would result from her death.

Most states require that a specified portion of a man's estate be granted to his wife, and she is given the power to elect this share against her husband's will. The share ranges from a life interest in one-third of the husband's real estate to half of his entire estate outright. The share varies from state to state and sometimes within a given state, depending on the number of children who survive the husband. In some states, the wife can waive these rights. In others, she can't. These rights usually do not apply against insurance proceeds. Sometimes the widow's rights cannot be asserted against property transferred to the children or to trusts by the husband during his life.

A divorce after making a will may automatically revoke all provisions in favor of and relating to a divorced wife. A marriage after making a will may give a surviving spouse a right to the intestate share in addition to the right to take against a will. These provisions vary from state to state. (See the table on pages T-34a-c.)

[¶203.1]   **The Marital Deduction**

It is necessary to consider that, if the wife should die before the husband, a loss of the use of the joint income tax return and the marital deduction for estate tax purposes will substantially increase current income tax liability and the estate tax liability on his death. This represents a financial loss which it may be desirable to cover by insurance.

Property bequeathed to the wife outright or in a trust qualifying for the marital deduction will be exempt from federal estate tax on the husband's death (the marital deduction is the greater of $250,000 or one-half of the adjusted gross estate (IRC §2056)). Property bequeathed to the wife in excess of the marital deduction is exposed to a second estate tax on the wife's subsequent death. For this reason, it may be desirable to have certain property available for the use of the wife, to the extent that it exceeds the marital deduction, placed in a trust where it will be taxed only on the husband's death and not taxed a second time when the wife dies. The wife's security can be protected by giving her income rights in this trust.

If, for income tax-saving purposes, it is deemed desirable to accumulate the income or distribute it directly to children, the wife can be given access to the principal of either the marital deduction trust or the children's trust. No limit is required on her access to the marital deduction portion for tax reasons, because that will be taxed in her estate in any event. To save estate taxes on her death, her access to the capital of the second trust should be limited to the trustee's discretion, based on maintaining living standards and emergency needs or, on her demand, up to $5,000 a year or 5% of the trust corpus, whichever is higher (IRC §2041 (b)(1)(A) and (2)).

In making provisions for a wife, these are the usual guidelines:

(1) Give her all the income for her life, unless the estate is so large that she will clearly not need it all and that giving her all the income would result in excessive income tax costs.

(2) In a two-trust plan, the wife must be given all the income from the marital deduction trust plus the right to consume capital from that trust and to have income distributed directly to children or accumulated in the other trust. This will reduce the amount of the estate which will be taxed on the wife's death. She can be protected against a falling off of income either by giving her withdrawal rights or by giving the trustee discretion to distribute principal from the second trust.

(3) Whenever there is a possibility that the income from the estate will be insufficient to maintain the wife adequately, give her the limited right to withdraw capital, and, in addition, give the trustees discretion to make additional distributions to her from capital when necessary to maintain her living standards and to meet illness or other emergency costs.

(4)(a) *Trust which qualifies for the Marital Deduction.* On the wife's death, the capital which qualified for the marital deduction trust must be distributed according to the wife's general power of appointment (a general power of appointment allows the wife to decide who is to get the property held in trust). The husband's will can stipulate that the power can be exercised in the wife's will only by specific reference to the power granted; the husband's will can include a determination of the recipients of the capital in the event that the wife does not exercise this power of appointment.

(b) *Residuary Trust.* In the second, or residuary trust, the wife must not hold a general power of appointment or the property will be included in her estate; however the husband can give his wife a limited power of appointment, so she decides only how much of the trust will go to the eventual beneficiaries who are specified in the husband's will. The capital from this trust cannot be distributed to the wife's estate, creditors or anyone else but those named in the husband's will. This way, when the wife makes her last will, she can decide how the capital is to be distributed (depending on the financial conditions, needs and the instant circumstances of the beneficiaries) at a time subsequent to her husband's death. If the husband does not give his wife this limited power of appointment, he must specify in his will not only who is to receive the capital, but if it is to be distributed outright after his wife's death or continue in trust until the beneficiaries reach stated ages.

[¶204]   **CHILDREN AS BENEFICIARIES**

Provisions for children require special care. The property owner must formulate his philosophy as to when children should come into possession of money, whether they should have access to the capital or merely use of the income. If there is small capital, they usually get it outright at some appropriate age; if there is large capital, it may be considered that the income will be enough for them, or that a portion of the capital will be enough for them, or that they should get all the capital in two or three payments separated by from five to ten years, rather than at one time.

Where capital is tied up, it is important that a mechanism be established so that children will be able to get sums large enough to meet educational requirements and perhaps set up a home or get started in business. This can readily be done by appropriate capital invasion provisions, either in the discretion of the trustee or on call of the children. There are no serious adverse tax consequences as to the latter provided a single year's invasion is limited to 5% of the corpus or $5,000, whichever is higher (IRC §2041 (b)(2), 2514(e)).

Unless the estate is fairly large, it is customary to provide no benefits for the children until the wife dies. Where there is a large estate, it may be desirable to make gifts to the children during life and to set up trusts for them under the father's will. Whether the children are provided for by gift, bequests, trusts created directly for them under the will, or distributions from a trust created for their mother after her death, there is the problem of when to make the funds available to the children and whether to take advantage (in the estate of the surviving spouse) of the orphan's exclusion. Where property is left to the child, there is a limited deduction of up to $5000 per child for each year between the child's age at the death of the surviving parent and his achieving the age of 21. A decision is necessary as to whether it is healthy and wholesome to permit the children to come into substantial funds at 21, or is it better to have the funds conserved until a more mature age and more experience are attained? Should all the funds be made available at once? Or is it safer to distribute the funds in two or three installments? Using the multiple distribution, if they are going to lose the money they will not be able to lose it all at once, and it is possible they might gain some experience from their first financial disaster.

Some parents want to have the child's share held in trust for life so that they would control who gets the property after the child's death and in order to save estate tax on his death. It is doubtful whether either of these reasons is good enough to keep property tied up in trust for a child's life so that the child will never be able to use anything but the income from the property.

It will be necessary to decide whether all children are to be treated alike. A parent usually spends funds in accordance with the needs of the children, making no attempt to equalize the amount spent for education, medical care and such things. By postponing a division of the estate into separate shares until the youngest living child reaches a designated age and by directing that, until that time, income and principal shall be used for the benefit of the children in accordance with their needs in amounts not necessarily equal, the practical situation can remain the same after the parent's death as before. This plan is particularly sensible where the estate is modest and the children are young. Another way to accomplish this result is to permit the estate to be divided into separate shares but to direct that specified expenditures for any one child such as medical and educational expenses be charged equally against all shares rather than against the share of the particular child benefited by the expenditures.

There are other problems with children arising from the special protection which the law gives them and from the many different kinds of children that can exist—grandchildren, stepchildren, adopted children, illegitimate children and posthumous children. (A posthumous child is one born after the death of a parent and generally inherits along with the other children under a broad provision in a will or in intestacy.)

In most states, the law provides that when a child is born after the will is executed, the child is entitled to his intestate share just as if no will had been drawn. In certain states, an afterborn child may result in the revocation of a will. Usually, however, any mention of children as a class in the will circumvents this problem. (See the table on pages T-34a-c.)

Most states recognize that adopted children have the same rights as children born of the marriage. However, the protection given to children in wills is not always accorded in life insurance beneficiary arrangements. If a father neglects to change his life insurance beneficiary arrangements after a child is born or if he dies while his wife is pregnant, the child will not receive any of the proceeds. Similarly, unless an adopted child is specifically named as the beneficiary, he will not receive any insurance proceeds.

In most states, illegitimate children inherit from their mother but not from their father unless his parenthood is formally recognized. Again, this protection does not follow over into life insurance.

The draftsman should be careful to see that the will is written in accordance with the estate owner's wishes in regard to all children. Although state law frequently makes provision for afterborn children and creates a presumption for adopted children, these should not be enough for the careful draftsman since there is always the possibility that the testator may move to another state. Cover the status of these children expressly.

The kind of provisions which should be made for children would depend upon the parents' analysis of their character, capabilities and objectives in life.

[¶205]　　　**THE INCOMPETENT CHILD**

The problem of providing for an incompetent child is one of custody and adequate financial provision for life. This overriding requirement may call for all the capital the parents have been able to amass. There may not be enough capital to provide lifetime assurance and this may suggest the possibility of public institutional care at some point. This may call for a change of residence so that the parent can assure himself that the most satisfactory public institution will be available to the child if that should ultimately be necessary.

Where there are enough funds, a trust should be created to provide maintenance, including institutional care. The important thing is to provide independent financial support for an incompetent or possibly incompetent child, not only to assure the child's security but to remove the burden from the siblings; this is in the incompetent's interest as well as that of the siblings. It is especially important that a guardian or committee be appointed to control the incompetent's money.

[¶206]   **GRANDCHILDREN AS BENEFICIARIES**

The problems of income provision and capital distribution are the same for grandchildren as for children; however, there is frequently a problem of how best to spread out the family wealth among grandchildren after their parents, the grandparent's children, die. The usual provision is that, on the death of children, property held in trust for them should be distributed "in equal parts per stirpes." This provision divides the property into as many equal parts as there are children living or children dead with issue living, with one part passing to each living child and one part passing to the issue, collectively, of each deceased child. A per stirpes distribution treats each branch of the family equally.

It may be more equitable to provide for a per capita distribution that gives an equal amount to each individual grandchild. Thus, if there are two children, one of them having only one child and the other having five, a per stirpes distribution will make one of the six grandchildren five times richer than the other five. A per capita distribution would give them all an equal amount. The problem of afterborn grandchildren and of some children living much longer than others and thus keeping property put in trust for them tied up that much longer makes a per capita distribution very complicated to work out, which may account for the greater popularity of the per stirpes distribution. However, careful draftsmanship can work out satisfactory per capita arrangements.

[¶207]   **GUARDIANSHIP**

When property is left to a minor, he can't get the property himself. Neither the bank holding the parent's bank account, the corporation which has issued stock owned by either parent nor the executor or administrator of the parent's estate can make payment to a minor. Transfer of the property to a person under 21 (from 18 to 20 in some states) may be made to him only if a guardian is appointed by the court for his benefit. Unless husband and wife select a guardian to take their place in the event both should die, the court will have to appoint one without their help.

Guardianship has two aspects: (1) Who is to have personal control of the minor? (2) Who is to manage the minor's property? Both functions may be joined in the same person, or a separate guardian of the person and a guardian of the property may be appointed. Neither parent can appoint a guardian of the person of the child other than the surviving spouse, unless the survivor is incompetent or otherwise clearly incapable or unfit. But the first spouse to die, like any other person, can appoint anyone as guardian of the property which he leaves to the child. The surviving spouse will generally have the right to designate a guardian in his or her will, of both the property and the person of the child.

If the parents make no such appointment or appoint different persons and die in a common disaster, the probate court will appoint the guardian. The child then becomes a ward of the court, and the court will determine which appointment will best serve the welfare of the child and select the guardian accordingly, with next-of-kin ordinarily given preference. Frequently, the same person will be appointed guardian of both the person and the property, but sometimes a separation of these functions is justified. For example, an aunt of the child might clearly be the right choice to be guardian of the person, but she may be so inexperienced in investment and finances that another person will be appointed guardian of the property.

The selection of the guardian is a matter which should be given very careful attention and not overlooked. The assumption is that the surviving spouse will perform the function and while this is correct as far as it goes, it fails when both parents die in a common disaster or the surviving parent fails to consider the problem and neglects to designate a guardian. Not only should the selection of the guardian be given careful thought before the selection is made but the matter should be discussed with the prospective guardian. It is advisable for an alternate or successor guardian to be named in case the first one is dead, declines to act or undertakes the responsibility and later wants to resign or is unable to complete the work.

The rules concerning guardianship vary from state to state. The handling of property by a guardian is always a cumbersome and expensive process. Unless the will exempts an individual named as guardian, he will generally be required to provide bond either by putting up his own property or buying a surety bond which will constitute a charge against the infant's property (a bank is not usually required to post a bond, but most banks are unwilling to act as guardian of the person). The guardian must meet the expense of periodic accounts out of the infant's property.

The consent of the court is usually required before any of the child's money is spent; and if the guardian is a parent, the court will not permit the use of any of the infant's funds if the parent has the means to support the child. However, if a widowed mother is a guardian and has insufficient means of her own, a court may permit an invasion of the infant's property to permit the mother to maintain a home for the child.

On occasion an uncle or aunt is expected to take care of a child after the death of the parents without consideration being given to the financial burden that it will represent. It may mean a larger house, it will almost certainly mean expenses over and above those which the court will allow on behalf of the child. This should be faced, discussed and, where possible, covered with an adequate financial provision of some kind for the putative guardian.

There is one way to avoid all the red tape which goes with guardianship; the will can authorize either an executor or trustee to hold the property and to administer it as though he were a guardian. The best way is to put the property in trust for the infant and to give the trustee the right to pay the income and a portion of the principal when needed for support directly to the child, to his personal guardian, to the person with whom he lives or to others for the benefit of the child; the trustee can then be given the power to accumulate any balance which is not needed for the child's care. The trustee should be given this power with respect to any portion of a trust fund which, by virtue of the death of prior beneficiaries or otherwise, becomes distributable to an infant.

[¶208] ## PARENTS OR OTHER ELDER MEMBERS OF THE FAMILY

Frequently a property owner will have been making regular contributions to (or otherwise supporting) his parents or uncle or aunts or older siblings, and may want to continue this support after his death. This can be done by having the will provide for income payments, or by setting up a trust to last for the duration of the beneficiary's life, with the property reverting to the property owner's wife or children or a trust set up for them. Or, if there are trusts set up by the will, it can be directed that these trusts pay out the required income. It is sometimes desirable to direct or authorize the executor to buy an annuity to continue payments to a relative, which can avoid tieing up the estate for the rest of the relative's life in some instances.

The least expensive way of providing for elderly relatives may be a short-term trust. Or, where it's desirable to retain a dependency exemption, the mere purchase of tax-exempt bonds may do the trick. See ¶1407.

[¶209] ## THE FORGOTTEN WOMAN

A former surrogate of New York applied this term to daughters-in-law; sons-in-law are much less of a problem, but sometimes there is a lot of money from a mother's side which has accustomed the children to a certain kind of living which will make it difficult for the son-in-law if his wife should die and her share of the family money should be placed in trust for the children.

The acute problem is with the daughter-in-law. Grandfather will provide that the father will have the income from the trust for life, and upon his death the principal is to go to his children, with the daughter-in-law completely by-passed. When her husband dies, therefore, she must rely on her children for support. If they are infants, she must act under cumbersome red tape and expensive bond as their guardian and go to court to obtain annual decrees permitting her to make modest use of the children's funds for their mainte-nance and her own. Then when the children come of age, she is no longer entitled to any relief from the court and becomes wholly dependent on her children and on her own earning capacity.

The best way to deal with this problem is to give the son a limited power of appointment over a portion of the trust so that he can make appropriate provisions for his wife. Make sure that he knows about the existence of the power of appointment and prod him into making proper use of it. In addition, grandfather can provide for maintenance of his daughter-in-law while her family is growing up when he provides for his son and grandchildren in his own will. The important thing is to provide something for the daughter-in-law after the grandchildren, her own children, have attained their majorities so that she is protected from being entirely dependent on them.

SECTION III.   THE ASSETS OF
THE ESTATE

After getting an understanding of the beneficiaries and their needs, the next step is to analyze the assets available to meet their needs—and to consider the possibility of creating additional assets by converting present investments or income into additional life insurance.

In analyzing the assets item by item, we will consider their liquidity (see the table on page T-21), their income-producing capacity, the valuation problems they present, their investment qualities, the special problems they might create for the estate, the special testamentary instructions which might be called for and the authority which the executor and trustee should be given in order to manage each specific asset.

[¶301]   **TANGIBLE PERSONAL PROPERTY**

Personal property will be part of the taxable estate. If personal property which might be included in the estate really belongs to somebody else, steps should be taken to make the real ownership clear. In some states, there is a presumption that furniture in a house owned or rented by the husband belongs to him. If in fact it belongs to the wife, recitations in the will and a record showing the true ownership should be enough to make its ownership clear (evidence of gifts from the wife's family, bills or checks showing payment by the wife, etc.).

Always dispose of the personal property by separate will provisions. Section 662 provides that all amounts distributed to the beneficiary for the taxable year shall be included in the gross income of the beneficiary to the extent of the distributable net income of the estate. Section 663 excludes from this rule any amount which, under the terms of the will, is distributed as a gift of specific property and which is distributed all at once or in not more than three installments. Thus, by separately disposing of the tangible personal property in the will and calling for its distribution to specified legatees all at once, we avoid having this distribution taxed as income to the legatee to the extent of income of the estate.

In disposing of personal property, it is advisable to mention specifically those items of personal property which may have special value. We should say, "including automobiles, together with all insurance on such property."

Careful provision for the person to whom personal property is to go can avoid a lot of headaches for the executor. If the gift is to a class of children or persons, the testator's children for example, it may be enough to make it a simple class gift and allow the members of the class to make whatever division they desire. If it is possible that the class of beneficiaries may be unable to agree on a division, add a provision that, if there is no agreement, the property is to be divided among the class in substantially equal proportions by the executor. A more complicated method is to provide that a division is to be made by giving the members of the class alternate choices until all the property has been taken.

A simple and frequently satisfactory method is for the will to give all the testator's tangible personal property to a single member of the family or a friend in whom he has confidence, with a precatory request that the articles are to be distributed as the designated individual believes the testator would wish or to persons whom the testator has subsequently designated. (A subsequent letter or list has no binding power unless executed and proved as a codicil.) The testator may be satisfied that the individual he names, while having no legal obligation to distribute the articles in any specified manner, or to distribute them at all, may nevertheless be the best vehicle for dealing with a shifting class of beneficiaries.

Points to remember: where personal property is to be given to a minor, provision should be made for its delivery to a designated adult; the bequest of personal property to a trust requires the trustee to sell it and get income out of the proceeds; unless the will provides that all inheritance and estate taxes on tangible personal property are to be paid out of the residuary estate, the executor may have to collect a proportionate part of the tax from each legatee.

[¶302]   **BANK ACCOUNTS AND SECURITIES**

In getting a list of securities owned, check to see that they are registered properly in order to avoid confusion after death. Make sure that securities or a bank account held as nominee or in any fiduciary or agency capacity are clearly indicated and that the real interest of the parties involved is stated in writing. Have the securities kept in one place, preferably in the state of domicile, to avoid possible double taxation and requirements of ancillary administration. For the same reason, it is desirable to maintain all bank accounts in the state of domicile.

In reviewing the security portfolio, consider eliminating those which may present troublesome valuation problems. If there are any notes of children or other members of the family, determine whether they are to be forgiven, collected or set off against a legacy.

[¶303]   **DEBTS AND OBLIGATIONS**

It is important to get complete information about the obligations of the estate owner. This information is necessary to estimate death taxes, liquidity requirements and the value of the estate remaining after administration.

In the case of a mortgage debt or any other debt which is a lien on real estate or other property which is specifically bequeathed, it is vital to determine whether the beneficiary is to receive the property subject to the lien or not. In some states, the law provides that in the absence of a specific direction to the contrary, the devisee of real estate subject to a mortgage takes subject to the mortgage.

Be careful about the usual general provision calling for payment of all debts. Does the testator really mean that he wants the mortgage on his home, for example, paid off? In some states, an insurance beneficiary may have a claim against a decedent's estate for the amount of a debt which was paid from the proceeds of a life insurance policy placed as collateral for the debt; provisions for handling this type of debt should be specifically spelled out in the will.

[¶304]   **REAL ESTATE**

If the family is to continue to live in the family residence after the husband's death, it is best to leave it outright to the widow or to the children if they are of age. It's important to determine the state law with respect to any mortgage on the real estate and to provide whether or not the real estate is devised free and clear of the mortgage and whether or not the executor is to leave the mortgage outstanding or pay it off.

Real estate should not be left outright to a minor because of complications in selling it. It's better to leave real estate in trust for a minor until he reaches majority, or later.

Where a house is put in trust and the income beneficiary of the trust is to live in the property, specify that the right of occupancy is to be free of rent. (This avoids requiring the beneficiary to pay rent to the trustee and then take it back as taxable income.) Where real estate is put in trust, the will should specify who is to pay taxes, insurance premiums, repair bills, and other carrying charges; whether or not improvements should be made; and under what conditions the real estate can be sold. The will should either set up a fund to pay the expenses or give the trustee enough power either to force the beneficiary to pay the expenses or sell or mortgage the property.

With respect to real estate other than the family residence, it is important that the estate not be burdened with the carrying charge of unproductive real estate, and authorization or direction to sell unproductive real estate should be provided.

[¶305]   **REAL ESTATE SYNDICATE INTERESTS**

If the estate owner is a participant in one or more real estate syndicates (usually of the limited partnership variety), special provisions should be inserted in his will:

(1) The executor should be authorized to comply with all the terms and provisions of the syndicate agreement and to execute and deliver to the general partners the requisite designation of a successor to the estate owner's

interest. (A similar authorization, except for the designation of a successor, should be given to any testamentary trustee.)

(2) Fiduciaries should be empowered to vote and exercise all rights and also to execute all required consents in regard to such property, just as if they were the absolute owners.

(3) If such property is not specifically bequeathed, then it might be a good idea to authorize the executor to make distributions in kind.

(4) Where an interest in a real estate syndication is to be used as corpus in a trust, the trustees can be directed to allocate all distributions to income if this is the estate owner's desire, regardless of the fact that a portion of such distributions may be a return of capital for accounting and tax purposes. Also to be considered is the question of whether or not to treat mortgage amortization payments as income.

[¶306]   **FARMS**

A farm asset has the attributes of real estate and of a business. In transferring a farm by will or deed of trust, the draftsman must deal with land, buildings, machinery, equipment, livestock, accounts receivable, bank accounts, insurance policies, crops, real estate mortgages, etc. If the farm is incorporated, all these assets are reflected in the shares of stock and the problem is greatly simplified. In addition, there may be income tax saving and capital-building opportunities in the incorporation of the farm.

In devising farm land, it is necessary to decide whether the devisee is to be exonerated for mortgage debt from the balance of the testator's estate. In some states, unless he is explicitly made responsible for the mortgage debt, this will occur. (In any event, the burden of the mortgage debt should be explicitly fixed.) Also specify whether debts incurred in connection with the improvement of buildings or the purchase of equipment are to be assumed by the devisee or paid out of the general estate.

Specifically bequeath insurance policies covering farm buildings and equipment to the devisee. Livestock, machinery, stored crops and other farm personal property should be bequeathed in specific or general terms. State the rights to growing crops if there is any doubt. Specify whether the beneficiary gets the accounts receivable owing by virtue of produce or livestock sold.

It is necessary to give the executor or trustee authority to carry on the farm operation alone, as a partner or shareholder; to hire labor and managers or get tenants; to buy and sell machinery, equipment or livestock; to reconstruct, repair and improve farm buildings; to borrow money; to carry on operations or to make improvements; to sell all or part of the farm business; to subdivide or otherwise convert the farm property to new uses; to retain income from working capital and to set up reserves out of income for cattle purchases, building improvements, fences, tilling, fertilizer, etc. Perhaps the trustee should also be authorized to incorporate the farm business, to sell it to the property owner's issue on special terms or options, to lease it to members of the family, to build new buildings, to continue and improve herds, to mortgage the farm to provide funds for beneficiaries.

[¶307]   **BUSINESS INTERESTS**

Closely held stock or a partnership interest or an individually owned business raises a large range of problems which are analyzed at ¶1201 et seq.

An individually owned business presents problems much like those of a farm.

See that executors and trustees are directed to sell or authorized to hold. In the absence of express authority to hold a business interest, state law may require them to sell. If they are to hold, the will must give the necessary authority and the indemnities necessary to operate.

The business estate presents a multitude of especially difficult problems. The real value of the business may depend on the skill and energy of the owner. The business usually represents a large percentage of the total estate which is not liquid, unless special arrangements are made to convert it into cash, and the value of this nonliquid asset is likely to create a large cash tax liability. Unless funds are made available to meet this liability, disastrous results may follow.

[¶308]   **MUTUAL FUNDS**

The same considerations as apply to securities generally apply to mutual funds and other investment company holdings. Some extra thought must go into planning for the disposition of these assets, however, if they are to be used as all or a part of the corpus of a testamentary trust or if there may be a prolonged delay before the estate assets are finally distributed to beneficiaries.

If mutual funds are already owned by the estate owner and he wishes them partially or fully to fund a testamentary trust, the will should provide in no uncertain terms that his executor and trustee be empowered to retain such shares and to invest further in such shares, notwithstanding any possible state statute or case law holding that such retention or purchase is not permitted. Otherwise, depending on local law, it might be necessary to sell the mutual fund shares, and it might be impossible for the trustee to reinvest in these types of shares.

The question of allocation of mutual fund capital gains distributions between income and corpus of the trust should also be resolved by an appropriate provision in the will. If this is done, local law will determine how these distributions are to be allocated. Many states, either by statute or case law, say that such distributions are principal, and the Revised Uniform Principal and Income Act says that they should be treated as principal. As long as the estate owner provides in his will to whom such distributions shall belong, the income beneficiary or the remaindermen (and the provision does not violate any state law such as possible law against accumulations), this provision will usually be followed.

From a federal tax point of view, capital gains distributions from mutual funds are treated as long-term capital gains regardless of whether they are treated as income or principal for trust purposes. How these distributions are treated for purposes of trust administration will affect only the question of who gets them, the income beneficiary or the remaindermen of the trust, and who pays the tax thereon, the income beneficiary or the trust. Where a substantial amount of mutual fund shares is involved, this may become an important area of planning for the estate owner. Who should receive the capital gains distributions and pay the tax thereon? And the same reasoning applies to state income taxation, whether such capital gains distributions be considered long-term capital gain or ordinary income under the appropriate state tax law. This is just another reason why the estate owner should be crystal clear in answering this question in his will.

In a given estate, it may prove necessary for the executor to withhold distributions for a relatively long time. And in the absence of a specific authorization to the executor to retain nonlegal investments, in a number of states the executor will be required to dispose of the mutual fund shares. It is therefore advisable that the will contain a clause specifically empowering the executor to retain, and even to reinvest distributions (if this is desired) in mutual fund shares.

[¶309]   **OIL AND GAS INTERESTS**

Special considerations occur where an estate owner possesses oil and gas interests. Years ago, it was a rather rare occurrence when someone outside the oil rich states possessed interests in oil and gas. Not so today. Many doctors, executives and others having nothing whatsoever to do with oil and gas have made direct investments in oil and gas ventures.

Usually, an oil interest turns out to be some sort of realty interest and, quite often, in a state other than where the estate owner lives. One problem, of course, is that the owner's will may have to be rechecked to see that it has been executed in accordance with the requirements of this other state; there is the possibility that the oil interest may devolve in accordance with that other state's intestacy laws. Another thing to check is whether or not the testator has made a general devise of his "real property"—this devise may unwittingly include his oil and gas interests. A further consideration, since these interests are generally realty, will have to be given to granting the executor the power to name ancillary executors or ancillary administrators if the need arises.

Oil and gas interests (leasehold interests, royalty interests, working interests, production payments, net-profit interests, etc.) can be very difficult assets to administer in the estate, and sometimes it is preferable to arrange for their disposition prior to or shortly after death. Where these interests are to be retained for beneficiaries, many estate planners urge that they be given to beneficiaries via bequests and devises rather than as part of the general or trust estate. They reason that leaving such interests in the general or trust estate sometimes places too serious an investment burden on the shoulders of the fiduciary. And, unless to do so might bar him from further participation in a venture, he may very well prefer to sit on his hands rather than commit further monies to the oil or gas venture.

Where, despite the above admonitions, oil and gas interests are to form a part of the general or trust estate, it will be necessary to grant the executor or the trustee a substantial array of special powers:

(1) This is a highly complex investment area; the fiduciary must be given the authority to rely on the advice of experts without incurring any personal liability for acting on this advice and, if necessary, to pay for this advice.

(2) Where a fiduciary is to be given the power to retain oil and gas interests, inquiry should be made as to whether the estate owner wishes their retention even if the interest is unproductive at his death. If the answer is yes, then a provision to that effect belongs in the will.

(3) Any authority to invest or reinvest in additional oil and gas ventures should specifically refer to the type of interest (leasehold, royalty, working, etc.) which the estate owner has in mind, or should be sufficiently broad to include any of these if this is his intention.

(4) In a *working interest*, it is a good idea to give the fiduciary power to participate in any reorganization and to invest any additional monies as may be necessary for the further exploration, development and preservation of such interest.

(5) It is also a good idea to give the fiduciary specific leasing powers, as well as the power to drill, test and explore for further minerals.

(6) It is very important that the trustee be given broad authority to allocate income and expenses of oil and gas interests and to establish such depletion reserves as it deems desirable. Unless the governing instrument or local law permits or requires a reserve for depletion, the depletion deduction will be apportioned between the income beneficiary and the trustee on the basis of the trust income allocable to each (IRC §611(b)). Thus, proceeds allocable to principal might be taxable without an offsetting deduction. This drain on principal can be avoided or minimized if the reserve requirement is present in the instrument, as the deduction would then be allocated first to the trustee to the extent that income is set aside for the reserve and then apportioned between the income beneficiary and trustee in the same proportion that the receipts are apportioned.

There are numerous other considerations which must be taken into account when an estate owner has oil and gas interests. If these interests are substantial, the wisest precaution would be to call in an oil and gas specialist.

FOREIGN ASSETS

The warning flag should always go up whenever the estate owner possesses any property in a foreign country, especially if it is a country with which we are not, politically speaking, on the best of terms or one which is geographically rather far removed from the United States. Depending on the nature of the property, it might be necessary to determine who can qualify as ancillary executor or ancillary administrator in this foreign country. It will also be necessary to find out about the requirements of this foreign land concerning the disposition of property by will or otherwise, the administering of the property and any death or other taxes.

Foreign real estate used to be excluded from the gross estate. But this is no longer the case. This being so, foreign realty may well prove to be a more costly holding at the owner's death than domestic realty. The reason for this is that you not only have ancillary administration and other international red tape to contend with, but also the U.S. estate tax. So, an owner of foreign real estate will have to ask himself what role the former role of noninclusion in the gross estate played in his decision to purchase this property, while a prospective foreign land owner should make certain that he takes the current estate tax rule into account.

[¶311] **MISCELLANEOUS ASSETS**

Every asset which a person owns must be looked at and considered separately to determine the best disposition and the special directions necessary to preserve its value.

Sometimes, a person is not conscious of all the assets that may fall into his estate. Rights under employee benefit plans may have great value to an employee's family; but because the employee can not lay his hands on these assets until some time in the future, he does not think of these assets. Here are some of the additional assets to be woven into a proper estate plan.

[¶311.1] **Interests in Keogh, Individual Retirement Accounts (IRA), Pension or Profit-Sharing Plans**

The plan will ordinarily provide a mechanism for designating the beneficiary to receive the amount accumulated when the participant dies. By naming individual beneficiaries rather than his estate, the participant can avoid estate tax on the amount accumulated from the employer's contribution, as long as the post-death payout does not qualify for lump sum treatment for income tax purposes. For Individual Retirement Accounts, the post-death payment must qualify as an annuity and be payable over at least 36 months to be excluded. By naming an inter vivos or testamentary trust for his family as beneficiary, the participant can save estate tax at the death of his wife and other beneficiaries of the family trust.

Study the plan itself. What elections does it make available? Consider the income tax liability when the accumulated benefits are received. See that successor beneficiaries are named. See the complete treatment of the employee estate beginning at ¶1301.

[¶311.2] Stock Options

Study the plan and the option contract. How much time is allowed to exercise the options after death? Will any income tax liability accrue at death? Has the executor been specifically authorized to exercise the options and to borrow money or sell assets quickly for that purpose? Should insurance be provided to facilitate the exercise of options? See ¶1308 et seq.

[¶311.3] Deferred Compensation Contracts

Are any benefits available to the employee's family? What can be done to minimize income tax liability? Should the executor be directed as to how to distribute these rights? See ¶1305.

[¶311.4] Contract Rights, Uncollected Bills, etc.

Give the executor authority to collect and adjust and flexibility to spread these assets so as to minimize income tax liability. See ¶1509.6.

[¶311.5] Insurance Policies

These will constitute the most important part of many estates. For a full discussion, see ¶701 et seq. Here, we will stress only the importance of reviewing the policies. Don't take the insured's word on ownership and beneficiary designation. Many times he's under a false impression. Don't overlook policies owned on somebody else's life. Who should get these policies? If they go to the insured, the present value will be taxed in the owner's estate and the full proceeds on the insured's death. If they stay in the estate and then go into trust, the will should give proper discretion as to the payment of premiums maturing between the death of the owner and that of the insured. Should the policy be transferred by bequest or sale to the insured, or should it be cashed in or converted to paid-up insurance, or should it be carried as an investment and, in that event, where will the premium money come from?

In reviewing these questions, bear in mind that IRC §2042 allows a man to transfer policies on his life to the ownership of his wife or children in order to keep the death proceeds out of his estate.

SECTION IV. VALUATION OF ESTATE PROPERTY

The rules set forth below generally apply to valuation for both estate or gift tax purposes.

Valuing estate assets is both simple and certain, complicated and uncertain. Valuing items that are available in the open market is simple and certain; there are definite rules for valuing and, as long as you follow them, the Treasury won't question your valuation. Determining the value of a going business, an interest in a partnership or a closed corporation, on the other hand, is complicated; even after you have done your best to arrive at a fair figure, you may find that the Treasury has a different idea of the value.

The basic rule provided by §2031 of the Internal Revenue Code is that assets are to be valued for estate tax purposes at their value on the date of the decedent's death. Section 2032 gives the executor an election to value assets as of six months after the decedent's death. If the election is made and the executor disposes of an asset within the six months, the date of disposition becomes the valuation date for that asset.

[¶401]   **STOCKS AND BONDS**

The value of stocks and bonds listed on a stock exchange or sold over-the-counter is the mean between the highest and lowest quoted selling prices on the valuation date (Reg. §20.2031-2(b)). A lower value may be justified where the decedent's holdings are so large that throwing them on the market all at once would depress the price. This is known as the blockage rule (Reg. §20.2031-2(e)).

If there were no sales on the valuation date but there were sales within a reasonable period before and after that date, use a weighted average of the mean between the highest and lowest sales on the nearest dates before and after the valuation date (Reg. §20.2031-2(b)). If there were no sales within a reasonable period before and after the valuation date, use the mean between the bid and asked prices on the valuation date; if none, take a weighted average of the means between the bid and asked prices on the nearest trading dates before and after the valuation date (Reg. §20.2031-2(c)). Mutual funds used to be valued at net asset value plus the sales charge, if any, that would be charged if the same number of shares were being bought (Reg. §20.2031-8(b)). But this Regulation has been declared invalid by the Supreme Court (*Cartwright, 93 Sup. Ct. 1713*). The value of mutual fund shares is now deemed to be their redemption price at the date of the owner's death (or the optional valuation date, if elected).

37

The special rule valuing U.S. Treasury bonds redeemable at par to pay federal estate tax is set forth on page T-32.

[¶402]　　　　**UNLISTED AND CLOSELY HELD STOCK**

The Code (§2031 (b)) and Regulations provide special rules for these stocks. Where the stock of corporations engaged in a similar business are listed, their value must be considered. Other elements considered are: for bonds, soundness of security, interest yield, maturity date and other relevant factors; for stock, net worth of the company, prospective earning power, dividend-paying capacity, good will or other intangible value and other relevant factors (see *Rev. Rul. 59-60*, 1959-1 CB 237; *Rev. Rul. 65-193*, 1965-2 CB 370) as set out below:

[¶402.1]　**Risk Factor**

IRS will check the past history and the financial position for signs of stability or instability, growth or lack of growth, diversity or lack of diversity in operations. It will look at the nature of the business, its products or services, operating and investment assets, capital structure, plant facilities, sales record and management. These will be studied as of the date of appraisal, with most stress on recent changes and nonrecurring events discounted. For a successor corporation, the predecessor's record will be studied, too.

[¶402.2]　**Economic Situation and Labor Conditions**

These include adverse world conditions, labor problems, effect of "cold war" developments. IRS will look at both the general economic picture and the prospects within the industry.

[¶402.3]　**Balance Sheets**

IRS will want comparative annual statements for two or more years immediately preceding its appraisal, plus a current balance sheet, if possible, and supplemental schedules where necessary for clarification. Balance sheets will be compared for significant financial changes. In computing book value, distinction will be made between operating and investment assets, the former generally being presumed to carry greater earnings potential. If the corporation has more than one class of stock, IRS will examine the charter to compare voting power of the different classes and preference as to dividends and distributions in liquidation.

[¶402.4]　**Profit and Loss**

IRS will consider the profit and loss statements for five or more years before its appraisal to determine earnings potential. IRS will separate recurring from nonrecurring income and expense, distinguish between operating and investment income, ascertain whether there are consistent loss lines that could be abandoned by the business, and determine percentage of earnings retained for expansion.

[¶402.5]   Dividend-Paying Capacity

Earnings must be capitalized, based on the nature of the business, the risk, stability and regularity of earnings, and allowing for fluctuations common to the industry. The aim is to find what can be paid after fair allowance for the needs of the business. IRS gives comparatively minor weight to the dividend-paying factor because owners of a closed corporation distort it by overpaying themselves to increase the corporation's tax deduction.

[¶402.6]   Good Will

The value of good will, says IRS, is based on earning capacity. The presence of good will rests on the excess of net earnings over the fair return on the net tangible assets. Prestige, renown, brand name and record of successful prolonged operation in a particular locality all go towards establishing the value of the good will.

[¶402.7]   Sales of Stock

While prior sales of the corporation's stock are an element in proving value, IRS will give little weight to forced or distressed sales, or to isolated sales. A higher value may be placed on stock sold in a block that carries corporate control with it.

[¶403]   VALUING A PARTNERSHIP OR PROPRIETORSHIP

The value of an interest in a partnership or proprietorship is arrived at by (a) fairly appraising as of the valuation date all the assets of the business, tangible and intangible, and including good will; (b) taking into consideration the demonstrated earning capacity of the business and (c) weighing all the factors considered for stock that apply to a nonstock ownership.

The Regulations require that full supporting data be submitted with the estate tax return, including copies of reports of accountants, engineers and any other technical experts who may have participated in the estate's valuation (Reg. §20.2031-3). This Regulation also warns that special attention will be given to valuing good will in partnership cases where the decedent didn't arrange a buyout agreement with his partners.

[¶404]   **REAL ESTATE**

Case law rather than the Regulations enables us to set a value on real property. The value of income-producing real estate is established by one or more of the following methods: (1) expert appraisal; (2) assessed value; (3) replacement cost; (4) income produced; (5) sales price of similar property.

One of the most common and widely accepted methods of proving the value of real estate is through the testimony of well-informed, experienced real estate brokers, operators and investors who qualify as experts. In general, they base their opinions on the assessed valuation of the property, keeping in mind the percentage of assessed value which the average sales in the area have realized in the period immediately preceding the appraisal, as well as the earning power, replacement cost and sales of similar property. Since each piece of realty is unique, it is difficult to determine to what extent two prices are comparable. The present rental value may be misleading since it may not be indicative of the true value. The presence or absence of a long-term lease and the type of tenant must be taken into consideration. In normal times, replacement cost is a limiting factor in the determination of value of improved realty; but when there is a shortage of labor or materials, this factor may become inapplicable.

Real property which is not used for income-producing purposes is limited almost exclusively to personal residences, where values are influenced by elements of residential desirability rather than income production. In most instances, residential property which costs in excess of $200,000 will not bring anything near its cost, while smaller residences in the $25,000 class have appreciated greatly.

[¶405]   **VALUATION OF CERTAIN FARMS AND REAL
                PROPERTY USED FOR BUSINESS**

The general rule for valuing real property used in a farm or in a closely held business is to value the property on the basis of its highest and best use, even though the property is not being utilized at its highest and best use. For example: land presently being used in farming which could be converted into either a residential sub-division or industrial park has a greater value than if it remained as farmland. Thus, the IRS would value the land at this higher and better use, even though the property would continue to be used as farmland. This valuation method has caused hardship on those who wanted to continue using the property in a family business and, therefore, an executor may elect to value the qualified property based on its actual use as a farm or small business property.

[¶405.1]   **Requirements for the Special Use Valuation (IRC §2032A)**

(1) The decedent must be a citizen or resident of the United States at his death and the real property must be located in the United States.

(2) The real property must be used as a farm or in a closely held business at the time of the decedent's death.

(3) The special valuation cannot reduce the decedent's gross estate more than $500,000 below the value under the regular valuation method.

(4) The value of a farm or closely held business (both real and personal) must be at least 50% of the decedent's gross estate.

(5) At least 25% of the value of the gross estate must be the qualified real property.

(6) The values used in tests (4) and (5) are to be determined without the use of the special valuation method and it is reduced by any debts attributable to the property.

(7) The real property must pass to a qualified heir.

(8) The real property must have been owned by the decedent or a member of his family and there must have been material participation by the decedent or a member of his family in its operation, for five (5) of the last eight (8) years immediately preceding the decedent's death.

[¶405.2]   **Special Valuation Method**

If the real property meets the above requirements, then the executor can value the land under the following rules:

(1) *Farm Method.* The value of a farm that qualifies for special use valuation can generally be determined by:

(a) Computing the average annual gross cash rental for comparable land used for farming purposes in the same locality as the farm being valued,

(b) Subtracting the average state and local real estate taxes for the comparable land,

(c) Dividing the result by the annual effective interest rate for all new Federal Land Bank loans.

The average annual amounts are calculated from the five calendar years before the date of decedent's death. This formula cannot be used if there is no comparable land from which the average annual gross cash rental may be determined, or if an executor elects to value the farm by applying the multiple factor method.

(2) *Multiple Factor Method.* For farms which do not use the farm method and for closely held business property, the valuation of real property is determined by applying the following factors:

(a) The capitalization of income that the property can be expected to yield for farming or closely held business purposes over a reasonable period of time under prudent management using traditional cropping patterns for the area, taking into account soil capacity, terrain configuration and similar factors.

(b) The capitalization of the fair rental value of the land for farmland or closely held business purposes,

(c) Assessed land values in a State which provides a differential or use value assessment law for farmland or land used in closely held businesses,

(d) Comparable sales of other farm or closely held business land in the same geographical area far enough removed from a metropolitan or resort area so that nonagricultural use is not a significant factor in the sales price, and

(e) Any other factor which fairly values the farm or closely held business value of the property.

[¶405.3] Recapture of Estate Tax Saved

If, within 15 years after the death of the decedent (but before the death of the qualified heir), the property is disposed of to nonfamily members, or ceases to be used for farming or other closely held business purposes, all or a portion of the federal estate tax benefits which resulted through the special use valuation, will be recaptured. There can be full recapture of estate tax saved if the disposition is within 10 years of the decedent's death and, over the next five years, if there is a disposition, the amount will be phased out on a ratable monthly basis.

To protect the IRS, there is a special lien on the real property during this 15 year period (§6324 B).

[¶406] NOTES

Notes, whether secured or unsecured, are valued at the amount of the unpaid principal, plus interest accrued to the date of death, unless the executor can establish a lower value or worthlessness. An inadequate interest rate or provision for maturity might establish a lower value. Worthlessness can be established by proving uncollectibility due to insolvency or other cause, and that the note wasn't secured (Reg. §20.2031-4).

[¶407] BANK CHECKS AND DEPOSITS

Bank deposits are included in the estate the same as cash. Amounts covered by bank checks issued by the decedent to pay bona fide obligations and subsequently honored by a bank are not included if the obligation is not claimed as a deduction on the estate tax return (Reg. §20.2031-5).

[¶408]   **HOUSEHOLD GOODS AND PERSONAL EFFECTS**

Reg. §20.2031-6 gives comprehensive provisions for these. It suggests a room by room itemization, with each item separately named and valued. But articles in the same room, none of which is worth more than $100, can be grouped. The executor can, in lieu of itemization, submit a written statement of aggregate value based on estimates of experts.

There's a special rule for articles of intrinsic worth, such as furs and jewelry, paintings, rugs, valuable books and stamp and coin collections. If the total value exceeds $3,000 an appraisal by experts under oath must be filed with the return.

[¶409]   **ANNUITIES, LIFE ESTATES, TERM INTERESTS**
AND REMAINDERS

Where a decedent's estate contains a remainder, reversion, life estate or term interest, the value of the interest may be included in his estate. If the decedent's estate's continuance of this interest is to be circumscribed by the lifetime of another, the value of the interest to the estate is computed by the use of actuarial tables which appear in the estate tax regulations (§20.2031-7). The same computations may be required where there is a gift of an annuity, life estate, term for years or remainder or reversion or where a private annuity is being valued. The tables which appear in the estate tax regulations are contained in the gift tax regulations (§25.2512-5). See tables starting on page T-22a.

SECTION V. THE UNIFIED ESTATE AND GIFT TRANSFER TAX AND HOW IT WORKS

Lifetime transfers made after 1976 will count in determining the estate tax to be paid for death time transfers. Thus, the unified federal estate and gift tax is a tax on the privilege of transferring property during one's lifetime and at death.

A federal estate tax return (Form 706) must be filed within nine months after death if the estate at decedent's death is valued at more than $120,000 in 1977; this gradually increases to a valuation of $175,000 for decedents who die in 1981 and later.

The property to be included in the decedent's gross estate is determined by reference to §2031-2044, inclusive, of the Internal Revenue Code. Another excellent and most understandable source is Form 706 itself, Schedules A to I, inclusive. [Revised form 706 unavailable at time of publication so schedule references may vary.]

[¶501]   **CHECKLIST OF PROPERTY INCLUDIBLE IN THE GROSS ESTATE**

(1) Real estate (Schedule A).

(2) Stocks, including dividends payable though not yet paid to the decedent at the date of his death (Schedule B).

(3) Bonds, including accrued interest up to the date of death (Schedule B).

(4) Mortgages, notes and cash (Schedule C).

(5) Insurance proceeds payable to the decedent's estate (Schedule D).

(6) Insurance proceeds payable other than to the decedent's estate, but with respect to which the decedent owned incidents of ownership in the policies (Schedule D). (See ¶704.)

(7) Joint tenancy and tenancy by the entirety property (including joint bank accounts and co-owned U.S. Savings Bonds). For tracing and for special rules where such property was acquired by gift or inheritance, see Reg. §20.2040-1 (Schedule E). (See also the discussion at ¶601.3.)

(8) Other miscellaneous property including: debts due decedent, business and partnership interests, income accrued to the date of death, unpaid compensation for work performed prior to death, insurance policies owned on another's life, accumulated dividends on insurance policies listed in Schedule D, employee death benefits contracted for by decedent, enforceable claims, rights, patents and copyrights, royalties, leaseholds, judgments, unexercised stock options which can still be exercised by the estate or by beneficiaries,

44

vested remainder interests, household goods and personal effects, automobiles, farm machinery, livestock, growing crops, etc. (Schedule F).

(9) Property transferred during lifetime in contemplation of death (Schedule G).

(10) Property transferred during lifetime in which decedent retained certain legal or beneficial interests (Schedule G). For details, see ¶502.

(11) Property subject to a general power of appointment possessed by the decedent (Schedule H).

(12) Joint and survivor annuities, refund annuities and other payments received under similar contracts or agreements, to the extent that the decedent contributed to the purchase price (contribution by employer if not made pursuant to a qualified plan is deemed to be a contribution by decedent) (Schedule I).

[¶502]   **SCHEDULE G—TRANSFERS DURING
DECEDENT'S LIFETIME**

Property which was transferred by the decedent during his lifetime may nevertheless be includible in his gross estate under certain circumstances. These include: (a) transfers made in contemplation of death; (b) transfers with retained life estate; (c) transfers taking effect at death; (d) revocable transfers.

[¶502.1]   **Transfers Made in Contemplation of Death (IRC §2035)**

(1) **Transfers After 1976:** Lifetime transfers made after 1976 and within three years prior to death of the decedent will automatically be included in the gross estate, except for those transfers which qualify under the $3,000 annual exclusion for the decedent. This is an absolute rule; thus there is no presumption or opportunity to argue that the gifts were not made in contemplation of death. However, if the decedent made deathbed transfers of $3,000 per donee, these transfers would be excluded from the decedent's gross estate if they qualify for annual exclusion.

Not only is the gift included at the day of death value, or if alternate valuation is elected, the value six months after death, but the gift taxes paid or incurred by the decedent will be added back to the gross estate. If, however, the spouse elected to treat half the gifts as made by her and paid the gift tax on one-half of the gifts, the spouse's payment of gift taxes will not be added back. If the total gift was under $3,000 and qualified for the annual exclusion at the time of the transfer, and the value of the gift has appreciated beyond $3,000 at decedent's death, the appreciation may be included in the estate.

(2) **Transfers Before 1977:** Transfers by decedents are, *unless shown to the contrary*, deemed to have been made in contemplation of death if they were made within three years prior to death. Any transfer made more than three years prior to the date of the decedent's death are absolutely excluded

from this category regardless of the motivations which prompted the transfers.

The Regulations point out that a transfer within this three-year period is prompted by the thought of death if (1) made with the purpose of avoiding death taxes, (2) made as a substitute for a testamentary distribution of the property or (3) made for any other motive associated with death.

While it is necessary to rebut the presumption that a transfer made within three years prior to death is one made in contemplation of death, this presumption is frequently overcome by showing that the donor was healthy, life minded and active, or that the motives behind the making of the gift were lifetime rather than death motives. Examples of lifetime objectives might be: a desire to be of current assistance to beneficiaries (as by buying a home for beneficiaries, starting up a college fund, etc.); Christmas presents and presents on other occasions such as births, communions, bar mitzvahs, birthdays, graduations, weddings, etc. (For some special life insurance considerations, see ¶702.)

Should the Treasury be successful in maintaining that a gift made before 1977 was made in contemplation of death, the results would still be better than if no gifts had been made. The gift tax paid or incurred would be available as a credit against the Federal estate tax and since the gifts occurred before 1977, the gift tax would not be included in the gross estate.

[¶502.2] Transfers Not Complete Until Transferor's Death (IRC §2036-2038)

Briefly, §2036 is intended to impose an estate tax on lifetime transfers under which possession or enjoyment is retained by the transferor until his death; §2037 causes a tax to be imposed on lifetime transfers under which the transferee can obtain possession or enjoyment only by surviving the transferor; §2038 taxes lifetime transfers under which the transferor reserves for his lifetime significant powers over the possession or enjoyment of the property.

Section 2036: This section is broken down into two separate subsections: §2036(a)(1) taxes transfers where the decedent has retained the income for himself for life, or for a period which is not ascertainable without reference to his death, or for any period which does not in fact end before his death. An example of a transfer which would be taxed under this provision is:

X creates a trust to pay the income to himself for life, remainder to Y or his estate.

For transfers after June 22, 1976, the mere retention of voting rights is sufficient to cause inclusion of the stock in the transferor's taxable estate.

Section 2036(a)(2): This section taxes transfers where the decedent has retained during his lifetime the right, either alone or in conjunction with any other person, to designate the person who shall possess or enjoy the property or the income therefrom, this right being treated as the equivalent of the retention of the enjoyment itself. Here are two examples of transfers which would be taxed under this provision:

> X creates a trust to pay the income to Y for life, remainder to B's estate. X retains the right (alone or in conjunction with another) to invade corpus for the benefit of Z.
>
> X creates a trust to pay the income to Y for life, remainder to Z. X retains the right to accumulate income and add it to corpus.

Section 2037: This section taxes transfers which are essentially testamentary in nature, the transferee's possession or enjoyment of the property being deferred until the death of the transferor. This provision will be applied only if the decedent had retained a *reversionary interest that is in excess of 5%* of the value of the entire property at the time of his death. The thought behind this reservation is that in order for the property to be taxed in the transferor's estate, he must have retained an expectation of return which was something more than just theoretical. An example of a transfer which would be taxed under this provision (assuming reversionary interest exceeds 5%) is:

> X creates a trust to pay the income to Y or his estate during X's lifetime, with remainder to Z. Should Z die before X, then reversion to X's estate.

Section 2038: This section taxes transfers where the decedent, either alone or in conjunction with any other person, retains the right to alter, amend, revoke or terminate the arrangement. In addition, if the decedent relinquishes the above rights within three years before his death, this would result in the inclusion of the property in the decedent's gross estate. This section obviously covers the revocable trust situation, which incidentally is also covered by §2036(a)(2). In fact, many transfers caught within the framework of §2038 are also subject to §2036(a)(2). For example, the two cases cited under the preceding discussion of §2036(a)(2) can also be cited as examples of transfers encompassed by §2038.

However, there are situations where despite the fact that a particular transfer is covered by both these sections, the amount includible in the decedent's estate may be greater where the Commissioner imposes one section than if he imposes the other:

> X creates a trust to pay the income to Y for life, then to A and B during their joint lives, then to the survivor for life, remainder to Z. X retains the power to vary the income interests of A and B.

It's clear that §2038 applies; X retained the power to alter the distribution of income from the trust. Since X also retained the power to designate the persons who should enjoy the income of the property, §2036(a)(2) also is applicable. When applying §2038, only those interests are taxed which may be affected by the decedent's exercise of his retained powers. Thus, in the above example, only the joint life interests of A and B would be taxable, not the life interest of Y or the remainder interest of Z. On the other hand, under §2036(a)(2), the entire trust corpus less the value of Y's life interest would be taxable.

In situations where both §2036(a)(2) and §2038 seem to cover a given lifetime transfer and the amount includible under one section exceeds the amount includible under the other, the Commissioner will probably invoke that section which causes the most property to be included in the gross estate.

Besides this overlap between §2038 and §2036(a)(2), there is also overlap between §2037 (assuming we have the 5% reversionary interest) and §2036(a)(1) and, in fact, with §2036(a)(2) and §2038 as well.

[¶503]   **ALLOWABLE DEDUCTIONS AGAINST**
                  THE GROSS ESTATE

The next step in the estate tax computation process is valuing the property included in the gross estate. This subject is dealt with separately at ¶401 et seq.

Once the value of all the property in the decedent's gross estate has been determined, the next step is to compute and itemize allowable deductions against the gross estate. These deductions follow right after the includible items in Form 706 in Schedules J through N (§2053-2057 IRC), as follows:

(1) Funeral and administration expenses (Schedule J; also Schedule L);

(2) Debts of decedent and mortgages and liens (Schedule K);

(3) Losses during administration (Schedule L);

(4) Marital deduction (Schedule M);

(5) Orphan's exclusion (Schedule —);

(6) Charitable deduction (Schedule N).

[¶503.1]   **Funeral and Administration Expenses**

Includible in the category of *funeral expenses* are items such as undertaker's charges, burial costs, cemetery plot costs, costs of headstone, etc. *Administration expenses* include attorneys', executor's, accountants' and appraisers' fees; court costs; publication fees; and other expenses necessary to estate administration. (See table on pages T-31a-d for a checklist of approximate probate and administration expenses for estates of various sizes. The actual figures will vary, of course, from case to case, depending on the nature of the estate property, its intended distribution pattern, place of probate and location of the property.) Note: The executor has an election to deduct administration expenses from the gross estate or from the estate's income tax return. (See ¶1509.7.)

[¶503.2]   **Debts of the Decedent, etc.**

This needs little explanation except that it may include income taxes due on decedent's earnings prior to death, interest accrued prior to death and unpaid taxes. Expenses of the decedent's last illness would also be included under this category. Debts secured by mortgages and liens are deductible separately but only if the encumbered property is included in the gross estate.

[¶503.3]   Losses during Administration

Losses are only deductible if they arise from casualty or theft and then only to the extent that they are not compensated for by insurance or otherwise.

[¶503.4]   Marital Deduction

To a decedent's surviving spouse, this is perhaps the most important of the deductions from the gross estate. The amount of the deduction depends on two amounts and cannot exceed either of them:

(1) The amount of property which is left outright, or tantamount to outright (whether by will, intestacy, joint tenancy survivorship, disposition of life insurance proceeds, or otherwise), to the surviving spouse.

(2) The greater of $250,000 or fifty percent of the *adjusted gross estate* (the adjusted gross estate being all the property listed in Schedules A through I of Form 706, less the deductions claimed in Schedules J through L—the gross estate minus funeral and administration expenses, debts and losses during administration).

If the decedent has made lifetime transfers to his spouse of less than $200,000 after 1976, there is an adjustment to the estate tax marital deduction. After 1976, the gift tax marital deduction is allowed in full for the first $100,000 of gifts to the spouse; on the next $100,000, no marital deduction is allowed; and when the gifts go over $200,000, half of the gifts are allowed as a marital deduction. The maximum estate tax marital deduction is reduced by the amount of the marital deduction allowed for lifetime transfers in excess of 50% of the value of the lifetime transfers. For example, if the decedent were to give his spouse $100,000 after 1976, he would have a full gift tax marital deduction of 100% of the gift, the estate tax marital deduction would be reduced by $50,000 (gift marital deduction $100,000 less 50% of the gift = $50,000 adjustment). Note: the adjustment can never be more than $50,000.

The above adjustment to the estate marital deduction would appear to be required even if the gift to the spouse was included in donor's estate as a transfer in contemplation of death.

The idea behind the grant of the marital deduction in the estate of the first spouse to die is that the property upon which the deduction is based, assuming it is retained, will subsequently be taxed in full when the surviving spouse dies or, if transferred during lifetime, will be subject to gift tax. (See ¶603 for a review of marital deduction trusts, ¶612 for a brief summary of how a common disaster can affect the marital deduction, and ¶703 for special considerations relating to life insurance.)

[¶503.5] **Orphan's Exclusion**

Where a decedent has children under the age of 21, who have no known surviving parent (thus, if a divorced parent is still alive, this deduction is not available), there is a deduction of $5,000 per child for each year between the child's age at the death of the surviving parent and until he reaches 21 years of age. For example, if the child is 10 at the decedent's death, the deduction would be 11 (21−10) × $5,000 or $55,000. The amount of deduction is limited to the amount actually passing from the decedent to the child. If the amount is not left outright to the child, it can be left in trust for him, as long as the terms qualify under the rules for the marital deduction under Code §2056(b) pertaining to life estates or other terminable interest, as if the interest were left to a surviving spouse. Thus, the child must eventually receive the property or have a power of appointment over it. However, the interest will not be treated as a terminable interest if the property will pass to another person due to the child's death before the youngest child of the decedent reaches the age of 21.

[¶503.6] **Charitable Deduction**

The value of all property *included in the gross estate* and transferred by the decedent, whether in his lifetime or by will, for public, charitable and religious purposes, may next be deducted.

Note that the charitable deduction comes after, not before, the marital deduction. Thus 50% of the entire estate can be made tax free under the marital deduction, and all or any portion of the remaining estate is tax free to the extent bequeathed to charity.

[¶504] **TAXABLE ESTATE AND TENTATIVE TAX BASE**

Having reduced the gross estate by the deductions allowed under Schedules J through N and explained above, we have arrived at the *taxable estate*. Form 706 goes through two procedures to arrive at this taxable estate. There's a complete recapitulation, on page 3 of the form, of all the property included in the gross estate and of all the deductions allowed from the gross estate. After the taxable estate has been computed, we must add all adjusted taxable gifts made by the decedent after 1976 to this figure and thereby we arrive at the tentative tax base. If there were taxable lifetime transfers, this would cause the estate to be taxed at a higher bracket. Then the computation of tax, on page 1, sets forth the following:

(1) Total gross estate $

(2) Total allowable deductions $

(3) Taxable estate (item 1 minus item 2) $

(4) Adjusted post-1976 taxable gifts $

(5) Tentative taxable base (items 3 & 4) $

[¶505]   **COMPUTATION OF THE ESTATE TAX**

The next step is to compute the estate tax on the tentative tax base. The following table shows the computation as it appears in the Code (§2001) and at Table A of Form 706 Instructions.

COMPUTATION OF ESTATE TAX ON TENTATIVE TAX BASE

Tentative taxable base exceeding (1)	Tentative taxable base not exceeding (2)	Tentative tax on amount in column (1) (3)	Rate of tax on excess over amount in column (1) (4)
$ —	$ 10,000	$ —	18%
10,000	20,000	1,800	20
20,000	40,000	3,800	22
40,000	60,000	8,200	24
60,000	80,000	13,000	26
80,000	100,000	18,200	28
100,000	150,000	23,800	30
150,000	250,000	38,800	32
250,000	500,000	70,800	34
500,000	750,000	155,800	37
750,000	1,000,000	248,300	39
1,000,000	1,250,000	345,800	41
1,250,000	1,500,000	448,300	43
1,500,000	2,000,000	555,800	45
2,000,000	2,500,000	780,800	49
2,500,000	3,000,000	1,025,800	53
3,000,000	3,500,000	1,290,800	57
3,500,000	4,000,000	1,575,800	61
4,000,000	4,500,000	1,880,800	65
4,500,000	5,000,000	2,205,800	69
5,000,000	—	2,550,800	70

[¶505.1]   **Credits against Estate Tax on Tentative Tax Base**

After the estate tax on the tentative tax base has been determined, this tax is reduced by the gift taxes paid on post-1976 gifts, because the tentative tax has been applied on cumulative transfers both lifetime and death time. After this adjustment has been made, there are a number of credits which may be deducted if applicable:

(1) Unified credit

(2) Credit for state death taxes actually paid

(3) Credit for federal gift taxes previously paid by decedent on pre-1977 transfers

(4) Credit for federal estate tax on prior transfers to decedent

(5) Credit for foreign death taxes paid

[¶505.2]   Unified Credit

The unified credit has replaced the $30,000 gift tax lifetime exemption and the $60,000 estate tax exemption. The credit is phased in between the years 1977 and 1981 as follows:

Year	Credit	Exemption equivalency
1977	$30,000	$120,667
1978	34,000	134,000
1979	38,000	147,333
1980	42,500	161,563
1981 and later	47,000	175,625

The above credit is available for lifetime gifts and for estates of decedents dying after 1976, however credit against gift tax from January 1, 1977 to June 30, 1977 is only $6,000.

[¶505.3]   Credit for State Death Taxes

The state death tax credit is given for any such taxes paid with respect to property included in the decedent's gross estate. The credit equals the lesser of:

(a) The total of such taxes actually paid, or

(b) The amount determined by use of Table B in Form 706 Instructions, reproduced below, which also appears at §2011 of the Code.

COMPUTATION OF MAXIMUM CREDIT FOR STATE DEATH TAXES

Adjusted taxable estate exceeding* (1)	Adjusted taxable estate* not exceeding (2)	Credit on amount in column (1) (3)	Rate of credit on excess over amount in column (1) (4)
$ 40,000	$ 90,000	—	0.8%
90,000	140,000	$ 400	1.6
140,000	240,000	1,200	2.4
240,000	440,000	3,600	3.2
440,000	640,000	10,000	4.0
640,000	840,000	18,000	4.8
840,000	1,040,000	27,600	5.6
1,040,000	1,540,000	38,800	6.4
1,540,000	2,040,000	70,800	7.2

COMPUTATION OF MAXIMUM CREDIT FOR STATE DEATH TAXES

Adjusted taxable estate exceeding* (1)	Adjusted taxable estate* not exceeding (2)	Credit on amount in column (1) (3)	Rate of credit on excess over amount in column (1) (4)
2,040,000	2,540,000	106,800	8.0
2,540,000	3,040,000	146,800	8.8
3,040,000	3,540,000	190,800	9.6
3,540,000	4,040,000	238,800	10.4
4,040,000	5,040,000	290,800	11.2
5,040,000	6,040,000	402,800	12.0
6,040,000	7,040,000	522,800	12.8
7,040,000	8,040,000	650,800	13.6
8,040,000	9,040,000	786,800	14.4
9,040,000	10,040,000	930,800	15.2
10,040,000	—	1,082,800	16.0

* Taxable estate less $60,000.

[¶505.4]   **Credit for Federal Gift Taxes on Pre-1977 Transfers**

It is possible that the decedent has made transfers during his lifetime prior to 1977 and paid gift taxes thereon, only to have the transferred property included in his gross estate either as a gift made in contemplation of death or otherwise. The purpose of this credit is to prevent both gift tax and estate tax being imposed on the same property. This credit, permitted by §2012, cannot exceed that proportion of the gross estate tax less credit for state death taxes that the value of the included gift(s) bears to the gross estate less the marital and charitable deductions.

[¶505.5]   **Credit for Federal Estate Tax Previously Paid**

Sometimes a decedent's estate may contain property which was previously taxed in the estate of another decedent who was a transferor. Where this is the case and where the property was included in this transferor's taxable estate within ten years before or two years after the current decedent's death, §2013 allows a credit for the federal estate tax previously paid. Under the Tax Reform Act of 1976, the federal estate tax previously paid includes the recapture of estate tax if a farm or real property is disposed within 15 years of transferor's death (See ¶405.3) and transferor's estate elected to use the special valuation. In addition, if there was a generation skipping tax (See ¶1403.5) imposed on transferred property, the credit will include this tax. How to compute the maximum amount of this credit is explained in the Schedule P Instructions of Form 706. Where the present decedent predeceased the other decedent (who had transferred property to him) and not more than two years separated the deaths, the credit allowed is 100% of the maximum amount. Where the present decedent was the survivor, the percent of the maximum amount which is allowed as a credit for prior transfers depends on the number of years which elapsed between the dates of death in accordance with the following table:

Period of time exceeding	Not exceeding	Percent allowable
—	2 years	100
2 years	4 years	80
4 years	6 years	60
6 years	8 years	40
8 years	10 years	20
10 years	—	none

[¶505.6]   **Credit for Foreign Death Taxes**

Sometimes when a citizen or a resident of the United States has property in another country, that country may impose a death tax. Pursuant to IRC §2014, the amount of tax paid to such a foreign government may be taken as a credit against the gross estate tax, with certain limitations, to the extent that the property taxed by the foreign government is included in the gross estate under Schedules A through I of Form 706. If the foreign country is one with which we have a treaty covering this situation, then the credit is computed in accordance with the treaty. Details of this are set forth in the Schedule O Instructions of Form 706.

[¶506]   **STATE DEATH TAXES**

State death taxes can be broken down into three categories: (1) inheritance tax, (2) estate tax, and (3) additional estate tax to absorb the maximum credit for state death taxes allowable under the federal estate tax law. (See the state death tax table on page T-1a-d.)

[¶506.1]   **Inheritance Tax**

An estate tax (like the federal tax) is imposed on an estate before its distribution. It is levied on the right of the deceased to *transfer* property at death. An inheritance tax, on the other hand, is levied on the right of the beneficiaries to *receive* property from the deceased. The tax is measured by the share of the estate passing to each beneficiary.

Beneficiaries are divided into classes, with those closely related to the decedent forming one class, those related to another degree forming another class, and those unrelated forming still another class. Different exemptions usually are established for each class of beneficiary. The same can be said of the tax rates which apply for each class of beneficiary. The general effect is that a lower inheritance tax results when property passes to a close relative than when the same amount of property passes to a more distant relative or a nonrelative.

Note: When we say that different exemptions apply for each class of beneficiary, we don't mean that there is one exemption for the class; each beneficiary is allowed the exemption granted to the beneficiaries in his class.

[¶506.2] **Estate Tax**

Less than a dozen states impose estate taxes which are similar in principle to the federal estate tax. In most of these cases, a flat exemption is given to the estate. A few of these states, however, group the beneficiaries in classes and allow an exemption for each beneficiary before imposing a single tax rate on the entire remaining estate.

[¶506.3] **Additional Estate Tax**

Most states have the provision that if their inheritance and/or estate taxes bring into their treasuries less than the maximum credit for state death taxes allowed by the federal tax law, then the amount payable to the state is automatically increased to absorb the difference.

Example: Assume that the maximum credit allowed against the federal estate tax for state death taxes amounts to $3,600. Yet the total state death taxes amount to only $3,000. Most states impose an additional estate tax so that they, rather than the federal government, get the extra $600.

[¶507]   **FILING REQUIREMENTS**

The requirements for filing federal estate tax Form 706 reflect the phase-in of the unified credit. The requirements are as follows:

Calendar year	Gross estate more than
1977	$120,000
1978	134,000
1979	147,000
1980	161,000
1981 and later	175,000

The amounts are reduced by the sum of the adjusted taxable gifts made after December 31, 1976 and for specific gift exemption allowed for gifts made after September 8, 1976.

SECTION VI. TRANSFERS AT DEATH

Property transferred at death falls subject to the estate tax. There are four broad methods by which transfer at death is made:

(1) Joint ownership of the property where ownership is transferred by operation of law.

(2) Through the process of estate administration, either under a will or by intestacy.

(3) Creation of a revocable trust, which becomes irrevocable at death, into which additional assets can be poured over by will.

(4) Life insurance.

[¶601]   **JOINT OWNERSHIP**

Here are the major ways available to hold property in joint name:

(1) Tenancy in Common: Each owns undivided interest in the property. Each may sell his own portion. Heirs of each take his portion. This means that when X dies, his half interest isn't forfeited to Y; it belongs to X's heirs or passes according to his will.

(2) Joint Tenancy: All the property passes to the survivor on death of either one. While both are alive, either joint owner can break up ownership even against the will of the other joint owner, but, if the joint tenancy is not broken up, it is a gamble who will be the survivor and wind up owning the property.

(3) Tenancy by Entirety: Used only by legally married persons. The entire property goes to survivor on death of one; neither may sell without approval of other. This is, in effect, a special kind of joint tenancy between husband and wife, recognized only in certain states. Cannot exist after a divorce—all property previously held this way is assumed to be held as tenants in common—each holds undivided interest.

(4) Community Property: Still another type of plural ownership and existing in only eight of our states, it has features shared by both tenancy in common and tenancy by the entirety to some extent. The states concerned are Arizona, California, Idaho, Louisiana, Nevada, New Mexico, Texas and Washington. There are important differences from one of these states to the next. It is not safe to speak of the law of community property as if there were just one law. However, the underlying theory is that one half of what either husband or wife earns while married belongs to the other.

[¶601.1]   **Joint Property and the Income Tax**

Each co-owner reports his proportionate share of the income from the joint property. Where a husband and wife file a joint return, all of the income will be reported on this return. Note the following:

(1) If local law recognizes an agreement between the parties that one of them shall own the income, then the tax liability will fall on that person under the theory that the tax follows the income.

(2) The purchaser of U.S. Savings Bonds is taxed on the increment even though he allows the co-owner to receive it. If he gives his interest in the bond to the co-owner before maturity, he is only taxed on the increment in value up to the date of the gift.

(3) Since the death of one joint tenant (or tenant by the entirety) vests the property in the survivor by operation of law, the income subsequent to death is taxable entirely to the survivor, not at all to the deceased co-owner's estate.

(4) For purposes of the surviving tenant's determination of gain or loss upon subsequent disposition of the property, the basis to the survivor of a joint tenancy or tenancy by entirety equals:

(a) The acquisition cost of the property (both the portion included in the decedent's estate and the part not included), *plus*

(b) The appreciation, if any, attributable to the portion includible in the decedent's gross estate for the period between the date of acquisition and December 31, 1976 (see ¶802.1 and ¶802.2) and possibly the death tax attributable to the decedent's appreciation which occurred after 1976 (see ¶803).

Where there was a tenancy in common, the basis to the surviving co-tenant is not affected by the other's death. This is because only the decedent's share of the property is affected. Its carryover basis inures to whoever inherits the decedent's portion of the property.

[¶601.2]   **Joint Property and the Gift Tax**

Transfer of property to the names of the donor and another person as joint owners usually amounts to a taxable gift of an amount equal to the recipient's interest in the property. Note the following:

(1) The creation of a tenancy by the entirety or any joint tenancy by husband and wife in real property is not treated as a transfer subject to gift tax unless the donor chooses to have it so treated. In this case, any subsequent termination of the tenancy during the spouses' lives will result in a gift, the amount of which will be in proportion to the original contributions of the spouses. This rule does not apply to tenancies by the entirety created before 1954.

(2) Where a joint bank account is opened, since either party has the right to withdraw at any time, there is no gift. But when the noncontributing co-

depositor makes a withdrawal, there is a gift to the extent of the amount withdrawn.

(3) The same rule as in (2) applies to U.S. Savings Bonds, there being no gift until the co-owner redeems the bonds and retains the proceeds.

[¶601.3] Joint Property and the Estate Tax

Joint Interest Created Prior to 1977: The entire value of joint tenancy and entirety property, including joint bank accounts, is included in a decedent's gross estate unless the executor submits facts sufficient to show that property was not acquired entirely with consideration furnished by the decedent or was acquired by the decedent and the other joint tenant(s) by gift, devise, bequest or inheritance (IRC §2040). This is called the "consideration furnished" test rule.

Thus, where a husband buys with his money securities in his and his wife's joint names, on his death their value will be included in his estate. Note the following:

(1) Where decedent and spouse acquired property by gift, bequest, devise or inheritance as tenants by the entirety, only half the value is included in the decedent's gross estate (Regs. §20.2040-1(c)(7)).

(2) Where the decedent and any other person acquired property by gift, bequest, devise or inheritance as joint tenants, divide the value by the number of joint tenants and include only the fractional share in the decedent's gross estate (Regs. §20.2040-1(a)(1)).

(3) Where the decedent paid the purchase price for property owned by the survivor prior to its conversion into a tenancy by the entirety, the property will usually be included in full in the decedent's gross estate (Regs. §20.2040-1(a)(2)).

(4) If a husband makes a gift of property to his wife, who then creates a joint tenancy with him with this property before predeceasing him, it would appear that her estate isn't taxable (Regs. §20.2040-1(a)(2)). However, if he died first, his estate would probably be taxed in full (Regs. §20.2040-1(a)(2) and 20.2040-1(c)(4)).

(5) Property passing from one spouse to another via a joint tenancy (or tenancy by the entirety) qualifies for the estate tax marital deduction (IRC §2056).

(6) Where U.S. Savings Bonds are purchased in joint names, the redemption value at death will be included in the decedent's estate to the extent of his or her contribution to the purchase price (*Rev. Rul. 68-269*, CB 1968-1, 399).

(7) To the extent that the creation of a joint tenancy (or tenancy by the entirety) is subject to gift tax, a credit for the gift tax paid will be allowable against estate tax if the property is includible in the gross estate. This credit is reduced if the property qualifies for the estate tax marital deduction on the theory that only property subject to estate tax should qualify for the credit for gift tax. (See IRC §2012 and related regulations.) For gifts made after 1976,

under the unified gift and estate tax system imposed by 1976 Tax Reform Act, the gift tax is not allowed as a credit under IRC §2012.

"Qualified Joint Interest" between Husband and Wife after December 31, 1976: The "consideration furnished" test rule for joint interest created before January 1, 1977 will apply for all joint interests created after December 31, 1976 with one exception: Where husband or wife creates a "qualified joint interest" only one-half of the value of the jointly owned property will be included in the gross estate of the decedent, regardless of which joint tenant furnished the consideration. This is called the "fractional interest rule."

In order for the joint interest to qualify, the following four conditions must be satisfied:

(1) The joint interest must have been created by the decedent, his spouse, or both (inherited property does not qualify).

(2) In the case of personal property, the creation of the joint interest must have been a completed gift for gift tax purposes.

(3) In the case of real property, the donor must have elected to treat the creation of the joint tenancy as a taxable event at that time.

(4) The joint tenants cannot be persons other than the decedent and his spouse.

In the case of joint bank accounts, this rule does not apply, since either spouse is entitled to make withdrawals. Therefore, the creation of such a bank account (or additional deposits to it) is not considered a completed gift for gift tax purposes.

For real estate to qualify, the donor must make an election by including the creation of the joint interest in a timely-filled gift tax return. Once the election is made, it applies to all subsequent additions in value, and additional gift tax returns are required if gifts to the donee spouse exceed the $3000 annual exclusion. Additions in value would include mortgage principal payments as well as improvements made to the property; however, appreciation in value of the property is not an additional gift.

Planning Considerations: (1) From an estate-planning point of view, holding too much property as joint tenants (or tenants by the entirety) may be a costly proposition because you usually can't plan with such property; it will, by operation of law, belong to the surviving joint owner. An estate planning arrangement such as the non-marital deduction trust (¶604), which is designed to avoid death taxes, in the surviving spouse's estate, cannot be funded with joint property, so there is the possibility of double tax in the estates of the husband and wife.

(2) The estate owner should give serious consideration to the desirability of severing existing pre-1977 joint tenancies (or tenancies by the entirety) and creating a new joint tenancy (or tenancy by the entirety) to be eligible for fractional interest treatment. If the estate owner supplied the entire consideration for the original purchase, a transfer back to him would not constitute a gift, although creation of a new joint interest would be a gift. However, the gift tax marital deduction on the first $100,000 would probably eliminate a taxable

gift. Another possibility is to convert the joint tenancy into one in common (see item (3) below).

(3) Unlike joint tenancy and tenancy by the entirety, only the decedent's interest in a tenancy in common will be included in his estate. The Regulations (§20.2040-1(6)) specifically exclude tenancy in common property from their definition of "property held jointly."

[¶601.4] Community Property

While community property concepts are of importance primarily to residents of community property states, they might also come to the fore in noncommunity property states. This is especially true today as more families move from one state to another.

Example: John and Mary Jones live in New Mexico. John buys XYZ stock in his name with community funds. This stock becomes community property under New Mexico law. Then they move to New Jersey. Do the shares now become John's separate property? No—that which was community property in the state of acquisition does not change in status merely by being carried into another state where it would have been separate property if acquired there. (Reversing the situation, suppose John and Mary move from New Jersey to New Mexico after the shares have been purchased in John's name in New Jersey. Applying the same reasoning as above, John's separate property would not now automatically be transformed into community property.)

Property acquired by husband and wife during marriage while residing in Arizona, California, Idaho, Louisiana, Nevada, New Mexico, Texas or Washington is generally community property and the income therefrom is community property also.

Community property laws do not apply to property which belonged to either spouse at the time of the marriage or to property acquired after marriage by means of gift, devise or descent. This remains separate property. Also, it is generally possible for spouses to agree that certain of their property is not to be community property. For example, in some, though not all, community property states, it is possible for a husband and wife to have title to property as joint tenants if they so desire.

It is important to realize that the laws of the several community property states differ in many respects. Although all community property states make the earnings of spouses during marriage community property, only some apply the same treatment to damages for personal injuries. While income, profits and improvements relating to separate property of a spouse are held to be community property in some states, they constitute separate property in others.

In some community property states, on the death of one spouse half the community property belongs automatically to the survivor. In at least one, all the community property will vest in the surviving spouse except where there are children, in which case only half the community property will so vest. In at least one state, although a surviving wife will automatically take title to half the community property, a surviving husband, on the other hand, will automatically take title to all the community property.

Generally speaking, the husband as manager of the community usually controls and may even dispose of or exchange community property during the continuance of the marriage.

Here is a brief rundown of some of the more important federal income, gift and estate tax treatments of community property:

Income Tax: Community income is taxed one-half to each spouse regardless of whether they file joint or separate returns. At the death of either spouse, the entire community property may get a stepped-up basis, depending on whether at least one-half the property was taxable in the decedent's estate (IRC §1014(b)).

Gift Tax: There is no gift at the time property which is earned or acquired by one spouse automatically takes on the characteristic of community property. There may be a gift where one spouse's separate property is transformed into community property (IRC §2523, especially §2523(f)). Note the following:

(1) Where community property is transformed into separate property, there may be a gift (as determined by state law) (IRC §2523, especially §2523(f)).

(2) Where spouses make an inter vivos gift of community property to a third person, both spouses are subject to the gift tax on the value of their respective half interests (IRC §2513).

Estate Tax: Ordinarily, one-half the community property is included in the estate of a deceased spouse. For example, if the wife died first, in most community property states one-half the community property would be included in her estate despite the fact that her husband alone had earned all the community property. Although the marital deduction normally does not apply to community property, because community property already has its own marital deduction built into its structure, if one half of the community property is less than $250,000, the excess is eligible for the marital deduction.

[¶602]   **HOW TO TRANSFER THE MOST BY WILL**

Generally, the biggest item of cost in transferring estate property is the estate tax. The easiest and most convenient way to keep this cost at a minimum is to make a judicious use of the marital deduction, which exempts from tax the greater of $250,000 or 50% of the adjusted gross estate provided it goes to the spouse in a form that qualifies it for the deduction (IRC §2056). The marital deduction property will be taxed in the surviving spouse's estate, unless consumed or given away during the period between the two deaths. The remainder of the property will be taxed in the first estate but need not be taxed a second time when the surviving spouse dies. We can give her the income from it (and the property itself if she needs it) without making it a part of her taxable estate simply by leaving it in trust for her use, but not subject to her control.

[¶602.1]   **Minimizing Estate Tax for Both Husband and Wife**

The estate owner can transfer his estate without incurring an estate tax, whether he leaves his entire estate to his spouse, or gives her $250,000 (marital deduction), if his adjusted gross estate is less than $250,000, plus the exemption equivalent of the unified credit. The combination of the $250,000 and exemption equivalent of the unified credit is as follows:

Year of death	Adjusted gross estate
1977	$370,667
1978	384,000
1979	397,333
1980	411,563
1981 and later	425,625

The above figures must be adjusted for lifetime transfers which effect the marital deduction and the unified credit, as well as other credits allowed on the estate tax return.

When the estate owner's adjusted gross estate is less than the amounts shown above, the use of the maximum marital deduction of $250,000 may not be advisable because the amount going to the surviving spouse may be greater than necessary to reduce the estate owner's federal estate tax to zero, and thereafter result in unnecessarily high tax on the surviving spouse's subsequent death. This is also true if the estate owner's entire estate is left outright to his wife. For example, if the estate owner dies in 1981 and has an estate of $350,000 (and assuming the spouse has no assets of her own) and she receives the maximum marital deduction of $250,000, the decedent's federal estate tax would be zero, but the tax on the spouse's subsequent death would be $23,800.

If, instead of leaving the maximum marital deduction, the estate owner's will had a marital deduction clause leaving the *lesser* of (a) the maximum marital deduction allowable for federal estate tax purposes or (b) the marital deduction which shall be necessary to reduce the federal estate tax to zero after allowance of all available credits and deductions, the surviving spouse

	Maximum marital deduction		Minimum marital deduction	
	Husband	Wife	Husband	Wife
Assets	$350,000	—	$350,000	—
Marital Deduction	250,000	250,000	174,375	174,375
Taxable Estate	100,000	250,000	175,625	174,375
Gross Tax	23,800	70,800	47,000	46,800
Unified Credit	47,000	47,000	47,000	47,000
Federal Estate Tax	-0-	23,800	-0-	-0-

would receive approximately $174,375 (assume estate owner's death in 1981) and the result would be no federal estate tax for either estate. This formula clause can be used in both the pecuniary bequest or fraction of the residue formula (see ¶603.9).

If the estate owner left his entire estate outright to the surviving spouse, his estate still would incur no federal estate tax, but on the subsequent death of the surviving spouse, there would be federal estate tax of $57,800, as illustrated below:

	Husband	Wife
Assets	$350,000	—
Marital Deduction	250,000	$350,000
Taxable Estate	100,000	350,000
Gross Tax	23,800	104,800
Unified Credit	47,800	47,000
Federal Estate Tax	-0-	57,800

To recapitulate the different tax results of each method in tabular form:

	Total death taxes	Net to children
Minimum Marital Deduction (so husband's estate pays no federal estate tax)	-0-	$350,000
Maximum Marital Deduction of $250,000	$23,800	326,200
Estate Left to Spouse Outright	57,800	292,200

Where the adjusted gross estate is over $500,000, leaving 50% of the adjusted gross estate to the spouse outright or in trust, which qualifies for the marital deduction, will minimize the tax in both estates, assuming the wife has no substantial property in her own name.

[¶602.2] **Methods of Transfer by Will**

This table illustrates, for deaths after 1980, the tax savings by use of the maximum and minimum marital deductions as compared to an outright bequest by the estate owner to the surviving spouse. Clearly, the most expensive method of transferring the estate is the outright bequest, then the maximum marital deduction, and the least expensive way is the minimum marital deduction. Once the adjusted gross estate exceeds $425,625, the maximum marital deduction will become the least expensive method. This table is based on the wife having no assets in her own name and the federal estate tax is computed with the unified credit of $47,000, without taking into consideration the credit for state taxes paid, or administration expenses.

HUSBAND'S ESTATE IN 1981

	Adjusted gross estate	Maximum marital deduction	Minimum marital deduction	Tax
(a)	200,000	200,000	24,375	-0-
(b)	300,000	250,000	124,375	-0-
(c)	400,000	250,000	224,375	-0-

WIFE'S SUBSEQUENT ESTATE

	Tax if outright bequest of entire estate	Tax with max. marital deduction	Tax with min. marital deduction	Tax saving by using minimum mar. deduction
(a)	7,800	7,800	-0-	7,800
(b)	40,800	23,800	-0-	40,800
(c)	74,800	23,800	15,600	59,200

In deciding which of the three methods is most advisable for the estate owner, consideration should be given to overall tax savings, and to the needs of the surviving spouse and children; tax saving by itself should not be the only guide. By giving the spouse only the amount which qualifies for either type of marital deduction, she does not have the full sole management of all her husband's assets. For this reason, in small estates (especially under $175,000), it is usually better to give the wife the entire estate outright. However, if the wife has substantial property in her own name, there may be an overall saving in both estates if she is given a life estate in her husband's estate, so that it does not qualify for the marital deduction in her husband's estate, but will not be included in her estate on her subsequent demise. As the estate gets larger, she can be given the amount which qualifies for the marital deduction either outright or in trust. If the marital deduction portion of the property is left to her outright, she may do as she pleases with those funds. If left in trust, she must be given the minimal right to direct to whom and how the property shall be distributed at her death. (This appointive power is designed to qualify such trust for the "marital estate tax deduction.")

If the estate owner has a will executed before 1977 which contains a formula clause stating that the surviving spouse is to receive the "maximum marital deduction" and the estate owner dies before 1979, the surviving spouse will not receive the full $250,000 if the estate is smaller than $500,000 (unless the domiciliary state has enacted a law to the contrary). This should be closely examined and may require an amendment to the existing will.

[¶603]   **THE MARITAL DEDUCTION TRUST**

The outline of one widely used form of the marital deduction trust method of property distribution is as follows:

(1) The husband would first direct in his will that the estate which he leaves at his death should be divided into two parts.

(2) He would secondly direct that the first half be placed in a trust at his death for the benefit of his wife. The income from the property in the trust would be paid to his wife for life. She would be given the right to direct in her will how and to whom the property should be distributed at her death. He would finally direct in respect of this trust that the trust property would pass to his children at his wife's death (or a further delayed date) in the event she failed to exercise the privilege of directing to whom it should go at her death.

(3) He would then direct that all the taxes, charges and expenses against his estate be paid out of the second part of his estate.

(4) He would finally direct that the balance remaining of the second part of his estate be transferred to a second trust. The income of this second trust would likewise be paid to his wife for life. The property itself would be distributed to his children at his wife's death or some other selected date.

The above four-step outline sets forth the bare mechanics of one form of the marital deduction trust method. Many additional precautions must be taken in its actual formulation to satisfy the requirements of §2056 of the Internal Revenue Code.

[¶603.1]   Trust Management

If the husband wishes to give his wife a voice in the management of the trust funds, he may do this by appointing her and another individual (or trust institution) as co-trustees. Efficient and trained management of the trust funds is assured by this approach since the wife and the other trustee must agree and act in unison in every step of the administration of the trust. In effect, this approach arms her with the management experience and training of the other trustee and blends both these skills and her personal viewpoint into the management of the property.

The potentials of the trust management feature do not end at this point. It also gives to the creator of the trust the opportunity to dictate whatever investment instructions he wishes to have applied to the trust property. These instructions may take several different forms:

(1) He may wish to limit the investment of the trust funds to specific securities or types of securities.

(2) He may wish to have certain of his investments disposed of immediately.

(3) He may wish to forbid the sale or other disposition of certain of the trust investments.

[¶603.2]   Trust Flexibility

It should be noted that the husband may give the wife substantial powers over the trusts without destroying their tax-savings features. With respect to the trust which is designed to qualify for the marital deduction, the wife may be given the broadest possible rights including the power to withdraw principal funds at will. With respect to the other trust, the rights which may be given to her without affecting the tax savings include such powers as the following:

(1) The right to consume, invade or appropriate trust principal in emergency situations necessitating additional funds for sickness, accident, support or maintenance.

(2) The noncumulative right to withdraw up to $5,000 or 5% of the trust principal each year for whatever purposes she desires.

In addition to these rights, the trustee could be given the discretionary right to apply the trust principal to the care, support or maintenance of the wife and a similar right coupled with educational powers for the children.

Where the husband desires to utilize the marital deduction, he can either give the portion of his estate which qualifies for the marital deduction to his wife outright or transfer the property to an "estate" or "power of appointment" trust naming his wife as beneficiary. The estate trust is one in which the trustee has the power to distribute or accumulate and the corpus becomes part of his wife's estate on her death. In the power of appointment trust, the wife receives the income for life, payable at least annually, together with a general power of appointment over the trust property. Use of one of the marital deduction trusts has the advantage of not burdening the widow with the management of the estate. Moreover, the superior experience of the trustee will generally mean that more of the estate will be conserved for the remaindermen.

[¶603.3]   The Power of Appointment

A bequest in trust will qualify for the marital deduction if these five conditions are met:

(1) The surviving spouse must be entitled to the income from the trust for life.

(2) This income must be payable annually or at more frequent intervals.

(3) The surviving spouse must have the power, exercisable in favor of herself or her estate, to appoint the entire corpus free of the trust.

(4) This power must be exercisable by the surviving spouse alone, either by will or by deed during life, and it must be exercisable in all events.

(5) The corpus of the trust must not be subject to a power in any other person to appoint any part of the trust to any person other than the surviving spouse.

One of the advantages of the power of appointment trust is that it affords the testator the opportunity to specify in his own will the ultimate beneficiaries of the trust corpus in the event his wife fails to exercise her power to appoint. He can thus indicate his wishes and make it easy for his wife to abide by them just by doing nothing.

He may give her power to appoint by deed of trust during life. The power to appoint by deed during life is necessary if the wife is to have the opportunity to minimize estate tax on her death by making lifetime gifts. It gives her full control unless she is restricted to appointing to a particular group which does not include herself.

The husband can limit her to appointing the trust corpus by will, which will conserve it for her use during life. But he has only inadequate protection against the possibility that she will appoint the property to someone other than his children or others who he thinks should be the ultimate beneficiaries. See Regs. §20.2056(b)-5(a).

The appointive property is not usually considered an asset of the wife for state law purposes since she is merely being used as an instrument to pass title of the husband's property. This being so, the power of appointment trust generally prevents the trust property from becoming subject to the wife's creditors or claims which could result from a later marriage. It also prevents the corpus from being subjected to a new set of probate expenses, attorney's fees, and other administration costs. In some states, the power of appointment trust may escape state death taxes on the wife's death.

[¶603.4]   The Estate Trust

When Congress passed the technical requirements for using a trust for the marital deduction which in effect made it possible to qualify certain terminable interests, it unintentionally left the door open for an estate trust to qualify. This is so because the estate trust gives the wife a remainder, which is an interest in property and not a terminable interest.

Thus, in drafting such a trust, there need be no concern over compliance with the five technical conditions of the Code. All that need be done is to make certain that all income and principal will *ultimately* be payable to the wife or to her estate when she dies.

Nor is there any limitation on the type of property which can be included in an estate trust. Thus, nonincome-producing property could be left in trust without worrying about the uncertain complexities of a ban against nonincome-producing property.

The disadvantage of this type of trust is that it forces the trust property into a second administration with its concomitant costs and exposes it to claims of the wife's creditors.

The advantages are:

(1) It is simpler to draft and offers a convenient repository for unproductive property, such as stock in a family corporation that doesn't pay dividends.

(2) The income can be accumulated, paying tax at the trust's lower tax rate, thus building capital faster than if it had to be distributed; the widow, having lost the benefit of income splitting, would pay a heavy tax if the income was distributed to her.

(3) It enables the widow to establish new trusts, measured from the time of her death rather than from the time of her husband's death. A new trust

created by her will can be measured by the lives of heirs born after her husband's death; if she merely exercises a power of appointment, she is restricted in establishing new trusts to lives in being at the time of her husband's death.

[¶603.5]　Asset Selection for the Marital Deduction Trust

Proper selection of assets for the marital deduction trust can be a crucial factor in saving taxes. The executor should be directed to exclude certain assets such as insurance on the life of the wife (it will be taxable at a much larger figure in the estate of the wife than that allowed for the marital deduction), foreign assets (part or all of the credit for foreign death taxes may be lost) and income in respect of a decedent's assets (part or all of the income tax deduction followed for estate tax paid with respect to such assets may be lost if they are not excluded). In addition, there should be a blanket direction to exclude all nonqualifying or "tainted" assets which would otherwise result in a reduction of the marital deduction allowed to the extent of their value. The absence of such a direction will reduce the marital deduction by the value of all tainted assets which might have been used to satisfy the marital legacy whether or not they were actually so used (Regs. §20.2056(b)(5)).

When a power of appointment trust is used, provision should be made for unproductive property to be excluded or compensated for in other ways.

On the other hand, there should be a direction to either include specific wasting assets or wasting assets in general to lessen the amount of marital deduction assets subject to estate tax on the wife's subsequent death.

[¶603.6]　Invasion Provisions

An additional tax-saving purpose may be served by giving the wife power to deplete the corpus of the marital deduction trust. This right may be limited to an annual amount equal to a percentage of the income of the marital trust or to the income of the family trust. In states that permit accumulations for adults, instead of making the wife the income beneficiary of the family trust, its income may be accumulated until the corpus of the marital trust is exhausted or at least until her death. This method generates both income and estate tax savings. The wife is taxed on income but not principal distributions of the marital trust, and the income of the family trust will be taxed to the trustee until the marital trust is exhausted. Estate tax in the wife's estate will be saved to the extent that the marital trust principal is used up by the time of her death.

[¶603.7]　Allocating the Death Tax Burden

The marital deduction is defined as the greater of $250,000 or 50% of the adjusted gross estate. Since the adjusted gross estate is arrived at without reduction for death taxes (federal and state), apportioning any part of such taxes to the marital share, whether under the will or under state law, may result in the reduction of the marital deduction to the extent of the tax charged against the bequest which qualifies for the marital deduction. For this reason, any marital deduction wills should contain a provision charging all death taxes to the nonmarital portion. This is equitable since it results in having the tax charged against the property on which the tax is based.

Caution should be exercised when using a fractional share formula in setting up the marital legacy to avoid the usual allocation of death taxes to the residuary estate. The taxes should be specifically charged against the non-qualifying portion of the residue to avoid the apportionment problem.

[¶603.8] The Use of Tax Formula Clauses for Achieving the Maximum Benefits of the Marital Deduction

The draftsman of the will who wants to obtain the maximum overall estate tax savings in both the husband's and wife's estate must realize it is impossible to figure out the exact values of both future estates at the time of their demise. In moderate estates, leaving the wife $250,000 does not accomplish the minimum estate tax when considering both estates; in estates of $500,000 or more, the estate owner wants to leave his wife one-half of the estate in order to achieve the minimum tax on both estates, assuming she has little or no property in her own name (see ¶602.1).

The only sure way of accomplishing the minimum estate tax in both estates is by use of a formula marital deduction clause in the will. Without such a clause, the property owner can only estimate whether he is giving his wife an amount which would accomplish his goal in lowering taxes in both estates. This is because any subsequent increase or decrease in his estate can cause either an underqualification or overqualification for the marital deduction. On the other hand, a tax formula clause based on the value of the estate at the time of death (or alternate valuation date) assures that the wife will receive exactly an amount equal to the desired marital deduction.

In cases where the wife has substantial property of her own (but less than that of her husband), the maximum overall estate tax savings in both estates will usually be achieved if both spouses end up with approximately the same taxable estate. To achieve this goal, the draftsman should use an equalization formula clause in the husband's will. This clause gives the wife only one-half of the difference between the value of the husband's estate over the value of her own estate. (This is computed as if both spouses had died on the same day.) For example, if the estate of the husband (who is assumed to have died first) is $600,000 and the estate of the wife is $400,000, she would receive $100,000 by using the equalization formula clause. If the wife outlived her husband for a long period of time, the equalization formula clause might not be the most beneficial as the overall savings in tax in both estates is diminished by the loss of earnings on the higher taxes paid in the husband's estate, since he did not utilize the full marital deduction. Therefore, the draftsman may want to limit the use of the equalization formula clause to older estate owners.

Formula clauses have been criticized by some draftsmen primarily on the ground that there is too much of an obsession with the idea of hitting the marital deduction which would benefit both estates on the nose. For example: (1) other (nontax) considerations may call for the wife's receiving more than the marital deduction desired; (2) the testator, being assured that his wife will receive an amount equal to the marital deduction desired regardless of subsequent events, may haphazardly cause substantial changes to be made in his estate plan (as by changing beneficiary designations in life insurance policies) without first seeking legal advice and may mess up what was at its creation a good estate plan.

The above objections can be countered by the argument that the draftsman who knows what he is doing will only use a marital deduction formula clause in those cases where its use is definitely warranted and will advise the property owner not to unilaterally make any changes in his estate plan.

A somewhat more valid objection is that there might be a conflict of interest between the widow and other beneficiaries which might cause the executor quite a bit of embarrassment. For example, the marital deduction tax formula may be larger or smaller depending on whether the executor elects to take certain administration expenses as estate tax or income tax deductions or on whether the estate is valued as at the date of death or at a date six months later. The answer to this objection is that a testator will usually indicate to his executor by a provision in his will just who it is who is to be preferred when a problem arises involving the use of the executor's discretion. Within this framework, the executor should not have too much difficulty in working with a tax formula clause.

How tax formula clauses work out will become apparent in the discussion which follows, where we compare the two major types of formula clauses: the pecuniary bequest and the fractional share bequest.

[¶603.9]   Pecuniary Bequest or Fraction of the Residue Formula

Although there are variations, the two main types of formula clauses are the pecuniary bequest and the fraction of the residue formula. The first provides for an amount equal to the maximum or minimum marital deduction to go to the wife; the second gives the wife that fraction of the residue which will equal the maximum or minimum marital deduction. In substance they both aim to achieve the same thing—the exact maximum or minimum marital deduction. But they may result in important differences.

The pecuniary bequest has the tremendous advantage of allowing the executor, in making a distribution in kind, to consider the impact of carryover basis to the widow (marital deduction share) and nonmarital share. Any property which is part of the marital deduction share does not get an adjustment to the basis for estate tax (see ¶803). This means that in a pecuniary bequest, the executor can sort out the assets with the high basis for the widow and give the assets with lower basis to the nonmarital share, thereby making an adjustment for estate tax purposes to the assets which have the greatest appreciation. If the nonmarital share gets the high basis assets, these assets may not get the full adjustment to basis for estate tax paid, because when the adjustment for death taxes is added to the basis, it may be greater than day of death value.

Since the pecuniary bequest is in the nature of a general legacy, it has the effect of creating a dollar legacy. Unless there is a provision to the contrary in the will, assets used to satisfy a legacy of any kind must be valued at the date of distribution values. Paying such a dollar legacy (of, say, $200,000) with assets which were worth $150,000 at date of death but have appreciated between the date of death and the date of distribution will subject the executor to capital gains tax on the appreciation, even though no gain is recognized on the difference between carryover basis and value at date of death. This problem can sometimes be overcome by allocating to the bequest both appreciated and depreciated assets, if any, in proportion so that the gains and losses balance out.

An even more serious problem which may result from the use of a pecuniary formula is the possible distortion of the testamentary plan if there is any substantial appreciation or depreciation in the estate assets between the date of death and the date of distribution. For example, if the adjusted gross estate is $500,000 on the date of death and $750,000 on the date of distribution, a pecuniary bequest would still only entitle the spouse to $250,000 or one-third of the date of distribution value of the estate. Likewise, if the value of the estate depreciates from $500,000 to $250,000 at distribution, the spouse gets the entire estate. Both the risk of loss and the potentiality for gain are shifted to the residuary estate. This is all right provided it reflects the testator's intent.

Both this distortion problem and the capital gain problem are avoided by the use of the fraction of the residue formula clause. Since the wife is a residuary legatee, she takes the appreciated assets at the carryover basis and realizes no gain at that time. When she sells the appreciated assets, she will recognize gain to the extent of the difference between the sales price and the carryover basis.

The fraction of the residue formula, although it avoids these problems, has problems of its own. The major one is that physical assets have to be divided into fractional shares or sold, and the sharing in appreciation or depreciation must be applied to each asset on an individual basis. This can severely limit flexibility, and can be a real problem where this is important. In addition, the executor does not have a choice as to distributing high basis assets to the widow, since she is physically entitled to a portion of all the assets. On the other hand, the problem discussed immediately below does not arise with a fraction of the residue formula. This fact alone may be worth the trouble arising from its cumbersomeness.

[¶603.10]   **Distribution at Estate Tax Values—Rev. Proc. 64-19**

Some pecuniary formula bequests contain provisions which permit the executor to satisfy the pecuniary bequest by distributing assets at their estate tax values. For example, if the amount of the marital bequest was $100,000 and the estate consisted of two blocks of stock, each worth $100,000 at date of death but at the time of distribution one block was worth $75,000 and the other $125,000, the executor could satisfy the marital bequest by distributing the $75,000 block of stock. The entire marital deduction will be denied if the will permits this (*Rev. Proc. 64-19*, 1964-1 CB 682).

For wills executed before October 1, 1964, IRS will allow the marital deduction if the executor and the surviving spouse enter into side agreements by which they agree to apply a construction to the will that will achieve the result desired by IRS, that is, a distribution of assets fairly representative of appreciation and depreciation.

In the case of wills executed on or after October 1, 1964, and also where the executor refuses to execute a side agreement on a pre-October 1, 1964 will, the power to distribute at estate tax values will bar the marital deduction unless the executor can show that the interest of the surviving spouse is ascertainable as of the date of death and that it can't be shifted to anyone else by the actions of anyone other than the surviving spouse. This burden might be met by showing that local law required this result, that is, that the executor is required to consider any appreciation or depreciation in the value of all property in making distribution to a surviving spouse. IRS has ruled that New York law meets this requirement, and it is likely that it will so rule in the case of other states with similar laws. Many states have enacted such legislation.

IRS agrees that the problem does not arise in the case of a fraction of the residue type formula bequest or in the case of a pecuniary formula bequest which does not permit in-kind distribution of property at estate tax value. And it would seem that a provision in a pecuniary formula bequest for distribution at the lower of estate tax or date of distribution value should be all right since, according to the terms of the instrument, the widow cannot get less than the amount of the pecuniary bequest. Distribution at date of distribution values, however, will not by itself satisfy IRS. It must be required by the governing instrument.

[¶604]　　　THE NONMARITAL DEDUCTION TRUST

The nonmarital deduction property, if left outright, will be taxed both in the decedent's estate and again in his spouse's estate upon her subsequent death unless consumed or given away in the period between the two deaths. This means that there is a good possibility that by the time the property reaches the children, it will have been depleted by estate taxes in the husband's and wife's estates.

By placing the property which qualifies for the deduction in a marital deduction trust and the remaining property in a second trust, a double estate tax on the nonmarital deduction property can be avoided.

The second trust, in a typical two-trust arrangement will be set up primarily for the protection of the wife during her life, but without giving her such control over the trust as to make its principal taxable on the wife's subsequent death. Income may be made payable to the wife alone or to the wife jointly with the testator's children. The testator may restrict himself to setting up one trust out of the residuary estate (or the balance of the residue after the marital deduction trust has been carved out), or he may set up a number of trusts, one for each of the children who survive him. Whether the trust is one or more will depend on whether the dollar amount available is sufficient to provide a sound economic funding for more than one trust and whether any tax savings can be provided by an authorization to accumulate excess income.

Here are some objectives and possibilities for this kind of trust:

(1) Income tax savings may be made available by setting up a separate trust for each child beneficiary so that each trust will be considered a separate taxpayer. This accomplishes a division of the total income among several taxable entities, bringing lower annual income tax brackets into play.

(2) We may provide that the wife shall receive the annual income from the trust property.

(3) We may not wish to direct the income to the wife if it will put her into an excessively high income tax bracket at a time when she will no longer enjoy the benefit of split income. We can, in this case, provide for the accumulation of trust income, state law permitting, or the distribution of trust income to the children and protect the wife by giving the trustee discretion to apply the principal for the support and maintenance of the wife and children if necessary.

(4) The trustee may be directed to "sprinkle" so much of the income of the nonmarital trust among the wife, children and grandchildren of the testator as their maintenance and educational requirements dictate.

(5) The ultimate distribution of the corpus of the second trust must be specified. We may provide for the distribution of the corpus of each of the separate trusts when the child beneficiary attains a specified age or portions of the corpus at various ages, or we can save further estate tax by deferring distribution of the trust property until the death of the child beneficiary, passing it to grandchildren or surviving sisters and brothers or their descendants if that beneficiary has no children.

(6) We may give each child beneficiary of a nonmarital deduction trust a special power of appointment to grant what remains of his share of the trust at his death among those specified descendants or other relatives: spouses and descendants of the beneficiaries; spouse and descendants of the testator; spouses of any of these descendants. This type of power is tax free.

[¶605]   **WILL CHECKLIST**

There is an infinite variety of detail which should be considered and discussed preliminary to the preparation of a will. Much of this detail comes out of the testator's own experience, his appraisal of his property and his heirs and his aspirations for them. There are some technical matters about which he should think and develop his own ideas, so that he can discuss them properly with the estate planner.

The following series of questions provides a useful check, both for the estate owner (to stimulate his thinking prior to the preliminary conversation with his estate planner) and for the planner to make sure he has obtained all necessary information.

Any Special Instructions for Funeral Arrangements, Upkeep of Cemetery Plot, etc? Instructions can be spelled out in your will. Burial instructions in a will are useless where the provisions of the will remain secret until some date after death and after burial has already taken place. The matter can be left to the discretion of your family, or you may leave a special letter addressed to your executor or to your family to acquaint them with your wishes.

Who Should Get Your Personal Belongings? If you do not provide for the disposition of clothing, jewelry, furniture, etc., such articles, unless state law provides otherwise, will go into the residue of your estate and possibly impose on your executor the obligation to sell them. Tangible personal property should always be disposed of by separate will provisions. This is because under IRC §662 all amounts distributed to a beneficiary for the taxable year must be included in the gross income of the beneficiary to the extent of the distributable net income of the estate. Under IRC §663, any amount which, under the terms of the will, is distributed as a gift of specific property all at once or in not more than three installments is excluded from the operation of IRC §662. Thus, if the tangible personal property is separately disposed of in the will and is distributed to the legatee all at once, its distribution will have no income tax consequences. However, if disposed of as part of the residue, its distribution might be taxable as income to the legatee. It may be wise to specify the individuals who are to receive the most valuable of your personal possessions and leave the balance to someone in whom you have confidence, with instructions to divide it at his discretion among those close to you.

Do You Want to Make Any Cash Bequests? When you leave a specific amount of money to an individual or to a charity, your executor is required to pay that amount in full before he makes any distribution to the beneficiaries who are to share the balance of your estate. If your estate should be smaller than you expect, such a cash bequest could result in your unintentionally having made inadequate provision for other beneficiaries. You can guard against this by providing that cash bequests are to be paid only if the total estate exceeds a specified minimum, or bequests to individuals and charities can be made in fractions or percentages of the estate rather than in fixed dollar amounts.

What Do You Want to Do with Your Real Estate? Do you want to leave your solely owned real estate outright, place it in trust (possibly a residence trust in which your wife has the rights to the house), have it sold and the proceeds distributed or give one beneficiary—for example, your wife—the right to use it for life with ownership going to your children on her death? Under the law of some states, your spouse may have dower or curtesy rights in your real estate.

Do You Want to Leave an Income for Anybody? You may want to assure a regular income for your parents, dependent relatives or others. You may do this through a trust established by will or by directing your executors to buy annuities for named beneficiaries. In the event that you establish the trust, you can specify the individual to whom the trust property will go after it has produced the required income for a specified period of time.

Whom Do You Want to Have the Remainder of Your Estate? Decide who is to share in the bulk of your estate; then divide the balance, after specific bequests, in fractions or percentages. By being overly exact in allocating particular assets to certain beneficiaries or in specifying interests in dollar amounts, you can frustrate your own objectives in the event of important changes in the size or value of your estate. If you divide the bulk of the estate by fractions of a share, you won't be in the position of having to revise your will repeatedly because of changes in asset values. Be sure your will names alternate or contingent beneficiaries who are to receive the share of any beneficiary who fails to survive you.

What Can You Do to Protect the Interests of Minor Beneficiaries? It is usually necessary to have a guardian appointed by the court to manage a child's property until he or she attains majority. The guardian must furnish bond, make periodic accountings and secure court approval on many of the actions he will have to take. Guardianship, except for small sums of money, can be both burdensome and expensive. Your will can simplify this matter by directing that the property be turned over to a trust to be held for the benefit of minors until majority. The trustee can be authorized to use the trust property to provide maintenance, support and education for the minor.

What Can You Do to Protect the Interests of Adult Beneficiaries? Adult beneficiaries can dissipate outright gifts quickly. You should decide whether you want to leave your property outright, turn it over to beneficiaries in installments or have it held and managed for their benefit by an experienced trustee.

How Do You Want Trust Property Handled? Subject to local law, you can determine whether the income of trust property is to be distributed or accumulated in order to build up future value. You can determine how much of the income is to be distributed and how much of it is to go to each beneficiary. You can authorize the trustee to distribute some of the trust principal to your beneficiaries if income is insufficient to maintain living standards or meet emergencies. Again subject to local law, you can decide when the trust is to terminate—for example, whether it should be distributed to your children or held for your grandchildren. You should decide at what age your beneficiaries should be capable of handling the property themselves. You may wish to have them receive trust principal gradually in installments.

Whom Do You Want as Executor and Trustee? An executor and possibly a trustee must be designated to handle the settlement and management of your estate. This responsibility must be accepted. The details of settling an estate must be handled. Your property must be managed until it is turned over to your beneficiaries, and this calls for a high degree of skill and experience. The choice of an executor and trustee may determine whether your plans for your family and your property succeed or fail.

Other Points to Consider: Whether or not you have a will, changes in the law and new developments in your own affairs may have made your will obsolete. Here are points you should discuss with your lawyer, unless you have reviewed them very recently:

(1) Does your will take full advantage of the maximum or minimum marital deduction?

(2) Are your insurance arrangements integrated with your will?

(3) Are inheritance taxes to be paid by each beneficiary or by the estate?

(4) Have safeguards been established to minimize the possibility that your property will be taxed twice—once when you die and again when your wife dies?

(5) Has provision been made for the possibility that you and your wife may die under such circumstances that it is impossible to determine which of you died first?

(6) Should your executor have authority to carry on your business, or should he be directed to dispose of it?

(7) Does your executor have the right to borrow money, to pledge estate assets and to renew existing obligations?

(8) Should your executor have the power to retain real estate or to sell, mortgage or lease it?

(9) Should your executor have the right to retain assets owned by you at the time of your death, whether or not they constitute a legal investment for trust and estate funds?

(10) Does your trustee have broad discretion in the investment and reinvestment of trust funds? Do you want to give him any specific instructions?

(11) Have income provisions for trust beneficiaries been protected against inflation?

(12) Does the trustee have the right to make special provision for beneficiaries in the event of emergencies?

(13) Will there be enough liquid funds to meet estate tax obligations and other cash requirements which will confront your executor and trustee?

(14) Has the future distribution of your property been studied with a view to minimizing the tax drain on the income it will produce?

[¶606]   **TESTATOR'S DOMICILE**

Theoretically, a man can have only one domicile. While we know that for tax purposes, at least, he may have two, three or even more domiciles, the problem for the testator is not one of multiple domiciles but one of which one is *the* domicile.

An estate owner may spend his winters in Florida, summers in Maine and commute between New York and Washington, D.C., during the rest of the year, maintaining residences of a more or less permanent nature in all four places. Which of these jurisdictions is his domiciliary state for purposes of will probate, estate administration and the like? It could be that potential administration expenses in his estate would be considerably less in one jurisdiction than in any of the others; all other things being equal, he would probably prefer that this state be treated as his domicile, inasmuch as the legality and administration of a testator's will and estate are determined by the laws and practice of the domiciliary state. And how about inheritance taxes? To which state should they be paid? Or can part be paid to one state and part to another?

All discussions of domicile center on one question: *Where is the testator's principal home?* In many cases, this question is easier asked than answered. The solution lies in a two-pronged affirmative approach: (i) assert which state you wish to be your domicile; (ii) act accordingly. Adhering to the following set of rules should help to set a one-state domicile:

(1) Integrate your activities to coincide with your assertion as to your state of domicile. If necessary, adjust your pattern of living if it will give added weight to an otherwise questionable choice of domicile.

(2) Label your choice of domicile as *your home,* your *legal residence, your address,* reserving to the others such titles as *summer home, winter home, vacation home, business home,* etc. Recite your domicile in your will.

(3) File *resident tax returns* in the state you select for your domicile, nonresident returns in the others.

(4) Keep the bulk of your valuable assets within your claimed domiciliary state. Not only is this further evidence of your intentions, it is also a much easier and less expensive matter for your personal representative to collect and distribute such property than if it had been scattered here and there.

(5) Consider whether it is advisable to hold real estate in any state other than your claimed domicile. Not only may this bring up the question of what is your domicile, it may also involve costly ancillary proceedings. It might be better to rent in a nondomiciliary state.

(6) Use the address of your claimed domicile for purposes of bank accounts, automobile and driver's licenses, securities registration and dividend payment notices, life insurance, etc.

(7) Register and vote in the state in which you wish to be domiciled.

(8) File for homestead or veterans' real estate tax exemptions in the state in which you assert your domicile.

After an estate owner has died, if there remains some doubt as to what was his domicile at the date of his death, his personal representative should first examine all the available evidence so that he can come away with a good idea as to which state seems to have the most support as the domicile. If there is still substantial doubt, then there are a number of choices which may be available:

(1) *Before the will has been probated,* assuming there are two competing states, it is possible to negotiate a *settlement* so that each state agrees to take a percentage of any tax due and that the will shall be probated and the estate

administered in one of them (preferably the state in which the bulk of the decedent's assets are located).

(2) *After the will has been probated* in the state which seems to be the testator's proper domicile, it still might be possible to compromise tax claims of competing states via a *settlement* between the states. (This assumes that a state other than the one in which the executor qualified is actually in a legitimate bargaining situation.)

(3) *Also after the will has been probated,* it might be possible to refer any tax dispute between states to arbitration. This will insure that only one state will collect a resident inheritance tax. This, however, is much more drawn out and much more expensive than a settlement.

(4) As a last resort, actual litigation may be attempted; but it will be difficult to interplead the taxing authorities of competing states.

Remember, it is best to avoid the necessity for a settlement, arbitration or litigation involving different states for purposes of establishing a probate or a tax domicile. And the way to do this is to clearly favor during lifetime, by assertion and by action, one state as the domicile.

[¶607]   **DRAFTING THE WILL**

Here are points to check when drafting a will.

[¶607.1]   **Charitable and Religious Pledges**

Are these expressly included as debts or otherwise directed to be paid? If not, the executor may not be authorized to pay them; or, if he does pay them, he may not be authorized to deduct them taxwise.

[¶607.2]   **Jurisdiction**

Does the testator own real property in another state? If so, what does the law of that state require to effectively transfer title by will?

Does the law of another state where some of testator's property is located give dower, curtesy or community property rights inconsistent with the provisions of the will? This also ties in with any provisions for a spouse in lieu of dower, right of election, etc.

If there are property interests in other states, are they treated as personalty or realty? This is especially important in the case of oil and mineral rights.

If a power of appointment is to be exercised or given, there may be a conflict of laws as to jurisdiction between states which have had or may acquire jurisdiction over the parties. The exercise may be construed and administered under the laws of the state of residence of either the donor or donee. Consider this especially if there is to be any adding of lives in a subsequent trust created under the power.

[¶607.3]   Tax Apportionment

The impact of estate and inheritance taxes may be charged against the residuary estate, apportioned, or treated differently as to varying interests. Does the tax fall where it will be least felt?

A beneficiary of a gift of real or tangible personal property may have difficulty in paying a proportionate share of the tax without liquidating the gift.

Cash legacies when reduced by a pro rata share of the tax may not give full effect to the intention of the testator.

Where there is substantial taxable property passing on death otherwise than under the will, such as insurance or inter vivos trust property, charging all taxes to the residuary estate under the will, unless contemplated in the testamentary plan, could create difficulties in carrying out that plan.

Where the residuary estate is divided up, is it more advantageous to have one portion bear all the taxes? Where the marital deduction is utilized, should taxes be charged to the nonmarital portion?

Where there is a percentage gift, is it clear whether it is to be computed before or after taxes?

[¶607.4]   Marital Deduction Provisions

If the intention is to keep the taxes down in successive estates, is the spouse given only the minimum amount of property necessary to obtain the least amount of tax in both estates?

If a formula clause is used, does it make provision for property passing to the spouse under other clauses of the will or otherwise than under the will?

If there is a marital deduction trust, is the power of appointment broad enough to qualify and does the spouse receive all the income? If the trustee is given broad powers over allocation of receipts between income and principal, etc., should a tax-saving clause be used to qualify his power?

Would a survivorship presumption clause be helpful in saving the marital deduction in the event of a common disaster? If used, is it consistent with the language of the bequest? Is the bequest conditioned on survivorship or is it one which can only be divested by proof of prior death? Who must carry the burden if there is little or no proof?

[¶607.5]   Eliminating Beneficiary Uncertainty

Inadequate identification of beneficiaries is a fault frequently found in wills. If a gift is to a relative, is the relationship stated? Even then there may be two nephews with the same name so that further identification should be included. In most instances, a designation of residence will solve the problem.

Gifts to charities require careful checking. The legal name may be very different from the testator's description. Exact names, addresses and even the state of incorporation may be required to insure that the gift is received by the intended beneficiary.

Are there provisions for "children," "issue" or "descendants"? These designations have been given various interpretations. Does it clearly appear from the text whether one generation or more is to be included? If more, are the interests *per stirpes* or *per capita*? If the word "legitimate" has been used in referring to these groups, has it been done advisedly? Under the present conflicts of laws on divorce, the status of a child may vary from state to state.

Who is to receive the interest of a beneficiary who predeceases the testator? The states are not in accord, and in a given state the rule varies with circumstances such as the degree of relationship of the beneficiary to the testator. But if the will makes provision, it is controlling.

Are the disposing provisions sufficiently exhaustive to insure against partial intestacy? A lapsed legacy, especially one involving a remainder interest, can cause trouble.

If there are specific legacies, should there be alternative provisions or gifts in the event of ademption?

Should there be a testamentary guardian for infant beneficiaries? If so, the same precautions should be taken as in selecting the other fiduciaries. If payments to be made are to be used for the infant, should they be made directly by a trustee, through a guardian or otherwise? Legal restrictions upon guardians may be determinative.

[¶607.6] Executor and Trustee Provisions

Is there a clear statement of intention as to the number of acting executors or trustees required?

Has a sufficient number of fiduciaries been named? Has adequate provision been made for nominating them so as to obviate any possible necessity for judicial designation? Using or including a corporate fiduciary in the first instance or as a successor gives protection.

Can each named fiduciary qualify under the laws of the state of domicile by reason of residence, relationship or other requirements? The same tests should be applied with respect to any ancillary proceedings which will be required for property located in other states.

Will the designated fiduciaries serve? The size and nature of the fund may make the administration of an estate or trust attractive or unattractive. Commission provisions in the instrument—state law permitting—may induce or discourage the required service. When state law controls, splitting up a residue into a number of small trusts can increase the detail work to a point where it would be a financial burden to the fiduciary. Conversely, in substantial estates, limitations on compensation may be justifiable. If there is any question, it may be advisable to consult the proposed fiduciaries before they are named.

[¶607.7] Powers of Fiduciaries

Administration provisions can be as important as the dispositive provisions in carrying out the testamentary plan, especially where they are interlocking. These are primarily the responsibility of the draftsman.

Broad fiduciary powers are generally necessary and advisable to permit flexible administration. Sufficient protection from personal liability for acts performed in good faith permits them to act freely. Trustee powers should be enumerated, since they do not have the implied and inherent powers common to executors.

Draftsmen usually have stock provisions defining routine fiduciary powers in general terms. These are helpful but frequently inadequate to provide for a workable and advantageous administration of the immediate estate. Unique situations, which seem to be the rule rather than the exception, require special treatment. There may be a particular problem involving liquidity, taxes, investments, distribution, a close corporation or some other factor.

Realty Interests: The greatest particularity is required in listing powers covering real estate and mortgage interests. Implied, inherent and statutory powers of fiduciaries concerning these are generally much more restrictive than in the case of personalty. In enumerating applicable powers, verbosity should not be considered a fault. It may give the fiduciary that one particular authority without which he could not act advantageously under special circumstances.

When neither mortgages nor real property is included in the original estate, may powers applying specifically to such interests be omitted from the instrument? Weigh the possibility of subsequent acquisition of such interests as the result of a liquidation, or in an attempt to salvage a bad debt or through other unanticipated channels against the tremendous disadvantages to a fiduciary attempting to administer these interests without such powers. It may be safest to include these powers even though it seems there will be no immediate need for them.

If oil or mineral interests are involved, we will be dealing with a field that is highly technical. A study of the documents creating the interests and the applicable state law may be helpful in determining the nature and scope of the fiduciary powers necessary to permit realization of maximum income, profit and tax benefits. If it should become necessary to make additional investments or if this was originally contemplated to effect full exploitation of the interest, the extent of the fiduciary authority should be clearly defined. But even though authorized, a fiduciary may be reluctant to make any further investment if he considers it highly speculative. In such cases, it would not seem advisable to make it a "must"; an expression of the testator's wishes may be sufficient to influence the action. This should be coupled with adequate protective provisions for the fiduciary. If valuable oil or mineral interests are involved, the draftsman may find it advisable to consult a specialist on the technicalities.

Voting Rights: Fiduciaries are generally given the power and, in some instances, have a duty to vote stock held in the fund. But there are some situations where voting rights should be clearly defined.

If there are several fiduciaries, what happens in the event of absence or if there is a disagreement? How many votes are necessary for action or inaction? If there is a dispute, should one have the controlling vote? May there be a delegation of voting rights between fiduciaries?

Is a beneficiary-fiduciary disqualified from participation in any decision as to the discretionary distribution of income or invasion of principal to or for the personal use of that beneficiary?

If there is a corporate fiduciary, should it be authorized to vote its own stock held in the fund?

What are the rights of the fiduciaries in voting the stock of a close or controlled corporation? May they vote themselves into office? May they personally engage in business transactions with the corporation? Should the voting rights of a fiduciary who personally owns stock in the corporations be different from the nonowner-fiduciary? Frequently, a wife or other relative is in the position of holding stock in the family corporation both individually and as fiduciary. This does not necessarily create a conflict of interests but may give rise to many doubts as situations develop. These cases require a clear definition of specific powers.

Investments: Does the testator have any confirmed ideas on investment policy? Generally, a fiduciary is given the broadest powers to retain original property and to use his uncontrolled discretion in making investments. Most draftsmen are well equipped to supply appropriate language giving such powers and do so generously, sometimes without consulting the donor who might prefer to include a few restrictions. He may favor conservative investments or a degree of speculation. He may believe in broad diversification. He may have definite opinions on common trust funds, investment trusts, foreign or international securities, the percentage of the whole to be invested in bonds, whether a corporate fiduciary may hold or invest in its own stock, and other possible courses which may or may not be open to the fiduciary under the usual powers supplied by the draftsman.

Unproductive property, especially real estate, may give rise to apportionment difficulties if no guideposts are supplied. Guidance is also needed if there is a specified period of occupancy or life estate in a residence given to a wife or family. Fiduciaries should be permitted to hold unproductive property for a reasonable time; but, if the authorization is too broad, it may produce undesirable tax consequences.

Should interests in close corporations or partnerships be continued as investments to the extent possible? If not, should other interested parties be given special consideration when the fiduciaries liquidate? If the business is to be continued, should there be a time limitation, may additional funds be invested in the business and are there any special circumstances for which provisions should be made? Authorizing loans to the company may be instrumental in tiding it over a readjustment period resulting from the death of the testator, who may have been the key man.

Dealings Between Fiduciaries: An overall estate plan may include an inter vivos trust and a funded or nonfunded insurance trust. Frequently, the trustees and beneficiaries are identical with those named in the will. Trust powers and duties for all trusts should be arranged with adequate flexibility for the other trusts in mind.

Self-Dealings: There are times when expediency may warrant obtaining a loan rather than liquidating. Unless borrowing from a fiduciary with or without security is allowed, an available source from which to obtain funds may be lost.

Bankers, attorneys and accountants are often used as fiduciaries because of specialized knowledge. If so, they should be authorized to employ themselves or firms with which they are associated in a professional capacity. Unless they can pay for such services from time to time without prior court authorization, substantial tax benefits may be lost. Likewise, professional employment by a trust or estate beneficiary should not be a bar to similar employment by a fiduciary of the same trust or estate.

If a fiduciary is to be employed in the conduct or operation of a business owned or controlled by the estate, his compensation may be restricted to regular commissions unless the will contains a clear expression to the contrary.

Tax Saving Limitation: It is conceivable that situations may arise where certain powers may be given a construction which would deprive the estate of tax benefits. Broad discretion in the allocation of receipts between principal and income might be construed as denying the widow the right to all the income from a marital deduction trust, with the consequent loss of the marital deduction. Such powers could also be construed as broad enough to permit depletion of corpus in a charitable remainder trust, resulting in the loss of the charitable deduction. As a precautionary measure, it may be advisable to insert an all-inclusive clause revoking any power or authority which may be construed as depriving the estate of any tax benefits otherwise available.

Allocation of Assets with Different Tax Basis: The fiduciary should have the power to distribute assets in kind, including tangible and household effects, irrespective of the tax cost basis. Therefore, the fiduciary is protected from possible claims because the beneficiary would incur a larger capital gain tax on the eventual sale from one asset to another.

Protecting the Fiduciary: Protective provisions for the fiduciary are too often neglected. It is only reasonable for him to expect to be absolved from personal liability to the extent permitted by law if he acts diligently and in good faith. Provisions should include a right of indemnification or reimbursement from the fund for any individual obligation arising during or after administration, excepting such as may result from his own negligence. Adequate protection may give the insurance necessary to overcome timidity and stimulate efficient action especially in dealings with other trusts, operating property, conducting a business and giving effect to indicated preferences in discretionary matters.

[¶608]   **BEQUESTS AND DEVISES**

Bequests of personalty and devises of realty are generally classified into four principal types, as follows:

(1) A "specific" bequest or devise is a gift of a specific article or tract of realty;

(2) A "general" bequest is not a bequest of a specific article but is usually a bequest of money;

(3) A "demonstrative" bequest is one which is general in nature but is payable out of a particular fund;

(4) A "residuary" bequest or devise is one from what remains after all bequests, claims and administrative expenses have been paid.

This classification is necessary for two reasons. The first is that many things may happen to property specifically bequeathed or devised between the time the will is executed and the death of the testator. In the absence of a specific direction to the contrary, when such property is sold by the testator before his death, there is an ademption; that is, the legatee takes nothing. Similarly, where the property is mortgaged after the execution of the will but before the testator's death, depending on local law, the bequest or devise will probably be deemed to be one of the remaining equity in the property only. Again, a direction in the will to the contrary could change this result.

Unlike specific bequests, general and demonstrative bequests are not subject to ademption. Thus, even where a demonstrative bequest is to be paid out of the proceeds of the sale of specifically described property and the property is no longer owned by the testator at the time of his death, the legacy is not defeated.

The second reason for classifying bequests and devises is to establish an order of priority where an estate has insufficient funds to satisfy all its debts, costs and bequests or devises. Residuary bequests and devises abate first. If the residue is insufficient to discharge all the obligations of the estate, the general bequests will then abate. If there is still a deficiency, demonstrative and specific bequests will then abate. If necessary, the specific property will be sold; any balance of the proceeds remaining will be distributed to the specific (and demonstrative) legatees. Naturally, the above noted order of priority can be changed by specific provisions establishing a different order of abatement.

[¶609]   **HOW THE WILL CAN SAVE INCOME TAXES**

Although we commonly think of the will in terms of the estate tax and the disposition of estate assets, the will provisions also bear strongly on the income position of the beneficiaries.

The standard will plan divides the estate into roughly two parts, one part going into a marital deduction trust, the other part into another trust. The wife must receive all the income from the marital trust in order to qualify this trust for the marital deduction. It is customary to give her the income from the other trust, too, so that she will be well taken care of, with the remainder interest of this trust going to children so as to keep it out of the wife's taxable estate.

The result is to give the wife a lot of taxable income. Unless she remarries, she won't be able after the first two years to reduce her tax through income splitting (income splitting with the executor is available for only the first two years).

Here are four income tax saving points to consider:

(1) We can protect the income of the nonmarital trust from high taxation by providing for its accumulation, giving the wife a limited right to invade corpus if she needs extra funds. Thus, after the income has been accumulated in and taxed to the trust, the wife can, in effect, obtain it without paying income tax. Here, of course, it will be necessary to look out for the throwback rule which attempts to tax beneficiaries retroactively on certain accumulated income.

(2) Provision for family members other than the wife and children is generally made by outright bequest. It may be wiser to add the amounts of these bequests to the trusts we set up for the wife and children, giving the other relatives shares of the trust income. Annual income may serve the other relatives better than a lump-sum bequest, which can be quickly dissipated.

(3) Assuming we wish to give $25,000 to charity, is it better to give the charity $25,000 outright or $1,000 of income annually for 25 years? Assuming we leave a widow in a 50% income tax bracket, it would cost her only $500 of after-tax income if we diverted $1,000 a year of income away from her and to the charity. So it costs her a total of only $12,500 to give the $25,000 of income to charity. It will cost her two times as much if we give capital.

(4) An executor's compensation is taxable income. But you can give him the same amount as a bequest income tax free provided it is not conditioned upon his continuous performance as executor (*U.S. vs. Merriam*, 263 U.S. 179). In other words, attach no conditions. This may be one way of inducing an able man to serve. However, note that you sacrifice a deduction for estate tax purposes.

[¶610]   TESTAMENTARY TRUSTS IN INCOME PLANNING

The usefulness of trusts in minimizing the tax burden on the income from an estate turns on these attributes:

(1) The ability to divide income among beneficiaries and between trust and beneficiaries.

(2) The power to accumulate income and use it for family purposes within the trust.

(3) The ability to give a trustee the discretionary authority to distribute income and capital as the needs and the tax position of the beneficiaries indicate.

The fundamental thing to bear in mind here is that a testator can set up provisions in a trust for a beneficiary which the beneficiary could not set up for himself without running into tax complications. If a beneficiary created a trust and retained income rights, the property would be includible in his estate. If he directed that trust income be used to carry insurance on his life, the income would be taxed to him. However, if the testator created these trusts for the beneficiary, the right to income does not bring the proceeds into the beneficiary's taxable estate, and the carrying of insurance on the beneficiary's life does not make the trust income taxable to the beneficiary.

Here are the kinds of trusts found most useful in income planning for an estate:

[¶610.1] Residence Trust

The family residence is willed to a trust together with income-producing securities with instructions to the trustee that the wife is to be permitted to use the house rent free and income is to be used first to maintain the house and the balance distributed to the wife. The value of occupancy is not taxed to the wife. Money spent on repairs, insurance and upkeep of the property will be taxed at lower rates to the trust than to the wife. Money spent on interest and taxes will be deductible either way. Money spent by the trust for the wife's enjoyment of the property, like light bills and domestic help, will be taxed to her.

[¶610.2] Insurance Trust

Income-producing property is transferred to a trust charged with carrying insurance on a son's life. The income will be taxed to the trust at lower rates than to the son. It will carry more insurance than the same property would support if given outright to the son. Both the income-producing property and the insurance can be kept out of the estates of the son and his wife. Thus, the income placed in such a trust can provide family protection which would require two or three times as many of the son's earned dollars to carry directly.

[¶610.3] Sprinkling Trust

The trustee is given unfettered discretion to accumulate or distribute income among specified beneficiaries as he thinks best. The income tax position of beneficiaries will be one of the factors considered in the exercise of this discretion. For example, income can be distributed so that each child gets $850 of tax-free money ($750 exemption plus $100 dividend exclusion) while the balance of the income may be accumulated (taxed to the trust subject to subsequent throwback) or distributed to a widow who will still have a $750 exemption for each of her children.

[¶611] WHAT THE WILL SHOULD DO TO FACILITATE POST-DEATH TAX SAVINGS

Here are some of the things a will can do to facilitate post-death tax savings:

(1) Authorize the executor to join in a final tax return with the surviving spouse.

(2) Authorize the executor to assume whatever portion of the liability on the final tax return he deems fit.

(3) Give the executor express authority to make the elections available to him under the tax laws and also absolute discretion to determine whether the interests of the beneficiaries affected by the election made should be adjusted; and, if so, the nature and extent of the adjustments to be made. The clause may also be drawn to direct that no adjustment shall be made.

(4) To facilitate disclaimers in a will creating a trust, a provision can readily be inserted to the effect that if any beneficiary disclaims his interest in the trust property, such property shall thereafter be administered as though the beneficiary's death had occurred. A testator can also facilitate partial disclaimers by making two or more obviously severable separate bequests or devises to the same individual or, in the case of an otherwise indivisible gift, by expressly providing that it may be disclaimed as to any part.

(5) To avoid capital gain where distributions are to be made in kind or in cash, bequeath fractional shares of the residue rather than fixed dollar amounts. This is because an estate realizes income when a bequest of a fixed dollar amount is satisfied in kind with property which is appreciated in value since the testator's death. (This is also an argument in favor of fractional-type marital deduction formula clauses over a pecuniary type formula.)

(6) To preserve the marital deduction in the event both spouses perish in a common disaster and it cannot be determined who survived, provided that, if valid under local law, the wife shall be deemed to have survived. See ¶612.

Much is said about postmortem estate planning (¶1509) and the executor's tax choices (¶1509.2). Yet it should be realized that to a great extent the testator in his will can grant to his executor certain authorizations (and also make specific directions if he chooses), the purpose of which is to make the executor's task that much easier and to insure that his (the testator's) wishes will be carried out properly.

[¶612] COMMON DISASTER, SIMULTANEOUS DEATH AND SHORT-TIME SURVIVORSHIP

Short of actual proof of survivorship in a common disaster situation, the law will not presume that one person survived another by reason of age, physical attributes, etc. This means that the burden of proof as to survivorship will usually fall upon whoever is making a claim. This burden has been obviated by the enactment of the *Uniform Simultaneous Death Act* in practically all of our states.

Under this Act, *where there is no proof as to survivorship and no instrument provides for its own presumption,* then automatic common disaster provisions shall, in effect, be written into every will (and intestate distribution arrangement), every life insurance policy and every joint tenancy. For example:

(1) John and Marsha White had each been married previously, and each had a child of the former marriage. There were no children of the present marriage. They were killed in a bus accident, and it was impossible to determine who died first. By application of the Uniform Simultaneous Death Act, John's *individual property* would be distributed *as if he had survived.* Assuming he leaves no will, it would probably go to his own child. And the same would apply to Marsha's property. (This is an illustration of the Act's provision that the *property of each would be distributed as if each one had survived the other.*)

(2) John and Marsha owned their home as tenants by the entirety, and some securities as joint tenants. The Act would call for a *50-50 distribution* of this property. (This is an illustration of the Act's provision that property so held would be distributed *one half as if one had survived and one half as if the other had survived.*)

(3) Marsha was named beneficiary under all the insurance policies on John's life. Unless the policies provided for contingent beneficiaries, the Act would have the proceeds *payable to John's own child* (*Chown*, 428 F.2d 1395; *Old Kent Bank & Trust Co.*, 430 F.2d 392; *Lion*, 438 F.2d 56; *Meltzer*, 439 F.2d 798; *Wien*, 441 F.2d 32). (This is an illustration of the Act's provision that *proceeds are to be distributed as if the insured had survived the beneficiary.*)

A reverse common disaster clause can be used to create the presumption that the wife survived and thus preserve the marital deduction. See ¶612.2.

[¶612.1]　Short-Time Survivorship

Many testators make use of a short-time survivorship clause in their wills to provide against the possibility that one death may follow another within a relatively short period of time. The idea is that the testator wishes to make the alternative disposition of his property rather than leave it up to the primary beneficiary. One of the motivating factors behind this might be the desire, in the case of a husband and wife, to avoid double probate and administration expenses. An example of such a clause is:

> To my wife, Marsha White, if she is living at the end of 30 days after my death, and if she is not then living, to my son George White.

It is possible to couple such a clause with a reverse common disaster clause in the same will. The conflict that occurs can be obviated by providing that the short-time survivorship clause will be rendered inoperative in the event of a common disaster which is covered by the reverse clause.

[¶612.2]　Common Disaster

In order to make use of the marital deduction allowed in computing the federal estate tax liability (and certain state death taxes), *there must be a surviving spouse.* Where a husband and wife die under circumstances where it cannot be determined who died first, the Uniform Simultaneous Death Act may come into play with its presumption that the property owner survived the beneficiary. And the marital deduction may be lost with a corresponding increase in death taxes. For example:

Assuming in 1981 John White had an adjusted gross estate amounting to $350,000. If Marsha were to survive him, the combined federal estate tax would run in the area of $23,800. If Marsha were to predecease him, the combined tax would approach $57,800—a difference of some $34,000.

Bear in mind, in viewing the above situations, that *the Uniform Simultaneous Death Act does not apply in the case of wills, living trusts, deeds or contracts of insurance which contain provisions coping with such a contingency which are in conflict with the Act's provisions—i.e., these instruments take precedence over the Act.*

A clause such as the following, reversing the presumptions of the Uniform Simultaneous Death Act, would guaranty against the marital deduction being lost in the event of a common disaster.

In the event that my wife, Marsha White, and I die under circumstances where it cannot be established who died first, then it shall be presumed that my wife survived me, and this will and the dispositions thereunder shall be construed on that presumption.

The same type of clause can be inserted in living trust agreements, deeds and insurance policies.

A short-time survivorship clause will not cause an automatic disqualification for the marital deduction (under the terminable interest rule) provided the period of required survivorship does not exceed *six months* (IRC §2056)(b)(3)).

Before using a reverse common disaster clause to preserve the marital deduction in the event of such a contingency occurring, it is imperative that the estate planner go through some rapid calculations to determine what the total death costs will be in both estates if there was a common disaster. The estate tax savings will be offset somewhat by a doubling up of probate and administration expenses. The question is: Will these latter expenses eat up whatever savings have been made on the estate tax? Usually, they won't, and it will pay to use the reverse presumption clause.

[¶613]   **EXECUTION OF THE WILL**

The formality of having a will executed must be approached carefully, for failure to comply with the applicable technical requirements of execution may invalidate some or all of the dispositive provisions.

First we must find out what the applicable technical requirements are; we approach this by looking to the local law. Under common law for valid disposition of land and other immovables, the testator must have complied with the law of the situs or location of the property; to validly dispose of movables, compliance with the law of domicile at time of death was required. The common law rule for immovables presents no problem, since the location of an immovable remains the same always. Applying the common law rule for movables is, however, another story, for the testator can't be sure at the time he executes the will exactly where he will be domiciled at the uncertain moment of his death.

Fortunately, most states have taken care of this problem by modifying the common law rule so as to make a disposition of movables valid if there has been compliance with the formalities of execution of any of the following:

(1) The jurisdiction in which the will is executed;

(2) The testator's domicile at the time of execution;

(3) The testator's domicile at the time of his death;

(4) The jurisdiction where the movables in question are situated.

This broadens the common law rule so that the disposition has four chances to qualify instead of only one. However, since there are variations in language and detail among these state statutes, you can lessen the possibility of something going wrong by making sure that you meet the requirements of the laws of situs, domicile and place of execution as you know them to be at the time of execution. Then, the entire factual situation with respect to the disposition will have to change before there can be any danger at all of failure to meet the formal requirements of execution.

Bear in mind that this takes care only of movables. If the testator owns immovables in a common law jurisdiction, then each immovable asset should be disposed of in accordance with the formalities prescribed by the laws of the place where it is located.

[¶613.1]　Checklist of the Formalities

Under the common law, there are two kinds of wills, namely, the witnessed will and the unwitnessed will. The witnessed will is accepted in all jurisdictions, the unwitnessed will only in some. It is wise to avoid using the unwitnessed will, particularly if the testator is likely to leave assets in more than one jurisdiction, since the use of this type of will would increase the possibility of some of the dispositive provisions failing.

Although there are some variations in the state statutes with respect to preparing a witnessed will, we can list the following requirements as essentially applicable in all common law jurisdictions:

(1) The will should be declared in an instrument in writing.

(2) The testator should sign it; if he can't do so, another person should sign for him in his presence and at his request.

(3) This signature of either the testator or the person who signs for him must follow the text of the will immediately and without leaving any intervening space.

(4) At least three witnesses should attest the testator's signature (see state table on page T-33).

(5) None of the witnesses should be any of the following:

(a) Beneficiary, executor or trustee under the will;

(b) Spouse of a beneficiary, executor or trustee;

(c) Business partner of a beneficiary, executor or trustee;

(d) Officer or stockholder of a corporation which is a beneficiary, executor or trustee;

(e) Resident of a city, town, county or state which will receive a gift under the will that would alleviate its tax burden.

(6) The testator should expressly ask the attesting witnesses to attest "the execution of his will."

(7) All the witnesses to the testator's signature should either·

(a) See him sign or

(b) Hear him say that he acknowledges as his own a signature that is already on the instrument and which is pointed out to them and actually seen by all of them. If he can't write his signature, all the witnesses should observe that: (i) the testator expressly requests the person who signs for him to sign, and (ii) the person requested does sign in the presence of the testator. (See state table on page T-33.)

(8) The witnesses should be told that the instrument is to be the testator's will.

(9) Each witness should sign his name and write his address in the testator's presence, within the latter's unobstructed line of vision.

(10) All the witnesses, the testator and the one who signs for the testator, if that is the case, should be present simultaneously throughout the entire process of execution. (See state table on page T-33.)

(11) The will should be dated by fully and correctly stating the place, the day, month and year it was executed.

(12) The attestation clause should expressly recite the observation of all these formalities except numbers (3) and (5); this clause should also state the number of pages constituting the will.

[¶613.2]   Revocation

In any discussion of the execution of a will, something must be said about revocation, which is the way the testator undoes what he did by execution.

A will can be revoked either by some intentional positive act, such as cancellation, obliteration or destruction, or by operation of law.

As for revocation by operation of law, the statutes have modified the common law rules under which a marriage or the birth of a child after the will was executed revoked the will. The inclination now is merely to give the new spouse or child a share in the estate. In a few states, divorce may automatically invalidate a provision in favor of the spouse.

Revocation by operation of law is something it is difficult to guard against. No attorney drafting a will can foresee events that will occur subsequently in his client's life and which might invalidate all or parts of the instrument. Continual review of the will to see if anything that has occurred may affect the will or require some change is important. A table of various state laws on automatic revocation appears on page T-34a.

[¶613.3]   Reinstatement after Revocation

Suppose the will has been revoked by operation of law contrary to the testator's wishes or has been revoked by him and he now wishes to restore it. What can be done to revive the will?

This is a matter of complying with the applicable provisions of the state law. Some states treat revocation of a will as final and absolute holding that the only way it can be revived is by republishing it; that is, by re-executing it just as it was originally executed. This may be varied where revocation was accomplished by a subsequent inconsistent will or codicil or by a revoking clause in a subsequent will. In some jurisdictions, revocation of the revoked will revives the original will provided the terms indicate this was the testator's intention. In others, even an indication of the testator's intention isn't enough.

Many states, however, adhere to a rule that the destruction or revocation of a second will automatically revives the first will; they presume an intention to revive the first will from the fact that the testator didn't destroy it when he made the second one.

[¶614]   CODICIL TO THE WILL

A codicil to a will is treated as part of the will and is executed the same way. A codicil generally is an elaboration of, or amendment to, the will rather than a replacement for it; hence, it varies the will's provisions only to the extent necessary in order to be effective. Thus, where the codicil is subject to two possible interpretations, one of which is consistent with the will provisions and the other inconsistent, the consistent interpretation will be adopted. However, where the codicil definitely conflicts with the will, the codicil will generally prevail. If the codicil makes a specific change in the will, the fact that the codicil was so specific in what it was intended to accomplish indicates the absence of an intention to make any other change.

Even though the will and all its codicils are construed together, that doesn't necessarily mean that revocation of the codicil destroys the will or that destruction of the codicil restores the will to its original form. To illustrate, by execution of a codicil after intervening codicils have been revoked, the will can be republished in the form that includes the intervening codicils.

[¶615]   POUROVER OF ASSETS FROM A WILL
TO A LIVING TRUST

A pourover trust is one which exists outside the will, is independent of the will and serves as a receptacle for property which is given it by the will.

The basic advantages of this device are:

(1) All provisions for ultimate disposition appear in the living trust—it is not necessary to repeat the terms of the trust in the will.

(2) The provisions of the living trust need not be made public as must the provisions of the will.

(3) Since all the poured-over assets will be administered under the living trust, many of the costs and inconveniences involved in probate administration will be avoided.

(4) The testator gets a chance to see his representative, as trustee, manage a segment of his estate before death makes the arrangement irrevocable.

There is a serious hurdle which must be cleared before an estate planner can plan to make use of the pourover trust in those states which have not enacted legislation making the living trust-pourover will technique clearly effective. The validity of this type of trust and subsequent pouring over of assets to it from a will depends upon local law. Usually, the requirement is that the will and all of its dispositions must be wholly in writing and signed by the testator in the presence of witnesses or that he acknowledged his signature to them. Therefore, for such a trust to be effective, it would seemingly have to be incorporated in the will itself as a testamentary trust, subject to all of the inconveniences of probate administration.

However, if the state in which the will is to operate either recognizes the doctrine of *incorporation by reference* or is willing to admit proof as to fact of *independent legal significance,* then the pourover arrangement will be available. And a number of states have arrived at this line of reasoning, primarily on the basis of independent legal significance.

Where an attempt is made to incorporate the trust instrument into a will by *reference* (and only a few states permit this other than by statute), the will must specifically refer to the trust as a then existing instrument which must be properly identified. By then existing instrument is meant that it must have been in existence at the time the will was executed. And this fact will have to be proved. In the event that the trust is amended after the execution of the will, the doctrine could not apply because the amended trust was not in existence at the time the will was executed.

Many states allow pourovers on the theory of facts of *independent legal significance.* Since the will becomes operative at the time of the testator's death, a reference in the will to a fact determinable at that time (at the testator's death) is valid, according to this theory.

Of noteworthy interest in this area is the fact that uniform legislation, *The Uniform Testamentary Additions to Trusts Act,* has been adopted by many states, in some cases with modifications. This Uniform Act is actually a liberal codification of the *incorporation by reference* doctrine. It permits the pourover where the will specifically refers to and identifies the living trust which is to be the recipient of the poured-over assets. It makes no difference that the trust has not come into legal existence by delivery of the corpus to the trustee, as long as the instrument creating the trust was already in existence or came into existence concurrently with the execution of the will. Also, the trust need not be one which was created by the testator. And finally, it makes no difference that the trust is amendable, revocable, or even if the trust is in fact amended subsequent to the will's execution or subsequent to the testator's death. Revocation or termination of the trust subsequent to the testator's death will however cause a lapse.

It remains imperative that the estate planner ascertain the current law, whether statutory or case law, of the jurisdiction where the estate owner resides before he attempts to make any specific use of the pourover device, bearing in mind that this area is in a constant state of flux, at least until all states adopt the substance of the Uniform Act.

[¶616]   INTESTATE PROPERTY

If you make no will, your state makes one for you. Generally, the law gives the lion's share of your property to your spouse and children, but if there are no surviving children, under the laws of certain of our states, a share also goes to your parents, brothers and sisters, nephews and nieces, grandparents, uncles and aunts, and cousins.

Generally, the descent of realty is governed by the law of the place where the realty is located. The distribution of personalty is governed by the law of the state of domicile (usually the law of the state of the deceased's residence).

In addition, certain points should be kept in mind. Most states provide: (1) special allowances for the surviving spouse and children, such as rights to the homestead and specified amounts of personalty in addition to the intestate shares; (2) right to the surviving spouse to elect to take the intestate share if less is provided by will; (3) provisions for the payments of debts, funeral and administrative expenses before any distribution is made to the heirs. Marriage settlements conferring certain property rights upon a spouse are recognized in most states. Special provisions cover divorce and minors who die intestate.

Distinctions are sometimes made between ancestral property (property acquired from an ancestor) and nonancestral property (property acquired by the intestate's own efforts).

Eight states (Arizona, California, Idaho, Louisiana, Nevada, New Mexico, Texas and Washington) and Puerto Rico have community property. In those states, the surviving spouse's share of community property automatically goes to her and the deceased's share of the community property goes as otherwise directed by state law.

Many states have dower or curtesy. These are rights of wife and husband to claim an interest (frequently one-third), for life or outright, in all real property owned during marriage. In some states, dower and curtesy extend to personal property.

SECTION VII.   LIFE INSURANCE

Life insurance is frequently the major family asset. For many, it is the only sure way to build an estate and provide added liquidity to protect an existing estate. A life insurance policy is a method of transfer as well as an asset. Beneficiary designations can determine how the proceeds will devolve on one or more future generations.

While life insurance has important tax advantages, the premiums must be paid out of after-tax income. This may make it desirable to have them paid by a corporation or a trust funded with income-producing assets rather than by an individual with highly taxed personal income. Sometimes, insurance is carried with borrowed dollars. Then the carrying cost may be deductible as interest.

The death proceeds are received income tax free. If someone other than the insured owns the policy and the proceeds are not payable to the insured's estate, they may be received free of estate tax, even though the insured pays the premium. There may be a taxable gift when transferring the policies or paying premiums on policies owned by someone else.

[¶701]   **HOW TO ANALYZE INSURANCE POLICIES**

To plan an estate properly, it is essential to get the insurance policies and look at them. To be sure that this is done carefully, have a written record made on these points:

(1) What ages do the policies show? If there are different ages, get proof of age and make the appropriate corrections.

(2) Who are the beneficiaries?

(3) Who are the contingent beneficiaries? Are new marriages and new births reflected?

(4) What settlement options have been elected? Have they been left optional or made automatic?

(5) Are proceeds protected from claims of creditors?

(6) Are proceeds judgment-proof to beneficiaries?

(7) Will the proceeds qualify for the marital deduction?

(8) Is there an automatic loan provision to make the policies lapse-proof?

(9) Is there a waiver of premium on disability?

(10) Is there an accidental death benefit? Would it be preferable to take additional terms rider to provide added benefits if death is from sickness instead of accident?

(11) Can worthwhile savings be made by shifting premium payments to an annual basis, by discounting future premiums?

(12) Are dividends on participating policies being used to best advantage—to buy additions, to maintain amount of risk account over increasing cash value?

(13) Are there any loans? If loans have been paid up, have assignments of policies been released? Should loans be refinanced? Is it clear whether loans will be payable out of proceeds only or can repayment be demanded from residual estate?

(14) If owner is other than insured and beneficiary is a different person, has the gift tax risk been considered?

(15) Are simultaneous death and short-time survivorship contingencies accurately provided for? Do they furnish maximum protection for marital deduction or against diversion of proceeds and double administration?

(16) What savings can be achieved by change of ownership?

(17) What savings or added flexibility can be achieved by change of beneficiaries?

[¶702]   HOW INSURANCE CAN ESCAPE ESTATE TAX

When you own insurance on your life, the value of that insurance protection to your family is whittled down by the estate tax.

Even though you pay the premiums, the proceeds of insurance on your life can be protected from the impact of the estate tax. All you have to do is to transfer the policy and all incidents of ownership to your wife or child or to a trust. (See IRC §2042.)

The value of the policy for gift tax purposes is the cost of replacing it. This is usually the policy's interpolated terminal reserve.

The proceeds of life insurance transferred within three years of death are automatically included in the insured's estate.

Where the policy had been transferred more than three years before death but the insured paid premiums within the three-year period, the courts have been virtually unanimous in holding that only the premium payments should be included in the estate (*Gorman*, 288 F. Supp. 225; *Coleman*, 52 TC 921; *Chapin*, TC Memo 1970-7; *First National Bank of Midland*, 423 F. 2d 1286). This in spite of *Rev. Rul. 67-463*, 1967-2 CB 327, which said that a proportionate part of the proceeds should be included in the estate. That ruling has been superseded by *Rev. Rul. 71-497* which follows the cases. But see *Bel*, 452 F. 2d 683, which taxed the full proceeds of an annual renewable accidental death policy.

[¶703]   HOW TO QUALIFY LIFE INSURANCE
FOR THE MARITAL DEDUCTION

The following conditions must be met:

(1) The life insurance policies must have been owned by the decedent.

(2) The spouse must be the unconditional beneficiary entitled to the proceeds at the time of the death of the insured (this requirement is relaxed in the case of common disaster and six-month survivorship clauses).

(3) Since insurance proceeds payable through an optional mode of settlement constitute a terminable interest under IRC §2056(b)(1) whenever the mode of settlement requires a designation of a successor beneficiary, one of the following two sets of circumstances must be met in order to qualify the proceeds for the marital deduction:

(a) Assurance that no part of any remainder interest goes to anyone other than to the surviving spouse or to her estate. This may be done either by eliminating all possibility of a remainder interest or by arranging that the remainder interest passes to the surviving spouse or to her estate. Thus, provisions for the spouse to receive one lump sum, a straight-life annuity, or interest or installments for life all qualify and for convenience are grouped under the Code terminology of provisions which do not create terminal interests.

(b) The beneficiary provisions conform to specific conditions spelled out in IRC §2056(b)(6). The following five conditions must be met:

(i) The insurance proceeds shall be held by the insurance company subject to its agreement to pay them in installments or to pay interest thereon and that, as long as the surviving wife lives, all such payments must be unconditionally payable to her and only to her. If all five conditions apply to part of the proceeds of the policy, that amount can qualify for the marital deduction. A spendthrift clause which shuts off access to the policy proceeds to the claims of creditors and prevents assignment or alienation or pledge will not result in a failure to meet this condition.

(ii) Interest installment payments must be payable annually or more frequently, beginning not later than 13 months after the death of the insured.

(iii) The surviving spouse must have the power, exercisable in favor of herself or her estate, to appoint all the proceeds held by the insurance company. This condition is met if the wife has the right to withdraw the whole or any part of the proceeds held by the insured or the right to direct the payment of all the proceeds remaining at her death to her estate. As a practical matter, most insurance companies will allow withdrawal of proceeds held under an interest option but, with respect to insurance held under a settlement agreement calling for the payment of installments over a fixed period of time or for life, will allow only a single withdrawal of the commuted value of all unpaid installments as of the date of withdrawal.

(iv) The power of appointment must be exercisable by the surviving spouse alone and must be exercisable in all events.

(v) *Amounts payable under the policy must not be subject to any power of appointment in part to a person other than the surviving spouse.* We can qualify settlement payment plans for the marital deduction either by making the remainder interest absolutely payable to the estate of the surviving spouse or by giving the surviving spouse a power of appointment over the remainder.

[¶703.1]   Life Insurance Proceeds Payable to Trust

One way to get investment management and control, plus availability of insurance proceeds, to a surviving spouse is to have the proceeds made payable to a trust; in this situation, whether the insurance proceeds qualify for the marital deduction will depend entirely on the terms of the trust. If it is a trust in which the beneficiary's interest after the wife's death goes to her estate or over which she has a power of appointment *and which in other respects meets the five requirements outlined above,* the proceeds, through the trust, will qualify for the marital deduction.

The main advantage of the estate method is that it does not require that income be paid at least annually to the wife. Thus this method may be advantageous in situations where the insured wants to have the payments of the insurance proceeds concentrated in some period beginning more than a year subsequent to the date of death. It permits the accumulation of income from the policy proceeds for payment during some period in the future.

The power of appointment method allows the insured to name secondary beneficiaries to receive the proceeds left after the death of his surviving wife and how they are to get the proceeds, subject to his wife's right to cancel these arrangements and make other arrangements. Similarly, in most states the power of appointment method avoids state inheritance taxes on the remainder interest which would otherwise fall in the wife's estate, assuming of course that the wife has not exercised her power to bring the remainder proceeds actually into her estate.

Where the wife is the owner of the insurance so as to remove all proceeds from the owner's estate, she might wish to set up a trust to receive the proceeds or she may make a testamentary disposition of the policy. (The policy should not revert to ownership in the husband if the wife dies first.)

[¶703.2]   Exercise of Settlement Options Left to Wife

Another way an insured can qualify insurance proceeds for the marital deduction and still get the benefit of settlement options is to refrain from exercising the options himself, making his beneficiary designation so that his wife is entitled to receive the entire proceeds in a lump sum, leaving it to her to exercise the settlement options. Whether the insured exercises the optional mode of settlement or leaves it for the beneficiary to exercise, the annual payments receive the same income tax treatment. But the fact that the wife had the right to take down the proceeds in a lump sum would qualify the proceeds for the marital deduction. Placing them under an optional mode of settlement merely constitutes an investment of the proceeds.

[¶704]   HOW TO SET UP LIFE INSURANCE POLICIES

We must answer these questions:

(1) Who should own the policies?

(2) To whom should the proceeds be payable?

(3) How should the proceeds be paid?

[¶704.1] Who Should Own the Policies?

We can avoid estate tax by having someone other than the insured own the policies. The insured must decide whether this future estate tax saving is worth giving up the cash surrender value of the policy as an asset in his balance sheet. He can, to a degree, get the best of both worlds by converting existing policies to paid-up and having his wife use the premium money to take out new policies.

In transferring policies to new owners, these points should be considered:

(1) If the owner dies before the insured, the then value of the policies will be taxable in the owner's estate. This may argue for giving the policies to children or a trust rather than to a wife.

(2) If the insured continues to make the premium payments, each payment will constitute a gift to the owner. If a wife or children are the owners, this gift may be protected from gift tax by the $3,000 annual exclusion for each donee which is doubled if the wife joins in the gift. If the policy is owned by a trust (other than a IRC §2503(c) trust for a minor), the payment of premiums will be a gift of a future interest, the annual exclusion will not be available and, after consuming the unified credit, gift tax liability will be incurred with each premium payment.

[¶704.2] Who Should Get the Proceeds?

These are the points to consider:

(1) Are the proceeds likely to be taxed soon in the estate of the beneficiary? This argues for making the proceeds payable to the children rather than the wife. If the proceeds are payable to a trust, the wife and children can get the income and estate tax can be avoided over two generations.

(2) What assurance is there that the proceeds will be available to provide liquidity needed by the estate of the insured? Possibly the wife and the children will have a sufficient interest in the estate or can otherwise be counted on to feed the proceeds back into the estate by loan or by the purchase of assets.

There are only two ways to make sure that the proceeds will be made available to the estate:

(1) Make the proceeds payable to the insured's estate. This is bad, because it gets us back into an estate tax.

(2) Make the proceeds payable to a trust which is directed to buy assets from or lend money to the estate.

[¶704.3]   **Two Pitfalls to Watch Closely**

Here are two possible surprises which require the closest attention:

(1) If you have a policy in which your children are named as beneficiaries and you transfer that policy to your wife, you'll succeed in removing the proceeds from your estate at the cost of a possible gift tax. But, on your death, the proceeds will be deemed to have been received by your children as a taxable gift from your wife. (This is in addition to any gift tax you may have paid on the transfer of the policy to your wife.) Reason: during your life, while she had incidents of ownership, she had the power to change the beneficiaries. Having refrained from changing the beneficiaries, she is deemed to have made the gift at the last instant before she could no longer change the beneficiaries (see *Goodman*, 156 F.2d 218).

To avoid this type of result, consider making your wife the beneficiary as well as the owner and in her will she should make a disposition of the policy to the children or transfer the policy to an irrevocable trust, naming the trust the beneficiary of the insurance and the children as beneficiaries of the trust. The estate owner should not be the trustee of the trust since his fiduciary powers over a life insurance policy on his own life may be considered an incident of ownership for federal estate tax purposes (Rev. Rul. 76-261, IRB No. 1976-28, July 12, 1976). As an alternative, you can either:

(a) Fund the trust so that it has income to pay the premiums (any taxable gift will arise only on the transfer to the trust and that will be confined to the assets transferred to fund the trust—however the income earned by the trust will be taxable to you, if you or your spouse funded the trust); or

(b) Pay annual premiums to the trust (here, your gift will be confined to the premiums which will usually be preferable to having it applied to the proceeds).

(2) The second possible surprise can distort the distribution plan of the entire estate. More and more insurance is being financed by borrowed money. Where the insurance has been used as collateral for a loan on which the insured is personally liable and the lender repays himself out of the insurance proceeds, the beneficiary may be able to make the balance of the estate pay him the amount of the loan. This can inadvertently give the beneficiary of bank loan insurance, not the net value of the insurance, but its gross value at the expense of the residuary legatees of the estate. This result is not likely to occur where the insurance company has made the loan. The law varies from state to state. It is important that the credit paper and the will spell out the testator's intent as to whether an insurance loan is to be paid by the policy proceeds only or by the entire estate.

[¶704.4]   **How the Insurance Proceeds Should Be Paid**

Insurance proceeds may be paid outright to the beneficiary, or under one of the optional modes of settlement or to a trust. The trust offers greater flexibility in investment management and in application of the proceeds to meet family needs. Here are the advantages of payment to a trust:

(1) The trust may be a method of eliminating the trouble and expense of a guardian in the case of minor beneficiaries. The beneficiary clauses of the life insurance trust serve the same purposes as the special settlement provisions which are often attached to life insurance policies.

(2) The trust makes possible the elimination of successive transfer taxes in those instances where life estates in the trust income are given to elderly beneficiaries, with gifts of the principal to others at the death of such beneficiaries.

(3) Subject to statutory limitations in each state, income may be accumulated by the trustee until the beneficiary reaches a certain age, when the principal is to be turned over to the beneficiary. It is important to note that in many states, accumulations are permissible only during the minority of the beneficiary.

(4) A very great number of contingencies can be provided for in the directions to the trustee concerning distribution of income and principal of the trust.

(5) It is possible to grant the trustee discretion in the solution of many problems which the insurance company could not handle itself. This includes the selection of a member of the class of beneficiaries on the basis of need or any other discretionary yardstick.

(6) Restrictions and limitations on the use and enjoyment of the property by the beneficiary may be incorporated in the trust. Such restrictions would not be possible with the ordinary insurance options.

(7) Broad discretion in the selection of investments can be placed in the trustee's hands. Thus, with a capable trustee, it is possible that income realized through investments of trust funds may be greater than that guaranteed by the insurance company in the policy options—but without the guarantees.

(8) A life insurance trust can, by appropriate instructions to the trustees, provide estate liquidity for estate tax purposes and still keep important income-producing assets in the family.

Aside from the obvious reasons that payment of insurance proceeds under options rather than in a lump sum will prevent the improvident use of the proceeds or their capital loss through poor investment on the part of the beneficiary, there are at least six more good reasons why settlement options should be considered:

(1) By the use of the spendthrift trust clause, the proceeds will be protected against the claims of the beneficiaries' creditors. (Generally only the insured has the right to have this clause inserted in the policy.)

(2) The insured is permitted to direct who shall receive any excess insurance proceeds which the primary beneficiary does not consume.

(3) Common disaster complications can be avoided and probate expenses reduced.

(4) By using the investment services of the life insurance company, a guaranteed rate of return of 2% or more is assured. In addition, the beneficiary may participate in any excess interest which, although not guaranteed, may be awarded by the company.

(5) The payment of life insurance proceeds under a long-term option either for a fixed period of years or for life suggests the probability that life insurance proceeds will be received during both inflationary and deflationary periods thus resulting in dollar cost averaging of purchasing power.

(6) Insurance proceeds paid under the options may offer certain income tax advantages. The interest element payable to a spouse will be income tax free to the extent of $1,000 annually.

[¶705]   **HOW TO PROGRAM INSURANCE**

Programming consists simply of determining what kind and amounts of insurance a man should own in order to solve the particular problems with which he is faced. Programming consists of several steps:

(1) Determine the income needs of the man and his family.

(2) Determine how far present insurance and other assets will go in meeting these needs.

(3) Measure the deficiency, if any, between present assets and the income desired.

(4) Determine the amounts and kind of insurance needed to fill this deficiency, subject, of course, to the insured's ability to pay for it.

(5) Coordinate the old insurance and assets with the new insurance, selecting the most desirable settlement options and other policy provisions, such as spendthrift clauses, common disaster clauses, etc.

[¶705.1]   **Conventional Programming Method**

The conventional method sets up the job to be done by listing what Social Security will do and by calculating the new insurance necessary to produce the required income by utilizing the amounts guaranteed by the settlement options.

There are certain actuarial guarantees locked into the insurance policy package, handy in diagramming the distributive pattern for the payout period through use of settlement options. (See the tables on page T-18 et seq.) The insured is thus able to project the exact benefits he can bestow through the use of these options.

(1) Interest Option permits the insurance company to retain the proceeds and pay interest to the beneficiary in installments at a guaranteed rate. However, it is entirely likely that the actual interest rate may increase from time to time when financially justified. Arrangements may be made providing for withdrawal of principal either in whole or in certain prescribed amounts at periodic intervals. Interest received is fully taxable.

(2) Fixed Period Option allows for payment of principal and interest in systematic fashion for a stated period of time. The amount of the payment will depend on the proceeds, the applicable rate of interest and the period of time. Any change in the face amount of the policy will alter the amount of each payment but not the number of payments. Interest is fully taxable but the widow can receive up to $1,000 a year tax free.

(3) Fixed Amount Option stipulates specified amounts to be paid in periodic installments. The payments will continue as long as the principal and interest accretions last. The number of payments will be determined by the amount of proceeds and the interest rate. Partial withdrawal of proceeds can be provided because such withdrawal will merely affect the duration of installment payments. This privilege insures the duration of installment payments and flexibility and allows for dovetailing with Social Security.

(4) Life Income Option guarantees installment payment of proceeds for the entire life of the beneficiary. There are a number of factors which determine the amount of payments such as the age and sex of the beneficiary, when the payments are to commence in addition to the amount of proceeds and the interest rate. Further factors influencing the amount of periodic payments are the type of annuity option selected, i.e., 10- or 20-year certain, refund annuity, or joint and survivor annuity.

The interest portion of each payment in (3) and (4) is taxable, subject to a $1,000 annual exemption for a widow. The interest is computed by dividing the value of the insurance by the number of installments (stated number or life expectancy where payment is for life), and any amount received in excess of the amount so computed is treated as interest.

[¶706]   **HOW A FUNDED LIFE INSURANCE TRUST
CAN CARRY MORE INSURANCE**

The funded life insurance trust is one in which income-producing property is transferred to a trust and the trust is either given or directed to take out an insurance policy which may be made payable to the trust or to named beneficiaries.

If the trust carries insurance on the life of the person who set it up or his spouse, the income of the trust will be taxed to that person.

But if a man creates a trust and directs that the income be used to carry insurance on the life of his son, the trust income will be taxed to the trust. This offers an important opportunity to make investment income more valuable and carry more insurance on another person's life than could be carried if taxed personally to the grantor of a funded insurance trust.

[¶706.1]   **Buy More Insurance by Shifting Income**

Additional tax savings can be had by transferring top bracket income to another taxable entity—a child or a trust. This is particularly effective in building family security where investment income is received on top of salary or business income. If a father has adequate security he saves future estate tax and expands family income by the transfer of income-producing property to a trust.

Here's an approximation of how much insurance can be bought by a married individual filing a joint return with the tax savings from the transfer of $1,000 of investment income to a trust:

SHIFTING $1,000 OF INCOME TO TRUST

Taxable income (joint return)	Tax saving by transfer of $1,000	Non-par ordinary life (approximate)		
		Age 30	Age 40	Age 50
$20,000	$135	$10,000	$ 7,500	$ 4,500
30,000	245	17,500	12,000	8,000
50,000	355	25,500	17,500	11,500

[¶707] HOW TO USE ANNUITIES IN ESTATE PLANNING

Though usually thought of as a retirement vehicle, an annuity can also be a useful tool in estate planning. It can be used to provide for income lost when capital is given away to avoid having it subjected to estate tax. Thus, annuities can justify a gift program of an estate owner who wants assurance that he will not outlive his money and become dependent on his children. Or they can secure a fixed income for the wife so that the husband's business risks do not jeopardize her security. A joint annuity can be useful where the husband wants to qualify property for the marital deduction yet doesn't want his wife to have the power to dispose of his property after his death.

[¶707.1] Annuities as an Estate Asset

A survivorship annuity will be taxed in the estate of the annuity owner at a value determined from Government tables (which take into account the survivor's life expectancy). See the table on page T-26.

If the wife is given the survivorship benefits outright with full power over any part remaining at her death, the marital deduction applies. If her rights extend only to a portion of the benefits, the marital deduction applies only to that portion. If she merely has the survivorship benefits for life and at her death the benefits go to another, there is no marital deduction. But if the interest completely terminates at the wife's death it can qualify for the deduction.

SECTION VIII. CARRYOVER BASIS FOR INHERITED PROPERTY

The estate planner must be familiar with the Carryover Basis Rules for property acquired or passing from a decedent who dies after December 31, 1976. Since the recipient's basis for inherited property is no longer "stepped up" to the fair market value on the date of decedent's death (or alternate valuation date if that election is made), the estate planner now has many problems in determining the original basis, the effect of tax on eventual sale of the assets, and interpretation of these complex rules.

[¶801]   **CARRYOVER BASIS RULE**

The decedent's executor or beneficiary will take the same basis in the decedent's property as that of the decedent (subject to certain adjustments). Thus, appreciation occurring prior to the decedent's death will no longer completely escape income tax, since the recipient, upon disposition of the property, will have the decedent's basis, as adjusted, in computing gain.

[¶802]   **"FRESH START" ADJUSTMENT**

For property held (or treated as held) by the decedent on December 31, 1976, there is a "step-up" in the decedent's basis to reflect the value of the property on December 31, 1976. This is called the "fresh start" adjustment, so that appreciation up through that date will not be subject to tax on the eventual sale after the decedent's death.

A decedent is treated as holding the property on December 31, 1976, if he actually owned it on that date, received it as a gift from someone else who owned it on that date, or if he received the property in a non-taxable exchange after that date and the property he exchanged was held by him on December 31, 1976.

[¶802.1]   **Marketable Bonds and Securities**

The "step-up" in basis of marketable bonds and securities for determining gain (but not loss) will be the value as of December 31, 1976, even if the value on that date is greater than the estate value. For example, if the decedent's basis is 25 and the value on December 31, 1976 is 35, and the value at death is 30 (because the security goes up and down) and it is ultimately sold at 40, the fresh start basis will be 35. Marketable bonds and securities are securities which are listed on the New York Stock Exchange, the American Stock Exchange, or any city or regional exchange in which quotations appear on a daily basis, including foreign securities listed on recognized foreign national or regional exchanges; securities regularly traded in the national or regional over-the-counter market, for which published quotations are available; securities locally traded for which quotations can readily be obtained from established brokerage firms; and units in a common trust fund (Conference Report on Tax Reform Act of 1976). The fair market value is determined by using the normal methods of valuation for estate and gift tax purposes. There are various publications available listing the December 31, 1976 value and these publications should be a permanent part of one's library.

[¶802.2] Other Property

For assets such as works of art, patents, copyrights, oil interests, securities of closely held corporations, partnership interest, business interest, real estate, all kinds of tangible property, etc., held or treated as held on December 31, 1976, there is a different rule. If the value at day of death (not alternate valuation date even if that election is made) exceeds the decedent's adjusted basis immediately before death, there is an adjustment to basis. If the adjusted basis exceeds value at death, the decedent's basis is carried over. The value at December 31, 1976 is computed by a mandatory formula which assumes that the appreciation occurred at a uniform rate during the decedent's entire holding period. Thus, the actual value of the property on December 31, 1976 is irrelevant. For example, if a decedent acquired a piece of land on December 31, 1966 for $60,000 and subsequently dies on December 31, 1986 with the land valued at $160,000, the total appreciation is $100,000 ($160,000 − $60,000) of which $50,000 is deemed attributable to the period up to December 31, 1976.

$$\frac{12/31/66 \text{ to } 12/31/76}{12/31/66 \text{ to } 12/31/86} - \frac{3650}{7300} \times \text{Total appreciation } \$100,000 = \$50,000$$

Therefore, the stepped-up basis for determining gain (not loss) will be $110,000 ($60,000 original basis + $50,000). If the property was subject to depreciation, depletion or amortization, you must first add these items for the decedent's entire holding period to his adjusted basis before making the allocation. To determine the appreciation up to December 31, 1976, add to the net appreciation so calculated the adjusted depreciation, depletion or amortization for the holding period prior to December 31, 1976 to arrive at the addition to decedent's basis. The adjustment in basis cannot increase the basis of the other property above the estate value. Substantial improvements to any property are treated as separate property. As can be seen from this example, the longer the decedent lives, the lower the adjustment to basis will be.

The carryover basis rule has a drastic effect on art work in the hands of the artist's executor or beneficiary. When the property is sold, gain will be treated as ordinary income because of the peculiar interplay of the carryover basis rules and the definition of capital assets. Capital gain treatment is denied property created by decedent's personal efforts when the property is passed on to another who computes his basis with reference to the basis of the deceased creator (carryover basis).

[¶803]   **DEATH TAXES**

Besides the fresh start rules, the basis of the property is increased by the amount of federal and state estate tax and state inheritance tax attributable to the appreciation which occurred after 1976. This is computed by the following formula:

$$\frac{\text{Net appreciation beyond carryover basis}}{\text{Fair market value of all property subject to tax}} \times \text{Death tax}$$

However, this adjustment cannot increase the basis of any asset beyond the estate value. There is no adjustment for death taxes of property which qualifies for the marital deduction or charitable deduction. The state inheritance taxes must be paid by the recipient of the property.

[¶804]   **MINIMUM BASIS ADJUSTMENTS**

After both the fresh start and the estate tax adjustments have been made to the basis of the assets, if the aggregate basis of all carryover basis property is less than $60,000, then the basis of the appreciated property can be stepped up to a minimum of $60,000, provided the basis does not exceed the fair market value. Further, the executor may elect to exclude up to $10,000 of household and personal effects from the basis of the carryover basis rules and therefore be valued at fair market value. Any household or personal effects in excess of this exclusion would be subject to the carryover basis rules and would count in meeting the $60,000 minimum.

[¶805]   **INFORMATION REQUIRED TO BE FURNISHED**

Executors are required to provide information concerning the carryover basis property to the Internal Revenue Service, as well as provide each recipient of the property with the carryover basis for his future use. There are monetary penalties imposed on the executor for failure to provide this information.

[¶806]   **ESTATE PLANNING CONSIDERATION**

The estate planner should have all available information as to cost basis, date of acquisition, fair market value of marketable bonds and securities on

December 31, 1976, and current market value of all the estate owner's assets in order to make an intelligent decision regarding the minimizing of income tax costs when these assets will be sold. Insurance proceeds have been specifically excluded from the definition of carryover basis property; accordingly, the use of life insurance in estate planning has become even more significant. Insurance proceeds may now be needed to provide the funds to pay the income taxes on gains from disposition of appreciated property after the decedent's death.

Almost all estates including moderate estates where there may be no federal estate tax, will still feel the impact of the capital gains tax. In addition, buy-sell agreements, §303 redemptions and the use of Flower Bonds will have to be reviewed for the effect of the capital gains tax.

New concepts must be explored—traditionally estate planners have advised clients to hold appreciated property until death, so the estate or heirs would get a stepped-up basis for the appreciated property equal to the estate value. Now that post-1977 appreciation is no longer added to the basis of the property, it may be advisable for the estate owner to sell the appreciated property before death, so the estate will be reduced by the taxes on the capital gain. If the estate were to sell property after death, the tax on capital gain would not be a tax deduction in arriving at the taxable estate. The estate planner would have to make calculations to see if the sale before death would save taxes, and determine what adjustments to the basis would be made if the estate owner held on to the appreciated property until death.

SECTION IX.   LIFETIME GIFTS

The estate planner is deeply concerned with how the ownership of family property is distributed among various family members and how it should be redistributed after death. Delaying the transfer of property from one generation to the next, until death overtakes the older generation, maximizes transfer costs. Transfer of property from the older and wealthier members of a family to others during life reduces future estate tax liability on the appreciation of the assets. If the transferees are in lower income tax brackets, such transfers reduce the aggregate family income tax bill and thus increase either the family spending money or the aggregate amount of family assets. Where this is accomplished by gift, there will be gift tax liability whenever the unified credit against the gift tax of $47,000 in 1981 ($94,000 for man and wife) and the $3,000 ($6,000 for man and wife) annual gift tax exclusion for each donee have been exhausted.

When property is transferred from one member of a family to another, whether by gift or for value, we are keeping future appreciation of his estate as well as future increases in income out of his income tax return. And when a man does not want to incur gift tax liability, he may sell property to another member of the family; the proceeds of sale replace the property transferred in the estate of the transferor, but future appreciation gets over to the transferee without transfer tax.

Where we want to transfer property to another member of the family so that income and future appreciation will accrue to the transferee but the transferor wants to retain the use of the property, we may accomplish this by gift and leaseback or sale and leaseback.

Appreciated property may be transferred from one member of a family to another in return for the obligation of the transferee to pay a fixed amount of money to the transferor for life. This is the private annuity. It enables one to transfer property free of estate tax or gift tax. The capital gains tax on the transaction is spread over the transferor's life expectancy. The rest of the fixed payments which the transferee pays to the transferor are received as annuity income so that a large portion of the payments will come tax free as a return of capital and, to this extent, the payments will continue to be received tax free even after the transferor has received the value of the property at the time it was transferred for the annuity. The private annuity is frequently a very valuable estate planning technique, although there are many tax complications to be measured and placed under control.

The family partnership is another technique available to spread the income of a family business among various individual family members, including low bracket taxpayers. It will also, to the extent of the interest of the other family partners, take the ownership of the business and future appreciation achieved in building up the business out of the father's taxable estate, thereby relieving a possible liquidity problem. A family partnership can be created by making a gift of a partnership interest to members of the family, by having them buy their interest or by having them make an investment in a partnership which either starts or purchases a business. Where minor children are involved, family trusts can be made partners in a family partnership for the benefit of such minor children.

Another method for dividing income assets among members of the family is the family corporation. This may be a corporation operating the family business or possibly an investment company holding and investing the family savings. The corporate entity facilitates the division of interest by the year-by-year transfer of a small amount of stock to other family members in a manner which, taking advantage of the $3,000 ($6,000 for husband and wife) annual exclusion, will avoid any transfer tax. By using a corporation with a common and preferred stock capital structure and having the older generation retain preferred stock and transfer common stock to the younger generation, the accumulation of capital and value which occurs in building up the corporation can be transferred to the younger generation. This transfer is accomplished free of transfer taxes by way of increments in the value of their common stock.

Another result which is sometimes accomplished by family transactions is the creation of deductible payments from the higher taxed members of the family to the lower taxed members of the family. These payments may take the form of rent, salary, interest or royalty. All transactions between members of a family, not being arm's-length transactions, will have to pass a test of economic reality. This means that the property interest producing the income or calling for a payment will be validly and irrevocably vested in the ownership of a person receiving such income or payment. The amount of the payment will have to be justified by the value of the property, services rendered, etc. To get the desired tax results, it will frequently be necessary to see that the transaction does not run afoul of various provisions designed to block artificial tax advantages resulting from transactions between family members. Thus, loss on a sale made by one member to another may be denied, gain on the sale may be treated as ordinary income rather than capital gain and the deductibility of expense payments may be lost if cash is not transferred within a specified period of time.

[¶901]   **LIFETIME PERSONAL GIFTS**

The most direct and effective method of reducing the taxable estate of future appreciation is by making gifts during one's lifetime to those who would be the beneficiaries under the will. Such gifts may be made currently tax free if kept within the unified tax credit and exclusions. A program of lifetime gifts of $3,000 ($6,000 if married) per donee when planned and carried out over a period of years may produce substantial savings in transfer taxes.

However, the prospective death tax savings to be achieved by a lifetime gift may not be as powerful a motivating force as the prospect of immediate income tax savings. These income tax savings, achieved for the family group when income-producing property is transferred to children outright or in trust or when a father's business is converted to a family partnership, can accumulate over the years to a substantial amount of capital which will also be outside of the taxable estate.

The donor must also be satisfied that his donees will handle their gifts wisely if he wishes to make the gifts outright. Otherwise, he should protect the property by using a trust. This is particularly true in the case of a gift of shares in a family corporation. Irresponsible voters of a minority stock interest in a closely held corporation can find ways to interfere with management of the business or block a sale, reorganization or liquidation.

[¶901.1] Unification of Estate and Gift Tax Rates

Prior to the enactment of the Tax Reform Act of 1976, there were separate and unequal estate and gift tax rate tables. In general, the old gift tax rate was approximately 75% of the federal estate tax rate in a corresponding bracket, making it obvious to most estate owners that an immediate savings was available if a lifetime gift was made rather than a transfer at death. In addition, there was a greater savings in estate tax than the apparent 25% because the property, which is the subject of the gift, would have been taxed at the highest effective estate tax rate, while the gift would be taxed at the lowest available gift tax rate. Also, both the gift tax and estate tax had separate exemptions.

Starting January 1, 1977, the Tax Reform Act of 1976 combined the estate and gift tax rates into a unified rate schedule, with progressive rates based on cumulative transfers during lifetime and at death (see ¶505). In addition, both the $60,000 estate tax exemption and the $30,000 lifetime specific exemption have been replaced with one unified credit which is available against either the gift or estate tax (see ¶901.4 for phase in of unified credit).

All transfers during lifetime (after December 31, 1976) and at death will be accumulated for applying the unified rate schedule in determining the estate tax, with an offset for gift tax paid after December 31, 1976 for lifetime transfers. Thus, since the transfer tax should be the same for a person who makes transfers during lifetime and for a person who retains his property until death, there is no longer any substantial tax savings by making lifetime gifts. However, future appreciation can be removed from the donor's estate by making current lifetime gifts of the property; also, gifts which qualify for the $3,000 annual exclusion can be removed from the estate each year without incurring either a gift tax or an estate tax. If the donor survives the gift by more than three years, the gift tax is not grossed up, and therefore gift tax paid reduces the taxable estate, but is nevertheless subtracted from the tentative tax in arriving at the estate tax.

[¶901.2] Income Tax Saving in Gifts

It is very expensive for a person in high tax brackets to give money to another member of the family. If, for example, a man in the 50% tax bracket gives his mother $200 a month, each payment costs him $400 in the sense that he must earn that much or have property yielding that much to have left after taxes the $200 with which to make a payment. On the other hand, a gift of property which will throw off an equivalent amount of after-tax income can result in a substantial reduction or even complete elimination of the tax bite, depending on the donee's tax bracket. For example, although a $2,000 yearly allowance is tax free to the recipient, it is costly to the donor. Here's a comparison of the income cost of a yearly gift with that of a gift of property yielding $2,200 annually, the amount necessary to net $2,000 assuming a $200 income tax liability to the donee.

Donor's effective tax rate	Income required to net $2,000 after taxes	Income from transferred property	Income retained	After-tax income saving
30%	$2,857	$2,200	$ 657	$460
40%	3,333	2,200	1,133	680
50%	4,000	2,200	1,800	900

[¶901.3]   **How to Weigh Gift Tax against Income Tax Saving**

When we do have a gift tax to pay, we must deduct the income on the capital consumed to pay the gift tax in order to appraise the income tax saving. The capital represented by the gift tax payment more than three years before death, will itself be more than washed out in estate tax saving, so that the primary concern may be with the loss of future income measured against income tax savings from the switch.

[¶901.4]   **What Gifts Cost**

Each person has a unified credit against the gift tax (which will reach $47,000 in 1981) which can be doubled if the gift is reported as being made by a husband and wife together. In addition, each year a $3,000 exclusion may be taken on account of each person to whom present-interest gifts are made. Up to $6,000 can be claimed by the donor and his spouse even though only one owns the gift property. For gifts after December 31, 1976, the Code permits a marital deduction on the first $100,000 of a lifetime gift from one spouse to the other; the second $100,000 is fully taxed; thereafter the deduction allowed is one-half of the total lifetime gifts to the spouse. Thus, the cost of a gift will vary depending on whether it is made by a single person, by a married person to his spouse or by a married person to someone else.

[¶901.5]   **How the Gift Tax Works**

For gifts made after 1976, no quarterly gift tax returns are due until the cumulative taxable gifts exceed $25,000. If, during the calendar year, no quarterly returns were required, then an annual return must be filed by February 15 of the subsequent year where the gifts exceed the $3,000 per donee annual exclusion.

In determining the applicable gift tax bracket from the unified rate schedule for current gifts, all taxable lifetime transfers including those made prior to January 1, 1977, are to be added together. After the tax is determined, you subtract the gift tax previously paid. For gifts made before January 1, 1977, you do not use the actual tax previously paid, but use a tax as computed by the unified rate schedule, even though the gift tax imposed under prior law may have been less. This can be illustrated as follows:

1965—Husband made a $200,000 gift to his wife
1981—Husband makes a $500,000 gift to his wife

1965

Total Gift		$200,000
Less Lifetime Exclusion	$30,000	
Marital Deduction	100,000	
Annual Exclusion	3,000	133,000
Taxable Gift		67,000
Gift Tax Paid		8,595

1981

Total Gift		$500,000
Marital Deduction	$250,000	
Annual Exclusion	3,000	253,000
Taxable Gift		247,000
Prior Taxable Gift		67,000
Total Taxable Gifts		314,000
Gift Tax		141,600
Less Gift Tax on Prior Gift		14,820*
Gift Tax Before Unified Credit		126,780
Unified Credit		47,000
Gift Tax Payable		79,790

* Note the actual gift tax was $8,595, but you subtract the tax based on the unified rate schedule.

The unified credit for gift tax is as follows:

Year Gifts Made	Unified Credit
January 1, 1977–June 30, 1977	6,000*
July 1, 1977–December 31, 1977	30,000
1978	34,000
1979	38,000
1980	42,500
1981	47,000

* The unified credit for gift tax purposes is identical as for estate tax purposes, except for the period January 1, 1977 to June 30, 1977.

There is a special rule for gifts made after September 8, 1976 and before January 1, 1977. The unified credit available for gift and estate tax purposes is reduced by 20% of specific lifetime exemption used for gifts made during that period.

[¶901.6]　Net Gift—Donee Pays the Gift Tax

Sometimes the donor may want the donee to pay the gift tax due on the gift. This can be done by making the gift on the condition that the donee agrees to pay the gift tax. Thus, the donor has made a net gift, equal to the value of the asset given away minus the amount of the gift tax paid by the donee (*Turner*, 49 TC 356). This can save the donor cash and will also reduce the value of the gift.

Where the donee pays the gift tax as agreed, the amount of the gift tax should be subtracted from the value of the gift property in calculating the gift tax. In *Rev. Rul. 71-232*, IRS described a method of computing the gift tax which can prove helpful:

The donor made a transfer of property having a fair market value of $300,000 at the date of the gift, with the understanding that the donee would pay the resulting gift tax. His timely filed federal gift tax return reflected a reduction in the value of the gift in the amount of gift tax paid by the donee.

IRC §2512 provides that if a gift is made in property, the value thereof at the date of the gift shall be considered the amount of the gift; if a donor transfers by gift less than his entire interest in property, the gift tax is applicable to the interest transferred (Regs. §25.2511-1(e)); the donor is primarily liable for the payment of the tax (IRC §2502(d)). Thus, if at the time of the transfer, the gift is made subject to a condition that the gift tax be paid by the donee or out of the transferred property, the donor receives consideration for the transfer in the amount of gift tax to be paid by the donee. Under these circumstances, the value of the gift is measured by the fair market value of the property or property right or interest passing from the donor, minus the amount of the gift tax to be paid by the donee.

Accordingly, the gift tax attributable to the transfer of property in this case may be deducted from the value of that property in arriving at the amount of the gift where it is shown, expressly or by implication from the circumstances surrounding the transfer, that the donor attached payment of the tax by the donee (or out of the transferred property) as a condition of the transfer. In such event, the resulting tax must, of course, actually be paid by the donee or from the subject property. *Rev. Rul. 71-232* (IRB 1971-21,11) spells out the working of the formula.

[¶901.7]　What Constitutes a Gift?

A gift is many things besides the familiar transfer from one person to another. It can take the form of the cancellation of a debt, the designation of a life insurance beneficiary, the setting up of a trust, the purchase of services for another's benefit.

Before we can apply the gift tax rules, we must know when we have made a gift. The following checklist shows the gift tax consequences of different types of transfers.

GIFT OF	TAXABLE?
Joint Property Holdings	
Anything put in joint names with right to survivor to take.	Yes—for half of the value.
Putting property in joint names as co-owners and taking mortgage on property later paid off by you; property is in names of you and another as joint owners with right of survivorship.	Yes—gift comes for what you pay for property (one-half of that). Also if you pay off mortgage, you have gift of half of that payment too.
Putting property into title called tenants by the entirety (only husbands and wives can do this). In this form neither spouse can defeat the right of the survivor to all of the property.	Gift would be one-half of cost if ages were about the same. Check tables issued by government where there is disparity in age. (If gift is of real property, there is no gift until the tenancy is terminated other than by a spouse's death unless election is made to treat transfer as current gift. This applies also to regular joint tenancy in real property between spouses.)
Putting property bought in form called tenants in common; in this each can sell his share of the property.	You are taxed for the share you have given other persons.
Joint bank accounts where you put in money subject to withdrawal by you and another.	Yes—but only when other person really withdraws funds for purpose other than those for which you are obligated to pay—such as household costs.

U.S. Savings Bonds

If you buy and put them in:	
Your name payable on death to someone else.	No.
Someone else's name.	Yes.
Another's name and have payable on death to still another person.	Yes.
Two persons' names as co-owners.	Yes—to both of these.
Your name and another as co-owner.	No—until the other person collects the proceeds.

GIFT OF *(cont.)*	TAXABLE? *(cont.)*

Life Insurance

Assigning your policy to someone so you can no longer borrow on it.	Yes—if your estate is not the beneficiary.
Paying premium for someone else.	Yes.
Merely changing beneficiary in policy.	No, if you can change beneficiary again.
Irrevocably naming beneficiary.	Yes, if you also give up right to borrow on policy or to surrender it for cash.

Other Transfer

Property sold for less than its value.	Yes—unless it is an ordinary business transaction.
Lending money without expectation of repayment.	Yes.
Cancellation of a debt due you when the borrower can repay.	Yes, except in a business transaction.
Payments for support of a wife or child.	No.
Contribution to a corporation.	Maybe—unless you own all the stock. Some cases say there is a gift to other stockholders if you do not own 100% of the stock.
Gifts by minor.	Not until he reaches maturity and does not recall gift.
Gifts you later take back—say, because you do not get the income tax saving you hoped to get.	Yes—and that might be a double gift—one from you on the way out—and another on the way back.
Transfers to a third person for the benefit of your donee.	Yes.
To a charity with income reservation to yourself for life and then to your wife.	Yes—for the value of your wife's life interest.
Formal declaration by you that you hold property given another.	Yes.
You keep property without formal declaration but intend it for another and give him the income.	Yes—but only for the income he gets.
You give up only part of a piece of property, keeping the rest for yourself.	Yes, to the extent of the part given.

GIFT OF (cont.)	TAXABLE? (cont.)
Surrender of a life income property even where your consent and another's are required for you to do that.	Yes.

[¶902] TRANSFERS TO MINORS

There are numerous advantages in transferring property to minor children. Income produced by the gift property may be shifted from the donor's top rates to lower rates applicable to the child or a trust. If the income is the child's and he is under 19 or a student, part or all of it may be absorbed by his own personal tax exemption without loss of his parents' dependency exemption. If the income is accumulated in a trust for the child until he reaches 21, the income can be taxed to the trust which has its own exemptions and credits. On subsequent distribution the accumulated income (before he was 21) will be tax free to the child, provided there are no other trusts making an accumulated distribution to the child in the same year.

A drawback to outright gifts to minors is the possibility that circumstances will arise making it necessary or advisable for the minor to dispose of the gift property. Most states hold that contracts entered into during minority are voidable, thus allowing a minor to reclaim property which he has transferred with the result that most persons will not deal with a minor directly.

There is also the possibility that restrictions imposed by the state of the donor on the minor's use of the property for the minor's own protection may cast doubt on the legality of the gift.

[¶902.1] Outright Gift—Savings Account

You can make a valid gift by opening a bank account in the minor's own name. Interest is taxable to the child, the funds are not part of the donor's estate. The bank will allow the child to make reasonable withdrawals provided he has attained the state's "banking age," which varies from state to state from age 8 to age 13. The so-called "savings bank trust," which reads "X, in trust for Y," is usually not considered a completed gift. As long as X retains the passbook, he has complete control and ownership of the account. He can close the account by withdrawing all the funds. Such an account is merely a tentative trust which becomes absolute only at X's death, assuming there are still funds left in the account at that time. Any interest earned in this account is taxed to X; and at his death, the funds in the account will be taxed in his estate.

[¶902.2] Outright Gift of U. S. Savings Bonds

The most popular way of buying U.S. Savings Bonds for children is by registering the bonds in the name of a child with the parent as co-owner. This is costly taxwise, since the parent will be liable for income tax on the income, whether annually or when the bonds mature, and will probably have the value of the bonds taxed in his estate. Another form of registration sometimes used is one which makes the bond payable on the child's death to the parent. Should the parent die, the bond will be taxable in his estate to the extent of his reversionary interest.

The Treasury permits you to avoid these tax results by registering the bond in the child's name alone. If the child isn't competent to redeem, the parent may redeem for him.

[¶902.3]　Outright Gift of Life Insurance Policy

A life insurance policy can be the subject of a gift to a minor, whether the policy is on the life of the donor, or on another's life or even on the life of the minor. The fact that the policy has no immediate cash surrender value will not disqualify the gift for the annual gift exclusion. To make the gift effective, the donor must transfer all the incidents of ownership. This may raise a practical problem in that the minor's age may prevent him from cashing the policy, borrowing on it, etc. without the intervention of a legal guardian. There is also the possibility that the policy might revert to the donor. Assuming a close relationship, should the minor die, the incidents of ownership might revert to the donor; or, if it is the minor's life which is insured, the proceeds might be payable to the donor. If there is a 5% chance that the policy will revert to the donor, the transfer would have no effect for estate tax purposes. This can be avoided by having the donor designate a contingent owner other than himself in the event of the child's premature death.

[¶902.4]　Outright Gift of Securities

It may or may not be difficult to register securities directly in the name of a minor. If the transfer agent has knowledge that the intended owner is a minor, he will usually refuse to permit registration in the minor's name. Even if the shares are successfully registered, should the minor subsequently attempt to transfer the shares and the transfer agent learns of his minority, the agent will probably refuse to effect the transfer without the appointment of a legal guardian. The consequences can be serious. Where closely held corporation stock is involved, the gift of stock to a minor may impede corporate action which requires the affirmative vote of the donated shares; a sale of the entire corporate business may even be impeded. One solution is to register the shares in the name of an adult *nominee* for the minor. The nominee must file Treasury Department Form 1087, designed to put the Treasury on notice as to the true ownership of the stock.

[¶902.5]　Outright Gift of Mutual Funds

The general rules applicable to securities apply here. Of course, the problem of management and sale for reinvestment is minimized, because the fund itself provides continuous portfolio supervision. Changes in the underlying investments of the fund are made without reference to the minor, and many funds provide for automatic reinvestment of all distributions.

[¶902.6]   Outright Gift of Real Estate

While real property may be given to a minor, it is usually not advisable to do so directly. This is because it would be virtually impossible without the interposition of a legal guardian to mortgage, lease or sell the realty without costly delay. A more proper holding vehicle for a gift of real estate to a minor would be a trust. Or perhaps a real estate holding corporation might be set up and a gift of shares in the corporation made to the child.

[¶902.7]   Custodianship and the Gifts to Minors Act

All states have enacted legislation that greatly simplifies the procedure for making gifts of securities (in almost all states, money, and in most, life insurance) to minors—statutory custodianship. The primary purpose is to permit an outright gift of securities to a minor by a simple form of registration or deed of gift where the gift is of a bearer security. This permits the donor to realize important income and estate tax savings with little or no gift tax liability while at the same time providing some adult control over the subject of the gift without the need for a guardian or trust instrument. The gift must be delivered to the custodian. Where a security in registered form is involved, the gift is made by registering it in the name of the custodian. Thereafter, by mere reference on the stock certificate to the statutory provision, the custodian is empowered to retain or sell it, reinvest the proceeds or hold them in a savings account. The custodian is not limited to statutory legal investments as are guardians and trustees (unless the trust instrument provides otherwise). He is subject only to the "prudent man rule" in handling the custodial assets. Once the gift is made, it is irrevocable and conveys an indefeasibly vested title in the minor. Even though the child is the legal owner of the custodial property, the custodian acts as his statutory manager over the property in question. (In a trust the trustee is the manager and the legal owner of the trust property.) If the donor acts as custodian and he should die prior to termination of custodianship, the custodian account will be included in the donor's taxable estate (*Chrysler*, 44 TC 55).

Under a statutory custodianship for a minor, the custodian is empowered to pay over to the minor or expend for the minor as much or all of the custodial property as he deems advisable for the support, maintenance, education and benefit of the minor, with all unexpended property and income going to the minor upon his attaining age 21 (in some states, age 20, 19, or 18) or to his estate if he dies before then. This is virtually identical with a trust which is set up to meet the requirements of IRC §2503(c) (see ¶902.8).

[¶902.8]   Gift in Trust

Despite the flexibility introduced into the making and administering of gifts to minors by the enactment of the custodian laws, the most satisfactory method for making a substantial gift is through a trust, because it is desirable to suspend the minor's control of the property until he or she reaches a more mature age.

Where the income is not required to be paid currently to the minor, IRC §2503(c) preserves the annual gift tax exclusion for the trust by an exception to the future interest rule. The exception is that the gift is not one of a future interest to the extent (1) that the gift property and income therefrom may be expended by or for the benefit of the donee before he reaches his majority, and (2) will to the extent not so expended (a) pass to the donee upon his reaching his majority and (b) if he dies before reaching his majority, be payable to his estate or as he may appoint under a general power of appointment (see IRC §2514(c)). Note that it is not required that the property or income *actually* be spent by or for the donee during minority, but only that it *may* be so spent.

A prospective donor will have to determine whether a $3,000 annual gift tax exclusion is worth the restrictions that will have to be written into the trust. If the donor believes it undesirable for the child to receive absolute control of the gift property and accumulated income at majority—wishing to postpone this until a more mature age, say 30—he will have to be satisfied with the annual exclusion on the value of the income interest only or forego it altogether. This will mean that a gift tax will be payable after the unified credit of $47,000 in 1981 ($94,000 for husband and wife) has been exhausted. Or, perhaps he should be satisfied with an exclusion equal to the present value of the beneficiary's right to the income from the property transferred to the trust, as distinguished from the trust corpus itself (*Konner*, 35 TC 727; *Herr*, 35 TC 732, aff'd 303 F. 2d 780, nonacq; *Weller*, 38 TC 790; *Thebaut*, 361 F. 2d 428; *Rollman*, 342 F. 2d 62; *Rev. Rul. 68-670*, 1968-2 CB 413). These cases, holding that a part of a gift to a minor can qualify for the annual exclusion, further held that as long as the gift property or part thereof (which could be an income interest only) was to go to the minor at majority, that requirement of IRC §2053(c) would be met; it's not necessary that the entire trust corpus go to the minor at that age, or at all.

The best way to handle the income is to take full advantage of the leeway allowed by the statute and leave the income to be spent or accumulated in the uncontrolled discretion of an independent trustee.

It would be unwise for a parent to make it mandatory to use the income for the child's support during minority. Not only would this make the income taxable to the parent, whether or not the income was actually used for support, but if the parent died during the child's minority, the parent's estate would be subjected to estate tax on the ground of retained interest (IRC §2036).

Much the same disastrous result might follow from a mandatory direction merely to use the income for the minor or pay it to him, without any specific requirement that it be used for support. Although in this case, the parent would be subject to income tax only to the extent the income was used for support, it is hard to see as a practical matter how the trustee could discharge his duty to distribute without using the money (much of it, at any rate) for things that are deemed to constitute support. If the donor (whether or not the parent) was trustee, he would be vulnerable to estate tax if the infant died during minority, again on the ground of retained interest.

[¶902.9] **Short-Term Trust**

A special tax rule permits a high-bracket taxpayer to accumulate income at a lower rate in a "short-term" or temporary trust, or in the beneficiary's lower bracket, and recover the trust property at the end of the trust period. While this type of trust is useful in many situations, it is particularly suited to building an education fund for a child or supporting an aged relative.

Certain rules must be obeyed. The trust must, at its inception, be expected to last for at least ten years or for the lifetime of the beneficiary. The income may be accumulated, but the trust must require that the accumulation be turned over to the beneficiary when the trust ends, with no restriction on the way he uses it (see IRC §671-683). If these conditions are obeyed, the income will be taxed to the trust during the trust period and the donor can take back the property when the trust ends.

How does this work out with an education fund? Let's say father, who is in a 50% tax bracket, wants to accumulate as close to $20,000 as possible to assure his being able to put his child through college some 11 or 12 years from now.

Suppose father owns a property (real estate, stocks, bonds, etc.) that provides $2,000 a year in before-tax income. If he's in the 50% tax bracket, it leaves him $1,000 after taxes. If he invests the $1,000 each year at 6%, it will take about 15 years to accumulate $20,000. But he needs the money a lot quicker than that.

If he can accumulate a larger portion of the $2,000 income each year, however, he'd get the necessary $20,000 faster.

Suppose he transfers the income-producing property to a short-term trust set up to last for somewhat in excess of ten years, until the year before the child is ready for college. The child is named beneficiary of the trust. And the trustee is empowered to accumulate the income and pay it over to the child when the trust ends, at which time the property is to revert to the father.

Look at the arithmetic: The $2,000 the trust will earn each year will be subject to a tax of approximately $300, leaving $1,700 to accumulate (instead of the $1,000 before the transfer to the trust). If the trustee invests that amount at 6%, it should be able to accumulate $20,000 or almost that much by the time the trust is to terminate (in ten years instead of 15 years).

And, if desired, it is possible to word the trust in such a way that the transfer of the income-producing property to it will qualify for the annual gift tax exclusion despite the fact that the trust corpus is to be returned to the father (see ¶1404.4).

Note that we have arranged for the accumulated income to be distributed to the child, not in the year that he starts college, but the year before. This is to avoid the possibility that some of the income might be taxed to the father as income used to defray his support obligation. Since the child already owns outright (presumably in a bank account) all of the monies which will be used to pay his college expenses, there are no grounds for taxing the father when these costs are incurred.

Instead of accumulating income, we can pay each year's income directly to a bank account for the child (with a parent holding the passbook) or perhaps to a custodian under the state Uniform Gifts to Minors Act (see ¶902.7). Although the transfer to the custodian does not appear to meet the requirement of a "new" gift, many planners suggest that this approach is a sound one, enabling continuing reinvestments in securities.

If, after the trust terminates, the assets of the trust are to go back to the grantor, then during the term of the trust, the grantor will be taxed on capital gains allocated to the principal of the trust. Also, the grantor's estate will include the present value of the reversion (Reg. §20.2031-10(f)). In order for the grantor to avoid the capital gains and inclusion of the trust assets in his estate, he can designate his wife as remainder beneficiary.

If the grantor retains a reversionary interest in a short-term trust created after 1976, the Tax Reform Act of 1976 could possibly create additional tax for his estate. If the present value of the income from the trust created a taxable gift, that amount must be added to the taxable estate of the grantor in arriving at his tentative tax base (see ¶504). The grantor's estate already includes the reversionary principal of the trust (or a percentage, if the trust is still in existence). The Act, by inclusion of the taxable gift in the grantor's estate, now creates additional estate tax. The estate planner must be aware that only the income from the gift during the term of the trust has been removed from the grantor's estate. Therefore, the estate planner must calculate whether the income tax savings exceeds the additional estate tax cost.

SECTION X. INTRAFAMILY TRANSFERS

How the ownership of family property is distributed among the various members of the family and how it should be redistributed after the death of the respective owners are important considerations in the estate planning process. Delaying the transfer of property from one generation to the next until death overtakes the former will usually tend to maximize estate taxes and other transfer costs; handling the identical transfers during lifetime will, as a rule, cut these transfer costs considerably. And, assuming the transferees are in lower tax brackets, such lifetime transfers will reduce the aggregate family income tax bill, causing an increase in both current spendable income and in the aggregate amount of family assets. Gifts in trust and all types of transfers to minors have already been considered in broad terms at ¶902. Special problems concerning business interests are analyzed at ¶1201 et seq. There are a few more special types of intrafamily transactions, some of which are intertwined with the material in those other sections, which are deserving of comment at this point: private annuities, family lease-backs, family partnerships and family investment companies.

[¶1001] **THE PRIVATE ANNUITY**

The private annuity is a device which may be used whenever one person desires to transfer property to another person for a consideration. As most frequently used, it is an arrangement whereby the transferor gives appreciated property to the transferee (who is not regularly engaged in the business of writing annuities) in exchange for the latter's promise to pay him a certain annual income for life.

The possible tax advantages are:

(1) Income from the property is diverted from a high bracket taxpayer to one in a lower bracket.

(2) The transferor will be taxed only on a portion of the payments which he receives.

(3) The transferor, by reason of the fact that gain is not immediately recognized, is able to obtain higher annuity payments than if he had first sold the property and invested the net proceeds (after setting aside an amount for capital gains tax) in a commercial straight life annuity.

(4) The property is removed from the transferor's estate, thus saving on death taxes, and there is no gift tax on the transfer.

123

[¶1001.1]   **Estate Tax**

Since the payments will cease upon the transferor's death, the value of the transferred property will not be included in his estate.

[¶1001.2]   **Gift Tax**

There is no gift as long as the annual income promised to the transferor is set at a figure which has the same actuarial value as the present value of the transferor's property. If the annuity promised is below this amount, then there is a gift subject to tax, but the annual exclusion and unified credit may reduce or eliminate any tax liability on the transaction.

[¶1001.3]   **Income Tax—Revenue Ruling 69-74**

Excluded from the transferor's taxable income each year is an amount found by prorating the cost basis of the transferred property over the transferor's life expectancy.

Suppose, as will almost universally be the case, the present value of the annuity is considerably higher than the transferor's adjusted basis in the property. The gain is reported ratably over the life expectancy of the annuitant.

During all this time, of course, the remaining portion of the annual income is treated as the interest factor in the annuity and accordingly is taxed as ordinary income (*Rev. Rul. 69-74*, 1969-1 CB 43; but see, also, *Bell*, 60 TC, 469, 1973).

[¶1001.4]   **Use and Tax Effects of Annuities**

Here are two typical situations illustrating the use and tax effects of private annuities, the income tax effects following *Rev. Rul. 69-74:*

(1) Mrs. Smith, age 70, has an estate of $300,000, including a securities portfolio worth some $120,000; her cost basis for the securities is $80,000. She transfers this portfolio to her son in exchange for his agreeing to pay her $12,000 a year for the rest of her life. What are the tax results to Mrs. Smith?

Estate Tax: The estate has been reduced from $300,000 to $180,000, and the potential estate tax, from $41,000 to $2,000.

Gift Tax: No gift tax. Annual income is as much or slightly more than straight life annuity which could have been purchased from insurance company for $120,000.

Income Tax: Of the $12,000 annual income, $5,330 is tax free for life. This figure is arrived at by applying the ratio of the $80,000 cost basis over the $180,000 expected return ($12,000 × 15) to the $12,000 annual payment. This assumes a 15-year life expectancy for a female age 70. Next, the $40,000 capital gain is prorated over 15 years so that $2,670 is reportable as long-term capital gain each year for 15 years, ordinary income after that. During all this time, the remaining $4,000 a year, representing the interest portion of the annuity, will always be taxed at ordinary rates.

(2) Mr. Jones has a total estate worth $810,000 which includes a business valued at $500,000. His cost basis for the business is $250,000. Jones enters into an agreement with his son whereby he transfers the business to the son in exchange for the son's promise to pay him $25,000 a year. At that time, Jones has a life expectancy of 25 years. What are the tax results to Mr. Jones?

Estate Tax: The estate has been reduced from $810,000 to $310,000, and the potential estate tax, from $224,000 to $44,000.

Gift Tax: No gift tax. Annual income is approximately equivalent to straight life annuity which could be purchased from insurance company with $500,000.

Income Tax: Of the $25,000 income, $10,000 is tax free for life. This figure is arrived at by applying a 40% ratio (250,000/625,000) to the $25,000 annual payment. Prorating the $250,000 gain over 25 years gives us $10,000 each year as long-term capital gain for 25 years. During all this time, the remaining $5,000 a year, representing the interest portion of the annuity, will always be taxed at ordinary rates.

[¶1001.5] Tax Problems of the Transferee in Private Annuity Setup

Where does the transferee stand taxwise in the private annuity arrangement? He has the property and also the obligation under the agreement to make the annuity payments for the rest of the transferor's lifetime.

(1) **Estate Tax:** Although the transferee under a private annuity arrangement usually has a longer life expectancy than the transferor, there is always the possibility that the transferee may die first. If this should happen, the then value of the transferred property would be included in his gross estate. But, since his estate has the continued obligation of meeting the annuity payments, the then actuarial value of the transferor's right to income for life will be allowed as a deduction from the gross estate.

(2) **Gift Tax:** In the usual case, if there is going to be a gift, it will be one from the transferor to the transferee, where he either agrees in advance to receive a reduced annuity or where he forgives a part of the payment due each year. Rarely does the gift flow the other way which would be the case where the transferee agrees to pay to the transferor considerably more than the same dollar amount the property could buy in the form of a straight life annuity from an insurance company.

(3) **Income Tax:** Efforts have been made on behalf of transferees in private annuity setups to have either the income from the transferred property excluded from their own gross incomes or to get deductions for all or at least a part (the portion treated as interest and taxed to the transferor as ordinary

income) of the annual payments made to transferors. To date, all efforts have failed, and the transferee gets no deduction for the annual payment which he is required to make to the transferor.

Of especial importance in the income tax picture of transferees under private annuities are the following: (a) premature death of the transferor and (b) determination of transferee's basis. These are discussed briefly below:

(a) Premature Death of Transferor: The question is: Does the transferee realize current income when the transferor dies before having received back the value of the transferred property? If the property transferred is worth $100,000 and the transferor dies after receiving payments totalling $10,000, does the transferee realize taxable income of $90,000? There have been no really clearcut answers to date. Yet the possibility exists where the transferred property is cash or its equivalent that the transferee realizes currently taxable income in the year in which the transferor dies. When the property transferred is neither cash nor its equivalent (instead is stock, real estate, a business interest, etc.), the possibility of immediate taxation becomes remote. No gain would be recognized immediately. Instead, the transferee has merely acquired property with a low-cost basis.

(b) Determination of Transferee's Basis: The transferee must know the basis of his property if he's to compute his gain or loss on subsequent sale, or if he's to compute his annual depreciation deduction if the transferred property is depreciable. *Rev. Rul.* 55-119, 1955-1 CB 352 presents a reasonably thorough explanation of this question.

(i) *The unadjusted basis for gain or loss on sale after the death of the transferor* is the total of the payments actually made under the contract. (See *Rev. Rul.* 55-119 for adjustment of gain or loss for events occurring subsequent to the sale of the property and for adjustment where there was a gift element in the original transaction.)

(ii) *The unadjusted basis for purposes of computing gain on sale prior to the death of the transferor* is the total of the payments made plus the actuarial value (using tables in the gift tax regulations—see page T22a-d of the payments remaining to be made to the transferor. (See *Rev. Rul.* 55-119 for possible adjustments.)

(iii) *The unadjusted basis for purposes of computing loss on sale prior to the death of the transferor* is the total of the payments actually made. (See *Rev. Rul.* 55-119 for further explanation and for possible adjustments.)

(iv) *The basis for depreciation* is the actuarial value (under tables in the gift tax regulations—see page T-22a-d) of the prospective annuity payments, until such time as the total payments made to the transferor equal the actuarial value of the annuity. Any subsequent payments are added to the basis of the property. The unadjusted basis for depreciation becomes the total of the payments actually made immediately at the transferor's death. (See *Rev. Rul.* 55-119 for any adjustments.)

[¶1002]   **INTRAFAMILY ASSIGNMENTS**

The tax savings that arise from shifting of income within the family come about for the most part because income is transferred from high tax brackets to lower tax brackets. Sometimes, too, an income shift permits picking up deductions that would otherwise not be available; and shifting the property that produces the income out of your estate cuts the later estate tax.

[¶1002.1] **Assigning Property within the Family**

A much used way to shift income and keep the benefits within the family is to assign income-producing property to family members in low tax brackets. This can be done without the formation of a partnership. However, make sure that the property is given up with no strings attached. Just assigning the *income* doesn't effect a transfer.

Keep in mind that you may still be able to get an exemption for a child even though you've transferred more than $750 of annual income to him if he's either under 19 or a student (IRC §151(e)(1)).

Also, if your dependent donee is 65 or older, you can only get one exemption of $750 for him. If you transfer income to him, he can file his own return and get two exemptions (worth $1,500) plus the standard deduction.

Suppose, for example, you are supporting your uncle who is over 65. Assume you give him $2,000 a year. If you're in the 50% bracket, you have to earn $4,000 before taxes to give him that $2,000. You get a $750 dependency deduction which reduces your taxes by $375. That gives you a net cost of $3,625. Suppose you transferred property to him that threw off $2,000 a year. With your uncle's own exemptions, etc., he'd owe no tax; so he'd have the same $2,000. And your cost in income would be $1,625 less than if you continued to give him cash. And you could arrange to get the property back at your uncle's death by using a short-term trust.

[¶1002.2] **How to Make an Effective Assignment**

The important thing to remember about these types of transfers is that they must be genuine. You should be able to prove the competency of yourself and your donee and your intent to part with the legal title and control of the property. You should also show that you've made an absolute transfer of the property by either delivering the property itself or the means to control the property.

If you keep control over the property, you may find yourself taxed on the income from the property even though you never really get it. Note: even if a state court has ruled that your donee is the legal owner of the property, where you still control the property IRS may pin the tax on you. This was brought out in a case where the donors transferred stock of a controlled corporation. Then, they borrowed the dividends, giving their notes in exchange. They also signed documents for the corporation on behalf of the donees. All this added up to control, and they were taxed on the dividends (*Anderson*, 164 F.2d 870).

[¶1002.3] Types of Income-Producing Property You Can Assign

Among the types of property you can give are real estate, stocks, bonds, rental equipment, oil wells, patents, copyrights, a business interest, etc. Here are some specific illustrations:

(1) If you are receiving income on a contract that doesn't involve your personal services (for instance, an interest in a royalty contract), this may be assigned (*Reece*, 24 TC 187, *acq.*).

(2) An interest in a nonpersonal service partnership may be assigned.

(3) If the assignor withdraws completely from any proprietary activities, an entire interest in a business may be effectively assigned even if he continues to give advice and do office work (*Henson*, 174 F.2d 846).

(4) You may have an interest in a process which is still in the development stage, such as a patent, copyright, etc. If you're an author or inventor, you can give your child or other relative an undivided interest in the copyright or patent (*Dreymann*, 11 TC 153). An "undivided interest" means an unseparated part of the whole patent, that is, a piece of all the rights, not a part or whole interest in one or some of the basic rights.

(5) You may be about to retire and sell your interest in a family corporation. By using a private annuity arrangement in which you transfer your stock in exchange for an equally valued private annuity from your company, you can avoid estate and gift taxes. Also, since the annuity is partly tax exempt, you add to your after-tax income by converting salary to annuity. Incidentally, this is also a good way to shift full ownership of the business to your children.

(6) Another possible way of shifting income is to give leaseable business property to a low bracket family member. Then, you can enter into a lease and get business deductions for the rent. *Caution:* the terms must be consistent with those normally found in the field. Otherwise, IRS may question the arrangement. (They'll probably question it in any event.) Bear in mind that this type of deal can be made with any type of rental property—not necessarily realty.

(7) You can open a trust account for your minor child in a savings and loan association and the interest paid on such an account will be taxable to the children if under state law the account legally belongs to the child and the parents are legally prohibited from using any part of the funds to satisfy their support obligations to the child (*Rev. Rul.* 58-65, 1958-1 CB 13). Or, you can buy securities in the name of your donee (custodian laws which simplify giving securities to minors let you buy stocks or bonds in the names of your minor children) (*Rev. Rul.* 59-357, 1959-2 CB 212 and *Rev. Rul.* 73-287, IRB 1973-27, 13).

[¶1002.4]   **Timing Your Transfer**

It is especially timely to give property that is about to realize a large amount of income, for instance, stock which is about to receive a large dividend or an oil well that is about to come in.

If you have a closely held corporation, there is an additional timing precaution which you should observe to transfer dividends effectively: make sure that you transfer the stock *before* the date the dividend is declared. Dividends on stock transferred after the declaration date but before the record date have been taxed to the donor of a close corporation (*Anton*, 34 TC 842). The Court distinguished this situation from the usual rule that the owner on the record date is taxed with the dividend.

Suppose you own stock of a company which is contemplating liquidation. By giving the stock before the liquidation is started, you can reduce the capital gains tax resulting from the liquidation. Although capital gains can't be taxed at more than 25% (35% after the first $50,000), they can be taxed at less. If your donee's tax bracket is lower than 50%, his capital gains tax is less than 25%. But, you should also check to what extent your gift tax liability will cut your tax savings.

[¶1003]   **LEASEBACKS WITHIN THE FAMILY**

One way of dividing income within the family is to give business property to family members (directly or in trust) and lease it back. The rent you pay is deductible, and the family member or trust which owns the property picks up the rental income.

As an example of the tax saving in the gift or sale and leaseback, take Dr. Skemp's operation. He gave a $40,000 clinic building to a bank as trustee for his children. He was deducting $650 a year for depreciation on the building. After the gift, the trust leased the building to him for $6,000 a year. The doctor's net income ran about $40,000 after deducting the $6,000 rental payment. If he had kept the building, he'd have paid an additional $2,600 in income tax. By shifting the earning power of the building to a trust for his children, the tax would be cut to under $1,000. Thus, there's an annual tax saving of over $1,600 plus the estate tax saving (*Skemp*, 168 F.2d 598).

The use of an independent trustee can be important in gift-leasebacks. This helps to show that the donor or seller has parted with all control over the property. What's more important, however, is that the rental arrangement stands up as reasonable.

Danger: There is still considerable danger in the family leaseback situation.

In *Hall*, 208 F. Supp. 584, a New York District Court disallowed a rent deduction in a case somewhat similar to *Skemp*. Here, too, the trustee was a bank. But Hall had some control over the trust and could get the building back after ten years (a so-called short-term trust). The Court disallowed the deduction because: (1) only the right to receive income was transferred, in effect (because of Hall's control) and (2) Hall really kept an equity in the building because it would revert to him when the trust ended and IRC §162(a)(3) denies a deduction to a tenant who also has an equity in the building.

The most sweeping denial of the rent deduction was in the *Van Zandt* case (40 TC 824, aff'd 341 F.2d 440). Here, too, a medical building was transferred to a short-term trust by a doctor. And, to boot, he named himself trustee.

First off, the case was distinguished from the *Skemp* case because Skemp was not his own trustee. Then the Court went ahead, *without even taking into account the reversionary nature of the trust*, which alone could have knocked out the rental deduction on the "equity" argument, and proceeded to make a broadside attack on family trust-leaseback arrangements in general.

The Tax Court said that the effect of this transaction, while valid, was to cause a shift of family income and thus subvert the rent deduction allowed by IRC §162(a)(3). Where this type of leaseback arrangement does not serve a utilitarian business purpose, the Court went on to say, but is really a camouflaged assignment of income, such expenses are not "ordinary and necessary," as required by IRC §162(a). While they may be ordinary, they were not necessary since Dr. Van Zandt owned and used the same building and the same equipment both before and after entering into the trust-leaseback.

In affirming the Tax Court, the Fifth Circuit looked for the business purpose for the transaction and emphasized that the result in each case ultimately depends on the particular factual situation. "Here, factors such as the short term of the trust, reversion to the settlors, predetermination of the right to possession of the property, and the like, while perfectly permissible so far as taxability of the trust and the settlors goes, bear heavily on the element of business purpose."

It should be obvious by now that Internal Revenue will fight you on any attempt to take a deduction for rent paid in a family trust-leaseback arrangement. So you'll have to be prepared to go to court.

Shortly after *Van Zandt's* affirmance, the Tax Court allowed the deduction in a similar situation which also involved a doctor, a medical building and a short-term trust (*Oakes*, 44 TC 524).

The big difference between *Van Zandt* and *Oakes* can be summarized in two phrases: "independent trustee" and "no reversionary interest." Van Zandt was his own trustee. Oakes used a bank. Van Zandt had a reversionary interest in the trust property; he was to get it back when the trust period ended. Oakes transferred his reversionary interest to his wife; when the trust term ended, she, not he, would get the building back.

[¶1003.1] **How to Proceed on Family Trust-Leasebacks**

It is apparent that very close scrutiny will be given to sales and gifts of property to family members in which the original owner recovers the use of the property and pays rent or royalties to the transferee. Nevertheless, if the transfer is a complete gift which really shifts underlying ownership of the property, the income derived from the property should be taxed to the donee and money paid for the use of the property should be deductible by the transferor. This method should be just as effective in shifting income to the lower brackets of the donee as any other real gift of income-producing property. To maximize the chances of securing this result, prudent counsel will advise the following:

(1) Transfer the property to an independent trustee charged with protecting the interests of the donee beneficiaries.

(2) Make the gift to the trustee outright, with no string attached, leaving the donor to negotiate an arm's length lease with the trustee.

(3) Keep the rental payments in line with the value of the property.

(4) Make the term of the lease shorter than the term of the trust.

(5) Avoid using reversionary or short-term trusts. But see *Duffy*, Dist. Ct., So. Dist. Ohio, 4/12/72. (You might be okay here where the property is rented, not to you, but to your corporation—e.g., a professional corporation. The corporation would be seeking the rental deduction, and it has no reversionary interest in the property.)

(6) Where possible, arrange the transaction so that you are leasing back considerably less than you are transferring to the trustee. The Fifth Circuit in *Van Zandt* placed heavy emphasis on the fact that the entire trust property was being leased back.

[¶1004]   **FAMILY PARTNERSHIPS**

A family partnership arrangement can fill an important role in the estate plan of an individual business owner. By giving or selling interests in his business to members of his family (particularly children), he can save both income and estate taxes, thereby increasing the family's spendable income and its capital. The problem is to establish the partnership as genuine.

The Code (§704(e)) specifically permits setting up a valid family partnership by gift or purchase even though the partners render no services. In many cases, the family partnership has become clearly preferable to the closely held corporation from a tax standpoint. In years gone by, the refusal by the Treasury to recognize many of these partnerships for tax purposes made for great caution in taking advantage of the tax-savings possibilities offered by the family partnership. Now, by meeting a clear-cut set of standards, we can use this method of dividing business income with children and other members of the family, bringing much of this income into lower income tax brackets to increase the family's spendable income and build up its capital at the same time.

[¶1004.1]   **Family Partnership Tax Savings and How They Accumulate**

You may be startled at the accumulation of annual income tax savings plus the estate tax saving which can result from creating a family partnership. The following tables will give you an idea of the annual income tax saving and the cumulative build-up over 20 years, together with the additional tax saving at death. The tax savings are estimated at levels of business income ranging from $25,000 to $300,000 a year. We assume that a father makes a gift of a one-third partnership interest to each of his two children and that the father will report 50% of the partnership income (25% for services and 25% for capital—split up on a joint return with his wife) and the children will report 25% each. The tax savings and the children's income accumulate at 5% compound interest. The estate tax savings are estimated at a 30% rate.

Net Business Income	Tax as Propri- etorship	Family Partner- ship Tax	Tax Savings	
			Each Year	Over 20 Years
$ 25,000	$ 6,020	$ 4,770	$ 1,250	$ 27,389
50,000	17,060	12,040	5,020	109,993
75,000	30,470	22,030	8,440	184,929
100,000	45,180	34,120	11,060	242,336
150,000	76,980	60,940	16,040	351,452
200,000	110,980	90,360	20,620	451,805
250,000	145,980	121,560	24,420	535,067
300,000	180,980	153,960	27,020	592,035

Assuming that other income is offset by deductions, etc., this is also the figure from which taxable incomes of parents and children are derived.

[¶1004.2] How to Establish a Family Partnership

We can establish a family partnership in these ways—

(1) Accept into partnership any child or other relative who can be expected to perform important work in the business on a regular basis. (This is the only sure way of creating a valid family partnership in a professional or personal service firm.)

(2) Take into partnership any child or relative who can contribute capital.

(3) Make a gift of a partnership interest to children or other relatives.

(4) Sell a partnership interest to children or other relatives (the sale can be substantially on credit) to be paid for out of subsequent partnership income (*Gould*, 182, F.2d 573).

[¶1004.3] Personal Service Partnership

The law doesn't recognize partnership interests created by gifts where capital is not a material factor in producing income. Thus, an interest in a personal service partnership, such as an accounting firm, cannot be created by a mere gift. The donee would have to participate actively in the firm for his interest to be recognized.

[¶1004.4]   **Partnership Established by Gift**

The Treasury will recognize gifts of family partnership interests but expects that certain conditions will be fulfilled:

(1) The capital interest must have been transferred so that, by the gift, the original owner gives up all incidents of ownership and the donee or purchaser acquires full and complete ownership.

(2) Capital must be a material income-producing factor. That is the case where the business requires substantial inventories or plant or equipment. It is usually not the case where income consists principally of fees, commissions, etc., for services of partnership members or employees.

(3) To have a capital interest in a partnership, one must own a proprietary interest in assets used by the partnership in the business. These assets must be distributable on withdrawal or liquidation. The mere right to participate in the earnings is not a capital interest.

(4) A parent who gives a partnership interest to a child may be held not to have made a sufficiently complete transfer if he retains:

(a) Control of distribution of income.

(b) Restrictions on the right of the donee to withdraw or sell his partnership interest without financial detriment.

(c) Control of assets essential to the business, such as holding assets leased to the partnership.

(d) Unusual management powers. (See *Cochran*, 201 F.2d 365.)

On all these points, remember that, although a transfer was made to save taxes, the resulting savings are not invalidated.

[¶1004.5]   **Steps to Establish the Reality of the Partnership**

Such steps as these will help to establish the reality of the partnership:

(1) Participation in management by the donee or a fiduciary acting for him.

(2) Actual distribution to the donee of all or the major portion of his share of the business income for his sole benefit and use.

(3) Holding the donee out publicly as a partner.

[¶1004.6]   **Sharing Partnership Income**

Here are the rules on sharing family partnership income:

(1) A reasonable allowance must be made for compensation for services rendered to the partnership by the donor-partner (*Gorrill*, TC Memo 1963-168).

(2) Partnership income attributable to donated capital may not be proportionately greater than that attributable to the donor's capital interest.

(3) Partnership income paid to a son in military service on a scale similar to that on which he had previously participated will be recognized.

These rules on income-sharing apply only where there is a gift of a partnership interest; any sale to a spouse, ancestor, or lineal descendent is tagged by law as a gift. A sale between brothers wouldn't be a gift, and the rules wouldn't apply.

[¶1004.7] **Partnership Created by Sale**

You can avoid gift tax and get back some of the income shifted to others in the family by selling an interest in your business on terms. For example, when we take two children into a business earning $100,000 a year, we save $11,060 in taxes each year. Each year, the two children get $32,940 after tax. Over 20 years, the children can build up $1,020,119 at 5% interest compounded. Perhaps half of this could be paid back to the parents as the purchase price.

When we sell an interest, on credit or otherwise, we must meet one of these conditions:

(1) The terms are those of an arm's-length transaction, particularly with respect to credit terms, security, interest rates, etc., or

(2) The sale is genuinely intended to promote the interests of the business by securing the participation of the buyer.

Where the sale is to a member of the immediate family, the same rules and standards applicable to a gift of a partnership interest apply. This means the same rules concerning the way profits are to be paid out apply. The fair market value of the partnership interest obtained (not what was paid) is treated as the donation to the capital of the partnership. This means you must make sure:

(a) The partner who makes the sale is credited with fair compensation for his services in addition to his share of the partnership income coming to him as a partner.

(b) The sharing of the net profits by the new partner—*after* the deduction for compensation to the seller—is no greater than the ratio of the sold share to the entire partnership capital. If a father sells to a nonworking son 25% of the capital, he can give the son only a 25% share of the profits after the compensation allowance to the father.

[¶1004.8] **Sale to a Relative Not a Member of the Immediate Family**

As in the case of a gift to a relative not a member of the immediate family, the reason for the sale is not important. That it is to cut taxes doesn't matter as long as the transfer of the interest is real. That the donor keeps the big part of managing the partnership or is a trustee for the new partner won't invalidate the new arrangement. But the power must be exercised for the benefit of the beneficiary. Having an independent trustee avoids the need to walk this delicate line.

If a family member buys an interest in the partnership from a partner other than the family member, the partnership is usually recognized.

If a family member invests in the partnership with borrowed capital—the partnership will be recognized *unless the capital invested is borrowed from the partnership itself;* that is, the new family member invests by giving the partnership notes. It may *not* be recognized where the new family member borrowed from a bank and:

(1) Another family member's property is pledged as collateral.

(2) The partnership pays off the loan.

But a partnership interest can be paid for in notes where the purchaser has sufficient assets.

If a family member invests in the partnership capital from his own funds —he is recognized as a partner *even if he doesn't perform any services.* The contribution may be small in comparison with the amount the business later earns. But in these cases, you may have to show that capital is an important income-producing factor to the partnership.

[¶1004.9]   Contribution of Regular and Valuable Services

Where capital is not an important income-producing factor but the family member contributes regular and valuable services, the partnership will probably be recognized. A small amount of work which has no income-producing effect is not enough. Office work can be important enough (see *Herndon,* TC Memo 1948).

[¶1004.10]   Trust as a Partner

Can a trustee be a partner? Yes. If permitted under state law, a trustee will be recognized as a partner. He must be independent of the grantor and subject to the ordinary responsibilities of a fiduciary. He should participate in management. If the donor is trustee or if the trustee is one "amenable to his will," the Treasury will take a hard look to make sure that the trustee actually discharges the obligation of a fiduciary and that he doesn't get fiduciary interests mixed up with his own interests. Where there is no independent trustee, special consideration will be given to whether the trust's share of the partnership income was distributed to the trust annually and paid to the beneficiary or reinvested solely for the interest of the beneficiary.

To safeguard the trustee-partner setup from Treasury attack, the above conditions should be met. In addition, special attention will be given to whether the trustee is functioning in his fiduciary capacity. The trust instrument cannot free the trustee from the normal responsibilities and liabilities of a fiduciary. The provisions of the partnership agreement must show, along with the conduct of the parties, that the trustee acts in his full fiduciary capacity as the real owner of the gift capital.

Ordinarily, if a partnership in good faith was intended, where the trustee is independent of the grantor-partner and subject to the ordinary responsibilities of a fiduciary, the trust will be accepted as the real owner of the partnership interest. See *Adolph K. Krause,* CA-6, 5/30/74, for an example of how not to set up the arrangement.

Short-Term Trusts: IRS insists that in the case of a gift of an interest in a family partnership to a child, the interest must be a capital interest. When the gift is made by means of a trust, the better strategy appears to be to use an irrevocable trust in which the parent retains no reversionary interests. This will eliminate one area of conflict with IRS which insists that a short-term reversionary trust is only an income interest, since the trust capital returns to the grantor at the end of the trust term. Thus, according to IRS, such a family partnership is ineffective to shift income from parent.

[¶1004.11]   Minor Child as Partner

The minor child must be the real owner of the interest in the partnership. The Treasury recognizes that in some instances a minor child may have sufficient maturity and experience to be treated by disinterested persons as competent to enter into business dealings and to conduct his or her affairs on an equal plane with adult persons.

Unless a minor child is shown to be competent to manage his own property, he will not be recognized as a partner (*Pflugardt,* 310 F.2d 412). To overcome the effect of lack of competence, have control exercised by a fiduciary for the sole benefit of the child.

[¶1005]   THE FAMILY INVESTMENT COMPANY

This vehicle has a twofold use—(1) to build the estate by accumulating income at more favorable rates than a high bracket individual can and (2) to shift the value represented by accumulated income and asset appreciation to younger members of the family by giving them common stock while the older generation takes preferred stock for assets put into the corporation.

The family investment corporation can protect income and build common stock values by participating in sale-leaseback, private annuity and partnership arrangements with members of the family. The most dramatic thing it can do is protect dividend income from the high personal tax rates applicable to the highest individual brackets. Where an individual receives dividend income, the first $100 (up to $200 on a joint return) is nontaxable under the dividend exclusion. Everything over that amount is taxable at rates as high as 70%. Although a corporation gets no dividend exclusion, it does get a deduction for 85% of the dividends it receives. As a result, only 15% of its dividend income is taxable, and that at a maximum rate of 48%. The maximum effective rate is therefore 7.2% (15% × 48%). And where the corporation's taxable income does not exceed the $25,000 surtax exemption, the effective rate can be as low as 3.3% (15% × 22%). However, for 1977 only, the normal tax is 20%

on the first $25,000 of corporate taxable income and then 22% on the second $25,000, and 48% on corporate taxable income over $50,000.

To accomplish these objectives, we have to avoid personal holding company status for the corporation. If we have a personal holding company, we end up paying a 70% penalty tax or we have to distribute all of the corporation's profits to the stockholders (in which case we defeat the whole purpose of using the corporation in the first place since the individuals would then have to pay ordinary tax rates on the distribution). The effectiveness of the family investment company has been severely impaired by the Revenue Act of 1964 which tightened up on the available means for avoiding personal holding company problems.

[¶1005.1] Personal Holding Companies: What to Do

Where a corporation has 60% of its gross income from personal holding company sources and more than half of its stock is owned by not more than five individuals, we have a personal holding company. Because there are constructive ownership rules under which family members are deemed to own the stock of other family members, in a family situation it is almost impossible to avoid the five-individual test. And since the income the family investment company will be receiving will be principally of the personal holding company type, the 60% test would likely be met, too.

To avoid personal holding company status, the usual course used to be to mix stock investments with rent-producing real estate investments in the same corporation. Dividends, interest, rents, royalties and other similar types of income are personal holding company income. However, if rents constituted 50% of gross income, they ceased to be personal holding company income. Thus, if you could meet this test, it was not possible to be a personal holding company.

The test is now on a net basis. For rental income not to be personal holding company income, you have to meet these two tests: (1) adjusted income from rents (rental income reduced by depreciation, amortization, property taxes, interest and rent to the extent allocable to rents received) must be at least 50% of adjusted ordinary gross income (gross income excluding capital gains and reduced by the same items as above); (2) other personal holding company income must not exceed 10% of ordinary gross income (gross income excluding capital gains).

You can see what this does to the family investment company. It will be impossible to shelter any dividend income where the deductions are large enough to wipe out enough of the rent income to flunk the 50% test. And even where this is accomplished, as in the case of a fully depreciated building, the amount that can be sheltered in any event is limited to 10% of noncapital gain income.

Suppose your other personal holding company income comes to 12% of the ordinary gross income. That makes all your rent personal holding company income.

In this case, you can distribute the excess of other personal holding company income so that what remains does not exceed the 10% limit and thus avoid personal holding company status. *Net effect:* You still continue to shelter only 10% of personal holding company income under the rent umbrella.

The distribution of this excess of other personal holding company income (in our example above, 2% of ordinary gross income) can be made in any one or combination of the following ways:

(1) A dividend paid during the taxable year that qualifies as a dividend distribution under IRC §562. That means it can't be a preferential dividend.

(2) A dividend paid the following year but no later than the fifteenth day of the third month of the following tax year. In that case, the amount of the dividend can't be more than: (a) the company's undistributed personal holding company income and (b) 10% of the dividends paid during the taxable year of payment. See Code §563.

(3) A consent dividend—where distributions are not made but the stockholders pick up the income as if a distribution had been made. Here, too, you cannot have the effect of preferential distributions.

[¶1006]   **INSTALLMENT SALES**

The installment sale rules of Code §453 can be used to set up a deal between family members whereby a large profit can be realized but with the capital gain tax spread over a long period of time.

In the case of someone who is not a dealer, the installment method of reporting income is allowed for sale of real property or a casual sale of personal property for a price exceeding $1,000. The only special requirements are:

(a) That the seller must not receive payments exceeding 30% of the selling price in the first year;

(b) The payments must extend over at least two tax years;

(c) The buyer must be directly indebted to the seller for at least part of the selling price; and

(d) The seller must elect the installment basis on his tax return.

Take a simple example: If a father has stock now worth $100,000 which originally cost him $10,000, he can sell the stock to his son for the $100,000, payable in ten annual installments of $10,000. Then, each year, he will have a $1,000 return of capital and a $9,000 capital gain. The son, however, has a $100,000 basis, so that he can immediately sell the shares on the market at no gain or loss and invest the proceeds. The advantage to the family group is that the capital gains tax on the $90,000 profit is spread out over a ten-year period instead of having to be paid in full at once. The use of this tax money for such an extended period of time can be a real advantage.

The above example is a very simple one, used just to illustrate the rules. To avoid any possible gift implication, the deal should be made on a businesslike basis with a contract and notes to cover the unpaid balances and with interest.

The interest element is also important because, if any deferred payment sale contract does not specify interest or specifies an unrealistically low rate of interest, Code §483 will be applied to impose an amount of "imputed interest" on the deal. Imputed interest will be imposed whenever less than 6% per annum simple interest is provided for in the contract.

To illustrate a deal between a father and son that has all of the earmarks of a true arm's-length business transaction, assume the father has stock which cost him $25,000 and which is now worth $85,000. He sells the stock to his son for $85,000 under a contract which obligates the son to pay the $85,000 over twenty-five years, including interest at a rate of 6% a year. This works out to $547.40 per month, including level interest payments of $261.09 each month. This means that each month the father will be treated as having received the following:

Interest Income	$261.09
Return of Capital	84.21
Long-Term Capital Gain	202.10
Monthly Payment	$547.40

The son will be entitled to an interest deduction for the $261.09 a month. He can sell the stock and invest the full $85,000, undiminished by any capital gains tax, to produce a greater yield than 6% and possibly even obtain some growth of principal as well.

If the father should die before the entire obligation has been paid off, the value of the debt, usually the full unpaid principal balance, will be subject to estate tax. Each installment payment after death will be subject to income tax in the hands of the estate or beneficiary just as before. The interest payments still constitute interest income. The part of each principal payment that is long-term capital gain constitutes income in respect of a decedent, under Code §691, and the payee is entitled to a deduction for the amount of estate tax attributable to that sum. See ¶1509.6.

SECTION XI. CHARITABLE TRANSFERS

By making gifts to charity during life, we get the benefit of an income tax deduction as well as getting the property out of the taxable estate. The gift of property to the extent of the applicable tax rate builds liquidity as the property is converted into cash which remains in the bank instead of being paid to the tax collector.

When property is left to charity under a will, the taxable estate is reduced by the amount of the bequest. As long as the property goes to a qualified charity, the estate is entitled to a deduction for estate tax purposes.

[¶1101] **LIFETIME CHARITABLE GIFTS**

Here are some of the estate planning objectives which can be achieved by lifetime charitable gifts:

(1) Build cash or finance life insurance by deducting the value of property given to charity.

(2) Reserve life income for a man and his wife while converting the remainder interest of the property into tax-saving cash.

(3) Get a lump of tax-saving cash immediately by giving some future investment income to charity.

(4) Add to gross estate and increase marital deduction by taking out insurance for charity. It may be possible to reserve incidents of ownership and make the policy payable to charity, increase the amount of property which can be given tax free to a wife and still deduct the premium paid to carry the insurance for charity.

Generally, charitable gifts are deductible each year up to 50% of an individual taxpayer's adjusted gross income (IRC §170).

Not included in the category of charitable gifts which are eligible for the 50% ceiling are gifts to private charitable foundations. Here, the 20% limit applies, except that the 50% ceiling is permitted for gifts to *private operating foundations* and to private foundations that pay out of principal an amount equal to all of their annual contributions to public charities within two and a half months after the end of the year in which the contributions were received.

[¶1101.1] **Contributions of Property**

There are special rules for gifts of *appreciated capital assets* on which a long-term gain would have been realized in the case of a sale. Here, the annual

140

ceiling is 30% of adjusted gross income. However, a taxpayer may deduct such a contribution under the 50% ceiling if he makes a special election.

Under this election, the charitable deduction otherwise available must be reduced by 50% of the amount of the appreciation in value that would have produced a long-term capital gain if a sale had occurred. In other words, the donor on gifts of capital gain assets not otherwise subject to special rules discussed below may either (1) deduct the full value but be subject to the 30% ceiling or (2) deduct the full value minus one-half of the increase over his basis and be subject to the 50% ceiling.

Where *tangible personal property*, which is capital gain-type property, is concerned, if it is not directly used by the charity in its charitable endeavors, the deduction is computed by subtracting 50% of what would have been long-term capital gain if the property had been sold for the fair market value at the date of the gift.

In the case of a gift of capital gain-type property to a private nonoperating foundation, the value is reduced by 50% of the appreciation.

A specific set of rules also applies to a donation of "ordinary income property." Examples of such property are works of art, books, letters, and memoranda given by the person who prepared them; stock held less than nine months in 1977 and twelve months in 1978 and thereafter; and stock (such as §306 stock) acquired in a nontaxable transaction which results in ordinary income if sold. While the deduction ceiling for gifts of such property to qualified charities is 50% (the special 30% ceiling applies only to gifts of capital gain-type property), the deduction for such a gift is limited to the donor's basis in the property. In the case of property purchased or acquired which has gone down in value since it was originally purchased, the deduction is equal to its fair market value at the date of the gift.

[¶1101.2] Five-Year Carryover

Deductions which cannot be taken in one year because of the ceiling limitation can be carried forward five years, except that there is no carryover allowance for deductions which cannot be taken because of the 20% ceiling.

[¶1101.3] Bargain Sales

An individual can realize a greater profit in some situations if he enters into a bargain sale arrangement with a charitable institution rather than disposing of the appreciated security on the open market and donating the "net" proceeds to a charity. Here the security is sold to the charity at the owner's tax basis (his cost).

The owner gets a charitable deduction for the difference between his selling price and the market value of the property transferred. For example, if you sell a block of stock worth $5,000 to a charity for $1,000 (your tax cost), you get a charitable contribution deduction of $4,000 ($5,000 value less $1,000 received).

However, the cost basis must be allocated between the part sold and the part donated. This means that you will incur some taxable gain on the bargain sale. For example, in your bargain sale to charity for your $1,000 basis of stock worth $5,000, you would allocate 20% ($1,000/$5,000) to the part sold and 80% to the part given away. So, you'd have a taxable gain of $800 ($1,000 purchase price minus $200 cost).

[¶1101.4]   Gift with Life Income Reserved

Sometimes a person may want to help a charity with income-producing property or securities but may feel it necessary to retain the income for his life or for the life of some other person. The charity will accept such a gift and undertake to pay each year to the donor, or to a person designated by the donor, or to one person and upon the death of that person, to a designated survivor, an annual income determined by applying to the agreed value of the donated property the average net rate of return earned by the charity on its own investment portfolio. Similar results can also be obtained by transferring this property to an irrevocable trust of which the charity is the remainderman, with the trust income being reserved to the donor or someone designated by him.

Under this type of arrangement, the charity does not get any benefit from the property until its obligation to make life income payments terminates. From the charity's viewpoint, it would be just as well if the property were left to it by bequest upon the death of the owner, if income is to be reserved for his life. However, there would be a substantial advantage to the owner in giving the charity the remainder interest during his life, rather than by will or upon his death. He is permitted to deduct on his income tax return the value of the remainder interest which the charity will be receiving. See the table on page T-22a for the method of computing the amount of the deduction.

[¶1101.5]   Charitable Remainders; Annuity Trusts, Unitrusts and Pooled-Income Funds

Under the pre-1970 rules, a trust could be set up with the income payable to an individual for life or for a term of years, with the remainder interest to or for charity, and the value of the remainder interest would be deductible. Where the trustee invested in high-income and high-risk assets, the charitable deduction might exceed the amount eventually available for charity.

To prevent this possibility, the Tax Reform Act of 1969 eliminated the deduction for the value of a charitable remainder, unless the trust qualifies as a charitable remainder *annuity trust* or a charitable remainder *unitrust.*

An annuity trust is one from which a certain or a specified amount (which must be not less than 5% of the net fair market value of the property placed in the trust) must be paid to the income beneficiary, not less frequently than annually.

A unitrust is a trust from which a fixed percentage (which is not less than 5%) of the net fair market value of its assets as determined each year must be paid at least annually. As an alternative, provision can be made for distribution of 5% of the said value or the amount of the trust income (excluding capital gains), whichever is lower. If the trust income is less than the stated amount, it can be made up in a later year when more than enough income is received. *Invasions for the life beneficiaries of the charitable remainder (which were permitted within ascertainable standards under the pre-1970 rules) are not permitted.*

To qualify, all such trusts must have only charitable remainder interests, which must pass to charity upon termination of the income interest. There may be more than one noncharitable income beneficiary, and the income interest may be a life estate or a term of not more than 20 years. Also, the assets transferred must have an ascertainable market value unless an independent trustee is solely responsible for making the annual valuations. Examples of property with no ascertainable market value include real estate and stock in a closely held corporation.

A similar charitable deduction is allowed for transfers to a *pooled-income fund* set up by a public charity, wherein the donor retains the life income interest. However, the fund cannot invest in tax-exempt bonds, the trust must pay out the income to the life beneficiaries annually, and no donor or income beneficiary can be a trustee. The charitable deduction allowed is determined by valuing the income interest on the basis of the highest annual rate of return during the three years before the taxable year of the transfer. If the fund has not existed for three years, then the rate of return is assumed to be 6% (unless IRS fixes a different rate). Subtracting the value of this income interest from the value of the donated property results in the value of the charitable deduction.

A charitable deduction will be allowed for a charitable remainder after a life estate not in trust but only if the property is a personal residence or a farm. An example of this is where a man makes a donation of his residence to charity but retains the right to live there for life. The value of the deductible remainder interest is computed by using straight-line depreciation discounted at a rate of 6% a year (unless IRS fixes a different rate).

In determining which type of charitable remainder trust to create, consider the differences in the statute and regulations. Consider also that the life beneficiary receives a fixed annuity in the case of an annuity trust; whereas in the case of a unitrust, his payments may increase or decrease depending on investment results, inflation, depression, tax law changes, and other future events. You should also compare the value of the charitable remainders. In the case of a 6% payout rate to the life beneficiary, the values are about the same. However, if the payout rate is set at less than 6%, an annuity trust will produce the larger charitable remainder; if it is more than 6%, a unitrust will yield the larger remainder value.

The Tax Reform Act of 1976 extended until December 31, 1977 the time to amend charitable remainder trust governing instruments to comply with the Tax Reform Act of 1969 for purposes of the estate tax deductions. The previous deadline for amending these governing instruments, or to start judicial proceedings to amend them, expired on December 31, 1975.

[¶1101.6]   **Additional Limitations on Trusts**

In order for a charitable deduction to be allowed for a gift to a nonexempt trust (an annuity trust or a unitrust), the trust instrument must contain language expressly prohibiting the trust from the following activities:

(a) Self-dealing.
(b) Retaining excess business holdings.
(c) Making speculative investments.
(d) Making lobbying and other taxable expenditures.

The effect of these rules is to require trust amendments in the case of most old trusts or the creation of new trusts that contain the required language in order to be used as vehicles for obtaining charitable deductions for new gifts.

[¶1102]   **CHARITABLE BEQUESTS**

When property is left to a charity by will, as long as the charity is a qualified one, the estate is entitled to a deduction for estate tax purposes.

It is not necessary that the donor leave the property outright to the charity on his death. He may want to provide for income (via annuity trust or unitrust arrangements) to his children or other relatives from the property first. Then, upon their death or attaining a certain age, the property can be transferred to the charity. This is usually done by leaving the property in trust and providing for it to go to the charity upon the termination of the trust (i.e., the charity gets a remainder interest). When a remainder is left to a charity, the deduction allowed for estate tax purposes is less than it would be on an outright gift.

The value of the remainder interest which enjoys exemption is determined by multiplying the value of the property by the fraction opposite the age of life beneficiary, as indicated by the table entitled "Value of Annuity, Life Interest and Remainder Interest," on page T-22a. Thus, if the life beneficiary is:

> 40 years old and female, 15.719% of the property is exempt
> 50 years old and female, 24.524% of the property is exempt
> 60 years old and female, 36.774% of the property is exempt
> 70 years old and female, 42.460% of the property is exempt

Take a $500,000 estate to be left to a 60-year-old sister. It consists of securities yielding 5%. If it were left outright, she would have $383,000 earning 5% after payment of $117,000 in combined New York State and federal death taxes. That would give her an annual income of $19,150. If she took that $383,000 and purchased an annuity, she'd get $22,500 a year, all but $4,200 of it tax exempt. The purchase of an annuity would, of course, consume the entire estate.

If, on the other hand, the $500,000 were bequeathed to her for life and then to a charity, the estate tax would apply to only about $316,000. The estate tax would recede to $62,000. She would enjoy annual income of $21,900 and the $500,000 would be preserved for use by a foundation or charity.

[¶1102.1]   **Power to Invade the Charitable Remainder**

Charitable remainder annuity trusts and unitrusts cannot contain provisions allowing payouts to the income beneficiary from the charity's remainder no matter what the standards.

[¶1102.2]   **How a Charitable Contribution Can Enlarge the Marital Deduction**

In the usual situation where property is transferred out of the estate during the owner's lifetime, there is a saving in future estate taxes and a smaller share of the estate left for the surviving spouse and family. However, where the transfer is to a charity, and the marital deduction is fully utilized, an inter vivos charitable gift may result in larger estate taxes and a smaller share for the wife than where the charitable gift passes under the owner's will. Moreover, these circumstances (charitable contribution-marital deduction) may give rise to the phenomenon of an increase in the gross estate which is accompanied by a decrease in the amount of estate taxes and a larger share for the beneficiaries.

Here is a simple example which will illustrate some of the foregoing. Assume that in 1981 Mr. Smith has an adjusted gross estate of $1,000,000 and desires to leave one-half to his wife and one-half to charity. If he makes an inter vivos gift of one-half of that amount to charity, his estate is reduced to $500,000. After taking the marital deduction ($250,000), we are left with a net taxable estate of $250,000, the estate tax on which is $23,800. Mr. Smith's spouse would receive $436,200.

On the other hand, if the $1,000,000 adjusted gross estate is preserved until Mr. Smith's death, his estate tax would be computed as follows:

Adjusted Gross Estate	$1,000,000
Marital Deduction	500,000
Balance	500,000
Bequests to Charity	500,000
Taxable Estate	-0-
Left for Spouse	500,000

Thus, if Mr. Smith follows the latter course of action, the charity receives the same $500,000 it would have received by inter vivos gift, his estate escapes the $23,800 in estate taxes, and his spouse receives an additional $23,800. This superior result with a testamentary bequest is, of course, made at the expense of some income tax savings, since there will be no charitable deduction against income if the charitable gift is postponed until death. (Note: You can give the charity $175,625 less—$324,325 instead of $500,000—and get the same zero tax result. The $47,000 unified credit and its equivalent exemption of $175,625 went unused in our example. Using it will mean that there is $675,625 left for Mrs. Smith.)

The reason for this result is apparent from the foregoing example. While the charitable bequest is deducted from the estate in determining the estate tax liability, it constitutes a part of the gross estate for purposes of the marital deduction. The marital deduction is thus increased by one-half of the nontaxable charitable bequest. These circumstances place a premium on making a testamentary rather than an inter vivos disposition of the property earmarked for charity. If at the owner's death the estate is increased by money intended for charity, additional benefits will likewise flow to the estate and beneficiaries, as explained below.

[¶1102.3] Preserving the Income Tax Deduction

If the charitable gift that might be made during lifetime is held off to be made as a bequest, as indicated above, current income tax deductions are lost. However, with the use of a life insurance policy, it may be possible to get both the income tax deductions and still get the benefits of a boosted marital deduction by including the amount going to charity in the gross estate.

One suggested method is to name the charity an irrevocable beneficiary of a life insurance policy. If the charity is given vested right to the death proceeds and joint rights with the insured in all the other rights in the policy, the premiums paid by the insured should be deductible as charitable contributions for income tax purposes. Since the rights in the policy other than to the proceeds are *joint*, it is argued that the insured cannot reinvest the economic benefits in the policy himself. And where he cannot do that *himself*, the Regulations say he has made a gift of the value of the premiums (Reg. §25.2511-1(h)(8)). Of course, the insured could divest himself of all the rights in the policy. But if he did that, the insurance proceeds would not be included in his estate and he'd not get the advantage of the increased joint gross estate and increased marital deduction. But retaining the joint rights, it is argued, he retains incidents of ownership in the policy and the proceeds are therefore included in his estate (IRC §2042(2)). Of course, the proceeds are then deducted from the nonmarital half of the estate as a charitable contribution.

Another suggested method of getting both an income tax deduction for the premiums paid and still having the proceeds included in the gross estate is through the use of a trust. Under this arrangement, you would transfer an insurance policy to a trust and provide that while the trustee is the beneficiary of the policy, the insurance proceeds are to be paid by him to charities which qualify for the charitable contributions deduction. Name yourself trustee. Permit the trustee to designate the charitable beneficiaries and to change them as long as the beneficiaries at all times are qualified charities. Permit the trustee to terminate the trust, in which case he must pay over the corpus and income to the charities. Let the trustee have the right to cancel the policy and invest the proceeds, paying out or accumulating the income for the charities and paying out the corpus and accumulated income to charities when the trust ends.

You should get the income tax deduction, because payment of a premium on a life insurance policy is deductible where a trust is named beneficiary and the trust must then use the proceeds for charitable purposes (*Hunton*, 1 TC 821, acq.). And the fact that a grantor-trustee can designate the beneficiaries does not prevent a charitable contribution as long as the payout must ultimately go to qualified charities (*Danz*, 18 TC 454, acq.).

The proceeds should be included in the estate for the following reason —where an individual, as trustee has the power to change the beneficial ownership in a policy or its proceeds, even though he himself is not a trust beneficiary, he has an incident of ownership in the policy (Reg. §20.2042-1(c)(4)). Since, here, the grantor is also trustee and, as trustee, has the right to change the beneficiaries of the policy (although he may name only other charities as beneficiaries), it would seem he has sufficient incidents of ownership to cause the insurance proceeds to be included in his estate. In addition, the trust property could be includible in the grantor's estate on two other theories—(1) that the enjoyment of the trust property was, at the date of his death, subject to his power to alter, amend or terminate (IRC §2038; see *Lober*, 346 U.S. 335); (2) that he retained the right during his life to designate who should enjoy the trust property or its income (IRC §2036; see *Struthers vs. Kelm*, 218 F.2d 810).

[¶1103]   **CHARITABLE FOUNDATIONS**

The Tax Reform Act of 1969 made substantial changes in the tax rules. For the first time, there is a statutory definition of a private foundation (Code §509). A whole new set of statutory rules of behavior are enforceable by special excise taxes pursuant to a new Chapter 42 of the Code (§4941 to 4948). In addition, a new annual tax equal to 4% of the net investment income is imposed on private foundations (§4940). The result is the end of the free-wheeling, sometimes uncharitable, use of charitable foundations.

A charitable foundation is more than just a repository for estate assets which are to be used to satisfy the creator's charitable instincts. It can be, among other things: (1) a vehicle through which the creator can manage and control investments without the usual tax burdens, (2) a means of cutting estate taxes while retaining control, (3) a means of cutting income taxes, (4) a partner in the creation of capital gains, and (5) a means of perpetuating the creator's name. In other words, the creator retains all of the advantages and benefits of controlling a substantial amount of wealth, except the receipt of the earnings. He gives up the earnings in order to save the tax.

[¶1103.1]   **Trust or Corporation?**

A foundation can be either a trust or a corporation. The latter is probably preferable since once the corporate charter is granted, the foundation has both permanence and flexibility. The creator's family can control the operations of the foundation through their power as stockholders or members to choose the officers and directors and thus set business and investment policy. A trust, on the other hand, may run afoul of a Clifford problem because of the creator's retention of control and may be restricted by state law in administration and investment policy.

[¶1103.2] General Requirements for Tax Exemption

In order to qualify for income tax exemption, the foundation must (1) be organized and operated exclusively for religious, charitable, scientific, literary or educational purposes; (2) its earnings must not inure to the benefit of any private corporation or individual; and (3) it must not carry on propaganda. (See Code §501 et seq.)

The Tax Reform Act of 1976 contains new rules for permissible lobbying activities for public charities. Churches, their auxiliary organizations, private foundations can not engage in lobbying activities.

[¶1103.3] Prohibited Transactions

In order to prevent use of a foundation for private advantage, certain transactions with specified persons are prohibited. The transactions barred to the foundation are: (1) lending income or corpus without adequate security and a reasonable rate of interest; (2) paying unreasonable compensation; (3) offering services on a preferential basis; (4) making substantial purchases of securities for more than adequate consideration; (5) selling a substantial part of the foundation's securities or property for less than adequate consideration; (6) engaging in any other transaction resulting in substantial diversion of the foundation's income or corpus (IRC §503(b)). The persons with whom the foundation must not do any of the above are: (1) the creator, (2) a substantial contributor, (3) a member of the family of such creator or contributor (whole or half-brothers and sisters, spouse, ancestors and lineal descendants), and (4) a corporation controlled by any of the above ("control" means direct or indirect ownership of 50% or more of the voting power or 50% or more of the value) (IRC §503(b)).

The penalty is loss of the foundation's exemption and loss of the deduction for contributions to it thereafter.

[¶1103.4] Unrelated Business Income

Unrelated business income is taxed to the foundation at the income tax rates applicable to either individual or corporation, depending on whether the foundation is a trust or a corporation (IRC §511). Unrelated business income is income derived from a business not substantially related (aside from the need of the foundation for income or funds or the use it makes of the profits) to the exercise or performance of the foundation's exempt purpose (IRC §513).

Prior to the enactment of the Tax Reform Act of 1969 in computing unrelated business income, a tax-exempt organization could leave out dividends, interest, annuities, rents from real property and royalties and gains from the sale, exchange or other disposition of property other than inventory and items held for sale to customers. The scope of what constitutes taxable unrelated business income has been expanded. The Clay-Brown type of debt-financed acquisition of a business interest and the investment income received in the form of rent, interest or royalties from a taxable subsidiary are now unrelated business income. Also the term "trade or business" includes any activity which is carried on for the production of income from the sale of goods or the performance of services.

SECTION XII.   THE BUSINESS ESTATE

The businessman and his professional advisors have no more challenging task than that of deciding whether a business should be preserved beyond the death of its owner and then making the arrangements to implement that decision.

[¶1201]   **CONSIDERATIONS IN DECIDING TO SELL OR HOLD THE BUSINESS**

Set out below are a series of questions which, if seriously pondered, discussed and acted on with professional advisors, will provide the owner of a business with assurance that he has met a real and important obligation to the family, employees and business associates who survive him.

(1) Is it a purely personal service? Does it depend entirely on the personal talent or following of the owner? If so, can it be turned over to other ownership with advantage to family, customers or employees?

(2) Does it have going-concern value in the form of tangible assets, reputation, trade position, location, know-how or other factors independent of the owner? Is it large enough to support a second tier of management which can be trained to carry on?

(3) Does the owner's family have potential capacity for ownership and management? If not, is the business substantial enough to support hired management? Is the family capable of supervision? Can other arrangements be made for adequate ownership supervision of hired management?

(4) Does the family have a financial cushion so that its security is not entirely dependent on a business under new management?

(5) Are the risks of continued family ownership justified by the promise of a much greater investment return or the desire to hold the business as a vehicle for maturing children?

(6) Can assets be withdrawn or additional funds created to hedge this risk?

(7) How much of a cushion can be created by using some of the business income to carry insurance on the owner's life?

(8) Is the business profitable enough to justify its continuance? What are its future prospects?

If the decision is to sell, the job is to find a market which will provide a good price for the business. If the decision is to retain, there are various degrees of retention. It may be sufficient to retain working control. The need to raise cash to pay death taxes on the value of the business and the desirability of providing a stake for successor management are factors which push in the direction of retaining only control rather than 100% ownership.

Here are the considerations which will determine the basic decision to hold or dispose:

(1) Successor Management: Unless a business owner can count on adequate successor management, which may come out of the owner's family or from within the organization, there is no point in doing anything but arranging for the disposition or liquidation of the business. There is also the problem of providing the proper incentive for successor management and holding it responsible for making the business function for the benefit of the owner's family. Management stock or stock options may provide the former; voting control, fixed dividend, interest or bond payments may provide the latter.

(2) Estate Liquidity: Can the owner's estate afford to retain the business? What are the owner's other assets and liabilities? Is there a source of net liquid funds which will meet the cash liability which arises when the estate tax rates are applied to the value of the business and the other assets of the deceased? It may be possible to create estate liquidity by having the corporation redeem some of its stock. Is there sufficient cash to pay the capital gains tax on the redemption? In the case of a closely held corporation, it is usually possible to get a long deferment on meeting the cash liability of the estate tax. But the answer to this problem is to minimize the tax liability and to develop the liquidity to meet it.

(3) Family Cushion: Unless the family has a cushion of capital apart from the business, its future security will be left hanging on the performance of a business which has lost its guiding hand and driving force. Does the owner want to take this risk for his family? What can be done to build up assets independent of the business? A profit-sharing plan, life insurance or sale or redemption of part of the stock are some of the ways to provide funds independent of the business so that the owner and his executor are not forced to the choice of selling the business to raise cash or using investment-type assets to meet estate and income tax liabilities, thus leaving the family entirely dependent on the future of a closely held business.

(4) Business Cushion: What will the business need to carry on after the owner's death? Is there a franchise which will be jeopardized? Will credit become more restricted? Will more working capital be needed by less skilled and experienced management? Will important customers be lost? If these factors are serious, they will argue for the owner to (a) sell during his life, possibly getting a top price by taking a purchase price contingent on earnings, or (b) take steps to indemnify the business for his loss by providing fresh funds to help new management deal with these problems.

(5) Markets: What kind of a market exists for the business? What can be done to create a market by building up funds within the business itself or in the hands of associates, by carrying insurance on the life of the owner or otherwise? Should an Employee Stock Ownership Plan ("ESOP") be set up as the vehicle to acquire the stock of the company? What is the chance that a market existing at the owner's death might disappear with a few years of bad management so that the capital value represented by the business would substantially disappear?

(6) Valuation: If ownership of the business is retained by the owner's estate, it will be necessary to pay estate tax on a theoretical value either fixed by the government, or agreed or litigated. On the other hand, sale of the business within six months of the owner's death would fix the value at the sale price for estate tax purposes. This valuation problem may be overcome by a purchase-and-sale agreement which is binding on the owner during life as well as after death. It may be minimized by recapitalization into a preferred stock having readily predictable value and a common stock carrying the volatile and debatable elements of value, and then transferring much of the common during life.

(7) Marital Deduction: Can the marital deduction be used to minimize the cash liability arising out of application of the estate tax to the value of the business? Does the will minimize the further cash drain on the death of a surviving spouse? Is there provision for the additional liability on the owner's death if his wife predeceases him?

(8) Bargain Purchase: Is it better from the owner's standpoint to plan to retain the stock in all events or to make a deal with his associates so that, if they die first, he gets their stock at a bargain price, giving them in return the opportunity to buy his stock at a bargain price if he should die first? A plan to retain stock is likely to forfeit this opportunity to acquire full ownership at a bargain price if one's co-owners die first. Is the owner of a partial interest more interested in acquiring full ownership or retaining the partial interest in his family?

(9) Ownership Form and Capital Structure: Frequently, the corporate form will make it possible to build up liquid assets more readily than a proprietorship or partnership form and make possible the technique of redeeming the deceased's stock as a method of raising the cash to meet the requirements of estate liquidity.

(10) Recapitalization: It is sometimes desirable to recapitalize a business to provide a preferred stock which will carry the value already created in the business and a common stock much reduced in value which will carry the future of the business. Recapitalization makes it possible to use preferred stock to secure the position of the owner and his wife and to provide, sometimes by sale or gift during life, an immediate participation in the future growth of the business to children and to the executives who constitute successor management.

(11) Contractual Obligations: It is sometimes desirable to have the business assume contractual obligations to make continued salary payments to the owners and their wives or to other executives and their wives. It will be necessary to justify these obligations on the basis of services rendered to the business in order to get the desired tax consequences; but, where that is possible, the existence of a binding and valid obligation to make annual payments to the owners' widows may facilitate planning for the future of the business. We can frequently minimize the need for a family cushion with lease payments or interest and principal on notes paid by the corporation to redeem stock or acquire assets or paid by executives or children to acquire stock. Also, contractual commitments and debt instruments may be very useful in dividing the estate between sons and daughters in a way which will give the sons all the risk and responsibility of the family business without short-changing the daughters.

[¶1202]   **THE NEED FOR CASH IN BUSINESS
CONTINUATION PLAN**

Planning for the continuation of a business beyond the owner's life requires the provision of cash. The amount will depend on the size of the business, the character of the plan adopted and the resources of the owner's family apart from the business. All the required cash may be needed when the owner dies, or some of it may be deferred and made payable in installments over a period of years. Cash will be needed for some combination of these purposes:

(1) To pay death taxes on the value of the business.

(2) To pay the capital gains tax if part of the business is sold after death.

(3) To give the owner's family the value of the business if all or part of it is to be disposed of.

(4) To create a cash reserve in the business to offset, at least temporarily, any loss of credit or loss of skill in turning over working capital that may result from the owner's death—or to attract and retain successor management if this has not been provided for.

(5) To create a cushion of family capital and income independent of the business so that the owner's family will not be entirely dependent on a business which has lost its leader.

[¶1202.1]   **How to Reduce the Needs for Tax Cash**

The cash needed to meet tax liabilities may be minimized by steps such as these:

(1) Making lifetime gifts of minority interests in the business, being careful, however, when making these gifts so the owner's estate will still qualify for §303 redemptions, or special valuation method for qualified real estate used in farming or other closely held corporations (see ¶405).

(2) Making full use of the marital deduction on the owner's death. (This requires planning for the higher tax liability which will result if the wife predeceases and for tax liability on the marital deduction property on the wife's subsequent death. When the cash to pay taxes is coming out of the corporation in a §303 redemption, it may be desirable to forego the marital deduction, pay all death liabilities when the husband dies and avoid further tax on the death of a wife and living children by having the business go into a testamentary trust.)

(3) Pegging the value of the business by a buy-sell agreement or by recapitalizing and keeping preferred stock and making gifts of the more volatile common stock.

(4) Avoiding estate tax on the business interest by transferring it for a private annuity.

The only way for the owner to reduce the amount of cash required to cushion loss of credit and efficiency (only a seasoned estimate at best) is for the owner to build up assets and scale down debts while he is at the helm.

[¶1202.2]   Substitutes for Cash in Business Continuation Plan

The family cushion is again only an estimate or an aspiration. It is a matter for the owner's judgment. The owner may feel that the amount of cash cushion required will be minimized by such cash substitutes as these:

(1) Preferred stock held by his widow or a family trust.

(2) A contractual obligation of the business to continue compensation payments to his widow in a fixed amount over a fixed number of years or life. This would be a deferred compensation contract based on the owner's service to the business.

(3) A debt obligation of the business calling for interest and annual payments of principal. This can be created by having the business retire part of the widow's interest in the business.

(4) An obligation to make annual rental payments on a lease of real estate or other assets needed by the business. This may be created by a spin-off or redemption of stock with assets or by the owner acquiring and holding certain assets outside of the business.

[¶1202.3]   Checklist of Possible Methods of Accumulating Cash

The difficulty of accumulating the cash needed to buy a business at an adequate price or to finance retention of a business has become so great that it may be necessary to use more than one method. Here is a checklist of possibilities:

(1) Life insurance is the fastest and least costly method of introducing new cash into the picture. For relatively small annual payments, we can get a guarantee that additional cash will become available on a tax-free basis at the maturing of the death-tax liability and the family-cushion requirement.

(2) Co-owners or employees can commit to buy all or some of the deceased's interest at his death. Their ability to pay can be assured by their carrying insurance on the owner's life.

(3) The corporation can redeem some of the deceased's interest. Here again, the corporation might carry insurance on the owner's life so that the cash will be available.

(4) The family's ability to accumulate dividend income into additional capital may be enhanced by transferring dividend-paying stock to a corpora-

tion, where it will be taxed at a 3.3% to 7.2% rate. If the corporation has gross operating income which is more than 40% of total gross income, the personal holding company penalty will be avoided.

(5) If the operator of an unincorporated business makes more than $40,000 a year, it may be possible to save taxes and create cash by incorporating the business and dividing the income between that taxed to the corporation and accumulated and that withdrawn as salary.

(6) Establishing a profit-sharing or pension plan will create independent funds for the owner's family based on his own participation. It will also create a large accumulation of liquid funds held in trust for all employees.

(7) Establishing an ESOP, so the corporation can contribute its own stock and get a tax deduction. The savings in taxes can be substantial, and there is no outlay of cash by the corporation.

(8) Creating a preferred stock by recapitalizing, having this preferred stock draw off dividend income and transferring it to a trust where the dividends will be taxed at lower rates. These dividends may be accumulated for the benefit of the spouse or children of the person creating the trust, or to carry insurance on the life of the owner's wife or on the owner's life if his wife has the stock to fund such a trust.

(9) Sale and leaseback of real estate or other assets of the business or mortgaging of these assets may be a method of getting cash to meet transfer costs and immediate business needs and even to get free funds to the deceased's family. This method will usually be available only when the credit and asset value of the business are strong.

[¶1203]   **HOW TO TRANSFER A FAMILY CORPORATION**

There are several ways to transfer a family corporation:

(1) Make a lifetime transfer, thus enabling the owner to work out the best deal himself.

(2) Create liquidity by selling part of the business to the public and starting a market in the stock.

(3) Enter into a buy-sell agreement with co-stockholders and fund it to establish a market at death.

(4) Sell or give part of the business to other members in the family, employees, or both, and work out a stock redemption plan that will give the estate cash from the business.

(5) Sell part of the stock to ESOP, actually a partial redemption at capital gain rates.

(6) Recapitalize to reduce the value of control stock and then proceed as in (4) above.

(7) Let the business pass by will and grant the executor power to get enough cash out to pay death costs and provide for the widow.

No matter what plan is pursued, these two steps are essential:

(1) Have the will explicitly give the executor all authority necessary to retain the stock and to operate the business.

(2) See that there is insurance or some other definite source of liquid funds to meet the obligations which mature at death.

[¶1203.1]   How to Transfer the Business to Children Who Will Work in It and Provide for Those Who Won't

Where the problem is one of equalizing the bequest of stock in a closely held business to participating children with a similar provision to children who do not participate, the following solutions apply:

(1) Insure the owner's life to make commensurate provision for the nonparticipating members of the family.

(2) Give the inactive children their share in stock but keep the stock in trust and make the active children the trustees so that they have management control. This is a poor solution because the active children are left with fiduciary obligations to the inactive children and the inactive children have no assurance that their trust assets will ever do anything for them.

(3) Provide contractually that the corporation has a right to buy stock of the family business bequeathed to the inactive children or to trusts for them with interest-bearing obligations of the corporation payable over a period of time. If the owner has $600,000 worth of property, of which $500,000 is stock in his family business, his will may direct that $300,000 of the stock go to the active children and that $100,000 of his other property together with $200,000 of his stock go to the inactive children, the stock going to the inactive ones being subject to an option on the part of the corporation to buy the stock for $200,000 with 6% bonds payable over 10 years. That way the active children get all the responsibility, risk, and future reward that the business offers, and the inactive children get a first call on assets and future earning power of the business, a promise of investable cash in the future, and interest payments, deductible by the corporation in the interim.

(4) The corporation can be recapitalized into voting and nonvoting stock or into common or preferred stock, giving the nonvoting preferred to the inactive children. This has the advantage that the payments to the inactive children on preferred stock will be nondeductible to the corporation. It may also freeze the inactive children into assets for which there may be no market and which may never provide them with either a satisfactory income or cash that can be invested in securities more suitable to their needs.

[¶1203.2]   How to Get Cash out of a Family Corporation

Care must be exercised to get cash out of a corporation without having it taxed as a dividend to the estate. We have this problem wherever the corporation has accumulated earnings and profits.

[¶1203.3]   **Redemption under §303 after 1976**

Section 303 of the Internal Revenue Code provides that a redemption of the stock included in a decedent's estate for federal tax purposes is to be considered a distribution in exchange for the stock, not a taxable dividend, to the extent that the distribution does not exceed the amount of federal and state death taxes, interest on those taxes and the deductible funeral and administration expenses of the estate. At the time of the redemption, if the value of the stock redeemed is greater than the carryover basis, there will be a capital gain tax on the appreciation. See Section VIII for the method of computing carryover basis. To avoid the dividend treatment, we have to meet specifications which are laid down by statute:

(1) The stock redeemed must be included in the decedent's gross estate.

(2) The redemption must be made from any shareholder who has the burden of paying the death taxes and funeral and administration expenses. Wills may have to be changed so the stock to be redeemed is not part of the marital deduction share.

(3) The federal estate tax value of all the stock of the corporation whose stock is redeemed, which is included in determining the value of the decedent's gross estate, must be more than 50% of the adjusted gross estate (gross estate less deductions for administration expenses, debts, taxes and losses and before the marital deduction).

The aggregate value includible in the estate of all classes of stock of the redeeming corporation is to be taken into account in determining whether the percentage requirement is met.

(4) The stock of two or more corporations is treated as the stock of a single corporation for the purpose of computing whether the stock makes up the required percentage of the gross or taxable estate provided more than 75% in value of the outstanding stock of each corporation is included in the gross estate. In meeting this 75% requirement, we can include the surviving spouse's interest in stock held by the spouse and the decedent together as community property.

(5) Redemptions qualify only in the combined amount of the following:

(a) Death taxes imposed because of the decedent's death, plus interest thereon. This includes federal and state estate, inheritance, legacy and succession taxes, and almost certainly similar foreign taxes.

(b) The amount of the funeral and administration expenses allowable as deductions for federal estate tax purposes.

Normally the redemption must take place within the period of limitations provided in IRC §6501(a) for the assessment of the federal estate tax or within 90 days after the expiration of such period. This gives us three years and ninety days after filing the estate tax return, irrespective of any extensions of the period for assessment. However, the redemption may be extended as long as 15 years after death if the estate qualifies under IRC §6166 for extension of time payment of estate tax. This section requires the value of the closely held business to exceed 65% of the adjusted gross estate. If the decedent has more than one business, the estate can meet the 65% test if he had more than 20% interest in each business.

There are special rules which limit the amount of qualifying redemption distributions that are made more than four (4) years after the decedent's death to either the amount of taxes, funeral expenses and administration expenses remaining unpaid at such a distribution, or those which are paid within a one-year period beginning at the distribution, whichever is less.

The Tax Reform Act of 1976 adds a new provision to extend time to pay estate tax as an alternative to one in existing law that allows an executor to elect to pay the installments over 10 years. (IRC §6166A). Under the new provision, if the closely held business qualifies under IRC §6166, the executor can elect not to pay any tax at all for the first 5 years. But interest on the tax for that period must be paid each year after the 5-year period, and the estate tax liability can be paid in 10 yearly installments.

[¶1203.4]   How to Take Money out without Qualifying under IRC §303

We may be unable to qualify a redemption under IRC §303 because:

(1) We want to take out more money than the amount of the death taxes, administration costs and funeral expenses, or

(2) The estate's stock in the corporation does not add up to the required portion of the estate.

We then have these alternatives in getting funds out of the corporation without having them taxed as a dividend:

(1) Qualifying the distribution as "not essentially equivalent to a taxable dividend," which is difficult but possible (see ¶1203.6);

(2) Effecting a redemption which reduces the estate's ownership by more than 20% and leaves it owning less than 50% of the company;

(3) Completely retiring the estate's ownership in the corporation;

(4) Liquidating the corporation entirely; or

(5) Effecting a partial liquidation of the corporation under IRC §346.

In the second and third of the above alternatives, it is essential to take into account any stock owned by heirs or beneficiaries of the estate whose holdings may be attributed to the estate.

A stockholder will be deemed to own stock actually owned by one of the following (IRC §318):

(1) By his spouse, parent, child or grandchild;

(2) By a trust or estate of which he is a beneficiary, and vice versa;

(3) By a partnership of which he is a member, and vice versa;

(4) By a corporation of which he owns 50% or more of the stock, and vice versa.

Usually the consummation of stock retirement plan completely retires the stock owned by the deceased stockholder. This can result in a taxable dividend, even though all the estate's stock is redeemed, if at the time of the redemption, either of these situations exists:

(1) Any beneficiary of the estate owns stock in the corporation; or

(2) A child, grandchild, spouse or parent of the deceased owns stock in the corporation.

This stock may be attributed to the estate so that the redemption, while terminating the estate's actual ownership, will not terminate ownership attributed to it.

It is possible, however, to have the redemption treated as not essentially equivalent to a dividend even though the acquisition rules prevent the redemption from being a total redemption. See ¶1203.6.

[¶1203.5] How to Protect a Stock Retirement Plan against a Dividend Tax

We have these possible methods of protecting against an unexpected dividend tax on a stock redemption which completely retires all the stock owned by a deceased shareholder:

(1) A provision in the agreement relieving the estate of its obligation to sell if the application of constructive ownership rules would result in a taxable dividend.

(2) Satisfying ourselves that even if the attribution to the estate of stock owned by a member of the family or estate beneficiary resulted in less than a complete termination of interest, the distribution would still qualify as a capital transaction under IRC §303 (the amount limited to death duties and administration expenses) or as a disproportionate redemption (the estate being constructively charged with less than 50% of the corporate stock and the retirement having reduced its actual and constructive ownership by more than 20%).

(3) Making sure that any family attribution is eliminated and eliminate any attribution between the estate and the estate beneficiary by having the estate satisfy its obligation to the beneficiary before allowing its stock to be redeemed. A person shall no longer be considered a beneficiary of an estate when all the property to which he is entitled has been received by him, when he no longer has a claim against the estate arising out of having been a beneficiary and when there is only a remote possibility that it will be necessary for the estate to seek the return of property or to seek payment from him to satisfy claims against the estate or expenses of administration. This makes it safe to provide for outright bequests to children without concern about the application of the attribution rules to a stock retirement plan. Proper handling by the executor can avoid any difficulty.

Special care must be exercised in providing for any testamentary trust. For example, suppose a man decided that he would prefer to leave a portion of his estate in trust with his wife as life beneficiary and his children, including his son, as remaindermen. This would mean that his wife and son would be beneficiaries of the same trust. As such, there would be stock attribution from the son to the wife through that trust, which would not depend on the family ownership rule.

This could have a disastrous effect, because it would mean that the link between the son's shares and the estate could not be broken under any condition; and so the complete termination test could not be met. Thus, if he wanted to establish a trust for his wife, he would probably find that he could not safely name his son as one of the remaindermen, although he might find that he could safely substitute the son's children, his grandchildren, as beneficiaries.

(4) Another danger is that a stock retirement contract, like a will, is ambulatory. It is drawn in the light of a certain state of facts which may be completely changed by the time of the stockholder's death. Changes in stockholders, especially transfers among related persons, can turn an arrangement mutually beneficial to all the parties when made to one that may be ruinous to the estate of a deceased stockholder. Thus, it is not only necessary to make an exhaustive analysis of the current situation when the agreement is made, but also to review it from time to time as changes in stockholders occur. Even the most minor and seemingly innocuous change, say a gift of a few shares to a child on graduation from college, may require a re-examination. This assumes that the parties will be able to make any change in the contract that may later be found desirable. Usually in a closely held corporation, it will be possible for the parties to make any changes indicated by changing events. But usually, the parties do not take advantage of the possibilities of periodic review. Any transfers of stock should be prospectively reviewed in the light of the effect the transfer may have upon the stock redemption agreement.

[¶1203.6] Distribution Not Essentially Equivalent to a Dividend

Even where the attribution rules apply to prevent a total redemption or disproportionate redemption, it's still possible to avoid dividend treatment by showing that the redemption is not essentially equivalent to a dividend.

Whether a distribution in connection with a redemption of stock is or is not equivalent to a taxable dividend *will depend on the facts in each case.* In some cases, where the distribution was not exactly pro rata among all the shareholders and its effect was to alter significantly the relative stockholdings of the shareholders, it has been held to be not essentially equivalent to a dividend. The question to be answered is whether the distribution produces results which are markedly different from the results which would be derived from the declaration of a dividend. Since different courts may rule differently on this question, it is a wise practice to plan a redemption of stock which meets the requirements of provisions of the Code which are more specific than IRC §302(b)(1).

In one case, a corporation redeemed more stock from an estate than was permitted under IRC §303 (the special provisions for redemption free of dividend problems of amounts equal to death costs; see ¶1203.3) and IRS claimed that the excess should be treated as a dividend distribution because the attribution rules left the estate with constructive ownership of stock after the redemption. However, there was substantial minority interest, which, without the attribution rules, owned more than the estate. Second, the executor and the stockholders whose stock ownership was attributed to the estate did not see eye to eye on the conduct of the business. The estate no longer controlled the corporation in a practical sense, even if it did under the attribution rules. So, said the Tax Court, the distribution was not essentially equivalent to a dividend (*Squier*, 35 TC 950, *acq.*).

[¶1203.7]   How to Avoid Tax to Surviving Stockholders

Where the corporation uses its surplus or insurance proceeds to retire the stock of a deceased stockholder, the surviving stockholders get the same increase in their proportionate ownership as if they had used their own money to buy the shares of the deceased in proportion to their interests. They have a proportionate interest in something of lesser value because funds have gone out of the corporation to buy the shares of the deceased. Nevertheless, the Treasury has tried to tax surviving stockholders as though they had received a dividend in the amount of corporate funds used to buy the stock of a fellow shareholder. Fortunately, the Treasury now agrees that there is no tax to the surviving stockholders, unless the corporation, in redeeming outstanding shares, in some way discharges a pre-existing obligation of the surviving stockholders (*Rev. Rul. 58-614,* 1958-2 CB 920).

If a stock redemption agreement places the obligation to buy firmly on the corporation and the corporation does buy, there will be no tax to the surviving stockholders.

If the surviving stockholders are committed by the agreement to buy if the corporation is lacking in surplus and the corporation buys, it would seem that there should be no tax on the stockholder.

It is only if the surviving stockholders incur a firm obligation to buy and the corporation either gives them the funds to discharge their obligation or assumes and discharges the obligation itself that the surviving stockholders can be taxed.

[¶1204]   THE CORPORATE BUY-SELL AGREEMENT

The best method of liquefying the business estate is to arrange and finance an agreement under which the stock of a deceased stockholder will be purchased at his death. If the objective is to keep the business in the family, only enough stock may be purchased to meet death charges in a stock redemption carried out under IRC §303. More frequently, the objective is to replace the interest of the widow and the family in the business with cash or investment-quality assets and to retire the interest of the family in the business so that the survivors can carry on without having new partners forced upon them. In planning this kind of transaction we must answer these questions:

(1) Should there be an obligation or merely an option to purchase the stock of a deceased stockholder?

(2) Should it be a stock-retirement agreement or a cross-purchase agreement?

(3) How should the price be determined?

(4) What should be the source and terms of payment?

(5) Should the payment obligation be funded by life insurance on the lives of the stockholders?

[¶1204.1]   **Obligation or Option?**

These are the basic kinds of buy-sell agreements:

(1) The survivors or the corporation are obligated to buy and the estate of a deceased stockholder is obligated to sell.

(2) The survivors or the corporation have an option to buy the stock of a deceased stockholder and, if this option is exercised, the estate is obligated to sell.

(3) The estate of a deceased stockholder has the right to offer the stock to the survivors or to the corporation; and, if it does, either the survivors or the corporation are obligated to buy.

(4) There is no obligation either to buy or sell, but if a stockholder or his estate wants to sell, the stock must first be offered to the other stockholders or to the corporation before it can be sold to an outside party.

Only an obligation on the part of the corporation or the survivors to buy will assure a stockholder that his estate will be converted to liquid assets which can buy investment-quality, income-producing securities. Unless the agreement places an obligation on the survivors or the corporation, any stockholder who dies may be leaving his family with an unmarketable asset and making them dependent on the surviving working stockholders for their income. We may hesitate to impose an absolute obligation to buy on the survivors or the corporation; it may be enough to give them an option to buy with the alternative of dissolution if the option is not exercised. Faced with the dilemma of imposing an obligation on the survivors and leaving the estate of a deceased stockholder high and dry, it usually seems preferable to put the responsibility on the survivors, who, presumably are still capable of earning income and who in the absence of an obligation have a distinct advantage in their ability to get many of the customers and the good will of the existing business if they should liquidate it and start another venture.

[¶1204.2]   **Stock Retirement or Cross Purchase?**

Should the corporation purchase the stock of a deceased stockholder or should the purchase be made by the survivors? In making this critical decision, we must consider these aspects:

(1) Source of Funds: The stock-retirement plan permits the use of corporate funds. The cross-purchase plan requires the use of funds which the stockholders have presumably taken out of the business and on which they have paid or will pay an individual income tax. If the income tax bracket of the stockholder is higher than that of the corporation or even if the corporate rate is higher but money used to make the purchase will have to be taken out as a dividend by the stockholders so that a double tax is involved, it will be cheaper to fund a stock-retirement plan.

(2) Enforceability: A cross-purchase agreement is clearly valid and enforceable, while a stock-retirement plan may not be enforceable if the corporation has or may have insufficient surplus to make the purchase and state law requires that stock may be redeemed only out of surplus. This potential deficiency in the stock retirement plan can be met by having the agreement provide that the survivors will either purchase or contribute sufficient surplus to the corporation in the event the corporation is prevented from retiring the stock of a deceased stockholder by state laws requiring that such purchases be made only out of surplus. In drafting the stock retirement agreement, the corporation should first be required to increase its available surplus by reducing its required capital or by increasing its capital to reflect a value for unrealized appreciation in assets. If this is insufficient and the survivors cannot either purchase or contribute additional funds to permit the corporation to meet the surplus requirement, the decedent's legal representative can be given the right to demand that the corporation be liquidated. (These supplementary steps will make the stock-retirement plan sufficiently valid and enforceable.)

(3) Complication in Ownership of Insurance Policies: If the plan is to be funded by insurance, the stock-retirement plan requires only one policy on each stockholder and permits the corporation to have continuous ownership of that policy. When one stockholder dies, the corporation can continue to carry the policies on the survivors in order to redeem the stock of the others on their death. In a cross-purchase plan, on the other hand, each stockholder has to carry insurance on the lives of the others. When there are four or five stockholders, this gets pretty complicated. Then, when one stockholder dies, the policies which he owns on the lives of the other stockholders have to be transferred to them; or, in the alternative, the corporation can acquire the policies. Transfer of a policy from the estate of a deceased stockholder to the surviving stockholders will result in the loss of the income tax exemption when these policies mature by death—unless the policies are transferred to those who are insured by the policies (IRC §101(a)(2)). Where there are only two stockholders to begin with, the survivor is the insured, and a transfer of the policy held on his life by the deceased stockholder will not result in the loss of the income tax exemption for any part of the proceeds. However, there may be more than two stockholders. Suppose there are three: Green, White and Black. Green dies holding policies on the lives of White and Black. It may be desirable to have the policy on White's life transferred to Black and the one on Black's life transferred to White. This will provide the survivor of the two with the funds to buy out the first of the two to die. But such a transfer of policies will cause part of the proceeds (in excess of any consideration and premiums paid by the transferee) to become subject to income taxes.

If the policies are transferred to the corporation, however, the income tax redemption is preserved (IRC §101(a)(2)). Thus, it is possible, without adverse income tax effects, to convert a cross-purchase plan into a stock-retirement plan—but not the other way around; a transfer of policies by the corporation to a stockholder other than the insured will cause the loss of the income tax exemption.

(4) Cost Basis of Stock: In a stock-retirement plan, the value of the stock of the survivors is generally increased when the corporation retires the stock of a deceased shareholder. However, the cost basis of the stock of the survivors remains the same. Thus, a latent capital gains tax liability is built up. On the other hand, in a cross-purchase plan when the survivors purchase the stock of a deceased shareholder, they step up the basis of the stock to the price at which they buy.

(5) Shift of Control: In a stock-retirement plan, the proportionate interest of the survivors automatically remains the same when the corporation buys the stock of a deceased shareholder. If the intent is to equalize the ownership of the survivors, it is necessary to give the survivor owning the smaller amount of the stock an option to buy additional stock from the corporation. In a cross-purchase plan, the result would be exactly the same if the survivors purchased in proportion to their present shareholdings. If it is desired to equalize the stock ownership, this can be done by merely having the stock-purchase agreement authorize each survivor to buy enough of the deceased's stock to produce the desired ratio of stock ownership as among the survivors.

(6) Burden of Insurance Premiums: In a stock-retirement plan with the corporation buying the insurance, the cost of the premiums is pooled and allocated to the stockholders in the ratio of their stock interests. The larger and the older stockholders pay most of the premiums while the smaller and younger stockholders, who stand to benefit most, pay a smaller portion. This inequity can be evened out by including a portion of the proceeds of the policy on the deceased stockholder's life in the purchase price formula. In a cross-purchase plan, the younger and smaller stockholders pay a larger portion of the premium because they have to carry enough insurance to buy out the largest stockholder and they have to pay rates based on the ages of the older stockholders. Sometimes this burden is so great as to make the financing of a cross-purchase plan impractical.

[¶1204.3] **How to Make the Purchase Price Binding for Estate Tax Purposes**

The price set in a mandatory buy-sell agreement will be controlling for federal estate tax purposes and if these requirements are met:

(1) The agreement is bona fide and entered into at arm's length. Agreements between members of the family where there may·be a donative intent

will be scrutinized carefully; and if the purchase price seems to be low in · relation to real value, it will not be accepted for federal estate tax purposes.

(2) The price has to be reasonable at the time the agreement is executed. The test is not whether the price is fair and reasonable at the time the agreement becomes operative. It is recognized that both parties carry the risk that they will be bought out by the other at the price at which they have agreed.

(3) Disposal of the stock during the lifetime of the parties must be either prohibited during life or restricted so that a stockholder cannot sell during life without first offering the stock to the other party at no more than the price established in the agreement to apply at death. The purchase price in the agreement will not be binding for estate tax purposes if, during life, the shareholder has been free to sell at any price he could get.

If the above conditions are met, the price in the agreement will be binding for estate tax purposes even if the agreement gives the survivors only an option rather than an obligation to buy. If the option is in the estate of the deceased stockholder or if the estate is merely obligated to make a first offer to the survivors, the price in the agreement has no effect for estate tax purposes. (See Reg. §20.2031-2(h); 20.2031-3(c).)

The Government takes the view that insurance in a stock-retirement plan must be considered to determine whether the price is reasonable. If the price is not binding, the insurance proceeds will be considered in determining the value of the shares. On the other hand, the Government recognizes that in a cross-purchase plan, the value of the insurance proceeds cannot be taxed on top of the value of the shares which are to be purchased by the insurance proceeds (*Est. of Tompkins,* 13 TC 1054, *acq.*).

[¶1204.4]   **How to Set the Price**

Actually, the valuation formula of closely held corporation stock is usually the most controversial factor in drafting any buy-sell agreement. But proper valuation is essential, and there are several ways of arriving at a fair sales price.

(1) **Fixed Price Method:** This is the most common method. The stockholders set a fixed price per share in the buy-sell agreement and leave room for revising this price, with the controlling price to be the last price stated prior to the death of the first stockholder. For example, the agreement may provide for a new price to be set annually at the close of the year; however, experience has shown that often the annual revaluation is never made. This raises the danger of an unfair (depressed or inflated) price being used. A possible solution is to use this method in conjunction with the appraisal method and to provide in the contract that if no revaluation was made within fourteen or more months prior to the death of a stockholder, the price of the stock will be determined by appraisal. Another way is to provide that the last agreed price is to be automatically adjusted by increases or decreases in earned surplus.

(2) Appraisal Method: With this method, price is left open for future appraisal. The buy-sell agreement provides that value be determined at the death of the first stockholder by a disinterested appraiser. Very often the agreement requires a panel of three appraisers—one appointed by the stockholder-purchasers, one by the decedent's estate and one by mutual agreement, such as a trust company. Time limits are set for the appointment of the appraisers and for their arriving at a decision, and provisions cover what is to be done in case of a dispute.

(3) Net Worth or Book Value Method: Here, valuation is based on the corporation's last balance sheet prepared prior to the death of the first stockholder, and the net worth is adjusted to the date of death; or the company's accountants may be required to determine book value as of the date of death. Neither way is adequate since the true value of the business as a going concern, including the earning power of intangible assets like good will, is not reflected. The use of a stated formula based on net worth usually corrects this shortcoming. When this method is used, the following items should be considered:

(a) *Inventory:* Will it be figured at cost or its real worth?

(b) *Accounts Receivable:* Will there be uncollectible accounts, and what percentage of these does not show up in the book figures?

(c) *Machinery and Equipment:* Does the present book figure fairly reflect the present worth? Has it become obsolete?

(d) *Buildings:* Does the book figure reflect current market value? Real estate is sometimes carried on books at cost and then depreciated substantially.

(e) *Insurance Proceeds:* If the company is to buy up the interest of the deceased associate and if there is insurance payable to the company, are the proceeds to be considered in determining book value?

(4) Straight Capitalization Method: With this method, the corporation's average net profits are capitalized at a specific rate, say 10%, and the result reflects the total value of the business including good will. The buy-sell agreement usually calls for averaging the net profits for the five years immediately preceding the death of the first stockholder, after which they are capitalized at the 10% rate. The resulting total value is then divided by the number of outstanding shares to determine the value per share. Adjustment must be made to reflect the absorption of profits in the form of stockholders' salaries, or the average net profits will be distorted. The multiple at which the profits are capitalized will depend on the nature of the business and the history of the particular corporation involved.

(5) Years' Purchase Method: This also relies on average net profits. The book value is averaged over a stated number of years, usually allowing a fair return of 6%. This is then subtracted from the average net profits, and the remainder, which represents excess earnings, is multiplied by the stated number of years' purchase to arrive at the value of good will. This good will is then added to the book value to determine the total value of the business and the corresponding value per share of stock.

(6) Combination of Methods: A combination of different valuation methods is sometimes used to overcome the shortcomings of one or the other method. The fixed-price method, for example, may be combined with the appraisal method. Other combinations utilized often involve the valuation of such assets as accounts receivable, fixtures and raw materials at book; assets, such as buildings and machinery by appraisal; and assets, such as good will at a multiple of earnings. Note that the years' purchase method is in itself a combination of different methods.

Here's a suggested formula for a valuation based on a combination of fixed assets and good will; capitalized value of the good will is added to the book value of the tangible assets. Determine the value of good will by reducing the average net profits of the corporation for a stated number of years by a specific rate of return on the fixed assets, say, 8%. Next, capitalize the balance of net profits at a rate customary for this type of business, say, 10%. Suppose a corporation has fixed assets with a book value of $25,000 and shows an average annual net profit for the past five years of $30,000. Take 8% of $25,000 (representing the rate of return on fixed assets) and subtract it from the $30,000 net profits. Thus:

Book Value of Fixed Assets	$25,000
Average Net Profit	$ 30,000
8% of Fixed Assets	2,400
Balance	$ 27,600
Capitalized Good Will (at 10%)	$276,000
Add Value of Fixed Assets	25,000
Total Value of Business	$301,000

[¶1204.5]   **Payment of Purchase Price**

The agreement must specify how and when the price is to be paid. The plan must provide for the source of the funds. (Life insurance on the stockholders will produce the necessary funds when they are needed.) The excess of the total price over the insurance proceeds and other free cash available can be made payable on an installment basis. This obligation should be evidenced by notes and secured by the interest being purchased. Additional security can be provided in the form of mortgages on assets or additional insurance policies. Provide the right to prepay the obligations and for acceleration of the full obligation in the event of default of payment, bankruptcy or sale of the business and other specified contingencies.

There may be a substantial advantage in paying for redeemed stock with appreciated securities or other acceptable assets owned by the corporation. The corporation can make the payment at the appreciated value without paying tax (IRC §311).

[¶1204.6]　**How Should Insurance Proceeds Be Reflected in the Price?**

If the commitment of the corporation is funded with insurance on the stockholders' lives, the question will arise whether the policies must be included in the computation of corporate values in determining the price to be paid for the stock. To make this concrete—suppose we have a corporation owned in equal shares by four stockholders. The corporation had previously acquired $75,000 insurance on the life of each owner. At the death of shareholder A, the worth of the corporation (not taking into consideration the proceeds of the insurance policy on A or any cash values built up in the other policies) is $300,000. But the corporation has now received an additional $75,000 in cash. It also has the present values of the policies on the lives of shareholders B, C and D, which have not been included in fixing the price. If the estate of the decedent receives only $75,000, he is not getting any benefit out of the premium money paid by the corporation. But his corporate share bore one-quarter of the burden. He has made as heavy a contribution as any of the other parties. If he receives no benefit, the three survivors have acquired a corporation worth $300,000 plus the cash values of the policies on B, C and D.

It would seem fairer that the decedent's estate should receive the same proportionate benefit as each of the others. Nevertheless, the parties must consider what the corporation has lost by the death of A. Its future earning capacity may be substantially decreased. The benefit of the insurance flowing only to the survivors may be justified on the theory that this may be necessary to offset the expected loss of corporate earnings for one or two or more years. The decision as to what to do will have to be made in the light of the particular circumstances in each case, and it should be made only after a thorough exploration of the facts to arrive at a fair and equitable result.

[¶1205]　　　　　　　　　**PARTNERSHIP INTEREST**

A partnership interest raises these problems:

(1) The partnership by law terminates at death.

(2) How to avoid harmful tax consequences from a doubling up of partnership income in the year of death.

(3) The best way for the deceased's partners and the survivors to liquidate an interest.

(4) What arrangements should be made during life.

The pattern and the legal mechanics of a partnership liquidation plan are comparable to those of a corporate buy-sell agreement. The buyout for the corporate interest can be an entity or on a buy-sell (cross-purchase) basis.

[¶1205.1]   **Entity vs. Cross-Purchase Agreements**

Whether the partnership itself will buy the deceased partner's interest (the entity approach) or each of the surviving partners will buy that interest (the cross-purchase approach), the funds to make the purchase are usually made available by carrying life insurance on the lives of each of the partners. Here are some of the pros and cons of each approach where insurance funding is used:

Entity Plan: The advantage here is that it is necessary to carry only one policy on the life of each partner. The proceeds are then received by the partnership on the partner's death and used to pay for his interest. What's more, after the death of a partner, the insurance policies on the surviving partners can continue to be held by the partnership without any transfers needed. With a cross-purchase plan, after the death of a partner, it is necessary to transfer the policies the deceased partner held on the lives of the surviving partners.

A disadvantage of the entity plan is that insurance premiums may be allocated unfairly among the policies. Presumably, the senior partners' interests will have greater value, and so larger policies will have to be carried on their lives. Presumably, too, they are older than the other partners, and the premiums on their policies will be higher for that reason as well. If the premium costs are allocated to the partners in their regular profit-sharing ratio, chances are the senior partners will be bearing the lion's share of the premium burden (since they presumably get the lion's share of the partnership profits). Yet, it's the younger, junior partners who stand to benefit the most from the insurance carried on the senior partners; in the normal course of events, the senior partners will die first, and the proceeds on the policies insuring their lives will be used to acquire their interests for the benefit of the junior partners. This disadvantage of the entity plan can be overcome, however, by allocating the premium burden among the partners on a cross-purchase basis (i.e., charging them with the same premium cost they'd have to bear if the plan were a cross-purchase plan).

Cross-Purchase Plan: One big drawback of a cross-purchase plan arises when there are quite a few partners. Each partner has to carry a life insurance policy on the life of each other partner. So, the number of policies involved can become unwieldy. For example, if there are five partners, each partner has to carry four policies—so there is a total of 20 policies. To avoid a large number of policies, a cross-purchase plan can provide for one policy on each partner to be owned jointly by the other partners. This is especially workable in small partnerships.

After the death of a partner, it will normally become necessary to transfer the policies he held on the survivors' lives to the other partners. Although these policies are transferred for value (sold by the estate to the other partners for the cash or replacement value), the full proceeds will continue to be income tax free when the surviving partners die as long as each policy is transferred to the insured, a partner of the insured or to the partnership itself (IRC §101(a)(2)). To maintain the same ratios of insurance ownership by the survivors on each of the other partners' lives, each of the insurance policies owned by the deceased on the survivors' lives should be transferred to the partners other than the insured. These policies could be jointly owned by them.

As previously indicated, the big advantage of a cross-purchase plan is that each partner pays premiums in proportion to the potential benefits he may enjoy. The junior partners pay the heaviest premiums, because they have to carry the policies on the older, senior partners whose interests are worth more. But then, the laws of probability favor the juniors' chances of acquiring the seniors' interests with the insurance proceeds.

[¶1205.2]   **Partnership Retirement Plan**

Normally, if a partner sells his partnership interest to an outsider or is paid out by the partnership, he gets capital gain treatment on his profits. But to the extent the purchase price covers unrealized receivables of the partnership or substantially appreciated inventory, he has ordinary income (IRC §741).

On a payout from the partnership itself, the partnership agreement under which the payout is made will, to a great extent, govern how the payments will be taxed. As indicated, payments for the partnership interest (other than for receivables and appreciated inventory) will be treated as a capital distribution. Payment for good will can be either ordinary income or capital distribution, depending on the provisions of the partnership agreement. If there is a provision in the agreement calling for a payment for good will, it is a capital distribution; otherwise, the payment for the good will value gives the retiring partner (or the deceased partner's estate) ordinary income. Similarly, guaranteed payments paid after retirement or death are ordinary income to the recipient (IRC §736).

The choice to be decided by the partners is whether or not the remaining partners are to get a deduction for the payouts to the retiring or deceased partner. If they are to get the deductions, then the payouts to the retiring or deceased partner should be in terms of guaranteed payments (these payments are deductible by the partnership, thus reducing the distributable income of the remaining partners). Then, of course, the retiring partner or the deceased partner's estate will get ordinary income. But the tax bite can be cut considerably by setting up a payout over a number of years. Alternatively, if the retiring partner or deceased partner's estate is to get capital gain, then the partnership agreement should provide a payment for good will (and set a reasonable value for it). In that case, of course, the remaining partners will get no deduction for the payout, since the partnership will get no deduction.

If the arrangement for the purchase of a partnership interest (either at death or retirement) is among the partners themselves, as opposed to an agreement to have the partnership buy up the interest, then, of course, the partners making the purchase get no deduction. In either case (payout by the partnership or cross purchase among the partners), if the partnership has made an appropriate election, any appreciation reflected in the purchase price of the departing partner's interest can be reflected in a stepped-up basis for the partnership assets (as to the purchased interest only).

[¶1205.3] How Individual Professional Practitioners Can Take Advantage of the Partnership Retirement Rules

The following examples show how an individual professional practitioner can plan for his retirement by taking in partners and taking advantage of the partnership retirement rules discussed above. These examples also show how these rules can work out:

How to Sell a Partnership Interest for Future Payments: A professional planning to retire in, say, ten years or so or who feels the work load is just too much may find that bringing in a partner helps solve both problems. He can sell the incoming partner a share in the physical assets and the good will and realize a capital gain. The payout can be over a period of years, so the incoming partner can use his share of partnership earnings to make the payments. On retirement, the balance of the good will can be sold, with payouts made over a period of years as a post-retirement annuity (again taxable at capital gain rates).

How It Works Out: Say Dr. Green, who has a substantial practice as a specialist, is willing to take in Dr. Brown as a partner. Brown is a bright, young, upcoming physician. Brown has a great potential but not much money; Green has an excellent location and a fine reputation that has considerable good will value. Green wants Brown to pay for the good will which Brown will now share. Also, when Green steps out of the picture in about ten years, Brown will be picking up additional good will. So, Brown agrees to pay Green immediately $5,000 for a half interest in Green's equipment plus another $25,000 for a half interest in the good will. Green gets a capital gain on the whole deal. But the $25,000 is paid over ten years (to let Brown use his partnership earnings to make the payment), and Green can report by the installment method—spreading his tax over that period. It's also agreed that when Green retires, Brown will pay another $30,000 ($5,000 for equipment and $25,000 for good will). These payments, too, will be paid over a ten-year period. Of course, these figures are merely illustrative; you can substitute your own to fit your own situation.

The reason the doctor is entitled to the favorable capital gain treatment in our example is that he sold a capital asset—good will. The courts have held that a professional can sell his good will without giving up his right to use his own name in his business. So, when the doctor sells half his good will and continues in practice, he can get capital gain on that. And when he sells out entirely, the same rule applies, of course (*Watson,* 35 TC 203; *Rees,* 295 F.2d 817; *Rev. Rul. 60-301,* 1960-2 CB 15; *Masquelette,* 239 F.2d 322).

IRS is very stingy in admitting the existence of good will in a professional practice. But at least it admits that it can exist in the case of the sale of an entire practice. However, IRS will fight for ordinary income in the case of an owner taking in a new partner. It will not follow the *Watson* and *Rees* cases but instead abides by *O'Rear* (80 F.2d 473) which held that such a transaction amounted to the relinquishment of a right to future income, taxable as ordinary income (*Rev. Rul. 64-235*, 1964-2 CB 18).

Another Approach: When a new doctor buys a share of the good will, he gets no tax deduction for that. As shown above, the new partner (or partners) can get a tax deduction if the retiring partner is willing to take ordinary income. Where the payout will be over a period of years and at a time when he will be in a lower bracket, the retiring partner may be willing to do that. These tax factors (capital gain v. ordinary income, for the retiring partner; deductible v. nondeductible costs, for the new partners) will enter into the calculations of any agreement.

How the Second Approach Works: Say Jones, a lawyer, is taking two young lawyers into his firm as partners. At first, it was thought that Jones would get 70% of the profits and the two new men, 15% each. In negotiating, however, it is agreed that Jones will take only 60% of the profits, with 20% going to each of the other two. But, on retirement, Jones is to receive guaranteed payments from the partnership for a number of years to compensate him for the 10% less profits he was taking out of the business. These guaranteed payments would be ordinary income to Jones (spread over the payout period) and deductible by the partnership (IRC §736).

[¶1205.4] How to Swap Tax-Deductible Dollars for Capital Gain in a Partnership Arrangement

Suppose Mr. Howe, a C.P.A., has a practice that has reached the point where he can use some help. He engages young Mr. Bell to assist him. Let's assume the understanding is such that as Mr. Bell's capacities and responsibilities develop—say, in about ten to fifteen years—he will be eligible for a share of the practice. In the meantime, the young accountant is a salaried employee.

Howe can set up a profit-sharing trust for his young assistant. He will probably have to include in the plan any other person in his employ. But he himself cannot participate in the benefits. The money which he contributes to the profit-sharing plan is tax deductible, however, so Uncle Sam pays a good part of the bill.

These dollars which go into the trust fund can be invested and any income earned escapes tax. In addition, the allocations to Bell and the other participants in the plan are not taxed to them at the time of the credit.

Bell can benefit still further. In addition to tax-free amounts paid into the trust for him, there is likely to be capital appreciation on the investments. Furthermore, forfeiture money, which is taken from the accounts of any employees who have left Howe's employ before all their benefits became vested, will be added to the account of those who stay—i.e., Bell.

The Payoff: By the time our young accountant is eligible for partnership status, he will have built up a substantial capital account in the trust fund.

When he ceases to be an employee, he must wind up his interest in the profit-sharing plan and settle his account. He is then entitled to get his share in a lump sum and take advantage of the favorable special ten-year forward averaging provision (see IRC §1302).

Bell now has the capital to buy a piece of Howe's accounting practice. Here too, Howe realizes capital gains for the sale of the partnership interest.

So the profit-sharing trust was used to build up capital with pretax dollars for a young employee. In turn, a good part of this accumulated capital was returned to the senior partner—again at capital gain rates.

[¶1205.5] How to Plan for Post-Death Partnership Income

Normally the death of a partner does not end the partnership's tax year (IRC §706). Where a partner and the partnership have different tax years, this rule is beneficial; it prevents the bunching of more than 12 months' partnership income into one taxable year of the deceased partner.

Example: The partnership year ends January 31, 1977. A partner who uses a calendar year dies November 30, 1977. If the partnership year ended on November 30 because of the partner's death, the deceased partner's share of the partnership's income for the 12 months ending January 31, 1977, would be picked up in his last return because that partnership year ended during his 1977 tax year. And, in addition, the 10 months' income of the partnership to November 30, 1977, would also have to be picked up because that partnership year ended with the partner's same tax year. By keeping the partnership year going to its normal fiscal closing, the bunching of 22 months' income in the partner's last return is avoided.

Look Out for the Tax Trap: Where partner and partnership have the same tax year, the rule that keeps the partnership tax year open on a partner's death can be a tax trap. Here's why:

The partner's tax year closes when he dies. But the partnership's tax year will close in the tax year of the beneficiaries or his estate (whoever succeeds him to that partnership interest). Thus, that entire year's partnership income will become the income of his successor. And the various expenses that are deductible in the partner's last income tax return may not be of any value because there's no partnership income picked up in that return against which to offset them.

What to Do: There are a few planning measures you can take:

(1) A partner can designate his widow as his successor in interest in the partnership after his death (the designation is made in the partnership agreement). Then, the distributive share of the partnership income is picked up by the widow and she can file a joint return with her deceased husband for the year in which he died. Thus, the income is available to be offset by the deceased husband's deductions (Reg. §1.706-1(c)(3)(iii)).

(2) Where possible, the estate can distribute sufficient income to the widow during the year of the deceased partner's death. This income, too, would be reported on the joint return and have the same effect as having the

widow get the partnership distributive share as a successor in interest. This route may not work as well as the first method, however. During the year before his death, the deceased may have drawn out a good deal of the distributive share of the partnership profits. So, the estate may get very little, if any, cash from the partnership and have nothing to distribute to the widow as income to her.

(3) The partnership agreement can call for a sale of the partner's interest to the surviving partners as of the date of his death. In that case, the partnership year as to the deceased partner ends at the date of death. So, his distributive share of the partnership income as of that date is picked up in his last return (Reg. §1.706-1(c)(3)(iv)).

[¶1205.6]   Checklist of Items to Consider in Working out a
             Partnership Buy-Sell Agreement

(1) Spell out the obligation of the survivors to buy the deceased's interest and the obligation of the estate of the deceased to offer the interest for sale on the agreed terms. You may want to set up an option on the part of either the survivors or the estate; but in most cases, you'll probably want a binding obligation to go through with the sale.

(2) The partners individually, the partnership (where it is going to make the purchase), the partners' wives (in some cases and definitely in community property states) and the trustee (if one is used) should all be parties to the agreement. The buy-sell agreement can be part of the partnership agreement or it can be incorporated into a separate agreement.

(3) As to how to fix prices for the partnership interest, see ¶1204.4. Also keep in mind the problems of valuing good will and the significance of putting a value on it in the agreement. See ¶1205.2. Spell out how the purchase price is to be paid. Keep in mind here that payments can be made, in effect, deductible by the partnership (and ordinary income to deceased's beneficiaries) or nondeductible to the partnership (and capital gain or nontaxable to the beneficiaries)—see ¶1205.2.

(4) Spell out what life insurance is to be acquired, who is to hold it (entity or cross-purchase), the kind of policies to be acquired, how the premium burden is to be shared (where entity insurance is used) and how the policies on the survivors held by the deceased are to be transferred.

(5) Indicate how insurance is to be reflected in the purchase price of a deceased partner's interest. For the considerations involved, see ¶1204.6.

(6) Provide for releasing the estate of the deceased of partnership obligations after the partnership interest of deceased is bought.

(7) Decide where the individual policies will be kept and by whom. Is an escrow agent necessary? Require notice to other partners before any partner can exercise any rights under the policies he holds. Consider use of trustee to hold the policies and carry out the terms of the agreement.

SECTION XIII. THE EMPLOYEE ESTATE

The special problems which must be taken into account in planning an estate for the modern executive are these:

(1) His company plan provides him a major build-up in capital value provided he remains on the job for a long enough time. If he dies before the company's promises are fulfilled, his family will lose this projected capital value.

(2) A substantial part of the estate is likely to be in death benefits or equities in a Keogh plan, individual retirement account, qualified pension, profit-sharing, stock bonus or savings plan which if properly handled can be transferred free of estate tax.

(3) Insurance benefits are likely to make up a large part of the estate, and it may be possible to have these values transferred free of estate tax. We must also be alert to the possibility that maturing insurance values may be needed to pay the estate tax which falls due on nonliquid assets or to conserve the values available to the estate in unexercised stock options.

(4) A large part of the taxable value of the estate may consist of rights to future income, to be realized by the estate and its beneficiaries only over a period of time. This may create a liquidity problem.

(5) A large part of the potential value of the estate may consist of stock options. If these are still unexercised at death, the executor will usually have to exercise them within a specified and limited number of months after death in order to conserve the value of any latent and unrealized appreciation in the stock to which the options apply.

(6) A substantial part of the value of an executive's estate may consist of rights to receive future income which, after the first $5,000, will be subject to income tax on receipt. If these rights to defer compensation go to the executive's widow, they will be subject, after two years, to income tax without benefit of splitting on joint return, unless she remarries. This may bring high income tax rates into play even though the executive's salary no longer swells the family income. These income rights can be more effectively converted to permanent capital for the family if the executive's will directs that they be distributed to a number of taxable entities such as the wife, the children directly or trusts for the wife and children.

(7) The executive's ability to accumulate capital outside the corporation will be impaired by the fact that investment income will be received by him on top of high earned income and thus fall subject to high income tax rates. This suggests the desirability of transferring investment assets to a reversionary trust or, if the executive can afford to part with the capital, to an accumulating trust for his wife and children or directly to his children if this can be done under the state law.

(8) Frequently executives will not be able to take advantage of one of the most effective estate tax saving techniques, that of making lifetime gifts, because most of their assets will somehow be tied in with their corporate employment so that it will not be practicable to make them the subject of a lifetime gift. It may make sense for such an executive to borrow to acquire assets that can be given directly to his family. The assets given to his family can thus be made free of estate tax, and the executive's borrowing will reduce his own taxable estate. Needless to say, this approach must be used with great caution in order to avoid impairing the executive's own personal security and peace of mind.

[¶1301]   WHAT THE EXECUTIVE CAN DO WITH EMPLOYEE TRUST BENEFITS

Amounts accumulated in a Keogh, pension or profit-sharing plan from the employer's contribution pass free of estate tax if made payable to a named beneficiary and the post-death payout does not qualify for lump sum treatment for income tax purposes. They are subject to estate tax if payable to the employee's estate. Estate tax can be skipped for the lives of a husband and wife if benefits are made payable to a trust (either inter vivos or testamentary) which suspends distribution until the next generation.

[¶1302]   HOW EMPLOYER CAN HELP THE EXECUTIVE'S PLANNING

Most corporations have installed plans which help the executive to build an estate within the corporation, or with a qualified employee benefit plan, or both. A contract to pay an executive or his family a stipulated amount after retirement or death or a deferred stock bonus plan are methods of building capital for an executive within the corporation. A company-sponsored and financed group life insurance plan, of course, also builds capital for an executive's family. By installing a qualified Keogh, pension, profit-sharing, stock bonus or thrift plan, a company can contribute pretax dollars for an executive's benefit, have them credited to his account without any personal income tax liability for the executive at that time, and have the investment earnings of the fund accumulate tax free. There is no tax to the executive or his family until the money is taken; then, if it's taken in a lump sum in the year of separation or death, normally only a capital gain tax applies except as to an amount equal to employer contributions for participation after 1973, for which there is a special ten-year forward averaging provision, provided the employee was a plan participant for at least five (5) years before the distribution. Starting in years after 1975, the recipient of the lump sum distribution from qualified plans can elect to treat the entire distribution, including pre-1974 participation, as ordinary income subject to the special ten-year averaging provision. This election could reduce the executive's tax liability by eliminating the potential minimum tax on the untaxed half of the capital gain income. Calculations would have to be made to see if this election would be beneficial.

The executive, on retirement or separation from his employer, can avoid income tax by complying with the special tax free rollover provisions of the law. He is permitted to withdraw his entire interest in a qualified plan without being subject to tax, if he recontributes all of it to another such plan within 60 days after receiving it.

The company which has installed some combination of these plans to build capital for its executives can consider the following modifications or supplementary steps to facilitate the executive's estate planning with respect to the capital which the company promises to accumulate for him:

(1) Equity in a deferred stock bonus plan, a stock option plan which makes additional options become exercisable with each year of service, a qualified Keogh, pension, profit-sharing or thrift plan, or any other plan in which an executive earns benefits with each year of service, will depend on his living to complete his projected service for the company. So, the company might well consider assisting him to underwrite the capital being built up for his family by carrying insurance. If he should die before completing his service, the insurance company will provide some or all of the capital which would otherwise accumulate for him under the plan.

This might be done by carrying group life insurance for the executives or for all employees. (The employee is taxed only on the cost of insurance coverage in excess of $50,000 (IRC §79).) Or a profit-sharing trust could carry insurance on the lives of executives, with the insurance proceeds accruing to their accounts if they die before completing their service. It might be done by the employer carrying a split-dollar insurance program for individual executives—without providing similar nondiscriminatory treatment for a large cross-section of employees, which might make the step too expensive. Under the split-dollar insurance program, the company advances a portion of the insurance premium each year, equal to the annual increase in cash value of the policy. The executive pays the balance. Usually this works out so that the executive pays most of the premiums in the first year, then a declining portion for several years, after which the company puts up all the money. The company as co-beneficiary of the policy will recover its advances from the insurance proceeds when the executive dies. So, the executive's family gets an annually decreasing amount of net protection from the policy unless the face value of the policy is maintained with supplementary term insurance or additional term is acquired with dividends on the policy. Even if the insurance protection does decline each year, the net equity available to the executive's family from accumulating benefits in profit-sharing, deferred stock bonus or other executive pay plans should increase. Thus, a split-dollar insurance program for executives, which would cost the company nothing except the use of the money it ties up in carrying the insurance policy, will underwrite the compensation plan for the family. The tax cost to the employee is minimal. He's taxed only on the value of the benefit received. IRS says this is the difference between the cost of term insurance at his age taken from a Treasury table and the amount he actually lays out (*Rev. Rul. 66-110*, 1966-1 CB 12; *Rev. Rul. 67-154*, 1967-1 CB 11; *Rev. Rul. 74-307*, IRB 1974-26, 11).

(2) When the amount payable to an executive on retirement or to his family on death under a deferred stock bonus has been increased by appreciation in the company's stock, income tax savings may be made available to the executive or his family by amending the plan to provide for distribution over a longer period of time.

[¶1303]   CONFLICT BETWEEN LUMP SUM DISTRIBUTIONS AND THE ESTATE TAX EXCLUSION

If the death benefits from a qualified Keogh or corporate plan are paid so as to qualify as lump sum distributions for income tax purposes, the recipient will receive favorable income tax treatment either under the special ten-year averaging rule or as capital gain, if applicable.

As a general rule, it would appear that receiving a distribution from a qualified plan so that it is considered a lump sum distribution for income tax purposes would result in a greater tax (combining the income and estate) to be paid, than receiving the distributions over a period of more than one calendar year for Keogh or corporate plan. However computations should be made to see if there would be an overall tax saving even if the death benefit is included in the decedent's estate. Especially with the combination of the exemption equivalent of the unified credit and the $250,000 marital deduction (see ¶602.1) many estates will incur little or no federal estate tax, thereby making the savings in income tax more beneficial.

If the death benefits are included in the estate and are subject to income tax, the distribution should qualify as income in respect of decedent (¶1509.6), therefore any estate taxes attributable to the death benefit can be taken as a deduction on the recipient's income tax return. The combination of lower income taxes paid on lump sum distribution and the benefit of deduction for estate tax paid may produce a better result than eliminating the distribution from the taxable estate. For the recipient to have the estate tax as a deduction, the beneficiary of the plan should not be the surviving spouse, so that no part of the plan distribution should qualify for the marital deduction. If the plan distribution qualifies for the marital deduction, there will be no estate tax attributable to the distribution, so no deduction will be available.

[¶1304]   EMPLOYEE STOCK OWNERSHIP PLAN (ESOP)

A special capital building opportunity is available through the use of the Employee Stock Ownership Plan. An ESOP is a qualified stock bonus plan where the employer contributes either cash or stock of the employer company. Just as in receiving accumulated benefits from any employee-benefit trust, there are the same estate tax rules and income tax rules on distribution. However, there is no income tax to the extent distribution consists of appreciation in employer securities. (The unrealized appreciation is subject to tax only if and when the stock is sold by the recipient.)

These provisions grant special flexibility in the distribution of stock of the employer company. Appreciation in employer stock can be taken out free of capital gain tax, at the cost of exposing it to estate tax.

[¶1305]   **DEFERRED COMPENSATION BENEFITS**

There are two main types of deferred compensation contracts now in use. One promises the executive a fixed sum for a term of years subsequent to his retirement or other severance of his employment relationship with the company. This commitment is usually subject to certain contingencies such as the executive's continuing to hold himself available for consulting services and/or refraining from engaging in competitive activities. A contract of this type usually provides that if the executive should die before receiving a stipulated number of payments, payments in the same or a reduced amount will be continued to his wife for a specified period of years or even for the duration of her life. The other main type of deferred compensation agreement is the deferred stock bonus, pursuant to which the corporation contingently credits the stock to the account of the executive each year and also credits him with dividends or an amount in lieu of dividends on the stock previously credited to his account. These accumulated credits are then distributed to him over a period of ten or fifteen years after he terminates his employment with the company. Again the payout of these credits is usually made subject to contingencies with respect to continued consulting and noncompetition. Usually if the executive dies before the stock is fully paid out to him, the company will continue making payments to his widow or other named beneficiaries.

[¶1306]   **WHEN IS SALARY CONTINUATION SUBJECT
TO ESTATE TAX?**

When it is contractual, says the Third Circuit Court of Appeals. An executive of Gimbel Brothers had an employment contract giving him salary of $50,000 a year, plus $6,000 a year for 15 years after he ceased to be an employee by reason of death or otherwise. The company's obligation to make these payments was contingent on his not competing with Gimbels. Any of these payments falling due after his death were to be paid to his estate or to a nominee named in his will. Reversing a District Court, the Third Circuit held that the deceased executive's interest in his employment contract is subject to estate tax at the present value of the right to the remaining payments, his death having extinguished all contingencies and matured a clear property right (*Goodman*, 234 F.2d 264).

But. salary continuation under a revocable plan not carrying any contractual obligation is not subject to estate tax even though the employer pursued and announced a practice of paying salary to the families of deceased employees. Decedent was an employee of Socony Mobil Oil Company. The company had a plan providing that two years' salary would be paid as a death benefit to the designated beneficiary of certain employees. The plan was stated to be noncontractual, and the company reserved the right to revoke it at any time. The decedent had no vested right to the benefit. Accordingly, it was not includible in his gross estate (*Molter Est.*, DC, NY, 146 F. Supp. 497). The IRS is attempting to include these benefits if the employee had the right to change the beneficiary (*Rev. Rul. 76-304*, IRB 1976-32,15).

[¶1307]   **HOW POST-DEATH COMPENSATION
PAYMENTS ARE TAXED**

Payments under a deferred stock bonus, a deferred compensation contract, and other nonqualified salary continuation plans have these income tax attributes:

(1) If they are paid pursuant to a contract between the executive and his employer, they constitute ordinary income when paid to his estate or other beneficiaries. Estate tax attributable to these payments may be deducted from income.

(2) If they are paid voluntarily by the employer, there is a split between the courts as to whether they constitute tax-free gifts or are taxable as additional compensation. Although a majority of the decisions have favored the tax-free-gift status, the question has become a moot one since the Code was amended in 1962 to limit company deductions for such gifts to $25 (IRC §274(b)). And although there's always the $5,000 death benefit income tax exclusion which is not subject to the $25 limit, as a practical matter, most of these post-death distributions to widows will now take the form of payments previously agreed on taxable to the widow and deductible by the company.

(3) The first $5,000 of such payments is tax free under a special exemption provided by IRC §101(b)(2)(A). Where the right to receive these future payments is subject to estate tax, the payments constitute income in respect of a decedent when received; and a pro rata portion of the estate tax, attributable to the right to receive these payments, may be deducted on the income tax return under IRC §691.

The main income-tax-saving opportunity with respect to these payments is to provide by will or otherwise for sprinkling them among as many taxable entities as the family facts and the practicalities justify. In this way, lower income tax rates will apply and a larger portion of the payments can be converted into permanent family capital.

For example, take a 50-year-old executive of a publicly held corporation. He already has about $425,000 of company stock and cash dividend accumulation to his credit under his employer's deferred stock bonus plan. The company has been crediting him with about $28,500 a year. At this rate, with dividend credits compounding at 6% a year, he will have $1,300,000 credited to his account at 65—without any further appreciation in the value of company stock.

Even without further appreciation, if this deferred compensation were paid out over 15 years to the executive's widow (where it would be taxed as ordinary income on top of pension and investment income) without benefit of income-splitting, most of it would be taxed away. However, if we make it payable to several trusts, with only the income to be distributed, we will do a much better job of converting these payments into family capital. Spreading an accumulating stock and cash bonus, which would reach $1,300,000 at 65 as previously described, over a period of time, say 15 years, to a number of trusts arranged for a wife and children instead of paying it directly to a wife will reduce future tax liability and increase family capital.

[¶1308] **PLANNING FOR STOCK OPTIONS**

In a stock option, an executive has an asset which occupies a unique position in the tax structure. It is also a unique kind of financial asset in that while it usually has cost the executive nothing, it may have appreciable value which will require a sizable cash investment if that value is to be realized. These attributes set up two estate planning possibilities with respect to stock options:

(1) The option may be exercised by the purchase of stock during life, presuming, of course, that the value of the stock is adequately in excess of the option price. The executive may be forced to sell valuable assets in order to raise the cash to make the purchase.

(2) To the extent that options are not exercised during life, the executive's will should authorize his executor to exercise those options which were not exercised during life by the executive himself, and his financial program should seek to provide his estate with the cash with which to exercise such options. This can be accomplished by insurance on his life, payable to his estate.

If the stock option is exercised by the executive during his life, the stock itself will become part of his taxable estate. It will be subject to estate tax at its date-of-death value. On the other hand if the executive dies with unexercised stock options, the option itself will be valued at the difference between option price and the value of the stock, plus possibly a small premium to reflect the ability of the executive or his estate to enjoy further appreciation without a cash investment. In short, the estate tax liability will be about the same whether the executive dies with stock acquired pursuant to an option or with the option unexercised.

[¶1308.1]   **Stock Options**

Prior to the Tax Reform Act of 1976, there was special treatment for qualified stock options. Basically the qualified options allowed the executive to buy stock of his employer at discount, without incurring a tax either at the time the option was granted or when it was exercised. When the executive disposes of the stock, he will pay a tax at capital gain rates.

For all stock options issued after May 20, 1976, this special treatment is no longer available, and rules for non-qualified stock options apply. Therefore, the executive must pick up ordinary income (value of the option less amount paid for the option) at the time the option is granted, if the option has a readily ascertainable fair market value. The IRS has taken the position that the option must be publicly traded in order to have a readily ascertainable fair market value. If the option is not publicly traded, the Tax Reform Act of 1976 has given the executive an election to value the option at the time it was granted. If ordinary income is not realized at the time of receipt of the option, then the executive must recognize ordinary income at the time the option is exercised, unless the stock is non-transferable or subject to a risk of forfeiture. The income at this point is the spread between the value of the stock and the option price.

Once the executive recognizes ordinary income either on the grant of the option, or the exercise of the option, when the stock is sold it will be subject to capital gain treatment. However, his basis for the stock will include the ordinary income recognized. In addition, the recognition of ordinary income either on the grant or exercise of the option will be subject to the 50% maximum tax on earned income.

[¶1309]   **POUROVER TRUST TO COORDINATE THE
               EXECUTIVE ESTATE**

The executive with an assortment of assets, those he owns outright and those which come to him from the corporation, has the problem of coordinating them into a coherent pattern and focusing them on his family objectives. One effective method of accomplishing this is to create an inter vivos trust and name it beneficiary in his will and in the beneficiary designations he gives to his insurance companies and to his employer to apply to Keogh, pension, profit-sharing, stock bonus and other deferred compensation rights. (For a discussion of the pourover technique, see ¶615.) Thus, by the terms of this trust, the executive can control how all of these assets are to be accumulated, distributed, and used for his family's benefit. He cannot give a lot of complicated directions to his corporate employer to govern the distribution of group insurance proceeds, pension and profit-sharing death benefits or deferred compensation payments. He could direct that these payments be made to his estate and then, by his will, provide that his executors and testamentary trustees follow his complicated directions. However, with the estate as beneficiary, we lose the estate tax exemption available for pension and profit-sharing death benefits arising out of the employer's contributions when these are made payable to a named beneficiary.

In the pourover trust created during lifetime, we have a named beneficiary and can preserve this death tax exemption. In fact, the use of the pourover trust can avoid the second tax which would be payable on the death of an individual named as beneficiary. If an executive directs his company to make his wife the beneficiary of its contribution to the death benefit, this portion may go to the wife free of estate tax. However, on her subsequent death, this portion will be subject to estate tax. On the other hand, if the executive creates a lifetime trust—which can be revocable until his death, names it the beneficiary to receive Keogh, pension and profit-sharing death benefits (other than in lump sum) and provides that trust income shall be distributed to his wife for life with the corpus going to the children on her death, we have avoided estate tax at the death of the executive's wife as well as that of the executive.

SECTION XIV.   TRUSTS

A trust permits an individual to provide for the continuous, trained and efficient management of the property or securities that he transfers to his beneficiaries either by way of gifts during his lifetime or legacies at his death. This trust feature will protect his property from speculative and mismanagement losses and assure its uninterrupted application to the financial and other purposes to which he wishes to apply it.

A trust is an arrangement whereby one person owns property but holds and manages it for the use of someone else. We have thousands and thousands of trusts for the benefit of employees, charities, and stockholders and for other business purposes. Here we are concerned with personal trusts—those created by individuals for individual beneficiaries.

A personal trust may be testamentary; that is, created by will, or it may be a living trust; that is, created by lifetime transfer. The latter is also known as an inter vivos trust.

A living trust may be revocable or irrevocable. The power to revoke may exist under an infinite variety of limitations and may be made subject to an infinite variety of conditions. In fact, the character and the purposes of trusts are as unlimited as the imagination of persons with property and their legal advisors.

One of our leading trust authorities, Gilbert Stephenson, says that personal trusts are created in order to supply one or more missing elements of ability or those aptitudes essential to the proper care, management and use of property. He lists their essential elements as: physical capacity, mental competence, providence or prudence, maturity, experience, interest in the management of property.

On this level, trusts are provided either to supply management of the trust property for the benefit of the beneficiary or to conserve the trust property for the beneficiaries and to protect them against their own tendency to mismanage, misuse or waste the property which is made the corpus of the trust.

Other common purposes in the establishment of trusts are the prospect of saving income and estate taxes and the desire to take advantage of the ease and privacy of property transfer which is available under the trust arrangement.

In establishing a trust, we may want to protect the trust property against our own indiscretion or against the improvidence of members of our family, or we may want to establish a flexibility with respect to dealing with problems as yet unknown. For example, life insurance proceeds may be made payable to a trust because the trustee can be given a much broader and more flexible discretionary authority as to the distribution of proceeds than any life insurance company would be willing to assume.

[¶1401] **WHY TRUSTS ARE CREATED**

A person may create a trust, having himself in mind as the primary beneficiary, for reasons and purposes such as these:

(1) He may want to obtain investment management and build up an estate by the steady and systematic transfer of his savings to a trust year by year.

(2) He may merely want to free himself from the burden of managing the property. Thus, a trustee may be utilized as a management agent by a person owning property whose only interest is in getting the income from the property.

(3) A businessman may create a trust for the purpose of building up assets entirely apart and separate from his business.

(4) A man going into a risky venture may decide to cushion his personal and family fortunes by transferring to a trust enough property to provide a living income before he makes the speculative plunge.

A man may create a trust for the benefit of members of his family or others for such reasons as these:

(1) To assure his wife an independent income.

(2) To provide his son with an independent income in order to permit him to pursue a career or line of activity which is either not particularly remunerative or would entail excessive financial risk.

(3) To provide a daughter with an income in the event that she should not marry or that a marriage should turn out unsuccessfully (a man may desire to make a gift to his daughter but not want her husband to have use of and access to the gift property).

(4) To provide for his parents or brothers and sisters, by a gift in trust for a variety of reasons including these: (a) he might lack confidence in their own prudence and ability to manage money; (b) he may want to avail himself of the tax advantages in transferring income-producing property to discharge such a responsibility rather than transferring annual chunks of income, which would come first to the transferor to whom it would be taxed in higher income tax brackets; (c) he may want to assure that the income will continue after his death; (d) he may want the fund to be supplied by a trustee rather than by personal gift for reasons of morale and psychological effect on the beneficiary.

(5) Finally, property may be transferred in trust for the purpose of establishing a working relationship between the trustee and the man's ultimate beneficiaries. The man transferring the property gets the opportunity to train and educate both the trustee and his beneficiaries, to see how his property would be managed in his absence and to guide the development of a satisfactory working relationship between those who would manage the property after his death and his beneficiaries.

[¶1402]   TAX SAVINGS AND CAPITAL ACCUMULATIONS THROUGH TRUSTS

The creation of a trust, by lifetime or testamentary transfer, can save taxes and accelerate the accumulation of capital in a variety of ways. These can be combined with each other. They include the following:

(1) Estate tax savings can be achieved by the transfer of property to an irrevocable trust. The transfer of the property to the trust will be a taxable gift, but the future appreciation of the property will be taken out of the estate's highest estate tax bracket.

(2) Annual income tax savings can be achieved by the transfer of income-producing property to a trust in which the income is taxed either to the trust or to the trust beneficiary. This step will transfer income from the top brackets of the settlor to the lower brackets of a trust or beneficiary.

(3) A trust arrangement may utilize the additional exemptions of the trust and the beneficiary to provide tax free income.

(4) Estate tax savings can be achieved by suspending the ownership of property in trust for one generation. For example, where, on death of the estate owner, a non-marital trust is funded with income to the wife for life, then corpus to the children, the estate tax is skipped on the transfer of property from the generation of the spouse to that of the children. There are other estate tax savings if we comply with the generation skipping rules (see ¶1403).

(5) Further estate tax savings result from the fact that the accumulated income of property transferred to a trust is not taxed to the estate of the settlor but accumulates in the trust or in the hands of the beneficiary for the use of the succeeding generation.

(6) Income tax savings can be achieved by the so-called "sprinkling trust," which gives the trustee discretion to distribute trust income among beneficiaries in varying proportions from year to year, depending on their needs. Trust income can be kept out of the higher income tax brackets by giving it to the beneficiaries in lower income brackets, who presumably need it more.

[¶1403]   TAX ON GENERATION-SKIPPING TRANSFERS

Prior to the Tax Reform Act of 1976, it was possible to shelter trust principal from estate tax for several generations. For example, a man creates a trust so the income is paid to his son during his life; on the son's death, the income is paid to grandchildren for life; on the death of the grandchildren, the principal is distributed to great grandchildren. Under the old law, the trust principal was sheltered from estate tax for several generations, as long as the rule against perpetuities was not violated (see ¶1415). The only tax in the above example which had to be paid was a gift tax on the original transfer to the trust and estate tax at the death of the great grandchildren.

[¶1403.1]   Explanation of the Generation-Skipping Transfer

Under the Tax Reform Act, there is a tax on generation-skipping transfers under a trust or trust equivalent whenever there is a distribution of the trust assets to a generation-skipping heir or when an intervening interest in the trust terminates. Trust equivalents include arrangements involving life estates and remainders, estates for years, insurance and annuities and split interests.

A generation-skipping trust is one having beneficiaries of two or more generations younger than the grantor's generation. For example, a man creates a trust so that income goes to his son for life and at the death of the son, the principal goes to the son's child. This is generation-skipping at the death of the son because all beneficiaries are in two or more generations below the grantor's generation. However, in the classical non-marital deduction trust, where the income goes to the wife for life, and on her death the principal goes to the children outright, there is no generation-skipping, because the spouse is considered to be of the same generation as the creator of the trust, regardless of any difference in age. If instead of all the principal of the non-marital trust passing outright to the children, part of the principal on the death of the wife went directly to grandchildren, there still would be no generation-skipping. This is not generation-skipping because the children were not beneficiaries of the same trust in which a distribution was made to grandchildren.

[¶1403.2]   Determination of Generations

(1) Family Members: The grantor's spouse and siblings are considered to be in the same generation as the grantor. Their children are the first younger generation, and their grandchildren are the second younger generation. Spouses of family members are assigned to the same generation as the family member (regardless of any difference in age).

(2) Non-Family Members: (a) Individuals not more than 12½ years younger than the grantor will be assigned the grantor's generation.

(b) Individuals more than 12½ years younger than the grantor, but not more than 37½ years younger, will be assigned to the first generation younger than the grantor.

(c) Each subsequent generation is measured in intervals of 25 years.

[¶1403.3]   Definition of a Beneficiary

A beneficiary is one who has either a present interest, future interest or power in a generation-skipping trust. A person has an interest if he has the right to receive income or principal during the duration of the trust, or a right to receive a distribution upon termination of the trust, or is a permissible recipient of income or principal under a discretionary power exercisable by himself or another. For example, if a trust provided that the income was to be paid for life to the grantor's child, then to the grantor's grandchild, with the principal to be distributed to the great grandchildren, then the child, grandchild and great grandchildren would all be beneficiaries under the trust, since all three generations have a present or future right to receive income or principal. A power is any right to establish or alter beneficial enjoyment of principal or income of the trust. However, an individual would not be treated as holding a power if he is limited to allocating income and principal among lineal descendants of the grantor who belong to a younger generation than the grantor. A power does not include the mere right of investment with respect to the trust property.

[¶1403.4]   Taxable Termination and Taxable Distribution

Upon the occurrence of either a taxable termination or taxable distribution, a generation-skipping tax would occur.

(1) A taxable termination occurs when a present interest or power ends for a younger generation beneficiary who is a generation older than any other younger generation beneficiary (IRC §2613(b)). For example, if the trust provides income to the grantor's child for life or a term of 20 years with the remainder to the grantor's grandchild, a taxable termination will occur upon the child's death or at the end of 20 years because the child belongs to a younger generation than the grantor and an older generation than the grandchild, who is the other beneficiary.

(2) A taxable distribution occurs whenever there is a distribution from a generation-skipping trust, other than a distribution out of current income, to a younger generation beneficiary and there is at least one other younger generation beneficiary who belongs to an older generation than the recipient (IRC §2613(a)). For example, if the trust income goes to a child for life with the remainder over to a grandchild and power to invade the principal for the child or the grandchild, then if any distribution of principal is made to the grandchild during the child's life, it is a taxable distribution. Reason: both child and grandchild are younger than the grantor, but the child is older than the grandchild to whom the distribution is made. The distribution to the child would not be a taxable distribution.

[¶1403.5]   Generation-Skipping Tax

The tax is substantially equivalent to the estate tax which would have been imposed if the property had been transferred outright from one generation to another. The value of the property subject to the generation-skipping transfer is added to the other taxable transfers of the deemed transferor (the parent of the transferee who is most closely related to the grantor). A tentative tax is computed on the total value of these transfers, then the tax on all transfers other than the generation-skipping transfer in question is subtracted. Neither the deemed transferor nor his estate is liable for the tax; it is paid out of the proceeds of the trust property.

[¶1403.6] $250,000 Exclusion

If the transfer is generation-skipping from the child of the grantor to the issue of the child, there is a $250,000 exclusion of property per child from the generation-skipping tax. In order to qualify for this exclusion, the transfer must be from the child of the generation immediately below the grantor to his children in a direct line. Thus, the second generation below the grantor must be the children of that particular child. In addition, the transfer must vest in the grandchildren at the time of termination or distribution, which means they either can get it outright or, if in trust, it must someday vest in them, and if they should die before they get it, it must go to their estate.

[¶1403.7] Effective Date

Generally, the generation-skipping tax will apply to taxable distributions and taxable terminations that occur after April 30, 1976. It does not apply in cases of transfers under irrevocable trusts in existence on April 30, 1976 or under a will or revocable trust in existence on and not amended after that date in such a way to create, or increase the amount of, any generation-skipping transfer, if the grantor dies before 1982.

[¶1403.8] Estate Planning

If any will or revocable trust which is in existence on April 30, 1976, where there is a future generation-skipping transfer, will be subject to tax had it been created after that date, no amendments or additions should be made to that instrument until after 1981, unless you are positive the amendments or changes would not cause a generation-skipping tax to be imposed if the grantor dies before 1982.

Instruments executed after April 30, 1976, may now have to be changed to take advantage of the $250,000 exclusion or to avoid generation-skipping transfer tax by creating separate trusts for separate generations.

[¶1404]   FOUR MAIN TYPES OF TRUSTS

The planner has four basic types of trust arrangements which he can use in his planning work. The ability to recognize which one or more of the four should be recommended in any specific planning situation is essential to a full realization of his client's objectives. A brief description of each of these basic trust arrangements is set out below.

[¶1404.1]   Testamentary Trust

This type of trust is created after an individual's death in accordance with the instructions in his will. While its use will not create any savings at its creator's death or during his lifetime, its use will insulate his property from the otherwise inevitable and successive levies of the estate tax and other death charges as it passes from one beneficiary to another after his death. The elimination of these future charges will create extremely substantial savings for his family.

[¶1404.2]   Irrevocable Living Trust

This type of trust is created by an individual during his lifetime by an irrevocable transfer of property to the trustee. Essential to this type of trust is the feature that its creator retains none of the rights over the trust income or property which would tax the trust income to him during his life or render the trust taxable for estate tax purposes at his death. The gift tax that may be imposed if the transfer exceeds allowed exclusions and unified credit is usually small in relation to the foregoing savings.

[¶1404.3]   Revocable Living Trust

This type of trust is created by an individual during his lifetime. Its principal distinguishing feature is that the creator retains rights over the trust which would permit him to cancel the trust at will and to retake possession of the trust property free of the trust. While this type of trust will not create any personal savings in income or estate taxes for its creator, it will eliminate the estate administration expenses which would otherwise be imposed against the trust property at the trust creator's death and effect savings in the estate tax and other death charges at his beneficiaries' future deaths.

[¶1404.4]   Reverter Trust

This type of trust is created by an individual during his lifetime. Its principal distinguishing features are as follows: (1) The life of the trust is expressly limited to a specified term of ten years or a longer period, or for the life of the beneficiary. (2) At the expiration of the specified period, the trust is automatically cancelled and the trust property is then returned to its creator free of the trust.

This type of trust will effect savings in its creator's income tax liability during its specified term by removing the income from his high bracket and taxing it to the income beneficiary or the trust itself. The creator of the trust may incur a gift tax on the present value of the income gift to the beneficiary to the extent that this value exceeds his annual exclusion.

[¶1405]   **SPECIFIC USES OF TRUSTS**

Apart from tax savings, here are some other needs and purposes which you can fill through a trust. You can provide:

(1) Built-in financial supervision and management safeguards to support your wife and children. Inexperienced and immature beneficiaries present serious planning problems to every individual who wishes to make sure that his property will yield the maximum benefits to his family.

(2) An income to your child until he attains his majority. Few minors have the experience, intelligence and capacity to handle any significant sums wisely. Besides, without a trust, the family would have to go through the "red tape" of appointing a legal guardian to transfer assets or sign agreements on the child's behalf.

(3) Income and principal for your wife and children with the same property at one and the same time.

For example, suppose you want to provide for the support of your wife after your death. But you also wish to combine this objective with the definite assurance that the property will pass to your two children at your wife's death. You can employ a trust arrangement to take on the following pattern:

(a) That the trust income be paid to your wife for life.

(b) That the trust be terminated and the property distributed to the two children in equal shares at your wife's death.

(4) For the passage of property to your blood relatives, i.e., you might want to exclude sons-in-law or daughters-in-law from taking the property if your own kin dies.

(5) Specific property for immediate distribution to a particular beneficiary. Property in a living trust is not involved in the administrative problems of an estate and the beneficiary continues to get the income from the trust when you die.

(6) A tie-up of principal for the benefit of a child for a number of years with periodic payouts at attainment of specified ages—e.g., one part at age 30, a further distribution at age 35 and the balance of the principal at age 40.

(7) Control of and ultimate disposition of your property long after your death. For example, you may not want your wife to have the principal if she remarries. In such event, you can stipulate that the income shall go to her for life with the further proviso that, in the event of her remarriage, the property shall then pass to the children.

(8) Restrictions on the sale of your assets. You can dictate the terms and conditions under which trust property should be sold by spelling out the details in the trust instrument. In that way, you can impress your own objectives and convictions when you're not around to advise.

(9) A temporary surrender of your assets. A short-term trust will permit you to reclaim the property after ten years, at which time you may have need for it.

(10) The disposition of life insurance proceeds to your family other than through lump-sum payments or settlement options of the policy. A trust may be named as beneficiary to reflect your wishes for distribution of the proceeds far better than the inflexible options of an insurance policy.

(11) Management of securities and other property during the period immediately following your death. Without a trust, the executor must assemble the estate assets, supervise the property and distribute it to the heirs—and he may need a court's approval. This can take months. Nor can he properly watch securities in a changing market. These hazards are not present with a living trust since experienced managers are in full command.

(12) Split-management. Through a trust, you can have several people share investment responsibilities. Your beneficiary can be one of them and can call on his co-trustees for guidance. In this way, there is a balance between one who is close to the situation and others who view the picture objectively.

(13) Protection against will contest through a living trust. You may wish to leave money to someone outside your family but not want to arouse any antagonism and hostility in your family. If you make the provision now through a living trust, you avoid a post-mortem feud, because no notice of the transfer will be given to your family or heirs as is required with a testamentary transfer.

[¶1406]   **HOW TO KEEP TRUST INCOME
FROM BEING TAXED TO GRANTOR**

If the grantor keeps no strings on the property transferred or its income, no control over the property or its income or over the administration of the trust, the situation is perfectly clear: The trust is a separate entity for property purposes and for tax purposes. The result is just as if the grantor were suddenly able to split income with another taxpayer, as he may under present law split his income with his wife.

Under the Internal Revenue Code §671-678, the trust income will be included in the grantor's taxable return, not that of the trust or the beneficiary, where the grantor has a reversionary interest, or economic control, or keeps certain administrative powers or the income is or may be used for his financial benefit.

Set forth below are (1) the powers which the grantor will not be allowed to keep if he expects to get the income produced by the trust property out of his own income tax return and (2) some powers that he can keep while still achieving this objective.

[¶1406.1]   **Where Grantor Has Reversionary Interest**

Whenever the duration of a trust is stated to be less than ten years and the grantor may then get the property or its income back, the income will be taxed to the grantor.

The income of an irrevocable trust for a term of years will not be taxed to the grantor if one of these conditions is met: (1) the trust will last for the life of the beneficiary, regardless of his life expectancy, or (2) the trust will last for more than ten years or until the happening of some event which is not expected to occur within a ten-year period, such as the death of the donor or of any other person if the donor or other person has a life expectancy at the date of transfer of at least ten years.

[¶1406.2]   **Where Grantor Has Beneficial Interest**

Under IRC §676-677, trust income will be taxed to the grantor in any of these circumstances:

(1) The grantor, or any person not having a substantial adverse interest in the corpus or income or both of them acting together have the power to revest title to the corpus in the grantor;

(2) The income may be distributed currently to the grantor or grantor's spouse, whether or not it is so distributed;

(3) The income may be held or accumulated for future distribution to the grantor or the grantor's spouse whether or not it is so held or accumulated;

(4) The income may be applied to the payment of premiums on insurance covering the life of the grantor or the grantor's spouse, whether or not it is so applied (policies irrevocably payable to charity are an exception);

(5) The income is actually applied or distributed for the support or maintenance of a beneficiary whom the grantor is legally obligated to support or maintain.

Note that in situations (2), (3) and (4), even the possibility of diversion to the grantor's use is sufficient to tax him. And if the income is not taxed to the grantor for any of the above reasons, it will be taxed either to the trust or to the beneficiary, depending on whether or not it is distributable.

[¶1406.3]   **Some Powers Can Be Retained**

The grantor can retain certain powers without being taxed (IRC §673, 674, Reg. §1.674). These are:

(1) Power (as trustee) to apply income for the support of a dependent—but he will be taxed to the extent he so applies it.

(2) Power to control the beneficial enjoyment of the trust provided this control can't be exercised until after the expiration of a ten-year period; but the grantor will be taxed on the income arising after the ten-year period unless he relinquishes the power.

(3) Power exercisable only by will, other than the power to appoint the income so it could be accumulated for disposition by the grantor without the consent of an adverse party (see Reg. §1.674(b)(1)(3)).

(4) Power to allocate corpus or income among (but not away from) charitable beneficiaries.

(5) Power to distribute corpus (a) to a beneficiary or class of beneficiaries in accordance with a reasonably definite standard (for instance, to meet medical or educational needs) set forth in the trust instrument or (b) to or for any current beneficiary provided such distribution is charged against such beneficiary's proportionate share of the corpus. This doesn't permit a power in any person to add beneficiaries or a class of beneficiaries, except to provide for after-born or after-adopted children.

(6) Power to distribute or accumulate income for a beneficiary provided any accumulated income is ultimately payable (a) to the beneficiary for whom held, his estate, his appointees, or those named as alternate takers in default of appointment or (b) to the current income beneficiaries on termination of the trust or in conjunction with a distribution of corpus (a provision for contingent beneficiaries is O.K. if the date fixed for distribution can reasonably be expected to occur during the lifetime of the primary beneficiaries).

(7) Power to accumulate income during the legal disability or minority of a beneficiary, even though the income becomes a part of corpus which is never distributed to this beneficiary.

(8) Power to allocate receipts and disbursements between income and corpus.

Note that income won't be taxed to the grantor merely because an independent person, neither related to nor subservient to him, can within reason (a) distribute, apportion or accumulate income to or for a beneficiary or class of beneficiaries and (b) pay out corpus to or for a beneficiary or class of beneficiaries. We have an independent trustee so long as not more than half of the trustees are subservient to the grantor.

[¶1406.4]   Reservation of Administrative Powers

Under §675, Reg. §1.675, trust income will be taxed to the grantor if he reserves any of these administrative powers:

(1) Power to purchase, exchange, or otherwise deal with or dispose of the income or corpus for less than adequate consideration.

(2) Power to borrow income or corpus, directly or indirectly, without adequate interest or security, except where a trustee other than the grantor himself is authorized to make loans without interest or security.

Points (1) and (2) apply too where the power is exercisable by a nonadverse party, either with or without the grantor. Where the grantor has borrowed income or corpus and hasn't completely repaid the loan with interest before the beginning of the taxable year, he will be taxed on the trust income unless the loan was made by an independent trustee with adequate interest and security.

(3) Power exercisable by any person without the consent of a fiduciary to (a) vote or direct the voting of stock in a corporation whose voting stock is held in significant amounts by the grantor or trustee, (b) control the investment of trust funds in a corporation in which the trust and grantor have significant

voting control, (c) reacquire trust property by substituting property of equivalent value.

(4) Power to amend which would permit the grantor to have any of the above powers.

[¶1406.5]   Adverse and Related Parties

Power exercisable by a nonadverse, related or subservient party may be attributed to the grantor so as to make him taxable. Similarly, he may be saved from tax by a requirement that his action must be consented to by a substantially adverse party. Here is an explanation of these rules.

An "adverse party" is one with a substantial beneficial interest in the trust which would be adversely affected by the exercise or lack of exercise of a power he possesses respecting the trust.

It is always necessary to determine whether an interest is "substantial" or not. For example, a person having a general power of appointment over the trust property has a substantial beneficial interest and is therefore an adverse party. A trustee, however, is not an adverse party just because he is trustee. A beneficiary of a trust is an adverse party; but if he has only a partial interest, he will be deemed an adverse party only with respect to that part.

A "nonadverse party" is one who does not come within the definition of "adverse party."

A "related" or "subordinate" party is a nonadverse party who is either a close relative (spouse living with grantor, father, mother, issue, brother or sister), employee of the grantor, a corporation or employee of a corporation in which the holdings of the grantor and the trust are significant or a subordinate employee of a corporation in which the grantor is an executive. The theory is that a party who is close to the grantor is subservient to him. However, persons who would otherwise be regarded as related or subordinate may be proven not to be so.

[¶1407]   HOW TO USE A LIFETIME REVERSIONARY
TRUST FOR AN ADULT RELATIVE

The short-term or reverter trust is very often misnamed the ten-year-and-a-day trust. This is because the section of the Code which allows (by indirection) such trusts refers to the ten-year period as the dividing line. Another part of the same section, however, also gives the green light to trusts which will last until the death of the income beneficiary, regardless of what this person's life expectancy is at the date of the trust's creation (IRC §673(c)).

This provision can be used with much effectiveness where it is the estate owner's desire to support a needy relative—say a parent—for the rest of the parent's life. Assume the estate owner has a reasonably substantial amount of income-producing property and is willing to part with this property, its income and the tax thereon during the parent's lifetime. The estate owner wants this property returned after the parent's death, for retirement or other purposes. A lifetime reversionary trust may provide the answer. Consider this example:

Mrs. Pecora, age 66, has been widowed for several years. Her income consists of a $229-a-month widow's benefit from Social Security, $100-a-month under a life insurance settlement option (such amount being guaranteed for another ten years or so), and $100-a-month which her son Fred has been contributing. The total of $429-a-month seems to be adequate to meet Mrs. Pecora's current needs (though this sum may not be adequate during inflationary periods).

Fred, however, is in a top 50% tax bracket. While he has been faring well financially and has been able to set aside a nice investment portfolio, the $100-a-month payout ($1200 annually) actually necessitates his earmarking almost $2400 of his annual earnings to make the payments, and he'd like to cut this down somewhat.

By setting up a lifetime reverter trust for his mother and depositing therein, say, $20,000 in securities yielding 6%, Fred would be giving her the same $1200 a year, while at the same time increasing his own spendable income by some $600. He'll get his securities back when the trust ends (at his mother's death). See ¶902.9 for additional tax costs.

Because of Mrs. Pecora's $1500 personal exemption and the fact that all of her other income is tax free, the $1200 distributed to her each year by the trust is not taxable. Fred is not taxed on any of this income either, since his mother has over $2000 of other annual income and the trust income is not being used for her support. Fred is only giving up $1200 of his pretax income (the income from the securities transferred) instead of $2400. His pretax saving is $1200 a year, approximately $600 (at 6%) after tax.

Note that Fred was at no time contributing more than half of his mother's support and so could not get a $750 dependency exemption. It might make sense in a situation where the son has been getting a dependency exemption to consider foregoing this trust arrangement in favor of the simple approach of purchasing tax-exempt bonds which throw off the same income and then give this income to the mother. She would be in the same no-tax situation, and the son would continue to take the $750 dependency deduction. All this would be without the expense and relative inflexibility of the short-term trust as compared with no trust.

[¶1408]   **APPLYING THE THROWBACK RULE
WHEN ACCUMULATED TRUST INCOME
IS DISTRIBUTED**

To prevent discretionary trusts from accumulating income at low tax rates and distributing such accumulations tax free in subsequent years to high bracket beneficiaries, the 1954 Code introduced the so-called "throwback rule." The throwback rule has been changed by the Tax Reform Act of 1969 and changed again by the Tax Reform Act of 1976.

The purpose of the throwback is to tax the beneficiary when he receives the distribution of accumulated income just as if he had received the income in the years in which it was earned and accumulated. The amount of the distribution in excess of the current year's income will be thrown back to the years in which it was accumulated and taxed to the beneficiary as if he had actually received income in those years. The taxes paid by the trust during the years of accumulation are added to the amounts deemed to have been given to the beneficiary. So as not to overtax the beneficiary, he's allowed a credit for whatever taxes were paid by the trust. However, the beneficiary cannot use this credit against the tax on income other than accumulation distribution, nor can this credit cause him to get a refund of tax which was previously paid by the trust.

There are a number of exclusions to the throwback rule. The following are specifically excluded from the application of the rule: (1) income accumulated for a beneficiary before his birth or before he attains the age of 21 (other than from multiple trusts); (2) capital gains distributed after 1975; (3) distributions not exceeding accounting income; and (4) prior years' accumulations aggregate less than $1000.

[¶1408.1]   **Computing the Beneficiary's Tax**

The accumulation distributions will be includible in the beneficiary's income in the year in which the distribution occurs. The beneficiary must use the following method in computing his tax for distributions after 1975:

Short Cut Method: This method requires the beneficiary to use the average of all accumulated distributions, determined by taking the total accumulated trust distributions divided by the number of years during which the income was earned. This average accumulated distribution is added to the beneficiary's taxable income for each of three of the five years immediately preceding taxable years, excluding the two years in which the beneficiary earned the highest and lowest income. A new tax is then recomputed for each of three years; then the average additional tax for the three-year period is multiplied by the number of years the trust accumulated the income. The result is the tax on the accumulations. Before the beneficiary can determine how much tax is owed, he reduces this amount by the taxes previously paid by the trust on the accumulated income which he is now adding to his taxable income.

[¶1408.2]   **Multiple Trusts**

If a beneficiary receives an accumulated distribution from three or more trusts attributable to the same prior years, the beneficiary cannot reduce his tax liability by the amount of taxes previously paid by the third trust.

[¶1409]   **GAIN ON SALE OF APPRECIATED PROPERTY**
           RECENTLY TRANSFERRED TO TRUST

The Tax Reform Act of 1976, in repealing the capital gain throwback rule, has added a new provision in the law to deter transferring appreciated securities to a trust and then have the trust immediately sell the securities and pay tax at a lower bracket than the grantor. For transfers of appreciated property to a trust after May 25, 1976, where the trust sells the property within two years after the transfer, the "built-in-gain" (the difference between fair market value at date of transfer less the adjusted basis of the property) is subject to tax at the grantor's tax rate.

For appreciated property transferred to an individual, the above rule does not apply. Also, if property which has depreciated in value is transferred to a trust and then the trust sells the depreciated property together with any appreciated property within the two years (thereby trying to have the losses from one property offset the gains from another) only the gains will be recognized. Reason: In determining a loss on sale of property acquired by gift, the basis of the gifted property is the lower of (1) the donor's basis or (2) the fair market value of the property at the time of the transfer. Therefore, the trust, in computing its basis for loss purposes, must use the fair market value at the time of the transfer as its basis (IRC §1015).

[¶1410]   **HOW TO KEEP TRUST PROPERTY**
           OUT OF THE TAXABLE ESTATE

Trust property will be taxed in the grantor's estate if the grantor alone, or in conjunction with another, retains the power to alter, amend, or revoke the trust or to designate who is to enjoy the trust income or corpus (IRC §2038). Retention of even the right to the income is sufficient to tax the grantor's estate.

The grantor's estate is taxed also if the transfer to the trust isn't intended to take effect until his death (IRC §2037). This applies where: (1) possession or enjoyment of the property could be obtained only by surviving the grantor, (2) the grantor has retained a possibility (called "reversionary interest") of regaining the property, having it return to his estate, or having a power of appointment over it, and (3) the value of this "reversionary interest" immediately before the grantor's death exceeded 5% of the value of the entire property (Reg. §20.2037-1).

Property put in a revocable trust remains in the taxable estate. The same thing is true if the grantor does not insist upon such complete control but merely keeps a power to change the terms of the trust or terminate it. It is immaterial whether he holds the power alone or in common with any other person. It is not necessary that the power to alter the terms of the trust be one that may operate in favor of the grantor. Even if he cuts himself off completely from economic benefits for himself but keeps the right to designate who is to enjoy the income or principal, the power has the same effect as if the principal itself were subject to recapture by him for his own benefit.

A grantor who is perfectly willing to forego the power to control the direction of trust benefits may still want to keep certain operative authority. The powers which he is most likely to want to hold are control over investments of the trust and voting rights in those investments. This is especially true if the funding of the trust includes close corporation stock. There are certain other administrative provisions which he may consciously want to retain or which the draftsman may include as part of his general recommendations. These include the right to allocate receipts and disbursements between the principal and income accounts; to set up reserves for depreciation, amortization or waste; to exchange assets and borrow trust funds for adequate collateral. The retention of such administrative powers would not, at first blush, appear to give the grantor any substantial control over who is to enjoy the benefits of the trust. Nevertheless, where the rights retained are numerous, the Internal Revenue Service sometimes contends that the grantor actually had dispositive control in the garb of administrative powers. In *State Street Trust Company*, 263 F.2d 635 (1959), the Court of Appeals in the First Circuit was persuaded that this "bundle of rights" retained by decedent as co-trustee with a bank had adverse estate tax consequences. The Supreme Court in the *Byrum* case (408 U.S. 125 (1972)) has seemingly held that no aggregation of purely administrative powers would amount to sufficient domain and control to be equated with ownership. (Also, see *Old Colony Trust Co.*, 423 F.2d 601 (1970).) However, transfers of stock to an irrevocable trust, after June 22, 1976, where the grantor retained voting rights, will now be included in the grantor's taxable estate. The retention of any voting rights in transferred stock is considered by the Tax Reform Act of 1976 to be a retention of the enjoyment of the stock.

[¶1411]   **HOW A LIVING OR TESTAMENTARY TRUST
CAN PROVIDE CURRENT BENEFITS
FOR BENEFICIARIES**

The trust can provide one or a combination of the following provisions:

(1) The net income of the trust is distributed to the beneficiary at specified intervals.

(2) The beneficiary gets only so much of the income as may be decided upon by the trustee, any balance being accumulated. This is permissible unless the state law prohibits accumulations.

(3) A specified sum is to be paid to the beneficiary at specified intervals, such payments to be made out of income to the extent available, the difference being distributed from principal.

(4) A specified percentage of the trust fund is to be distributed to the beneficiary at specified intervals.

(5) The trustee is authorized to make distributions of principal to the beneficiary as required to maintain previous or specified living standards or to meet educational, health or other emergency requirements.

(6) The beneficiary is authorized to withdraw specified amounts or specified portions of the trust fund at specified intervals.

[¶1412]   **INVASION OF TRUST PRINCIPAL**

Here are some special arrangements which we can set up for the beneficiary's lifetime use of trust principal, together with their effect on the includibility for subsequent death tax purposes in the beneficiary's gross estate:

(1) *Beneficiary has an unlimited right to withdraw all or any part of the trust corpus.* The entire trust corpus would be included in the beneficiary's gross estate (IRC §2041(a)(2)).

(2) *Beneficiary has a noncumulative right to withdraw up to 5% of the trust corpus or $5,000 annually, whichever is greater.* This right will cause the inclusion in the beneficiary's estate of only the amount of the unexercised withdrawal privilege in the year of the beneficiary's death (IRC §2041(b)(2)).

(3) *Beneficiary has a right to withdraw such sums from trust corpus as she deems necessary for her health, support and maintenance.* No part of the trust corpus would be included in the beneficiary's gross estate solely on account of this provision (IRC §2041(b)(1)(A)).

(4) *Beneficiary is to receive a fixed amount of principal each year, these payments to cease upon the beneficiary's death.* No part of the trust corpus would be included in the beneficiary's gross estate solely on account of this provision.

(5) *Beneficiary has no right of withdrawal, but trustee has the power to make payments of principal to the beneficiary for the beneficiary's support and maintenance or for any reason.* No part of the trust corpus would be included in the beneficiary's gross estate solely on account of this provision. (*Note:* Where a provision is made authorizing the trustee to invade principal for the income beneficiary's support and maintenance, sometimes the question comes up as to whether the trustee should take the beneficiary's independent income and/or capital into account. It is wise to make a clear-cut provision covering this in the governing instrument so as to avoid a costly construction suit later on.)

[¶1413]   **WHO GETS TRUST PRINCIPAL AFTER THE DEATH OF THE BENEFICIARY?**

One way to answer this question is to give the income beneficiary (or anybody else, for that matter) the power to appoint trust principal either during his or her lifetime or by will. Another way is to have the governing instrument itself specify when and to whom trust principal is to be distributed following the death of the income beneficiary.

A *power of appointment* can be created so as to put off this ultimate decision until the death of the holder of the power, as where a power is created which is exercisable only by will. The beneficial effect of this is that a final decision is being postponed until a time when more facts are at hand on which to base such decision. The creator of the power does have one important decision to make however: To whom should he entrust the final decision? Usually, it's the beneficiary.

For example, a man has a wife and young children. His will creates trusts. He can foresee what his wife's needs might be, but he can't know for certain what each of his children should eventually have; he doesn't know as yet what each child's financial requirements will be years hence or how each will fare as a money manager. Accordingly, he sets forth in his will the disposition he thinks he would want for the children but gives his wife the power to vary the disposition to the extent she thinks it is warranted by future events. (There should always be alternative provisions to take effect in the event of the holder's failure to exercise the power.)

If the power given is a *general power of appointment* so that the trust principal may be appointed to anybody at all including the holder, such principal will be included in the holder's gross estate whether or not the power is in fact exercised. (A beneficiary's absolute power to invade trust corpus for himself is the equivalent of a general power of appointment exercisable during lifetime.) A general power can be limited so that it can be exercised only by will.

If the right to appoint principal is limited to a certain class of beneficiaries, i.e., children, etc., then we have a *limited* or a *special power of appointment*. Thus, if a power is given to a wife as beneficiary to dispose of the trust corpus at her death only among her and her husband's issue, the trust corpus will not be included in her gross estate on account of this special power.

[¶1414]   **WHEN TO DISTRIBUTE TRUST CAPITAL**

To avoid the inadvertent exercise of a power of appointment, the instrument creating it should provide that it can be exercised only by explicit reference to the power and the instrument creating it.

The question of how long (apart from the perpetuities problem) and how much trust capital should be tied up in trust is one of personal and investment philosophy. There seems to be more reason for tying up trust capital for the life of a woman than for a man, and more reason to give a man a chance to work with and use some of the capital. There is much to be said for staggered distribution of trust corpus, i.e., one-third at age 25, one-third at age 30 and one-third at age 35. The concept here is that the beneficiary will not get the opportunity to squander all the money at once; and possibly, if he loses the first installment, he will have learned enough to make more prudent use of subsequent installments.

[¶1415]   **RULE AGAINST PERPETUITIES**

Many testators have a confirmed desire to control their estates in perpetuity from the grave. Thus the intentions of the testator frequently conflict with the so-called rule against perpetuities. The common law rule against perpetuities is measured by lives in being, plus 21 years. Currently, all states (except Wisconsin and Idaho) have some rule against perpetuities which limits the duration of a trust. The rules of different states are not completely uniform. The able draftsman is invariably alert to this problem and recognizes it immediately. He has his checks and tests which he applies to a proposed trust. He considers the legality of the period of suspension of the power of alienation, whether the final vesting of the remainder will be too remote and whether there will be an unlawful accumulation. The pitfalls and dangers, which vary under different state laws, are too numerous for generalization, but the warning sign is up whenever a trust is created by the exercise of a power of appointment or when one trust falls into another.

SECTION XV.   TRUST AND ESTATE ADMINISTRATION

To complete a sound estate plan, we must do more than maximize the net estate which will become available to beneficiaries and develop arrangements which will most effectively make that net estate available for family purposes. We must also make a sound choice as to who executes the plan.

Many people assume that careful selection of fiduciaries is important only for large estates, that the opportunities and dangers increase with the amount of property. Actually, the basic beneficiary needs are the same regardless of the size of the estate. And while poor management of the large estate may produce larger losses—there being more property involved—the beneficiary of the small estate will be the one who can least afford any loss.

[¶1501]   **CHOICE OF FIDUCIARIES**

Here is a rundown of the factors to be considered in the estate planner's choice of fiduciaries—the executor, the trustee, the guardian.

[¶1501.1]   The Qualities a Fiduciary Must Have

(1) Integrity: This might be termed the one indispensable ingredient of a good fiduciary. If you can't rely implicitly on his loyalty and honesty in carrying out your wishes, then the purpose of your careful estate planning may be defeated.

(2) Responsibility: This is companion to the quality of integrity. By years of labor and planning, the estate owner presumably has built up what he considers adequate provision for the support and comfort of his family. But his labors can come to naught if his estate is dissipated through irresponsible management after his death.

(3) Experience: The kind of experience we will look for in our fiduciary will depend, at least in part, on the type of assets that constitute the bulk of the estate. A businessman may be called for if there is a business to be continued, liquidated or sold. Where there are large real estate holdings, you want a man who has managed or owned real estate. An investment counselor may recommend himself to an estate consisting largely of stock and bond holdings.

(4) Sympathy: An estate is "property" only in a limited sense. More broadly, it is a means for taking care of the needs and wants of beneficiaries. Unless a fiduciary can provide sympathy and understanding for the beneficiaries, he will not be able to fully meet these needs and wants.

(5) Availability: To determine the availability of a candidate for a fiduciary role, we must answer two questions: (a) Will he be around enough? (b) Will he be around at all? A fiduciary whose business or profession keeps him traveling a lot may not always be on hand to attend to important matters as they arise or to meet developing emergencies. And a man who is older than the estate owner may not be alive to serve at all. Or, if he is alive, he may be living in retirement, too far out of touch with everyday affairs to be suitable for the estate's needs.

(6) Willingness: Even if the man we want has all the above qualities, they will not help if he is unwilling to accept appointment. Therefore, the first step is to find out whether the man we want is willing to serve.

[¶1501.2]   Individual or Corporate Fiduciary

The most compelling reason for naming an individual as fiduciary is the feeling that a particular individual has special knowledge, special experience, special familiarity and special understanding of the problems and needs of the estate owner's business and family. You may think that a corporate fiduciary will be timid and over-conservative with respect to your business affairs. You may find it difficult to visualize a financial organization serving in the role of parent toward your children.

Most individuals do not have enough financial responsibility to protect the beneficiaries from the financial loss that may result from mishandling. As a gesture of confidence to the individuals named in a fiduciary capacity, many wills direct that the posting of a surety bond be waived. Few individuals have the sheer administrative facilities to handle an estate systematically and properly.

The arguments for a corporate executor-trustee may be summed up as follows:

(1) It specializes in the handling of estates; the individual does not. It can give full time and attention to the estate; the individual will be distracted by his own business and personal affairs.

(2) It is experienced and responsible. Its work represents the combined knowledge and judgment of many seasoned men.

(3) It has information and experience which enable it to manage property so as to conserve the full value for the benefit of the heirs.

(4) It is fair, impartial and obedient to the directions of the will and trust instrument. The individual often finds it hard to handle the delicate situations that frequently arise in which personal wants and discretionary powers are involved.

(5) It takes over the affairs of an estate or trust as a matter of business. A friend or relative usually is not conversant with such details and finds them a burden.

(6) It never dies; the individual does, often with his work unfinished.

Do the personal interest in the welfare of the heirs, personal knowledge of the testator's business and personal concentration that a particular individual can bring to the administration of an estate and trust outweigh the greater experience, superior facilities and assured impartiality of the corporation? This is something for the testator to decide, bearing in mind that death may deprive him of the qualities sought in the selection of the individual while he can be reasonably sure a corporation will endure.

When a trust is involved, the setting up of the trust under the will furnishes a compelling argument for the naming of a corporate fiduciary as both executor and trustee. Administration will be more sound and orderly if the party who administers the property as an estate continues administering it after it has gone into the trust. The trustee's job is largely the day-to-day exercise of business judgment in managing the assets of the trust and making changes in the investments needed to maintain principal values and produce adequate income.

Because of its greater experience, wider access to information and superior facilities, a corporate fiduciary is better suited than an individual to the carrying out of trustee duties. Even if the individual selected has the necessary business judgment and knowledge to do the job properly today, it isn't likely the testator could count on these qualities being available throughout the life of the trust.

[¶1501.3] Individual and Corporate Fiduciaries Serving Jointly

The problem of whether to choose an individual or corporate fiduciary may be solved by choosing both. A combination of an experienced corporate fiduciary and a relative or friend, acting together, may be preferable to either one, acting alone. Even if the friend or relative is qualified to do the job alone, he may be unwilling to take on sole responsibility. He may be willing, however, to serve jointly with a corporate fiduciary better equipped than he to discharge the administrative burdens and with which he can share the responsibilities.

The combination can work very well in some cases, with the corporate fiduciary furnishing the experience and necessary facilities and the individual contributing insight into the workings of the estate owner's mind. A corporate fiduciary will seldom be as well equipped as an intimate family friend or relative for "reading between the lines" of the will or trust to discover what motivated the estate owner in granting a particular discretion and how he intended it to be exercised. There may be personal or business reasons why he chose to cover the matter in a discretionary provision, rather than by express direction.

In this case, appointment of the individual as co-executor and/or trustee will give the estate owner assurance that his true wishes will be fulfilled.

[¶1501.4] Risks in Naming Co-Fiduciaries

The naming of a co-fiduciary, however, may have certain disadvantages. For one thing, it means extra expense, since there will be two fees instead of one. There is also the danger that disagreement between the fiduciaries may mean delay in making necessary decisions; administration may be made more cumbersome.

All things considered, it will probably be better not to appoint two fiduciaries if the objective sought can be achieved some other way. In deciding this point, the estate owner might ask himself these questions:

(1) For the settlement of my estate and the subsequent management of my property, do I need more than one fiduciary?

(2) If so, what do I expect the two fiduciaries to accomplish that one acting alone could not accomplish as well?

(3) If I name more than one fiduciary, do I want them to act jointly on everything connected with my estate, or do I want one of them to do certain things and the others to do other things?

(4) If I have in mind special duties for each of them, shall I state the duties and powers of each of them separately, so that each may know what is his part in the handling of the estate?

(5) What provision shall I make for the compensation of each, so that each will be paid adequately and fairly for the services he renders?

(6) Is there any arrangement other than joint fiduciaries—such as advisers to the sole fiduciary or separate fiduciaries—that will accomplish what I have in mind better than joint fiduciaries?

[¶1501.5]   Use of an Adviser or Separate Fiduciary

As suggested by the last of the above questions, the problem may be solved by naming an individual adviser to the corporate fiduciary or a separate fiduciary for a special situation.

For example, the estate may include one or two assets that require management and eventual liquidation. Perhaps there is some one person who possesses the judgment, information or special skills that would be peculiarly suitable for this task but who is either unavailable or not generally qualified for official appointment as fiduciary. This person might be appointed as an adviser to deal with this asset or direct the fiduciary in dealing with it.

Since the intention is to fix the responsibility in this special situation on the adviser or special fiduciary, the general fiduciary should be expressly relieved of responsibility for failure to act in the absence of the required approval or direction or for the consequences of actions taken pursuant to any direction required by the instrument.

[¶1501.6]   Successor Fiduciaries

A sufficient number of persons should be named in the instrument to insure that there will always be a named person or corporation to act as fiduciary. If this is not done, provision should be made in the instrument for others to make the necessary nomination. Otherwise, the court will fill the gap.

The need for a successor arises in the event of death, resignation or refusal or inability of the original fiduciary to act. Where a corporate fiduciary is named either originally or as a successor, the problem is simplified, assuming its officers have been consulted before nomination and have agreed to have the corporation act. In naming individuals, even though there is to be but one acting at a time, due consideration must be given to the anticipated length of the period of administration, life expectancies, physical condition and willingness and ability to serve.

Thus, the problem is not merely to select a fiduciary, but also a number of successors, all of whom should be chosen with the same care and by the same standards as the original fiduciary. If a third person is to be given the power to name a successor to fill a vacancy, care should be taken in selecting the person who is to be vested with such power. Court nominations have their good points and shortcomings, varying in different jurisdictions, but should be avoided where possible, if only to minimize expenses.

[¶1502]   **THE ATTORNEY FOR THE ESTATE**

Generally, the executor has full freedom to choose his own attorney. The testator can suggest but cannot direct the selection. The executor will, however, usually respect the wishes of the testator. All things being equal, most trust companies will select the attorney who prepared the will. Nevertheless, if the testator believes the retention of a certain attorney will be beneficial to the estate—for example, a personal attorney who is fully familiar with his business and personal affairs—he should express this preference in the will.

[¶1503]   **PROBATING THE WILL**

The actual probate of the will, as distinguished from the entire process known as estate administration, is a relatively simple yet detailed procedure involving strict compliance with local law requirements.

Most states allow for at least two forms of probate: (1) probate in common form; (2) probate in solemn form. A will is probated in common form when it is presented to the appropriate court together with testimony from the witnesses as to its execution. Probate in solemn form is a much more formal matter. The will, together with a petition for probate, is filed. A date is arranged for a formal hearing on the petition. All interested persons are served and made parties to the probate. Arguments are heard for and, if any, against the admission of the will to probate. Then (sometimes after a jury has been given the opportunity of determining the facts), the surrogate enters the judgment for or against probate.

It is much easier at a later date to successfully contest a will that had been probated in common form. The reason is obvious: Where the will is offered for probate in solemn form, any objections would normally be brought out right then and there and all issues of fact and law determined at the probate proceedings. In a later will contest, the judge may rightfully inquire as to why these objections were not raised when the will was offered for probate in solemn form.

Where permitted, it is customary to offer a will for probate in common form where you are pretty certain that there will be no contest or any other difficulties. However, when a contest or other problems seem likely to arise, solemn form probate should be used. A number of states have other alternatives, some of which offer a compromise between common form and solemn form probate. In fact, it is often possible by family settlement contract to dispense entirely with probate where all the persons interested in the will or estate agree on a distribution different from that provided in the will.

The checklist below not only serves as a reminder of the steps to be taken in the actual probate of the will, but also of other steps which are usually taken through the time when the will is actually probated and the executor is appointed to take over officially the very detailed task of estate administration.

[¶1504]   **PROBATE CHECKLIST**

We have attempted to list the steps in their approximate order of occurrence in a typical estate. In all cases, of course, it will be necessary to check local law and practice to determine the precise steps to be taken in will probate and the various time limits and statutory waiting periods in the different jurisdictions:

(1) Notify banks where decedent had accounts and obtain data on them.

(2) Arrange for the collection and custody of decedent's personal property.

(3) Check insurance coverages on all of decedent's property.

(4) Investigate all of decedent's brokerage accounts.

(5) Make a preliminary estimate of the decedent's estate to determine what form the probate and the administration of the estate will take.

(6) Have additional copies of the will made for beneficiaries, taxing authorities, personal representatives, etc.

(7) List contents of decedent's safe-deposit box, if any, in the presence of member of the decedent's family and taxing authorities.

(8) Hold preliminary conference with family members and others named in will for the purpose of reading the will and determining whether there will be any objections or renunciations.

(9) Hold conference with decedent's personal representative(s) for the purpose of getting all the details needed for the preparation of the petition for probate.

(10) Make arrangements with the post office for custody of decedent's mail.

(11) File will and petition with probate court.

(12) Make copies of petition available to executor and taxing authorities,

accompanied by affidavit as to the total property affected by the will and the amounts going to the beneficiaries, together with their relationships to the decedent.

(13) Obtain copies of death certificate (as many as possible).

(14) Assist beneficiaries in collection of life insurance proceeds, obtaining necessary Treasury forms from insurance companies.

(15) Collect decedent's unpaid wages, salary or commissions.

(16) Inquire as to exact benefits due from company pension and/or profit-sharing plans and other company programs and from union or association benefit programs.

(17) Change automobile registration if in decedent's name.

(18) If decedent was a businessman, check for business continuation agreements, etc.

(19) Arrange for continued collection of loans, rents, interest, dividends, royalties, etc., and try to collect delinquent debts.

(20) Mail notice of hearing on petition together with order limiting time to file claims (all in accordance with local law requirements).

(21) Arrange for publication of order for hearing (in accordance with local law).

(22) File affidavit of mailing of notice of hearing (in accordance with local law requirements).

(23) Send copies of will and preliminary estimate of estate to appropriate heirs.

(24) Arrange for ancillary administration if necessary.

(25) Collect all pertinent information for income tax returns.

(26) If decedent was sole proprietor of a business, determine if there is an outstanding obligation for employer's tax.

(27) Collect all amounts due from retirement plans, etc.

(28) File Social Security claims.

(29) File VA claims if any.

(30) Arrange for witnesses to appear at hearing, obtaining written depositions if necessary.

(31) Send copy of will to widow and minor children, if not already done, and notify them as to their rights and advise them as to tax considerations.

(32) File affidavit of mailing of notice of widow's and children's rights (as required by local law).

(33) Assemble data on all nonprobate property (joint tenancy property, life insurance, living trusts, property subject to a power in the decedent, etc.).

(34) Inquire into all gifts above $3000 per donee made by the decedent within three years of his death and all transfers made in trust at any time.

(35) Make inquiry as to requirements for fiduciary bond, discuss it with named executor, and prepare application therefore, if necessary.

(36) Prepare executor's form of acceptance.

(37) Attend formal court hearing on petition for probate with witnesses and any required written testimony.

(38) File acceptance by executor.

(39) File fiduciary bond if required.

(40) Obtain certified copies of letters testamentary.

(41) To limit appeal time, serve copy of order on petition to interested parties.

(42) Have appraisers appointed, unless estate consists entirely of cash.

(43) Notify post office, banks, and others of executor's appointment.

[¶1505]   **DUTIES OF FIDUCIARIES**

An executor's duties are more circumscribed than those of a trustee, and usually of much shorter duration.

With the acceleration, beginning in 1971, of the due date for the federal estate tax return from fifteen months to nine months after death and elimination of most moderate estates filing federal estate tax form, there will be more pressure to close out estates within a relatively short period of time.

¶1505.1]   **Executor's Duties**

From the point at which the Probate Checklist at ¶1504 leaves off (right after the probate of the will) until the final distribution of the estate, we can, depending upon the nature of the estate, comprise a checklist of as many as 100 or more additional detailed steps to be taken by the executor (aided by the attorney).

Reaching back into the probate and pre-probate period as well as the post-probate period, the executor's overall duties generally encompass the following:

(1) The collection and conservation of the personal property of the estate. (Real property usually vests immediately in the devisees, with the executor being able to sell such property only in the event that personal property is inadequate to meet claims, etc.)

(2) The payment of all valid debts, including fees and expenses incurred in administration, death taxes, income and other taxes owed by the decedent, etc.

(3) The distribution of whatever property remains in accordance with the testator's wishes.

Intermeshed with these three overall duties may be any number of detailed duties which must be performed if these major functions are to be accomplished.

Such duties as the executor has are to be ascertained not only from the terms of the will, but also, except to the extent that the testator can and does decree otherwise, by reference to the statutes and case law of the state whose law governs the operation of the will. (This, of course, is also true for an administrator of interstate property, except that all his duties arise from local law.) An example of a duty sometimes imposed on an executor by operation of law is the duty to make unproductive assets productive when there is to be a relatively lengthy delay before distribution can be made.

[¶1505.2] **Trustee's Duties**

The duties outlined below are the usual duties of a testamentary trustee, although they might just as well apply to a trustee under a living trust. A testamentary trustee's duties begin at the point where the executor's duties leave off. Although state law may impose certain duties and restrictions on a trustee, particularly a testamentary trustee, most of his duties are derived from provisions in the testator's will. To a great extent, they overlap what is known as the "trustee's powers." The trustee's duties include:

(1) Taking possession and control of the trust property.

(2) Investing and reinvesting such property prudently for the production of income.

(3) Paying all necessary taxes and other reasonable expenses of trust administration.

(4) Exercising all mandatory directions recited in the governing instrument, except those which are impossible of fulfillment.

(5) Exercising any discretionary duties with "discretion" and impartiality.

(6) Keeping records and rendering accounts when required.

(7) Paying income (and principal, maybe) to those entitled to it.

(8) Refraining from dealing with the trust property personally and from commingling such property with its own.

(9) Refraining from delegating any of the above duties to others except to the extent permitted by the governing instrument or by local law.

[¶1506] **TAX DUTIES OF FIDUCIARIES**

Death of a decedent or the setting up of a trust creates a new taxpayer. The responsibility for filing the returns, paying the taxes and carrying out the other tax duties falls on the executor or trustee, as the case may be. The executor or trustee is more than just an agent in the carrying out of these duties; he acts in his capacity as a fiduciary taxpayer.

The duty to discharge the tax liability may be particularly onerous. For although normally the fiduciary is responsible for paying out only the funds entrusted to him as a fiduciary, in some cases he can become personally liable for the taxes.

[¶1506.1]   **Tax Returns**

The fiduciary must prepare and file not only the federal tax returns, but also those required by state and local authorities. Timely filing is important; valuable elections, such as the choice of the optional valuation date for the federal estate tax return, can be lost through failing to file on time (IRC §2032). Failure to file properly where penalties are provided may result in the fiduciary being personally surcharged.

[¶1506.2]   **Estate Tax Return**

The estate tax return, Form 706, must be filed within nine months after the date of death of a decedent. See ¶507 for filing requirements. A one-year extension may be granted. The tax return is to be filed with Internal Revenue Service Centers as follows:

Philadelphia, Pennsylvania, for decedents domiciled in Delaware, District of Columbia, Maryland, Pennsylvania;

Chamblee, Georgia, for Alabama, Florida, Georgia, Mississippi, South Carolina;

Cincinnati, Ohio, for Michigan, Ohio;

Austin, Texas, for Arkansas, Kansas, Louisiana, New Mexico, Oklahoma, Texas;

Ogden, Utah, for Alaska, Arizona, Colorado, Idaho, Minnesota, Montana, Nebraska, Nevada, North Dakota, Oregon, South Dakota, Utah, Washington, Wyoming;

Kansas City, Missouri, for Illinois, Iowa, Missouri, Wisconsin;

Andover, Massachusetts, for Connecticut, Maine, Massachusetts, New Hampshire, Rhode Island, Vermont, and New York except for New York City and its adjacent counties as listed below.

Holtsville, New York, for New Jersey and New York City and the surrounding counties of Nassau, Rockland, Suffolk and Westchester.

Fresno, California, for California and Hawaii.

Memphis, Tennessee, for Indiana, Kentucky, North Carolina, Tennessee, Virginia, West Virginia.

A nonresident files with the Director of International Operations, Internal Revenue Service, Washington, D.C. 20225.

Certain U.S. Treasury Bonds may be redeemed at par, even if they are selling below par, in payment of federal estate tax. See page T-32 for a further explanation of these useful bonds and a list of the available issues.

[¶1506.3]   **Income Tax Return of Estate**

If the estate has $600 or more of gross income, it must file a return on Form 1041 (IRC §6012(a)(3)). If there is a nonresident beneficiary, the return is required regardless of the amount of gross income. For purposes of filing, a taxable year for the estate must be selected. This need not be a calendar year and need not coincide with the date of death. It may be advantageous to use a short taxable year for the estate's initial return. Bearing in mind that the tax interests of the beneficiaries must be considered, the choice of a fiscal year may help split the income and thus reduce the tax.

The return must be filed by the middle of the fourth month following the end of the tax year (IRC §6072; estates and trusts can pay the tax quarterly (IRC §6152(a)(2)). It may be advisable to complete the return early to be able to give advance notification to distributees of the amounts they must include in their own returns.

[¶1506.4] Decedent's Income Tax Returns

The executor must also file the decedent's final income tax return on Form 1040 and, if necessary, delinquent returns for prior years. If death occurred between January 1 and April 15, there will generally be two returns to file, assuming decedent was on a calendar-year basis.

The decedent's return is a tougher proposition for the executor than the estate's return. He has the information for the latter; but unless decedent was the unusual taxpayer who keeps detailed records of such things as deductions, the executor may have to resort to making an estimate under the difficult-to-apply *Cohan* (39 F.2d 540) rule.

A joint return may be filed for a married decedent for the year of death, unless the surviving spouse should remarry before the close of the tax year or the decedent or the surviving spouse had a short tax year caused by a change of accounting period (IRC §6013(a)). Liability for the full tax in such cases is joint and several (IRC §6013(d)). Where the decedent's income was less than that of the surviving spouse and the latter isn't the sole beneficiary, the executor's consent to a joint return, without limiting the estate's liability, may expose him to a surcharge.

The surviving spouse may file a joint return if no executor has been appointed by the time the return is due. If the executor qualifies within a year after the due date (including any extensions for filing), he may disaffirm the joint return by filing a separate return within the one-year period (IRC §6013(a)). This rule protects the estate in the event the surviving spouse files a return that is detrimental to the estate; it will be up to the executor to disaffirm unless the estate is fully indemnified.

[¶1506.5] Declaration of Estimated Tax

Estates and trusts are specifically exempted from the requirement of filing estimated returns (IRC §6015); the estate isn't liable for the decedent's unpaid installments on his own estimate. The surviving spouse is liable for unpaid installments on a joint declaration; if she files an amended separate declaration, the credit for prior payments made on the joint declaration will be divided between the estate and the surviving spouse.

[¶1506.6]   **Withholding Tax**

Withholding for income tax and Social Security is required of estates and trusts who are employers; before making specified payments to a nonresident alien, the estate must deduct 30% tax (IRC §1441).

[¶1506.7]   **Information Returns**

Fiduciaries, like other persons, are required to file information returns (Forms 1096 and 1099) when paying $600 or more of income in any calendar year (IRC §6041). The fiduciary must report payments by both the decedent and the estate. This doesn't mean payments to distributees, for which the fiduciary tax return serves also as an information return.

[¶1506.8]   **Gift Tax Return Filed by Executor**

The executor should review the decedent's entire lifetime givings; a gift tax return may have been required (Form 709) even though no gift tax was payable. If there is doubt about the necessity to file, the executor should probably file anyway in order to start the Statute of Limitations running. The executor should always seek the surviving spouse's consent to have half the decedent's gifts attributed to her under IRC §1000 (f), so as to reduce any gift tax payable by the estate. Where it is the spouse who made the gifts, some thought would be required before giving consent to have half attributed to the decedent.

[¶1506.9]   **Notice of Trust Relationship**

Notice requirements for a trust are the same as for an estate, except that no preliminary notice is required.

[¶1506.10]   **Income Tax Return of Trust**

The trustee (whether the trust is testamentary or inter vivos) must file an income tax return (Form 1041) for any year where the trust has any taxable income or has gross income of $600 or more (IRC §6012(a)(4)). The principles governing the determination of an individual's income tax apply also to estates and trusts.

As with estates, the choice of fiscal year and method of accounting may be significant in determining the total tax impact on the ultimate beneficiaries. Remember too that there is a relationship between the amount of income taxed to the beneficiary and the amount taxed to the trust. To the extent the income is distributed and taxed to the beneficiary, the trust has a deduction; this provides a good opportunity to cut the total tax by some prior planning.

[¶1506.11]   **Estimated Tax, Withholding and Information Returns**

The rules for all these are the same for trusts as for estates.

[¶1507]   **PERSONAL LIABILITY OF FIDUCIARIES**

An executor or administrator who pays a due debt of the person or estate for whom he acts before he pays the federal tax liabilities becomes personally liable for any such taxes that remain unpaid (§3467 US Rev. Stat.). For purposes of applying this rule to estate taxes, the distribution of any portion of the estate to the beneficiaries is deemed payment of a debt. The rule making the executor personally liable applies only where the Treasury has a priority as a creditor against the estate's assets (§3466 US Rev. Stat.). Thus, funeral expenses and widow's allowances, to cite examples, could be paid with impunity by the administrator of even an insolvent estate, since these items have priority over *all* other debts.

Whether or not the executor is personally liable with respect to income tax liability, he is responsible for paying these taxes in his representative capacity. There is no doubt that he would be personally liable if the income taxes in question were those owed by the decedent and not those of the estate and he used up the estate's assets to satisfy other obligations. To protect himself, the executor would be wise to check not only the decedent's prior returns, but also all the decedent's transactions that might have produced income but weren't reported on his returns. The check should go back beyond the Statute of Limitations, since it is always possible the decedent committed fraud, for which there is no limiting period.

[¶1507.1]   **What Protection Has the Fiduciary?**

Although the possibility of personal liability is a serious problem for the fiduciary, he is not without protection. For example, unpaid gift taxes aren't likely to be charged against him, since the tax follows the gift and can be satisfied out of the gift property. Even if the donee has parted with the property, the fiduciary is still safe, since the gift tax then becomes a lien against the donee's other property. The fiduciary may be in some danger when the gift is in trust; because of the difficulty in reaching the beneficiaries, the Treasury may contend the trustee is to be treated as the donee.

With respect to the estate tax, the executor can ascertain the amount of estate tax due by making written request to the Commissioner. The latter must notify the executor of the amount within one year; if the executor pays this amount, he is entitled to a written discharge from personal liability (IRC §2204). Unfortunately, there is no such relief for the fiduciary with respect to income and gift taxes, although, as we have seen, this doesn't matter too much in the case of gift taxes.

There is a time limit on this personal threat to the fiduciary. Under the Code, any assessment against the fiduciary personally must be made not later than one year after the liability arises or not later than the expiration of the period for collection of the tax in respect of which the liability arises, whichever is later (IRC §6901(c)(3)). This is in addition to the Commissioner's six-year period within which he is permitted to collect a validly assessed tax.

Enforcement of personal liability against the fiduciary is made by the same processes (jeopardy assessment, distraint, etc.) and is subject to the same restrictions (90-day letter, etc.) as any other tax collection.

[¶1507.2] Transferee Liability

In addition to his representative and personal responsibilities, the fiduciary is also subject to transferee liability the same as any other taxpayer. (See IRC §6901(h).)

[¶1508]   INVESTMENT AUTHORITY AND POLICY FOR FIDUCIARIES

The general rule with respect to the duties of a fiduciary in investing funds entrusted to his care is that he is under a duty to the beneficiary:

(1) To conform to the terms of the governing instrument, if any;

(2) In the absence of provisions in the terms of the governing instrument, to conform to the statutes, if any;

(3) *In the absence of provisions in the terms of the governing instrument or of a statute otherwise providing,* to make such investments and only such investments as a *prudent man* would make of his own property having primarily in view the preservation of the estate and amount and regularity of the income to be derived.

The rule stated in this section is known as the prudent-man rule or the Massachusetts rule (see ¶1508.1). It is followed in most states by statute or by virtue of judicial decision.

A less liberal approach to the investment powers of a fiduciary is characterized as the legal-list rule, which limits fiduciaries to bonds or other forms of fixed income investment exclusively.

Some states have a modified prudent-man rule which generally permits discretionary investments by a trustee up to a stated percentage of the fund or expressly allows investments in common stocks under prescribed conditions or standards.

In the past twenty years there has been a decided movement in the direction of liberalizing fiduciary investment restrictions, and the majority of states which have adopted the prudent-man rule by statute or case law have done so since 1940. The prudent-man rule for fiduciary investments is currently the law in 31 states.

Some of the statutes are applicable only to banks and trust companies, some to all trustees and others to all fiduciaries. It is expressly provided in some of the statutes that where the terms of the governing instrument enlarge or restrict the investments which a fiduciary may make, these terms are controlling. In a number of the statutes, it is expressly provided that the statute shall not be construed as restricting the power of a court to permit a fiduciary to deviate from the terms of the instrument. In connection with the propriety of an investment, it is determined by the terms of the statute in force at the time the investment is made, not by the law in force at the time the governing instrument became effective.

[¶1508.1]   Duties of the Trustee in Investment of Trust Funds

The trustee's duty is to preserve the corpus of the trust and make it produce income. In general, it is his duty to invest trust funds in such a way as to receive an income without any improper risk of loss to the principal.

No definite standard can be established as to what constitutes proper trust investments. The trustee is regulated by the terms of the trust instrument, by statute and by court rules. With respect to the latter, certain principles can be set forth which the courts rely on in determining whether or not an investment is proper.

The only general rule continually used as a guide is the prudent-man rule. The rule involves three basic duties imposed on the trustee; namely, care, skill and caution. He must exercise a reasonable degree of *care* in the selection of investments, a reasonable degree of *skill* in making the selection and that degree of *caution* which a prudent man would employ where the fundamental consideration is the preservation of the funds invested. The standard fixed for the conduct of the trustee is an objective one and it is not sufficient that he invest the trust property in the same manner as he would his own property. The better view appears to be that he must exercise the care, skill and caution that a prudent man would exercise who has primarily in view the safeguarding of another person's property.

[¶1508.2]   Provisions of the Trust as to Investments

The power and duties of the trustee in making investments can be regulated by the provisions of the trust. As a general rule, a trustee can properly make such investments as are authorized by the terms of the trust and cannot properly make investments which are forbidden by the terms of the trust. But the trustee is not under a duty to make investments required by the provisions of the trust where compliance is impossible, illegal or would defeat the purposes of the trust, due to unforeseen circumstances.

The language in a trust with regard to investments may be permissive or mandatory. When discretion as to investments is conferred on the trustee by the provisions of the trust, it must be determined whether or not the settlor intended to enlarge the scope of permissible investments. In any event, the permissible scope of the trustee's discretion is based on the prudent-man test. If the trustee is authorized to invest in a particular kind of security, it does not mean that any investment in securities of that kind is proper. In making the selection, the trustee must use care, skill and caution. Thus, if a trustee is authorized by the terms of the trust to invest in common stocks, he may not invest in speculative common stocks or in any kind of common stocks. He may only invest in those common stocks which a prudent man would invest in under the circumstances then present.

[¶1508.3] **Types of Investments Which Are Proper for a Trustee to Make**

Although the rules with respect to proper trust investments differ in the various states, certain types of investments are almost universally deemed proper in all the states.

A trustee can properly invest in bonds of the United States, or of the state or of municipalities in the state. He can also invest in first mortgages on land within the state and in certain classes of corporate bonds. In any event, however, the propriety of such investments depends on the circumstances. An otherwise proper type of investment may be improper if it was improvident to make it under all the circumstances.

A deposit in a savings bank, although regarded as an unsecured loan, is usually proper as a method of investing trust funds. In some states such deposits are only permitted to the extent they are guaranteed by the Federal Deposit Insurance Corporation.

The fact that in making investments, funds of one trust are combined with funds of other trusts administered by the trustee does not make the investment improper provided it is in other respects proper. Thus, trust companies' practice of investing funds of a trust in participation certificates in mortgages held by them is generally regarded as proper.

In most states, corporate trustees are permitted by statute to invest trust funds in a common trust fund maintained by the trustee, subject to statutory restrictions.

The question whether a trustee can properly invest in stock or other securities of open-end investment companies (i.e., mutual funds) is still not settled. It is permitted by statute in several states; in others it is found objectionable on the grounds that such investments involve an improper delegation of his powers by the trustee and the payment of double commissions.

Investments outside the state in which the trust is administered are not ordinarily improper. Under the current trend of availability of information with respect to out-of-state investments, the following types of investments are ordinarily proper: mortgages on land outside the state, securities or bonds of a corporation incorporated and/or doing business in another state and bonds of another state.

By statute in most states, a trustee may purchase shares of preferred stock or common stock for trust investment. This is a proper investment if the company in which the shares are purchased has regular earnings, pays regular dividends and it is reasonable to anticipate that it will continue to do so in the future. In a period of general inflation, it would obviously be more prudent for the trustee to invest a larger proportion of the fund in stocks than in fixed-income bonds, to provide a hedge against the possibility of a continued inflationary spiral.

[¶1508.4] **How to Select Proper Investments**

In the Restatement of Trusts, certain suggestions are offered to the trustee for his consideration in making an investment. Apart from the general considerations with respect to the safety of principal and earning of income, the trustee should look to:

(1) The marketability of the specific investment.

(2) The maturity, call or redemption date of the investment.

(3) The probable duration of the trust.

(4) The probable condition of the market with respect to the value of the specific investment at the termination of the trust, particularly if at that time the investment must be converted into cash for the purpose of distribution.

(5) The probable condition of the market with respect to reinvestment at the maturity date of the particular investment.

(6) The total value of the trust and the nature and extent of other investments.

(7) The beneficiary's requirements of income.

(8) The other assets of the beneficiary, including earning capacity.

(9) The effect of the investment in increasing or decreasing liability for taxes.

[¶1508.5] **Trend Now toward Income Beneficiary**

Inflationary factors in the economy are the main reason for a developing trend toward emphasizing the needs of the income beneficiary. They are expressed in what is often called our "deflated dollar," meaning that it will take many more dollars to buy the equivalent of goods and services as could have been purchased in 1940. This trend accounts in part for the 1951 modification of the New York Rule to permit investment in equities, which are considered an effective hedge against inflation.

Until a generation ago, a trustee was expected to protect the fund for the benefit of the remaindermen, meanwhile investing it so that the life beneficiary would have income and in a way that was consistent with capital safety. The Second World War outmoded this choice; the absolute safety that testators counted on is a thing of the past. Now trustees are expected to invest in common stocks both to increase rates of income and to protect capital.

The best procedure is still to select a capable trustee and give him wide discretion in making investments.

[¶1508.6]   **Duty of the Trustee to Diversify Investments**

Diversification is a prudent investment practice as a general rule. The principle of diversification is to spread the risk of loss over a number of different kinds of investments. This is accomplished by making a number and variety of permitted investments. Where a trustee is given broad powers by the provisions of the trust, wide diversification can be achieved by investing in different types of government obligations located in different states and in securities of different corporations in different fields of enterprise. It is, of course, recognized that diversification would not be prudent for a modest estate. For example, if the trust fund amounts to a few thousand dollars, it may be proper to invest the whole amount in a single security or mortgage. In time of deflation, it might be proper to invest much or all of the trust in government bonds.

Under normal economic conditions, most courts regard diversification by the trustee as a sound investment policy, where the problem has been presented. However, opinion is divided as to whether diversification should be imposed as a duty on the trustee and as to what constitutes prudent diversification. In a few states, there are statutes which enforce a certain degree of diversification by imposing statutory maximums in terms of percentage or dollar limitations on single investments. For example, Wisconsin has had a statute which forbids trustees to invest in any one security more than 20% of the trust estate provided the trust estate exceeds $50,000, with larger percentages where the estate is smaller. But the absolute requirement of diversification by the trustee has been recognized as a rule of trust management in relatively few states.

In those states recognizing the requirement of diversification, the same rule applies to investments received from the settlor of the trust. But if the settlor of the trust has directed the trustee to retain the investments received, it would be improper for the trustee to dispose of these investments solely for the purpose of diversification. It is only where compliance with the provisions of the trust would endanger the trust fund or thwart the accomplishment of the trust purpose that the trustee may properly deviate from the course of investment prescribed by the settlor.

[¶1508.7]   **Duty of Trustee to Dispose of Improper Investments**

Unless otherwise provided by the terms of the trust, the trustee is under a duty to dispose of any part of the trust property coming into his possession which would not be a proper investment for the trustee to make. When a duty to convert arises, such conversion must be made by the trustee within a reasonable period of time after the creation of the trust. What constitutes a reasonable time depends on whether, under all the circumstances, the trustee acted with prudence in delaying or advancing the sale.

With respect to investments which were proper when acquired by the trustee but subsequently become improper after the creation of the trust, again the trustee is under a duty to dispose of the improper investments within a reasonable period of time.

What constitutes a reasonable holding period where there is a duty to convert a trust investment which no longer is proper again depends on the particular circumstance. Factors to be considered are as follows:

(1) The type of property and the risk involved in its retention.

(2) The amount to be received on an immediate sale as compared with future sale possibilities and past value.

(3) The available opportunities for reinvestment.

(4) The question of possible tax liabilities.

(5) The purpose and the size of the trust and the effect of a possible loss.

[¶1509]   **POSTMORTEM ESTATE PLANNING**

The draftsman of the will, the executor and the beneficiaries can collaborate to achieve important tax savings after the testator's death. The time to think of these is when or before drafting the will. But some opportunities will remain open to the executors even after the testator's death. The tax savings available here fall into these categories:

(1) Estate tax savings by altering the testamentary dispositions.

(2) Income tax savings for the estate in administration.

(3) Income tax savings for the beneficiaries.

[¶1509.1]   **Altering the Plan of Disposition**

This can be done by an election to take against the will, by contesting the will and effecting a settlement, by renouncing a bequest.

Failure to qualify for the marital deduction can be remedied by exercising the widow's right to take against the will if that election is provided by local law. Where property goes into a trust which does not qualify for the marital deduction, the election of the widow's share may not only save estate tax on the husband's death, but lifetime gifts by the widow to the children may save estate tax on the widow's death.

Where a will contest or settlement results in property passing to the surviving spouse, it will qualify for the marital deduction only if the surrender or assignment is a bona fide recognition of enforceable rights in the decedent's estate. A will contest or settlement which shifts property from a beneficiary named in the will results in the property being treated as though it had never passed to the named beneficiary. Thus, if the named beneficiary is a surviving spouse, the property surrendered or lost will not qualify for the marital deduction, nor will it be taxed in the estate of the named beneficiary on subsequent death.

Renunciation or disclaimer of a share in the estate can save income tax by shifting income to a successor beneficiary.

Property which passes to a surviving spouse by disclaimer qualifies for the marital deduction. Disclaimer by a widow of property in excess of the marital deduction amount can save the second tax on her subsequent death.

Renunciation of a property interest when a charity is the successor by terms of the will will obtain or enlarge a charitable deduction.

In order for disclaimer or renunciation not to be treated as a taxable gift when the interest is passed from the disclaimant to the recipient, the disclaimer must meet the definition of a "qualified disclaimer" (IRC §2518). A qualified disclaimer is defined as an irrevocable and unqualified refusal to accept an interest in property and must satisfy the following four conditions:

(1) The refusal must be in writing;

(2) The written refusal must be received by the transferor, his legal representative or holder of the legal title to the property, no later than nine (9) months after the day the transfer creating the interest is made;

(3) The disclaimant must not have accepted the interest or its benefits; and

(4) The interest must pass to another person; the disclaimant cannot have authority to direct the transfer to another person.

[¶1509.2] The Executor's Tax Choices

The executor has important decisions to make which will bear on the income tax liability of the estate and the beneficiaries and he has an obligation, as yet not fully defined, to make these decisions in the best interest of the beneficiaries.

[¶1509.3] Picking a Fiscal Year

By selecting a fiscal year which will produce a short year at the beginning of the estate administration and a short year at the end, income which will be taxed to the estate can be spread out to maximum advantage. In making this decision, consideration has to be given to when income will be received and when distributions which are deductible are likely to be made.

The ideal arrangement for minimizing taxes of the estate and all its beneficiaries would be to create, through properly timed distributions, a situation in which the tax brackets of the estate and the beneficiaries are the same. This can be accomplished where the estate is in a relatively high bracket before distributions and the beneficiaries are in lower brackets.

Frequently, an executor cannot make distributions to the beneficiaries in the calendar year of death without an unjustifiable risk. This is due to the fact that he must wait until six months have expired after probate of the will to be certain that there will be no will contest. Only by analyzing the situation of the particular will, will it be possible to determine whether there would be any great risk involved from a probate standpoint in making a distribution during the calendar year of death. If there is any great risk in making such a distribution, the executor or administrator may be well advised to select a fiscal year ending more than six months after the probate of the will. This will enable him to make distributions during the first tax year of the estate, thereby reducing the tax bracket to which the income of the estate is subjected.

The selection of a taxable year for the estate is important for two reasons —not only will it permit a leveling of income within tax periods of the estate, it will also determine when the beneficiary must include in his income distributions from the estate. The beneficiary must report the income during his taxable year within which the tax year of the estate ends.

The executor should be careful that his choice doesn't bunch two years of estate income in one income year of the beneficiary. Say the executor picked a fiscal year ending January 31 and distributed the income for a ten-month period to the beneficiary. He ends administration in December and distributes the income for eleven months. The beneficiary, on a calendar-year basis, must pick up the distributions for two years in one taxable year.

The executor can create additional taxpayers and lower brackets by activating testamentary trusts early in the administration. This also puts the estate in a lower income bracket.

One precaution is needed here: If the income of a trust must be distributed to beneficiaries who are in high income brackets, it might be wise to delay activation of that trust.

[¶1509.4]   Timing of Distribution

If the estate is in a lower bracket than the beneficiaries of the estate, the executor should accumulate the income of the estate in order to have it taxed as the income of the estate. If the beneficiaries are in lower brackets than the estate, the executor should accelerate the distribution of the income of the estate in order to have it taxed as the income of the beneficiaries.

It is only in connection with discretionary distributions that the executor is in a position to make substantial savings in taxes by proper timing of distributions from the estate. In the case of mandatory distributions of income, there is no choice as to the fact that the income will be taxed to the beneficiary rather than to the estate, and the only opportunity for tax saving lies in choosing the fiscal period for the estate which will result in the income being taxed to a beneficiary at the most advantageous time.

With this restriction in mind, the executor should consider these possibilities:

(1) Distribution of income to beneficiaries whose income tax brackets are lower than that of the estate.

(2) Relative merit of accumulating some or all income for the beneficiaries in higher tax brackets, so that this becomes taxable to the estate and can later be distributed free of tax to the beneficiaries.

(3) Desirability of making a partial distribution to a beneficiary shortly after a decedent's death, minimizing the extent of the shift to the higher bracket distributee by the selection of a short period for the first fiscal year and perhaps the payment of a portion of administrative expenses in that short period.

(4) Distribution of sufficient income to equalize income tax brackets of the joint return where decedent dies in the early part of the year and considerable income is received by the estate thereafter.

(5) Distribution of sufficient income so that the taxable income of the joint return doubles that of the estate's return, causing the top brackets of both returns to be the same and resulting in the lowest total income taxation.

It should be remembered that any distribution during administration is treated as a distribution of income, to the extent of the estate's distributable net income, unless it is payment of a bequest of a specific sum of money which is distributed in not more than three installments or unless it is a bequest of specific property (IRC §663(a)(1)).

[¶1509.5] Termination of Administration

Termination of the administration of the estate cannot be unduly delayed merely to secure the tax benefits inherent in having another taxable entity. The regulations state that the period of administration is the period actually required by the executor or administrator to perform the ordinary duties of administration, such as the collection of assets and the payment of debts, taxes, legacies and bequests. An estate is considered terminated when all the assets have been distributed except a reasonable amount set aside for unascertained or contingent liabilities and expenses. Termination of the estate closes its taxable year.

While the termination cannot be unduly delayed, wherever possible the executor should avoid having more than twelve months' distributions taxed to the beneficiaries in one year. If at all possible, the estate should be closed at such time as will bring the final distribution of income into another tax year of the beneficiary. On the other hand, if the final year of the estate is one in which excess deductions can be claimed by the beneficiaries under IRC §642(h)(2), the estate should be closed at a time when the beneficiaries can realize maximum benefit from such deductions.

[¶1509.6] Income in Respect of a Decedent

The type of income which comes to an estate as a result of it having been earned by the testator during his life will not be taxed in the last return of the decedent but will be taxed in the year received by the estate. The unpaid bills of a professional man or the contractual compensation of an officer of a corporation payable over a period of years will not be taxed in his last return. But they will be taxed either to his estate or to a person who is named by contract as having the right to receive that income, or to a person who has the right to receive the distribution by the estate before the cash is actually paid. In each of those three situations, the income will be taxed to the person who gets it at the time the cash or other property paid as income is received (IRC §691).

A value is placed on this right to future income for estate tax purposes. As part of the taxable estate, it carries the estate tax, and the estate tax can be taken by the recipient of the income as a deduction against the income when it is received (IRC §691(c)).

What do we do to minimize this income tax impact? Here are some possibilities:

(1) By will, these unpaid bills or future income can be given to a number of individual beneficiaries.

(2) Contractual arrangements set up during life can be used to spread out this income at death so it doesn't all come in one year.

(3) This kind of property can be used to provide for charitable dispositions.

(4) The executor can distribute the rights to this kind of income to several beneficiaries before, not after, receiving it.

Give the executor enough discretion so that he can move to distribute these income rights before they are collected. He can spread them over a number of beneficiaries rather than have them come into an estate which is taxed as a single taxpayer and doesn't get any benefit from income splitting. If we merely transfer the income from the estate to a married beneficiary before the income is realized, we produce an important income tax saving right there.

(5) This kind of income should be excluded from the marital deduction portion of the estate because, if it falls into that portion of the estate, we've lost the deduction for the estate tax against that future income. On the other hand, if this particular type of income is put in the nonmarital deduction portion where we have an estate tax burden, we set up a tax deduction against the receipt of that future income. This can be done under a broad discretionary authority which gives the executor the right to ascertain which assets will go into the marital deduction segment of the estate and which will go into the other segment.

[¶1509.7] Deduction of Administration Expenses

The executor must elect whether to deduct administration expenses from the gross estate or from the estate's income tax return. He has this election with respect to executor's commissions; attorney and accountant fees; appraisal, bond, custodian and court charges and expenses incurred in the administration of the estate. The election is made by taking these expenses on the return. A different election can be made with respect to different expense items and even parts of the same item.

In looking at the tax-dollar effects of his election, the executor cannot limit his examination to the rate tables. He must think in terms of effective rates. Where the full marital deduction is claimed, the effective rate of tax saving from an estate tax deduction of an administration expense is roughly one-half the estate tax rate.

The executor must consider not only the tax savings in the election, but also the effect of the beneficial interests. Where the income and residuary interests are not the same, the executor may find that an election, based on comparison of effective tax rates may warp the interests of competing beneficiaries. For probate accounting purposes, expenses of administration are usually principal charges which have the effect of reducing the residuary estate.

When the executor has determined his better election course from the tax-dollar standpoint and when he sees that his election will produce a benefit for one estate interest at the expense of another, what does he do? These are possible courses:

(1) Dodge the problem of adjusting for the warping effects of the election by deducting the expense on the return which does not produce distortion, at the cost of paying more taxes. However, an executor who pays more federal taxes than he must solely to preserve distribution symmetry risks complaint by the estate beneficiaries.

(2) Seek instruction of the probate court. This, however, may be costly and time consuming. If possible, he is best advised to—

(3) Bring together the affected beneficiaries, with their counsel, and seek their concurrence in his proposed course of election.

Excess deductions which the estate can't use in its final income year can be deducted by the beneficiary in that year. The returns should be planned with this in mind. A high bracket beneficiary receiving income from the estate on top of his or her own substantial income will find the extra deductions very helpful.

[¶1509.8]   Decedent's Final Income Tax Return

Except for medical expenses, (IRC §213(d)), death does not accrue income or expenses. Where both spouses had taxable income for the year of death, the executor has a problem of allocating tax liability between the estate and the surviving spouse if a joint return is elected. If the decedent was married at the time of his death, the executor and the surviving spouse can file a joint return for the decedent and the surviving spouse.

Although the executor may wish to file a joint return where this shows a lower tax than separate returns, this may not be permissible under local law, because the joint return subjects the estate to liability for the income tax on the surviving spouse's income. To eliminate uncertainty on this point, the will should contain explicit instruction to or authorization for the executor to join in a joint return. It may also be desirable to empower the executor to pay any part of the joint tax that he sees fit from the estate.

For additional pointers on what the will should contain to facilitate post-death tax savings, see ¶611.

ESTATE PLANNING TABLES

SUMMARY OF STATE DEATH TAXES

The chart that follows gives capsule descriptions of the death taxes levied by the various states. Where the type of tax is listed as "credit estate tax" the tax levied is the maximum federal credit for state death taxes. Where the tax is an "inheritance tax," the exemptions and tax rates listed are the maximum and minimum amounts (e.g., in California a spouse receives a $60,000 exemption and the tax rate is 6% to 14%, depending on the size of the distribution; a non-relative receives a $300 exemption and the tax is between 10% and 24%). Where both an "inheritance" or "estate tax" and a "credit estate tax" are listed, the "credit estate tax" is payable only if the tax under the basic state death tax is less than the maximum federal credit. "Payment" indicates the time after death when the state tax is due (unless an extension is granted and payable without penalty). "Assessed on" indicates whether the tax is payable from the "residuary estate" or is paid "proportionately" by the beneficiaries (unless the will provides otherwise).

Local law should always be checked for recent changes enacted by state legislation.

STATE DEATH TAXES

State	Type	Exemption	Rates	Payment	Assessed On
Alabama	Credit estate tax			15 months	Residuary estate
Alaska	Credit estate tax			15 months	Proportionately
Arizona	Estate tax	$100,000	0.8-16.0%	9 months	Residuary estate
	Credit estate tax				
Arkansas	Credit estate tax			9 months	Proportionately
California	Inheritance tax	$ 60,000	6.0-14.0%	9 months	Proportionately
		$ 300	10.0-24.0%		
	Credit estate tax				
Colorado	Inheritance tax	$ 30,000	2.2-8.8%	9 months	Proportionately
		$ 500	11.0-20.9%		
	Credit estate tax				
Connecticut	Inheritance tax	$ 50,000	3.9-10.4%	9 months	Proportionately
		$ 500	10.4-18.2%		
	Credit estate tax				
Delaware	Inheritance tax	$ 20,000	1.0-4.0%	15 months	Proportionately
		none	10.0-16.0%		
	Credit estate tax				
District of Columbia	Inheritance tax	$ 5,000	1.0-8.0%	18 months	Proportionately
		$ 1,000	5.0-23.0%		
	Credit estate tax				
Florida	Credit estate tax			9 months	Residuary estate
Georgia	Credit estate tax			9 months	Residuary estate

STATE DEATH TAXES (cont.)

State	Type	Exemption	Rates	Payment	Assessed On
Hawaii	Inheritance tax	$ 20,000	2.0-6.0%	18 months	Proportionately
	Credit estate tax	$ 500	3.5-9.0%		
Idaho	Inheritance tax	$ 30,000	2.0-15.0%	9 months	Proportionately
	Credit estate tax	$ 10,000	8.0-30%		
Illinois	Inheritance tax	$ 20,000	2.0-14.0%	15 months	Proportionately
	Credit estate tax	$ 100	10.0-30.0%		
Indiana	Inheritance tax	$ 15,000	1.0-10.0%	18 months	Proportionately
	Credit estate tax	$ 100	7.0-20.0%		
Iowa	Inheritance tax	$ 80,000	1.0-8.0%	15 months	Proportionately
	Credit estate tax	none	15.0%		
Kansas	Inheritance tax	$ 75,000	0.5-2.5%	9 months	Proportionately
	Credit estate tax	none	10.0-15.0%		
Kentucky	Inheritance tax	$ 20,000	2.0-10.0%	18 months	Proportionately
	Credit estate tax	$ 500	6.0-16.0%		
Louisiana	Inheritance tax	$ 5,000	2.0-3.0%	6 months	Proportionately
	Credit estate tax	$ 500	5.0-10.0%		

STATE DEATH TAXES (cont.)

State	Type	Exemption	Rates	Payment	Assessed On
Maine	Inheritance tax	$ 50,000	5.0-10.0%	12 months	Proportionately
	Credit estate tax	$ 1,000	14.0-18.0%		
Maryland	Inheritance tax	$ 150	1.0%	15 months	Proportionately
	Credit estate tax	$ 150	10.0%		
Massachusetts	Estate tax	$ 30,000 or net estate if under $60,000	5.0-16.0%	9 months	Proportionately
	Credit estate tax				
Michigan	Inheritance tax	$ 30,000	2.5-8.5%	9 months	Proportionately
	Credit estate tax	none	10.5-15.5%		
Minnesota	Inheritance tax	$ 30,000	1.5-10.0%	12 months	Proportionately
	Credit estate tax	$ 500	8.0-30.0%		
Mississippi	Estate tax	$ 60,000	1.0-16.0%	9 months	Residuary estate
	Credit estate tax				
Missouri	Inheritance tax	$ 20,000	1.0-6.0%	9 months	Proportionately
	Credit estate tax	none	5.0-30.0%		
Montana	Inheritance tax	$ 25,000	2.0-8.0%	18 months	Proportionately
	Credit estate tax	none	8.0-32.0%		

STATE DEATH TAXES (cont.)

State	Type	Exemption	Rates	Payment	Assessed On
Nebraska	Inheritance tax	$ 10,000	1.0%	16 months	Proportionately
	Credit estate tax	$ 500	6.0-18.0%		
Nevada	No tax				
New Hampshire	Inheritance tax	No tax on spouse or parent or child		12 months	Proportionately
	Credit estate tax	None	15.0%		
New Jersey	Inheritance tax	$ 5,000	1.0-16.0%	8 months	Proportionately
	Credit estate tax	none	15.0-16.0%		
New Mexico	Credit estate tax			9 months	Proportionately
New York	Estate tax	$ 20,000	2.0-21.0%	6 months	Proportionately
	Credit estate tax				
North Carolina	Inheritance tax	$ 10,000	1.0-12.0%	9 months	Proportionately
	Credit estate tax	none	8.0-17.0%		
North Dakota	Estate tax	$ 60,000	2.0-20.0%	15 months	Proportionately
Ohio	Estate tax	$ 5,000*	2.0-7.0%	9 months	Proportionately
	Credit estate tax	(*Plus $30,000 for surviving spouse, $7,000 for each child under 18 and $3,000 for each child over 18)			

STATE DEATH TAXES (cont.)

State	Type	Exemption	Rates	Payment	Assessed On
Oklahoma	Estate tax	$ 60,000* (*Complete exemption for spouse except for calculating credit estate tax)	1.0-10.0%	9 months	Proportionately
	Credit estate tax				
Oregon	Estate tax	$ 25,000	3.0-12.0%	9 months	Proportionately
	Inheritance tax	No tax on spouse, parents, or child $ 500	5.0-25.0%		
	Credit estate tax				
Pennsylvania	Inheritance tax	none	6.0% 15.0%	9 months	Proportionately
	Credit estate tax				
Puerto Rico	Estate tax	$ 60,000	3.0-70.0%	270 days	Proportionately
Rhode Island	Estate tax	$ 10,000	1.0%	15 months	Proportionately
	Inheritance tax	$ 10,000 $ 1,000	2.0-9.0% 8.0-15.0%		
	Credit estate tax				
South Carolina	Estate tax Credit estate tax	$ 60,000	4.0-6.0%	9 months	Proportionately

STATE DEATH TAX (cont.)

State	Type	Exemption	Rates	Payment	Assessed On
South Dakota	Inheritance tax	$ 60,000 $ 100	1.5-6.0% 6.0-24.0%	12 months	Proportionately
Tennessee	Inheritance tax Credit estate tax	$ 60,000 $ 1,000	5.5-9.5% 6.5-20.0%	9 months	Proportionately
Texas	Inheritance tax Credit estate tax	$ 25,000 $ 500	1.0-6.0% 5.0-20.0%	9 months	Proportionately
Utah	Estate tax Credit estate tax	$ 60,000	5.0-10.0%	15 months	Proportionately
Vermont	Estate tax Credit estate tax	$ 60,000	30% of Federal Tax on Vermont property	15 months	Proportionately
Virginia	Inheritance tax Credit estate tax	$ 5,000 $ 1,000	1.0-5.0% 5.0-15.0%	9 months	Proportionately
Washington	Inheritance tax Credit estate tax	$ 10,000 none	1.0-10.0% 10.0-25.0%	9 months	Proportionately
West Virginia	Inheritance tax Credit estate tax	$ 30,000 none	3.0-13.0% 10.0-30.0%	11 months	Proportionately

STATE DEATH TAXES (cont.)

State	Type	Exemption	Rates	Payment	Assessed On
Wisconsin	Inheritance tax	$ 50,000	1.25-6.25%	12 months	Proportionately
	Credit estate tax	$ 500	10.0-30.0%		
Wyoming	Inheritance tax	$ 60,000	2.0%	10 months	Proportionately
	Credit estate tax	none	6.0%		

INDIVIDUAL INCOME TAX RATES
Income Tax Rates for 1976 and later years

Taxable Income	Unmarried Individual Returns (Other than surviving spouses and heads of households)		Joint Returns (Married taxpayers and surviving spouses)		Head of Household Returns		Separate Returns (Married taxpayers)	
	Tax	Rate on Excess	Tax	Rate on Excess	Tax	Rate on Excess	Tax	Rate on Excess
20,000	5,230	38	4,380	32	4,800	35	6,070	48
22,000	5,990	40	5,020	32	5,500	36	7,030	50
24,000	6,790	40	5,660	36	6,220	38	8,030	50
26,000	7,590	45	6,380	36	6,980	41	9,030	53
28,000	8,490	45	7,100	39	7,800	42	10,090	53
32,000	10,290	50	8,660	42	9,480	45	12,210	55
36,000	12,290	50	10,340	45	11,280	48	14,410	55
38,000	13,290	55	11,240	45	12,240	51	15,510	58
40,000	14,390	55	12,140	48	13,260	52	16,670	58
44,000	16,590	60	14,060	50	15,340	55	18,990	60
50,000	20,190	62	17,060	50	18,640	56	22,590	62
52,000	21,430	62	18,060	53	19,760	58	23,830	62
60,000	26,390	64	22,300	53	24,400	58	28,790	64
64,000	28,950	64	24,420	55	26,720	59	31,350	64
70,000	32,790	66	27,720	55	30,260	61	35,190	66
76,000	36,750	66	31,020	58	33,920	62	39,150	66
80,000	39,390	68	33,340	58	36,400	63	41,790	68
88,000	44,830	68	37,980	60	41,440	64	47,230	68
90,000	46,190	69	39,180	60	42,720	64	48,590	69
100,000	53,090	70	45,180	62	49,120	66	55,490	70
120,000	67,090	70	57,580	64	62,320	67	69,490	70
140,000	81,090	70	70,380	66	75,720	68	83,490	70
160,000	95,090	70	83,580	68	89,320	69	97,490	70
180,000	109,090	70	97,180	69	103,120	70	111,490	70
200,000	123,090	70	110,980	70	117,120	70	125,490	70

INCOME TAXES SAVED ANNUALLY WITHIN A FAMILY WHEN PARENT
TRANSFERS INCOME-PRODUCING PROPERTY TO A CHILD OR TO A
TRUST WHICH PAYS THE INCOME TO A CHILD*

A. Where parent files an individual tax return:

Parent's Taxable Income Before Transfer	Tax Savings if Property Produces Annual Income of		
	$1,000	$5,000	$10,000
$ 20,000	415	1,385	1,900
30,000	495	1,875	3,100
40,000	545	2,065	3,540
50,000	565	2,255	3,940
60,000	585	2,355	4,220
70,000	605	2,455	4,420
80,000	625	2,555	4,620
90,000	645	2,655	4,820
100,000	655	2,705	4,920

B. Where parent files a joint tax return with spouse:

Parent's Taxable Income Before Transfer	Tax Savings if Property Produces Annual Income of		
	$1,000	$5,000	$10,000
$ 20,000	245	625	580
30,000	355	1,115	1,520
40,000	415	1,475	2,280
50,000	465	1,755	2,940
60,000	495	1,905	3,260
70,000	515	2,005	3,440
80,000	545	2,125	3,640
90,000	565	2,195	3,860
100,000	565	2,255	4,020

*Both tables disregard the maximum tax rate on earned income and assume the beneficiary receives all of his income from the transferred property.

HOW MUCH TAX-EXEMPT INCOME IS WORTH

Example of use of this table:

A tax-exempt bond builds up at a 2.50% rate. What is the equivalent taxable yield for a single individual with $50,000 of taxable income?

Answer: (From the $50,000 line in the table)..............6.58%

This table also applies to other tax-free investments. It can also be used to find the tax-free yield which equals a certain taxable return. For example, a single individual with $50,000 taxable income owns a taxable bond which yields 6%. If we check along the $50,000 income line, we find that a 6% taxable return is just slightly better than a tax-exempt bond yielding 2.25%. Therefore, if the individual gets a tax-exempt bond yielding better than 2.25%, he will have a higher after-tax income.

MARRIED PERSONS

TAXABLE INCOME		TAX-EXEMPT YIELD								
Separate Return	Joint Return	4%	4.5%	5%	5.5%	6%	6.5%	7%	7.5%	8%
$ 10,000	$ 20,000	5.88	6.61	7.36	8.09	8.82	9.56	10.29	11.04	11.76
12,000	24,000	6.25	7.03	7.82	8.59	9.37	10.16	10.94	11.73	12.50
14,000	28,000	6.56	7.38	8.20	9.02	9.84	10.66	11.48	12.30	13.12
16,000	32,000	6.90	7.76	8.62	9.48	10.35	11.21	12.07	12.93	13.80
18,000	36,000	7.27	8.18	9.08	10.00	10.91	11.82	12.73	13.62	14.54
20,000	40,000	7.69	8.65	9.62	10.58	11.54	12.50	13.46	14.43	15.38
22,000	44,000	8.00	9.00	10.00	11.00	12.00	13.00	14.00	15.00	16.00
26,000	52,000	8.51	9.57	10.64	11.70	12.77	13.63	14.89	15.96	17.02
32,000	64,000	8.89	10.00	11.12	12.22	13.33	14.44	15.56	16.68	17.78
38,000	76,000	9.52	10.71	11.90	13.10	14.28	15.48	16.67	17.85	19.04
44,000	88,000	10.00	11.25	12.50	13.75	15.00	16.25	17.50	18.75	20.00
50,000	100,000	10.53	11.84	13.16	14.47	15.79	17.11	18.42	19.74	21.06
60,000	120,000	11.11	12.49	13.88	15.28	16.67	18.06	19.44	20.82	22.22
70,000	140,000	11.76	13.23	14.70	16.18	17.64	19.12	20.59	22.05	23.52
80,000	160,000	12.50	14.06	15.62	17.19	18.75	20.31	21.87	23.43	25.00
90,000	180,000	12.90	14.52	16.12	17.74	19.35	20.97	22.58	24.18	25.80
100,000	200,000	13.33	15.00	16.66	18.33	20.00	21.67	23.33	25.00	26.66

SIMPLE INTEREST TABLE

Example of use of this table:

Find amount of $500 in 8 years at 6% simple interest.

From table at 8 yrs. and 6% for $1   1.48

Value in 8 yrs. for $500 (500 x 1.48) $740

Number of Years	Interest Rate							
	3%	4%	5%	6%	7%	8%	9%	10%
1	1.03	1.04	1.05	1.06	1.07	1.08	1.09	1.10
2	1.06	1.08	1.10	1.12	1.14	1.16	1.18	1.20
3	1.09	1.12	1.15	1.18	1.21	1.24	1.27	1.30
4	1.12	1.16	1.20	1.24	1.28	1.32	1.36	1.40
5	1.15	1.20	1.25	1.30	1.35	1.40	1.45	1.50
6	1.18	1.24	1.30	1.36	1.42	1.48	1.54	1.60
7	1.21	1.28	1.35	1.42	1.49	1.56	1.63	1.70
8	1.24	1.32	1.40	1.48	1.56	1.64	1.72	1.80
9	1.27	1.36	1.45	1.54	1.63	1.72	1.81	1.90
10	1.30	1.40	1.50	1.60	1.70	1.80	1.90	2.00
11	1.33	1.44	1.55	1.66	1.77	1.88	1.99	2.10
12	1.36	1.48	1.60	1.72	1.84	1.96	2.08	2.20
13	1.39	1.52	1.65	1.78	1.91	2.04	2.17	2.30
14	1.42	1.56	1.70	1.84	1.98	2.12	2.26	2.40
15	1.45	1.60	1.75	1.90	2.05	2.20	2.35	2.50
16	1.48	1.64	1.80	1.96	2.12	2.28	2.44	2.60
17	1.51	1.68	1.85	2.02	2.19	2.36	2.53	2.70
18	1.54	1.72	1.90	2.08	2.26	2.44	2.62	2.80
19	1.57	1.76	1.95	2.14	2.33	2.52	2.71	2.90
20	1.60	1.80	2.00	2.20	2.40	2.60	2.80	3.00
21	1.63	1.84	2.05	2.26	2.47	2.68	2.89	3.10
22	1.66	1.88	2.10	2.32	2.54	2.76	2.98	3.20
23	1.69	1.92	2.15	2.38	2.61	2.84	3.07	3.30
24	1.72	1.96	2.20	2.44	2.68	2.92	3.16	3.40
25	1.75	2.00	2.25	2.50	2.75	3.00	3.25	3.50
26	1.78	2.04	2.30	2.56	2.82	3.08	3.34	3.60
27	1.81	2.08	2.35	2.62	2.89	3.16	3.43	3.70
28	1.84	2.12	2.40	2.68	2.96	3.24	3.52	3.80
29	1.87	2.16	2.45	2.74	3.03	3.32	3.61	3.90
30	1.90	2.20	2.50	2.80	3.10	3.40	3.70	4.00
31	1.93	2.24	2.55	2.86	3.17	3.48	3.79	4.10
32	1.96	2.28	2.60	2.92	3.24	3.56	3.88	4.20
33	1.99	2.32	2.65	2.98	3.31	3.64	3.97	4.30
34	2.02	2.36	2.70	3.04	3.38	3.72	4.06	4.40
35	2.05	2.40	2.75	3.10	3.45	3.80	4.15	4.50
36	2.08	2.44	2.80	3.16	3.52	3.88	4.24	4.60
37	2.11	2.48	2.85	3.22	3.59	3.96	4.33	4.70
38	2.14	2.52	2.90	3.28	3.66	4.04	4.42	4.80
39	2.17	2.56	2.95	3.34	3.73	4.12	4.51	4.90
40	2.20	2.60	3.00	3.40	3.80	4.20	4.60	5.00

COMPOUND INTEREST TABLE

Example of use of this table:

Find how much $1,000 now in bank will grow to in 14 years at 4% interest.

From table 14 years at 4%   1.7317

Value in 14 years of $1,000 $1731.70

Number of Years	3-1/2%	4%	4-1/2%	5%	5-1/2%	6%	6-1/2%	7%
1	1.0350	1.0400	1.0450	1.0500	1.0550	1.0600	1.0650	1.0700
2	1.0712	1.0816	1.0920	1.1025	1.1130	1.1236	1.1342	1.1449
3	1.1087	1.1249	1.1412	1.1576	1.1742	1.1910	1.2079	1.2250
4	1.1475	1.1699	1.1925	1.2155	1.2388	1.2624	1.2864	1.3107
5	1.1877	1.2167	1.2462	1.2763	1.3069	1.3382	1.3700	1.4025
6	1.2293	1.2653	1.3023	1.3401	1.3788	1.4185	1.4591	1.5007
7	1.2723	1.3159	1.3609	1.4071	1.4546	1.5036	1.5539	1.6057
8	1.3168	1.3686	1.4221	1.4775	1.5346	1.5938	1.6549	1.7181
9	1.3629	1.4233	1.4861	1.5513	1.6190	1.6894	1.7625	1.8384
10	1.4106	1.4802	1.5530	1.6289	1.7081	1.7908	1.8771	1.9671
11	1.4600	1.5395	1.6229	1.7103	1.8020	1.8982	1.9991	2.1048
12	1.5111	1.6010	1.6959	1.7959	1.9012	2.0121	2.1290	2.2521
13	1.5640	1.6651	1.7722	1.8856	2.0057	2.1329	2.2674	2.4098
14	1.6187	1.7317	1.8519	1.9799	2.1160	2.2609	2.4148	2.5785
15	1.6753	1.8009	1.9353	2.0789	2.2324	2.3965	2.5718	2.7590
16	1.7340	1.8730	2.0224	2.1829	2.3552	2.5403	2.7390	2.9521
17	1.7947	1.9479	2.1134	2.2920	2.4848	2.6927	2.9170	3.1588
18	1.8575	2.0258	2.2085	2.4066	2.6214	2.8543	3.1066	3.3799
19	1.9225	2.1068	2.3079	2.5270	2.7656	3.0256	3.3085	3.6165
20	1.9898	2.1911	2.4117	2.6533	2.9177	3.2071	3.5236	3.8696
21	2.0594	2.2788	2.5202	2.7860	3.0782	3.3995	3.7526	4.1405
22	2.1315	2.3699	2.6337	2.9253	3.2475	3.6035	3.9966	4.4304
23	2.2061	2.4647	2.7522	3.0715	3.4261	3.8197	4.2563	4.7405
24	2.2833	2.5633	2.8760	3.2251	3.6145	4.0489	4.5330	5.0723
25	2.3632	2.6658	3.0054	3.3864	3.8133	4.2918	4.8276	5.4274
26	2.4460	2.7725	3.1407	3.5557	4.0231	4.5493	5.1415	5.8073
27	2.5316	2.8834	3.2820	3.7335	4.2444	4.8223	5.4756	6.2138
28	2.6202	2.9987	3.4297	3.9201	4.4778	5.1116	5.8316	6.6488
29	2.7119	3.1187	3.5840	4.1161	4.7241	5.4183	6.2106	7.1142
30	2.8068	3.2434	3.7453	4.3219	4.9839	5.7434	6.6143	7.6122
31	2.9050	3.3731	3.9139	4.5380	5.2580	6.0881	7.0443	8.1451
32	3.0067	3.5081	4.0900	4.7649	5.5472	6.4533	7.5021	8.7152
33	3.1119	3.6484	4.2740	5.0032	5.8523	6.8405	7.9898	9.3253
34	3.2209	3.7943	4.4664	5.2533	6.1742	7.2510	8.5091	9.9781
35	3.3336	3.9461	4.6673	5.5160	6.5138	7.6860	9.0622	10.6765
36	3.4503	4.1039	4.8774	5.7918	6.8720	8.1472	9.6513	11.4239
37	3.5710	4.2681	5.0969	6.0814	7.2500	8.6360	10.2786	12.2236
38	3.6960	4.4388	5.3262	6.3855	7.6488	9.1542	10.9467	13.0792
39	3.8254	4.6164	5.5659	6.7048	8.0694	9.7035	11.6582	13.9948
40	3.9593	4.8010	5.8164	7.0400	8.5133	10.2857	12.4160	14.9744

How Much $1 a Year Will Equal

Example of use of this table:

How much is $1,000 a year invested at 5% worth in 20 years?
At 5% for 20 years, the figure is   34.719
For $1,000 a year, the amount is $34,719

Interest Rate

Number of Years	3%	3½%	4%	4½%	5%	6%	7%	8%
1	1.030	1.035	1.040	1.045	1.050	1.060	1.070	1.080
2	2.091	2.106	2.122	2.137	2.153	2.183	2.215	2.246
3	3.184	3.215	3.246	3.278	3.310	3.375	3.440	3.506
4	4.309	4.362	4.416	4.471	4.526	4.637	4.751	4.867
5	5.468	5.550	5.633	5.717	5.802	5.975	6.153	6.336
6	6.662	6.779	6.898	7.019	7.142	7.394	7.654	7.923
7	7.892	8.052	8.214	8.380	8.549	8.897	9.260	9.637
8	9.159	9.368	9.583	9.802	10.027	10.491	10.978	11.488
9	10.464	10.731	11.006	11.288	11.578	12.181	12.816	13.487
10	11.808	12.142	12.486	12.841	13.207	13.972	14.784	15.645
11	13.192	13.602	14.026	14.464	14.917	15.870	16.888	17.977
12	14.618	15.113	15.627	16.160	16.713	17.882	19.141	20.495
13	16.086	16.677	17.292	17.932	18.599	20.015	21.550	23.215
14	17.599	18.296	19.024	19.784	20.579	22.276	24.129	26.152
15	19.157	19.971	20.825	21.719	22.657	24.673	26.888	29.324
16	20.762	21.705	22.698	23.742	24.840	27.213	29.840	32.750
17	22.414	23.500	24.645	25.855	27.132	29.906	32.999	36.450
18	24.117	25.357	26.671	28.064	29.539	32.760	36.379	40.446
19	25.870	27.280	28.778	30.371	32.066	35.786	39.995	44.762
20	27.676	29.269	30.969	32.783	34.719	38.993	43.865	49.423
21	29.537	31.329	33.248	35.303	37.505	42.392	48.006	54.457
22	31.453	33.460	35.618	37.937	40.430	45.996	52.436	59.893
23	33.426	35.667	38.083	40.689	43.502	49.816	57.177	65.765
24	35.459	37.950	40.646	43.565	46.727	53.865	62.249	72.106
25	37.553	40.313	43.312	46.571	50.113	58.156	67.676	78.954
26	39.710	42.759	46.084	49.711	53.669	62.706	73.484	86.351
27	41.931	45.291	48.968	52.993	57.403	67.528	79.698	94.339
28	44.219	47.911	51.966	56.423	61.323	72.640	86.347	102.966
29	46.575	50.623	55.085	60.007	65.439	78.058	93.461	112.283
30	49.003	53.429	58.328	63.752	69.761	83.802	101.073	122.346
31	51.503	56.335	61.701	67.666	74.299	89.890	109.218	133.214
32	54.078	59.341	65.210	71.756	79.064	96.343	117.933	144.951
33	56.730	62.453	68.858	76.030	84.067	103.184	127.259	157.627
34	59.462	65.674	72.652	80.497	89.320	110.435	137.237	171.317
35	62.276	69.008	76.598	85.164	94.336	118.121	147.913	186.102
36	65.174	72.458	80.702	90.041	100.628	126.268	159.337	202.070
37	68.159	76.029	84.970	95.138	106.710	134.904	171.561	219.316
38	71.234	79.725	89.409	100.464	113.095	144.058	184.640	237.941
39	74.401	83.550	94.026	106.030	119.800	153.762	198.635	258.057
40	77.663	87.510	98.827	111.847	126.840	164.048	213.610	279.781

How Much a Year $1 Will Bring

Example of use of this table:

If I put $1,000 in the bank, how much can I take out each year for 5 years to use up the entire sum if the interest rate is 4%?

From the table at 5 years 0.2246

For $1,000 (1000 x 0.2246) $224.60

Note: This does not necessarily represent the annuity payable under an annuity or insurance contract.

Interest Rate

Number of Years	3%	3½%	4%	4½%	5%	6%	7%	8%
1	1.0300	1.0350	1.0400	1.0450	1.0500	1.0600	1.0700	1.0800
2	0.5226	0.5264	0.5302	0.5340	0.5378	0.5454	0.5501	0.5608
3	0.3535	0.3569	0.3603	0.3638	0.3672	0.3741	0.3811	0.3880
4	0.2690	0.2723	0.2755	0.2787	0.2820	0.2886	0.2952	0.3019
5	0.2184	0.2215	0.2246	0.2278	0.2310	0.2374	0.2439	0.2505
6	0.1846	0.1877	0.1908	0.1939	0.1970	0.2034	0.2098	0.2163
7	0.1605	0.1635	0.1666	0.1697	0.1728	0.1791	0.1856	0.1921
8	0.1425	0.1455	0.1485	0.1516	0.1547	0.1610	0.1675	0.1740
9	0.1284	0.1314	0.1345	0.1376	0.1407	0.1470	0.1535	0.1601
10	0.1172	0.1202	0.1233	0.1264	0.1295	0.1359	0.1424	0.1490
11	0.1081	0.1111	0.1141	0.1172	0.1204	0.1268	0.1334	0.1401
12	0.1005	0.1035	0.1066	0.1097	0.1128	0.1193	0.1259	0.1327
13	0.0940	0.0971	0.1001	0.1033	0.1065	0.1129	0.1197	0.1265
14	0.0885	0.0916	0.0947	0.0978	0.1010	0.1076	0.1143	0.1213
15	0.0838	0.0868	0.0899	0.0931	0.0963	0.1029	0.1098	0.1168
16	0.0796	0.0827	0.0858	0.0890	0.0923	0.0989	0.1059	0.1129
17	0.0760	0.0790	0.0822	0.0854	0.0887	0.0954	0.1024	0.1096
18	0.0727	0.0758	0.0790	0.0822	0.0855	0.0924	0.0994	0.1067
19	0.0698	0.0729	0.0761	0.0794	0.0827	0.0896	0.0968	0.1041
20	0.0672	0.0704	0.0736	0.0769	0.0802	0.0872	0.0944	0.1019
21	0.0649	0.0680	0.0713	0.0746	0.0780	0.0850	0.0923	0.0998
22	0.0627	0.0659	0.0692	0.0725	0.0760	0.0837	0.0904	0.0980
23	0.0608	0.0640	0.0673	0.0707	0.0741	0.0813	0.0887	0.0964
24	0.0590	0.0623	0.0656	0.0690	0.0725	0.0797	0.0872	0.0949
25	0.0574	0.0607	0.0640	0.0674	0.0710	0.0782	0.0858	0.0937
26	0.0559	0.0592	0.0626	0.0660	0.0696	0.0769	0.0846	0.0925
27	0.0546	0.0579	0.0612	0.0647	0.0683	0.0757	0.0834	0.0914
28	0.0533	0.0566	0.0600	0.0635	0.0671	0.0746	0.0824	0.0905
29	0.0521	0.0554	0.0589	0.0624	0.0660	0.0736	0.0814	0.0896
30	0.0510	0.0544	0.0578	0.0614	0.0651	0.0726	0.0806	0.0888
31	0.0500	0.0534	0.0569	0.0604	0.0641	0.0718	0.0798	0.0881
32	0.0490	0.0524	0.0559	0.0596	0.0633	0.0710	0.0791	0.0875
33	0.0482	0.0516	0.0551	0.0587	0.0625	0.0703	0.0784	0.0869
34	0.0473	0.0508	0.0543	0.0580	0.0618	0.0696	0.0778	0.0863
35	0.0465	0.0500	0.0536	0.0573	0.0611	0.0686	0.0772	0.0858
36	0.0458	0.0493	0.0529	0.0566	0.0604	0.0684	0.0767	0.0853
37	0.0451	0.0486	0.0522	0.0560	0.0598	0.0679	0.0762	0.0849
38	0.0445	0.0480	0.0516	0.0554	0.0593	0.0674	0.0758	0.0845
39	0.0438	0.0474	0.0511	0.0549	0.0588	0.0669	0.0754	0.0842
40	0.0433	0.0468	0.0505	0.0543	0.0583	0.0665	0.0750	0.0839

How Much Must You Save a Year to Have $1
After a Specified Number of Years

Example of use of this table:

To find the amount of money which must be deposited at the end of each year to grow to $10,000 in 19 years at 8%.

From table for 19 years at 8%   .02413

Amount of each deposit ($10,000 × .02413) $241.30

Interest Rate

Number of Years	3%	3½%	4%	4½%	5%	6%	7%	8%
1	1.00000	1.00000	1.00000	1.00000	1.00000	1.00000	1.00000	1.00000
2	.49261	.49140	.49020	.48900	.48780	.48544	.48309	.48077
3	.32353	.32193	.32035	.31877	.31721	.31411	.31105	.30803
4	.23903	.23725	.23549	.23374	.23201	.22859	.22523	.22192
5	.18835	.18618	.18463	.18279	.18097	.17740	.17389	.17046
6	.15460	.15267	.15076	.14588	.14702	.14336	.13979	.13632
7	.13051	.12854	.12661	.12470	.12282	.11913	.11555	.11207
8	.11246	.11048	.10853	.10661	.10472	.10104	.09747	.09401
9	.09843	.09645	.09449	.09257	.09069	.08702	.08349	.08008
10	.08723	.08524	.08329	.08138	.07950	.07587	.07238	.06903
11	.07808	.07609	.07415	.07225	.07039	.06679	.06336	.06008
12	.07046	.06848	.06655	.06467	.06283	.05928	.05590	.05269
13	.06403	.06206	.06014	.05828	.05646	.05296	.04965	.04652
14	.05853	.05657	.05467	.05282	.05102	.04758	.04434	.04129
15	.05377	.05183	.04994	.04811	.04634	.04206	.03979	.03683
16	.04961	.04768	.04582	.04402	.04227	.03895	.03586	.03298
17	.04595	.04404	.04220	.04042	.03870	.03544	.03243	.02963
18	.04271	.04082	.03899	.03724	.03555	.03236	.02941	.02670
19	.03981	.03794	.03614	.03441	.03275	.02962	.02675	.02413
20	.03722	.03536	.03358	.03188	.03024	.02718	.02439	.02185
21	.03487	.03304	.03128	.02960	.02800	.02500	.02229	.01983
22	.03275	.03093	.02920	.02755	.02597	.02305	.02041	.01803
23	.03081	.02902	.02731	.02568	.02414	.02128	.01871	.01642
24	.02905	.02727	.02559	.02399	.02247	.01968	.01719	.01498
25	.02743	.02567	.02401	.02244	.02095	.01823	.01581	.01368
26	.02594	.02421	.02257	.02102	.01956	.01690	.01456	.01251
27	.02456	.02285	.02124	.01972	.01829	.01570	.01343	.01145
28	.02329	.02160	.02001	.01852	.01712	.01459	.01239	.01049
29	.02211	.02045	.01888	.01741	.01605	.01358	.01145	.00962
30	.02102	.01937	.01783	.01639	.01505	.01265	.01059	.00883
31	.02000	.01837	.01686	.01544	.01413	.01179	.00979	.00811
32	.01905	.01744	.01595	.01456	.01328	.01100	.00907	.00745
33	.01816	.01657	.01510	.01374	.01249	.01027	.00841	.00685
34	.01732	.01576	.01431	.01298	.01176	.00960	.00779	.00630
35	.01654	.01500	.01358	.01227	.01107	.00897	.00723	.00580
36	.01580	.01428	.01289	.01161	.01043	.00839	.00676	.00534
37	.01511	.01361	.01224	.01098	.00984	.00786	.00624	.00492
38	.01446	.01298	.01163	.01040	.00928	.00736	.00579	.00454
39	.01384	.01239	.01106	.00986	.00876	.00689	.00539	.00419
40	.01326	.01183	.01052	.00934	.00828	.00646	.00501	.00386

Present Worth of a Single Future Payment

Example of use of this table:

Find how much must be put at interest now to equal $10,000 in 12 years at a net rate of 4%.

From table for 12 years at 4% 6246
Invest now for $10,000 (10,000 x .6246). . . . . $ 6246

Interest Rate

Number of Years	3%	3½%	4%	4½%	5%	6%	7%	8%
1	0.9709	0.9662	0.9615	0.9569	0.9524	0.9434	0.9346	0.9259
2	0.9426	0.9335	0.9246	0.9157	0.9070	0.8900	0.8734	0.8573
3	0.9151	0.9019	0.8890	0.8763	0.8638	0.8396	0.8163	0.7938
4	0.8885	0.8714	0.8548	0.8386	0.8227	0.7921	0.7629	0.7350
5	0.8626	0.8420	0.8219	0.8025	0.7835	0.7473	0.7130	0.6806
6	0.8375	0.8135	0.7903	0.7679	0.7462	0.7050	0.6663	0.6302
7	0.8131	0.7860	0.7599	0.7348	0.7107	0.6651	0.6227	0.5835
8	0.7894	0.7594	0.7307	0.7032	0.6768	0.6274	0.5820	0.5403
9	0.7664	0.7337	0.7026	0.6729	0.6446	0.5919	0.5439	0.5002
10	0.7441	0.7089	0.6756	0.6439	0.6139	0.5584	0.5083	0.4632
11	0.7224	0.6849	0.6496	0.6162	0.5847	0.5268	0.4751	0.4289
12	0.7014	0.6618	0.6246	0.5897	0.5568	0.4970	0.4440	0.3971
13	0.6810	0.6394	0.6006	0.5643	0.5303	0.4688	0.4150	0.3677
14	0.6611	0.6178	0.5775	0.5400	0.5051	0.4423	0.3878	0.3405
15	0.6419	0.5969	0.5553	0.5167	0.4810	0.4173	0.3624	0.3152
16	0.6232	0.5767	0.5339	0.4945	0.4581	0.3936	0.3387	0.2919
17	0.6050	0.5572	0.5134	0.4732	0.4363	0.3714	0.3166	0.2703
18	0.5874	0.5384	0.4936	0.4528	0.4155	0.3503	0.2959	0.2502
19	0.5703	0.5202	0.4746	0.4333	0.3957	0.3305	0.2765	0.2317
20	0.5537	0.5026	0.4564	0.4146	0.3769	0.3118	0.2584	0.2145
21	0.5375	0.4856	0.4388	0.3968	0.3589	0.2942	0.2415	0.1987
22	0.5219	0.4692	0.4220	0.3797	0.3418	0.2775	0.2257	0.1839
23	0.5067	0.4533	0.4057	0.3634	0.3256	0.2618	0.2109	0.1703
24	0.4919	0.4380	0.3901	0.3477	0.3101	0.2470	0.1971	0.1577
25	0.4776	0.4231	0.3751	0.3327	0.2953	0.2330	0.1842	0.1460
26	0.4637	0.4088	0.3607	0.3184	0.2812	0.2198	0.1722	0.1352
27	0.4502	0.3950	0.3468	0.3047	0.2678	0.2074	0.1609	0.1252
28	0.4371	0.3817	0.3335	0.2916	0.2551	0.1956	0.1504	0.1159
29	0.4243	0.3687	0.3207	0.2790	0.2429	0.1846	0.1406	0.1073
30	0.4120	0.3563	0.3083	0.2670	0.2314	0.1741	0.1314	0.0994
31	0.4000	0.3442	0.2965	0.2555	0.2204	0.1643	0.1228	0.0920
32	0.3883	0.3326	0.2851	0.2445	0.2099	0.1550	0.1147	0.0852
33	0.3770	0.3213	0.2741	0.2340	0.1999	0.1462	0.1072	0.0789
34	0.3660	0.3105	0.2636	0.2239	0.1904	0.1379	0.1002	0.0730
35	0.3554	0.3000	0.2534	0.2143	0.1813	0.1301	0.0937	0.0676
36	0.3450	0.2898	0.2437	0.2050	0.1727	0.1227	0.0875	0.0626
37	0.3350	0.2800	0.2343	0.1962	0.1644	0.1158	0.0818	0.0580
38	0.3252	0.2706	0.2253	0.1877	0.1566	0.1092	0.0765	0.0536
39	0.3158	0.2614	0.2166	0.1797	0.1491	0.1031	0.0715	0.0497
40	0.3066	0.2526	0.2083	0.1719	0.1420	0.0972	0.0668	0.0460

Present Worth of Periodic Future Payments

Example of use of this table:

To find the cost now of $1,000 of income per year for 20 years at 7%.

From table for 20 years at 7%   10.5940

Cost of $1,000 per year ($1,000 X 10.5940) $10,594

Interest Rate

Number of Years	3%	3½%	4%	4½%	5%	6%	7%	8%
1	0.9709	0.9662	0.9615	0.9569	0.9524	0.9434	0.9346	0.9259
2	1.9135	1.8997	1.8861	1.8727	1.8594	1.8334	1.8080	1.7833
3	2.8286	2.8016	2.7751	2.7490	2.7233	2.6730	2.6243	2.5771
4	3.7171	3.6731	3.6299	3.5875	3.5459	3.4651	3.3872	3.3121
5	4.5797	4.5151	4.4518	4.3900	4.3295	4.2124	4.1002	3.9927
6	5.4172	5.3286	5.2421	5.1579	5.0757	4.9173	4.7665	4.6229
7	6.2303	6.1145	6.0021	5.8927	5.7864	5.5824	5.3893	5.2064
8	7.0197	6.8740	6.7327	6.5959	6.4632	6.2098	5.9713	5.7466
9	7.7861	7.6077	7.4353	7.2688	7.1078	6.8017	6.5152	6.2469
10	8.5302	8.3166	8.1109	7.9127	7.7217	7.3601	7.0236	6.7101
11	9.2526	9.0016	8.7605	8.5289	8.3064	7.8869	7.4987	7.1390
12	9.9540	9.6633	9.3851	9.1186	8.8633	8.3838	7.9427	7.5361
13	10.6350	10.3027	9.9856	9.6829	9.3936	8.8527	8.3577	7.9038
14	11.2961	10.9205	10.5631	10.2228	9.8986	9.2950	8.7455	8.2442
15	11.9379	11.5174	11.1184	10.7395	10.3797	9.7122	9.1079	8.5595
16	12.5611	12.0941	11.6523	11.2340	10.8378	10.1059	9.4466	8.8514
17	13.1661	12.6513	12.1657	11.7072	11.2741	10.4773	9.7632	9.1216
18	13.7535	13.1897	12.6593	12.1600	11.6896	10.8276	10.0591	9.3719
19	14.3238	13.7098	13.1339	12.5933	12.0853	11.1581	10.3356	9.6036
20	14.8775	14.2124	13.5903	13.0079	12.4622	11.4699	10.5940	9.8181
21	15.4150	14.6980	14.0292	13.4047	12.8212	11.7641	10.8355	10.0168
22	15.9369	15.1671	14.4511	13.7844	13.1630	12.0416	11.0612	10.2007
23	16.4436	15.6204	14.8568	14.1478	13.4886	12.3034	11.2722	10.3711
24	16.9355	16.0584	15.2470	14.4955	13.7986	12.5504	11.4693	10.5288
25	17.4131	16.4815	15.6221	14.8282	14.0939	12.7834	11.6536	10.6748
26	17.8768	16.8904	15.9828	15.1466	14.3752	13.0032	11.8258	10.8100
27	18.3270	17.2854	16.3296	15.4513	14.6430	13.2105	11.9867	10.9352
28	18.7641	17.6670	16.6631	15.7429	14.8981	13.4062	12.1371	11.0511
29	19.1885	18.0358	16.9837	16.0219	15.1411	13.5907	12.2777	11.1584
30	19.6004	18.3920	17.2920	16.2889	15.3725	13.7648	12.4090	11.2578
31	20.0004	18.7363	17.5885	16.5444	15.5928	13.9291	12.5318	11.3498
32	20.3888	19.0689	17.8736	16.7889	15.8027	14.0840	12.6466	11.4350
33	20.7658	19.3902	18.1476	17.0229	16.0025	14.2302	12.7538	11.5139
34	21.1318	19.7007	18.4112	17.2468	16.1929	14.3681	12.8540	11.5869
35	21.4872	20.0007	18.6646	17.4610	16.3742	14.4982	12.9477	11.6546
36	21.8323	20.2905	18.9083	17.6660	16.5469	14.6210	13.0352	11.7172
37	22.1672	20.5705	19.1426	17.8622	16.7113	14.7368	13.1170	11.7752
38	22.4925	20.8411	19.3679	18.0500	16.8679	14.8460	13.1935	11.8289
39	22.8082	21.1025	19.5845	18.2297	17.0170	14.9491	13.2649	11.8786
40	23.1148	21.3551	19.7928	18.4016	17.1591	15.0463	13.3317	11.9246

COST OF CHARITABLE CONTRIBUTION OF $100

Example of use of this table:

Find the actual out-of-pocket cost of the charitable contribution of a piece of property worth $100 which cost $60. The individual is married and has an income of over $50,000.

From the table on the $44,000 line.........$50.00.

Taxable Income More than Married Joint Return	Single Person	Cash Gift	Property with cost of						
			$30	$40	$50	$60	$70	$80	$90
$ 4,000	$ 2,000	$ 81	$ 74.35	$ 75.30	$ 76.25	$ 77.20	$ 78.15	$ 79.10	$ 80.05
8,000	4,000	78	70.30	71.40	72.50	73.60	74.70	75.80	76.90
12,000	6,000	75	66.25	67.50	68.75	70.00	71.25	72.50	73.75
16,000	8,000	72	62.20	63.60	65.00	66.40	67.80	69.20	70.60
20,000	10,000	68	56.80	58.40	60.00	61.60	63.20	64.80	66.40
24,000	12,000	64	51.40	53.20	55.00	56.80	58.60	60.40	62.20
28,000	14,000	61	47.35	49.30	51.25	53.20	55.15	57.10	59.05
32,000	16,000	58	43.30	45.40	47.50	49.60	51.70	53.80	55.90
36,000	18,000	55	39.25	41.50	43.75	46.00	48.25	50.50	52.75
40,000	20,000	52	35.20	37.60	40.00	42.40	44.80	47.20	49.60
44,000	22,000	50	32.50	35.00	37.50	40.00	42.50	45.00	47.50
52,000	26,000	47	29.50	32.00	34.50	37.00	39.50	42.00	44.50
64,000	32,000	45	27.50	30.00	32.50	35.00	37.50	40.00	42.50
76,000	38,000	42	24.50	27.00	29.50	32.00	34.50	37.00	39.50
88,000	44,000	40	22.50	25.00	27.50	30.00	32.50	35.00	37.50
100,000	50,000	38	20.50	23.00	25.50	28.00	30.50	33.00	35.50
120,000	60,000	36	18.50	21.00	23.50	26.00	28.50	31.00	33.50
140,00C	70,000	34	16.50	19.00	21.50	24.00	26.50	29.00	31.50
160,000	80,000	32	14.50	17.00	19.50	22.00	24.50	27.00	29.50
180,000	90,000	31	13.50	16.00	18.50	21.00	23.50	26.00	28.50
200,000	100,000	30	12.50	15.00	17.50	20.00	22.50	25.00	27.50
300,000	150,000	30	12.50	15.00	17.50	20.00	22.50	25.00	27.50
400,000	200,000	30	12.50	15.00	17.50	20.00	22.50	25.00	27.50

LIFE INSURANCE POLICY COSTS

The following tables give quick rule-of-thumb references to average costs of various types of life insurance contracts and cash values.

PRIMARY FORMS OF PERMANENT POLICIES

There are two primary kinds of permanent life insurance policies, namely Ordinary Life and Endowment.

Under an Ordinary Life policy, the benefits consist of the payment of the sum insured to the beneficiary at the death of the insured. The consideration for this policy usually takes the form of premium payments throughout the lifetime of the insured. If the premium payments are for a limited number of years, e.g., 20 years or paid up at 65, it is called a limited payment life policy (which is simply a variation of ordinary life).

An endowment policy provides for the payment of the sum insured in case of the death of the insured, and in addition guarantees the payment of the sum insured at the end of a stipulated period if the insured is then living. The premium for this policy may be paid throughout the whole period of the endowment, or it may be paid in a shorter number of years or in a single payment as in single premium Ordinary Life policies.

The table which follows illustrates the rates for the various types of basic policies as described. These are for non-participating policies (i.e., those which do not pay dividends). They are rule-of-thumb amounts only to give you a quick idea what the net cost of a particular policy at a particular age will be. To get exact premium costs and make comparisons, consult a life underwriter. There are numerous other forms of Specials. But these involve the primary principles in various combinations.

Basic Annual Premiums Per $1,000 of Insurance (Non-Participating)

Age	* Ordinary Life Male	* 20 Payment Life Male	Life Pay. to 65 Male	Life Pay. to 65 Fem.	* 20 Year End. Male	End. at 65 Male	Age	* Ordinary Life Male	* 20 Payment Life Male	Life Pay. to 65 Male	Life Pay. to 65 Fem.	* 20 Year End. Male	End. at 65 Male
5	7.02	14.07	7.65	7.19	41.41	9.49	38	19.84	29.16	24.07	22.08	43.23	30.73
10	7.94	15.37	8.66	8.12	41.41	10.80	39	20.67	29.97	25.32	23.22	43.48	32.37
15	9.11	16.97	9.97	9.32	41.47	12.50	40	21.55	30.80	26.68	24.45	43.76	34.16
16	9.37	17.32	10.28	9.60	41.48	12.89	41	22.47	31.67	28.15	25.80	44.08	36.10
17	9.65	17.68	10.59	9.89	41.49	13.30	42	23.43	32.57	29.74	27.26	44.42	38.23
18	9.93	18.05	10.93	10.19	41.51	13.74	43	24.44	33.50	31.48	28.87	44.80	40.34
19	10.23	18.44	11.28	10.51	41.53	14.20	44	25.49	34.48	33.39	30.63	45.21	42.88
20	10.55	18.84	11.66	10.85	41.55	14.68	45	26.58	35.49	35.49	32.57	45.67	45.67
21	10.87	19.26	12.05	11.20	41.57	15.19	46	27.71	36.54	37.70	34.62	46.17	48.13
22	11.22	19.69	12.46	11.58	41.60	15.73	47	28.87	37.63	40.26	37.00	46.72	51.52
23	11.57	20.13	12.90	11.97	41.62	16.30	48	30.06	38.77	42.85	39.43	47.31	54.98
24	11.95	20.59	13.37	12.39	41.66	16.91	49	31.30	39.96	46.04	42.40	47.95	59.22
25	12.35	21.07	13.86	12.84	41.69	17.55	50	32.61	41.19	49.66	45.79	48.65	64.05
26	12.76	21.56	14.38	13.31	41.74	18.23	51	34.01	42.48	53.81	49.67	49.41	69.60
27	13.20	22.07	14.94	13.81	41.79	18.96	52	35.50	43.83	58.62	54.19	50.24	76.05
28	13.66	22.60	15.53	14.34	41.85	19.66	53	37.08	45.24	63.48	58.78	51.13	82.33
29	14.14	23.15	16.16	14.91	41.92	20.47	54	38.76	46.71	70.07	65.01	52.09	91.15
30	14.65	23.73	16.83	15.51	42.01	21.35	55	40.57	48.25	78.10	72.59	53.14	101.88
31	15.18	24.32	17.54	16.15	42.10	22.28	56	42.52	49.93	....	....	54.33	....
32	15.75	24.94	18.30	16.84	42.21	23.27	57	44.62	51.70	....	....	55.63	....
33	16.33	25.58	19.12	17.58	42.33	24.34	58	46.85	53.57	....	....	57.04	....
34	16.95	26.24	19.99	18.37	42.47	25.48	59	49.21	55.56	....	....	58.58	....
35	17.61	26.93	20.93	19.22	42.63	26.71	60	51.71	57.68	....	....	60.26	....
36	18.31	27.65	21.84	20.05	42.81	27.91	65	66.65	....	....	....	....	....
37	19.05	28.39	22.91	21.02	43.01	29.33	70	87.76	....	....	....	....	....

CASH VALUE AND NET COST OF NON-PARTICIPATING POLICIES AFTER 10 AND 20 YEARS
(Per $1,000 - CSO 3%)

Ordinary Life

	Age 30		Age 35		Age 40		Age 45	
Annual Premiums.	$ 15.60		$ 18.75		$ 22.80		$ 27.70	
	10 Yrs	20 Yrs	10 Yrs	20 Yrs	10 Yrs	20 Yrs	10 Yrs	20 Yrs
Total Premiums	$156.00	$312.00	$187.50	$375.00	$228.00	$456.00	$277.00	$554.00
Cash Value	124.00	303.00	147.00	345.00	173.00	390.00	201.00	437.00
Net Cost or Gain*. . .	32.00	9.00	40.50	30.00	55.00	66.00	76.00	117.00
Average Cost or Gain*.	3.20	.45	4.05	1.50	5.50	3.30	7.60	5.85

Life Paid-Up at 65

	Age 30		Age 35		Age 40		Age 45	
Annual Premiums.	$ 18.00		$ 22.60		$ 28.77		$ 38.00	
	10 Yrs	20 Yrs	10 Yrs	20 Yrs	10 Yrs	20 Yrs	10 Yrs	20 Yrs
Total Premiums	$180.00	$360.00	$226.00	$452.00	$287.70	$575.40	$380.00	$760.00
Cash Value	145.00	355.00	181.00	430.00	228.00	538.00	300.00	716.00
Net Cost or Gain* . .	35.00	5.00	45.00	22.00	59.70	37.40	80.00	44.00
Average Cost or Gain*.	3.50	.25	4.50	1.10	5.97	1.87	8.00	2.20

20 - Pay Life

	Age 30		Age 35		Age 40		Age 45	
Annual Premiums.	$ 26.20		$ 29.50		$ 33.40		$ 38.00	
	10 Yrs	20 Yrs	10 Yrs	20 Yrs	10 Yrs	20 Yrs	10 Yrs	20 Yrs
Total Premiums	$262.00	$524.00	$295.00	$590.00	$334.00	$668.00	$380.00	$760.00
Cash Value	223.00	549.00	249.00	605.00	274.00	661.00	299.00	716.00
Net Cost or Gain*. . .	39.00	25.00*	46.00	15.00*	60.00	7.00	81.00	44.00
Average Cost or Gain*.	3.90	1.25*	4.60	.75*	6.00	.35	8.10	2.20

20 - Year Endowment

	Age 30		Age 35		Age 40		Age 45	
Annual Premiums.	$ 43.65		$ 44.30		$ 45.25		$ 47.00	
	10 Yrs	20 Yrs	10 Yrs	20 Yrs	10 Yrs	20 Yrs	10 Yrs	20 Yrs
Total Premiums	$436.50	$873.00	$443.00	$886.00	$452.50	$905.00	$470.00	$940.00
Cash Value	404.00	1000.00	403.00	1000.00	401.00	1000.00	399.00	1000.00
Net Cost or Gain*. . .	32.50	127.00*	40.00	114.00*	51.50	95.00*	71.00	60.00*
Average Cost or Gain*.	3.25	6.35*	4.00	5.70*	5.15	4.75*	7.10	3.00*

* Gain - Cash value exceeds total premiums

THE TERM POLICY

The benefits under a term policy consist of payment of the sum insured to the beneficiary at the death of the insured, provided death takes place within a stipulated number of years called the term of the policy. At the end of that period the policy becomes null and void. Premium payments are made throughout the term period.

Some term policies contain a conversion clause which gives the insured the privilege of changing his policy before it becomes null and void to one of the basic forms of permanent insurance, e.g., ordinary life or endowment policy, without having to submit new evidence of insurability.

Other term policies contain a stipulation giving the insured the privilege to renew his term policy at the expiration thereof at attained age rates.

Decreasing term policies are widely used in connection with mortgage risks. The insurance declines as the mortgage debt reduces. In the table below the insurance decreases ratably over the term - e.g., on 10-year term, the insurance coverage decreases 10% a year.

Basic Premium Rates For $1,000 (Non-Participating)

	5 YEAR TERM RENEWABLE TO AGE 65, CONVERTIBLE Minimum $5,000		10 YEAR NON-RENEWABLE TERM Minimum $5,000		TERM TO AGE 65 Minimum $5,000	
Age	Male Lives Flat Rate	Female Lives Flat Rate	Male Lives Flat Rate	Female Lives Flat Rate	Male Lives Flat Rate	Female Lives Flat Rate
20	4.35	4.32	4.37	4.34	7.55	6.94
21	4.36	4.33	4.38	4.35	7.73	7.10
22	4.37	4.34	4.40	4.36	7.93	7.26
23	4.38	4.35	4.43	4.37	8.13	7.43
24	4.40	4.36	4.46	4.38	8.34	7.61
25	4.43	4.37	4.51	4.40	8.56	7.79
26	4.47	4.38	4.57	4.43	8.79	7.98
27	4.53	4.40	4.66	4.46	9.02	8.17
28	4.61	4.43	4.77	4.51	9.26	8.37
29	4.71	4.47	4.90	4.57	9.52	8.58
30	4.83	4.53	5.05	4.66	9.80	8.81
31	4.99	4.61	5.23	4.77	10.10	9.06
32	5.19	4.71	5.45	4.90	10.42	9.32
33	5.41	4.83	5.69	5.05	10.76	9.60
34	5.65	4.99	5.96	5.23	11.12	9.89
35	5.92	5.19	6.26	5.45	11.49	10.19
36	6.20	5.41	6.57	5.69	11.88	10.51
37	6.50	5.65	6.90	5.96	12.28	10.83
38	6.82	5.92	7.27	6.26	12.71	11.18
39	7.19	6.20	7.68	6.57	13.16	11.54
40	7.60	6.50	8.15	6.90	13.64	11.92
41	8.05	6.82	8.67	7.27	14.14	12.32
42	8.52	7.19	9.23	7.68	14.67	12.73
43	9.05	7.60	9.83	8.15	15.22	13.16
44	9.65	8.05	10.54	8.67	15.82	13.62
45	10.35	8.52	11.31	9.23	16.47	14.12
46	11.16	9.05	12.17	9.85	17.18	14.68
47	12.06	9.65	13.10	10.54	17.96	15.29
48	13.04	10.35	14.10	11.31	18.77	15.92
49	14.08	11.16	15.20	12.17	19.60	16.56

T-15(a)

Basic Premium Rates For $1,000 (Non-Participating) Cont'd

	5 YEAR TERM RENEWABLE TO AGE 65, CONVERTIBLE Minimum $5,000		10 YEAR NON-RENEWABLE TERM Minimum $5,000		TERM TO AGE 65 Minimum $5,000	
	Male Lives	Female Lives	Male Lives	Female Lives	Male Lives	Female Lives
Age	Flat Rate	Flat Rate	Flat Rate	Flat Rate	Flat Rate	Flat Rate
50	15.16	12.06	16.40	13.10	20.42	17.16
51	16.21	13.04	17.66	14.10	21.24	17.74
52	17.24	14.08	18.98	15.20	22.06	18.30
53	18.36	15.16	20.40	16.40	22.90	18.86
54	19.69	16.21	22.00	17.66	23.75	19.40
55	21.35	17.24	23.83	18.98	24.60	19.94
56	23.30	18.36				
57	25.54	19.69				
58	27.95	21.35				
59	30.39	23.30				
60	32.75	25.54				
61	34.18	27.95				
62	35.50	30.39				
63	36.85	32.75				
64	38.27	34.18				

Decreasing Term

Male Age	Female Age	10 YEAR Flat Rate	15 YEAR Flat Rate	20 YEAR Flat Rate	25 YEAR Flat Rate	30 YEAR Flat Rate	Male Age	Female Age	10 YEAR Flat Rate	15 YEAR Flat Rate	20 YEAR Flat Rate	25 YEAR Flat Rate	30 YEAR Flat Rate
	20	5.37	5.39	5.42	5.45	5.49	37	40	6.41	6.69	7.11	8.02	9.14
	21	5.38	5.40	5.43	5.46	5.50	38	41	6.55	6.90	7.40	8.39	9.62
	22	5.39	5.41	5.44	5.47	5.51	39	42	6.74	7.15	7.73	8.83	10.16
20	23	5.40	5.42	5.45	5.48	5.53	40	43	6.98	7.45	8.13	9.33	10.78
21	24	5.41	5.43	5.46	5.50	5.58	41	44	7.28	7.81	8.59	9.91	
22	25	5.42	5.44	5.48	5.53	5.64	42	45	7.63	8.23	9.11	10.55	
23	26	5.43	5.46	5.50	5.57	5.72	43	46	8.02	8.69	9.68	11.25	
24	27	5.44	5.48	5.52	5.62	5.82	44	47	8.46	9.19	10.30	12.01	
25	28	5.45	5.50	5.56	5.68	5.93	45	48	8.94	9.73	10.96	12.82	
26	29	5.47	5.53	5.60	5.75	6.06	46	49	9.46	10.31	11.65		
27	30	5.49	5.55	5.64	5.83	6.20	47	50	10.02	10.93	12.38		
28	31	5.52	5.58	5.70	5.92	6.36	48	51	10.62	11.59	13.16		
29	32	5.56	5.63	5.77	6.04	6.54	49	52	11.27	12.30	14.00		
30	33	5.62	5.70	5.86	6.19	6.76	50	53	11.97	13.07	14.92		
31	34	5.70	5.79	5.97	6.37	7.01	51	54	12.71	13.88			
32	35	5.79	5.90	6.10	6.57	7.28	52	55	13.49	14.72			
33	36	5.90	6.03	6.25	6.80	7.58	53	56	14.32	15.62			
34	37	6.02	6.17	6.42	7.06	7.92	54	57	15.20	16.61			
35	38	6.15	6.34	6.63	7.36	8.30	55	58	16.16	17.71			
36	39	6.28	6.51	6.86	7.68	8.71	56	59	17.17				
							57	60	18.23				
							58		19.35				
							59		20.57				
							60		21.89				

FAMILY INCOME RIDER

The family income rider provides a monthly income in event of the death of the insured during the period selected. The period begins when the policy becomes effective. If, for example, the period selected is 20 years, and the insured dies after the policy has been in effect 10 years, the beneficiary will receive payments for 10 years under the family income rider. After the ten year period ends, the face of the policy will be paid. Each agreement may be written for any amount of monthly income from $10 to $50 for each $1,000 face amount of basic policy.

This plan was designed primarily to provide (a) income during the school period, (b) a life income to the wife and (c) funds to pay off a mortgage.

Tax Aspects of Family Income Rider - Proposed amendments to Regs. §§ 1.101-3 and 1.101-4 say that a portion of each monthly payment under a family income rider represents interest on the proceeds of the basic policy retained by the insurance company until the end of the term period. To that extent, a surviving spouse is taxed each year on such interest. The monthly yield per $1,000 face amount depends upon the rate of interest guaranteed under the policy; at 2-1/4% it would be $1.86; at 2-1/2%, $2.06, etc.

The balance of each payment under the family income rider is attributable to both principal and interest payable in installments from the term rider. To the extent that such installment payment reflects interest, it is taxable. But the surviving spouse is entitled to exclude from gross income an amount up to $1,000 a year. The commuted value of the family income rider is income-tax-free as death proceeds.

As an example of how IRS intends to tax a surviving spouse as beneficiary of a policy with a family income rider, let's assume the insured held a $100,000 ordinary life policy with a $1,000-a-month twenty-year rider. Suppose he died at the end of the seventeenth year so that there are thirty-six monthly payments to be made to his widow under the family income rider. At the time of his death, the commuted value of the $36,000 total payments ($1,000 x 36) is $28,409.

Assuming an interest rate of 2-1/4%, here's how to figure the amount of each $1,000 monthly payment includible in the widow's gross income:

First: Compute the annual interest on the $100,000 basic policy which is retained by the insurance company for the duration of payments under the rider ($100,000 x 2-1/4% = $2,250). When reduced to 12 monthly installments with the necessary adjustments for monthly payments, this comes to $185. The widow will include in her gross income the $185 monthly payments under Code § 101(c).

Second: Divide the commuted value of the family income rider by the number of monthly payments ($28,409 ÷ 36 = $789.14). So the $789.14 which represents distribution of principal under the rider is excluded under Code § 101(d).

Third: The balance of each monthly installment ($1,000 minus $789.14 minus $185 = $25.86), represents interest on the proceeds of the family income rider. Since the sum of $25.86 is being distributed to the widow along with the principal, it qualifies for the annual exclusion. And since the annual total is less than $1,000 ($25.86 x 12 = $310.32), the entire amount is tax free.

Fourth: At the end of the monthly payments under the family income rider, the $100,000 proceeds of the basic ordinary life policy will then go to the widow tax free under Code § 101(a).

Following are typical rule-of-thumb premiums for family income riders and the estimated commuted values of a typical policy.

FAMILY INCOME RIDER

MALE AGE	FE-MALE AGE	\$10 Monthly Income				\$20 Monthly Income			
		10 YEAR	15 YEAR	20 YEAR	25 YEAR	10 YEAR	15 YEAR	20 YEAR	25 YEAR
		FLAT RATE	FLAT RATE	FLAT RATE	FLAT RATE	FLAT RATE	FLAT RATE	FLAT RATE	FLAT RATE
	20	\$ 1.81	\$ 2.56	\$ 3.30	\$ 4.07	\$ 3.98	\$ 5.63	\$ 7.25	\$ 8.94
	21	1.81	2.57	3.33	4.11	3.98	5.65	7.32	9.03
	22	1.81	2.58	3.36	4.17	3.98	5.67	7.38	9.16
20	23	1.82	2.60	3.39	4.24	4.00	5.71	7.45	9.32
21	24	1.82	2.61	3.42	4.31	4.00	5.74	7.52	9.47
22	25	1.82	2.62	3.45	4.38	4.00	5.76	7.58	9.63
23	26	1.83	2.63	3.48	4.46	4.02	5.78	7.65	9.80
24	27	1.84	2.65	3.54	4.57	4.04	5.82	7.78	10.04
25	28	1.86	2.69	3.62	4.73	4.09	5.91	7.96	10.39
26	29	1.89	2.75	3.73	4.93	4.15	6.04	8.20	10.83
27	30	1.93	2.83	3.87	5.16	4.24	6.22	8.50	11.34
28	31	1.98	2.92	4.02	5.42	4.35	6.42	8.83	11.91
29	32	2.04	3.02	4.21	5.73	4.48	6.64	9.25	12.59
30	33	2.11	3.15	4.43	6.09	4.64	6.92	9.74	13.38
31	34	2.18	3.29	4.68	6.49	4.79	7.23	10.28	14.26
32	35	2.26	3.44	4.96	6.93	4.97	7.56	10.90	15.23
33	36	2.35	3.61	5.27	7.42	5.16	7.93	11.58	16.31
34	37	2.45	3.81	5.62	7.97	5.38	8.37	12.35	17.51
35	38	2.58	4.04	6.01	8.57	5.67	8.88	13.21	18.83
36	39	2.73	4.31	6.45	9.24	6.00	9.47	14.17	20.31
37	40	2.90	4.60	6.93	9.99	6.37	10.11	15.23	21.95
38	41	3.08	4.93	7.44	10.78	6.77	10.83	16.35	23.06
39	42	3.28	5.28	8.00	11.60	7.21	11.60	17.58	25.49
40	43	3.49	5.64	8.59	12.45	7.67	12.39	18.88	27.36
41	44	3.68	5.99	9.18	13.32	8.09	13.16	20.17	29.27
42	45	3.86	6.33	9.76	14.21	8.48	13.91	21.45	31.23
43	46	4.07	6.71	10.40	15.14	8.94	14.75	22.86	33.27
44	47	4.33	7.16	11.16	16.09	9.52	15.73	24.53	35.36
45	48	4.69	7.75	12.08	17.08	10.31	17.03	26.55	37.54
46	49	5.16	8.49	13.17		11.34	18.66	28.94	
47	50	5.73	9.34	14.39		12.59	20.53	31.62	
48	51	6.35	10.28	15.74		13.95	22.59	34.59	
49	52	7.01	11.27	17.23		15.41	24.77	37.86	
50	53	7.67	12.29	18.84		16.86	27.01	41.40	
51	54	8.32	13.33			18.28	29.29		
52	55	8.97	14.41			19.71	31.67		
53	56	9.65	15.54			21.21	34.15		
54	57	10.39	16.71			22.83	36.72		
55	58	11.21	17.92			24.64	39.38		
56	59	12.11				26.61			
57	60	13.07				28.72			
58		14.10				30.99			
59		15.19				33.38			
60		16.34				35.91			

COMMUTED AMOUNT OF EXTRA PROTECTION
PROVIDED BY FAMILY INCOME RIDER

Per $10 of Monthly Income

Balance of Fam. Inc. Period at Death of Insured	Commuted Value	Balance of Fam. Inc. Period at Death of Insured	Commuted Value
YEARS		YEARS	
25	$1,780	12	$991
24	1,728	11	919
23	1,675	10	846
22	1,620	9	770
21	1,564	8	694
20	1,506	7	613
19	1,447	6	532
18	1,387	5	449
17	1,325	4	364
16	1,261	3	276
15	1,196	2	186
14	1,130	1	94
13	1,061		

FAMILY MAINTENANCE RIDER

The family maintenance rider differs from the family income rider in that the insurance company will pay $10 per month per $1,000 of insurance for a designated period commencing at the date of death of the insured for the period specified.

The following table gives typical premium costs for the family maintenance rider.

Age	15 Year Rider Male	20 Year Rider Male	Age	15 Year Rider Male	20 Year Rider Male
16	$	$	35	$ 7.86	$ 11.68
20	4.25	5.61	36	8.44	12.55
21	4.31	5.70	37	9.07	13.49
22	4.35	5.76	38	9.76	14.48
23	4.39	5.85	39	10.51	15.58
24	4.48	5.97	40	11.32	16.79
			41	12.20	18.08
25	4.60	6.18	42	13.11	19.46
26	4.76	6.48	43	14.10	20.92
27	4.97	6.86	44	15.19	22.53
28	5.21	7.28			
29	5.48	7.76	45	16.40	24.29
30	5.79	8.29	46	17.72	.....
31	6.13	8.86	47	19.13	.....
32	6.49	9.46	48	20.65	.....
33	6.89	10.14	49	22.30	.....
34	7.35	10.87	50	24.10	.....
			51	.....	.....
			52	.....	.....
			53	.....	.....
			54	.....	.....

Optional modes of settlement provide that the whole or part of the net proceeds of a policy payable at death, or at maturity as an endowment or of the cash value of a policy in force, may be retained by the company for periodic disbursement in a number of ways.

To ascertain insurance requirements for income needs, it is necessary to determine what the settlement options will do in the way of income.

The following tables give the income payable, either at interest for a specified number of years, or for life under typical insurance policy settlement options. The tables show how long various amounts of insurance will provide stipulated amounts of monthly income at various rates of interest; and how much monthly life income will be available for periods certain for males and females.

Proceeds at Interest

The following table shows the monthly interest payable, at various guaranteed interest rates, where the proceeds are left with the insurance company to draw interest.

Interest Rate	Monthly Per $1000 Proceeds
2% guaranteed	$1.65
2½% guaranteed	2.06
3% guaranteed	2.46

Insurance Proceeds Payable in Equal Monthly Payments for Fixed Period of Years

No. of Years Pay-able	When 3% is Guaranteed Payments per $1,000 Proceeds	When 3% is Guaranteed Proceeds Required for Payments of $25	When 3% is Guaranteed Proceeds Required for Payments of $100	When 2½% is Guaranteed Payments per $1,000 Proceeds	When 2½% is Guaranteed Proceeds Required for Payments of $25	When 2½% is Guaranteed Proceeds Required for Payments of $100	When 2% is Guaranteed Payments per $1,000 Proceeds	When 2% is Guaranteed Proceeds Required for Payments of $25	When 2% is Guaranteed Proceeds Required for Payments of $100
1	$ 84.47	$ 296	$ 1,184	$84.28	$ 297	$ 1,187	$ 84.09	$ 298	$ 1,190
2	42.86	584	2,334	42.66	587	2,345	42.46	589	2,356
3	28.99	863	3,450	28.79	869	3,474	28.59	875	3,498
4	22.06	1,134	4,534	21.86	1,144	4,575	21.65	1,155	4,619
5	17.91	1,396	5,584	17.70	1,413	5,650	17.49	1,430	5,718
6	15.14	1,652	6,606	14.93	1,675	6,698	14.72	1,699	6,794
7	13.16	1,900	7,599	12.95	1,931	7,723	12.74	1,963	7,850
8	11.68	2,141	8,562	11.47	2,180	8,719	11.25	2,223	8,889
9	10.53	2,375	9,497	10.32	2,423	9,690	10.10	2,476	9,901
10	9.61	2,602	10,406	9.39	2,663	10,650	9.18	2,724	10,894
11	8.86	2,822	11,287	8.64	2,894	11,575	8.42	2,970	11,877
12	8.24	3,034	12,136	8.02	3,118	12,469	7.80	3,206	12,821
13	7.71	3,243	12,971	7.49	3,338	13,352	7.26	3,444	13,775
14	7.26	3,444	13,775	7.03	3,557	14,225	6.81	3,672	14,685
15	6.87	3,640	14,557	6.64	3,766	15,061	6.42	3,895	15,577
16	6.53	3,829	15,314	6.30	3,969	15,874	6.07	4,119	16,475
17	6.23	4,013	16,052	6.00	4,167	16,667	5.77	4,333	17,332
18	5.96	4,195	16,779	5.73	4,364	17,453	5.50	4,546	18,182
19	5.73	4,364	17,453	5.49	4,554	18,215	5.26	4,753	19,012
20	5.51	4,538	18,149	5.27	4,744	18,976	5.04	4,961	19,842
21	5.32	4,700	18,797	5.08	4,922	19,686	4.85	5,155	20,619
22	5.15	4,855	19,418	4.90	5,103	20,409	4.67	5,354	21,414
23	4.99	5,011	20,041	4.74	5,275	21,098	4.51	5,544	22,173
24	4.84	5,166	20,662	4.60	5,435	21,740	4.36	5,734	22,936
25	4.71	5,308	21,232	4.46	5,606	22,422	4.22	5,925	23,697
26	4.59	5,447	21,787	4.34	5,761	23,042	4.10	6,098	24,391
27	4.47	5,593	22,372	4.22	5,925	23,697	3.98	6,282	25,126
28	4.37	5,721	22,884	4.12	6,068	24,272	3.87	6,460	25,840
29	4.27	5,855	23,420	4.02	6,219	24,876	3.77	6,632	26,526
30	4.18	5,981	23,924	3.93	6,362	25,446	3.68	6,794	27,174

How Long Insurance Proceeds Will Last If Paid Out Monthly Until Principal And Interest Are Exhausted							

% of proceeds Paid each year or	Dollars per Mo. per $1,000 of proceeds	Fund will last - When Guaranteed Rate of Interest Is:					
		2%		2½%		3%	
		Yrs.	Mos.	Yrs.	Mos.	Yrs.	Mos.
5.0%	$ 4.17	25	5	27	6	30	2
5.4	4.50	23	0	24	8	26	9
5.5	4.58	22	6	24	1	26	0
6.0	5.00	20	2	21	5	22	11
6.5	5.42	18	3	19	3	20	5
6.6	5.50	17	11	18	11	20	0
7.0	5.83	16	9	17	7	18	6
7.2	6.00	16	2	16	11	17	10
7.5	6.25	15	5	16	1	16	11
7.8	6.50	14	9	15	4	16	1
8.0	6.67	14	4	14	11	15	7
8.4	7.00	13	6	14	0	14	7
8.5	7.08	13	4	13	10	14	5
9.0	7.50	12	6	12	11	13	3
9.5	7.92	11	9	12	2	12	7
10.0	8.33	11	1	11	5	11	10
10.2	8.50	10	10	11	2	11	6
10.5	8.75	10	6	10	10	11	2
10.8	9.00	10	2	10	6	10	9
11.0	9.17	10	0	10	3	10	6
11.4	9.50	9	7	9	10	10	1
12.0	10.00	9	1	9	3	9	6
12.5	10.42	8	8	8	10	9	1
13.0	10.83	8	4	8	6	8	8
13.5	11.25	8	0	8	2	8	4
14.0	11.67	7	8	7	10	8	0
15.0	12.50	7	1	7	3	7	5
16.0	13.33	6	7	6	9	6	10
17.0	14.17	6	2	6	4	6	5
18.0	15.00	5	10	5	11	6	0
19.0	15.83	5	6	5	7	5	8
20.0	16.67	5	3	5	3	5	4
21.0	17.50	4	11	5	0	5	1
22.0	18.33	4	9	4	9	4	10
23.0	19.17	4	6	4	7	4	7
24.0	20.00	4	4	4	4	4	5
25.0	20.83	4	1	4	2	4	3

MONTHLY LIFE INCOME PER $1000 OF PROCEEDS
AT VARIOUS AGES

(2-1/2% Interest)

Male	Age Female	Life Income Only	5 Years Certain and Life	10 Years Certain and Life	15 Years Certain and Life	20 Years Certain and Life	Install- ment Re- fund
25	30	$3.08	$3.08	$3.08	$3.07	$3.05	$3.01
30	35	3.27	3.27	3.26	3.24	3.22	3.17
31	36	3.31	3.31	3.30	3.28	3.25	3.20
32	37	3.36	3.36	3.34	3.32	3.29	3.24
33	38	3.41	3.40	3.39	3.36	3.33	3.28
34	39	3.45	3.45	3.43	3.41	3.37	3.32
35	40	3.50	3.50	3.48	3.45	3.41	3.36
36	41	3.56	3.55	3.53	3.50	3.45	3.40
37	42	3.61	3.61	3.59	3.55	3.50	3.44
38	43	3.67	3.66	3.64	3.60	3.54	3.49
39	44	3.73	3.72	3.70	3.65	3.59	3.53
40	45	3.79	3.78	3.76	3.71	3.64	3.58
41	46	3.86	3.85	3.82	3.77	3.69	3.63
42	47	3.93	3.92	3.88	3.82	3.74	3.68
43	48	4.00	3.99	3.95	3.88	3.79	3.74
44	49	4.08	4.06	4.02	3.95	3.84	3.80
45	50	4.15	4.14	4.09	4.01	3.90	3.85
46	51	4.24	4.22	4.17	4.08	3.95	3.91
47	52	4.33	4.31	4.25	4.15	4.01	3.98
48	53	4.42	4.40	4.33	4.22	4.07	4.04
49	54	4.51	4.49	4.42	4.29	4.12	4.11
50	55	4.61	4.59	4.50	4.37	4.18	4.18
51	56	4.72	4.69	4.60	4.44	4.24	4.26
52	57	4.83	4.80	4.69	4.52	4.30	4.33
53	58	4.95	4.91	4.79	4.60	4.36	4.42
54	59	5.07	5.03	4.90	4.69	4.41	4.50
55	60	5.20	5.15	5.01	4.77	4.47	4.59
56	61	5.34	5.28	5.12	4.86	4.53	4.68
57	62	5.48	5.42	5.23	4.94	4.59	4.77
58	63	5.64	5.56	5.35	5.03	4.64	4.87
59	64	5.80	5.72	5.48	5.12	4.70	4.98
60	65	5.97	5.87	5.61	5.21	4.75	5.08
61	66	6.15	6.04	5.74	5.30	4.80	5.20
62	67	6.34	6.22	5.87	5.39	4.85	5.31
63	68	6.54	6.40	6.01	5.48	4.90	5.44
64	69	6.75	6.59	6.16	5.56	4.94	5.57
65	70	6.97	6.79	6.30	5.65	4.98	5.70
70	75	8.32	7.95	7.07	6.05	5.14	6.48

LIQUIDITY VALUE OF ASSETS

Death produces debts where none may have existed during life. Cash will be needed to meet funeral expenses, executor's and trustee's fees, and estate taxes. It is a matter of sound business sense, therefore, that the potential liabilities and the ability to convert assets into cash to meet them be estimated as accurately as possible during life.

As a rule of thumb, the cash an experienced professional executor may reasonably expect to get for estate assets may be estimated by applying the percentages indicated below.

Assets	Percentage of Market Value Which Experienced Executor May Realize in Cash
Cash in bank	100
U.S. accumulation bonds	100
Government bonds	100
Municipals	90
Listed bonds	90
Listed common stocks:	
High-grade investment	85
High-grade speculative	70
Preferred stocks	90
Unlisted bonds:	
High-grade	85
Other	60
Unlisted stocks:	
High-grade	80
Other	30
Mortgages:	
High-grade	100
Other	70
Real estate	Your estimate
Close corporation stock:	
Subject to P/S contract	Price stipulated
Other	100-30
Partnership interests:	
Subject to P/S contract	Price stipulated
Other	Liquidated value
Proprietorship interests:	
Subject to P/S contract	Price stipulated
Other	Liquidated value
Interests in trusts and estates, based on underlying assets	100-30
Personal effects	Your estimate
Life insurance	100
Annuities	100
Other assets	Your estimate

The market value of a business that is to be liquidated is its liquidation value with some variation, depending upon the nature of the business. The ratio of the liquidating value of assets to their book value may reasonably be figured as follows:

Assets	Percentage of Market Value
Cash	100
Accounts receivable	85-25
Inventory	100-35
Realty	100-50
Fixtures	50-10
Equipment	75-25

VALUING LIFE ESTATE, ANNUITY AND
REMAINDER INTERESTS

Insurance company annuities are valued at replacement cost. But non-commercial annuities (e.g., $3,000 a year for life or a period of years under a will or trust), life estates and remainder and reversionary interests are valued under special Treasury Tables. For gifts made on or before December 31, 1970 and for estates of decedents dying on or before that date, the Treasury used tables that were based on 3-1/2% interest and with no distinction between life estates of men and women. However, for gifts made on or after January 1, 1971 and for estates of decedents dying on or after that date, the Treasury requires the use of a different series of tables, which use 6% interest, more modern life expectancies and different tables for male lives and female lives.

The value of a life estate is the value of the entire property less the present value of the remainder interest at the end of the life estate. The value of a term for years is the value of the entire property less the present value of the remainder interest at the end of the term. The value of a remainder interest is the value of the property times the appropriate figure under the remainder interest column. If the remainder interest follows a life estate, use the column opposite the age of the life tenant. If the remainder interest follows a term for years, use the column opposite the number of years.

The value of an annuity for life is the amount of annual payment times the figure in the "Annuity" column, opposite the appropriate age. If payments are at the end of other than annual periods, make this adjustment under the latest table:

If periods are	Multiply result by
Weekly	1.0291
Monthly	1.0272
Quarterly	1.0222
Semiannually	1.0148

If the first annuity payment is to be made at once, the value of the annuity is the amount of that payment plus the value of a similar annuity, in which the first payment isn't to be made until the end of the first period.

The value of an annuity for years is the amount of annual payment times the figure in the "Annuity" column, opposite the appropriate number of years. If payments are made at other than annual periods and are at the beginning of the period, make this adjustment under the latest table:

If periods are	Multiply result by
Weekly	1.0303
Monthly	1.0322
Quarterly	1.0372
Semiannually	1.0448

The annuity tables contained in Rev. Rul. 62-216 (1962-2 CB 30) should be used in valuing private annuity contracts for estate and gift tax purposes (Rev. Rul. 67-39, 1967-1 CB 18).

Present Worth of Annuity Life Interest and Remainder Interest Following Life
Estate for Gifts Made on or After January 1, 1971.

Table A(1)

Single life male, 6%, showing the present worth of an annuity, a life interest
and a remainder interest

Age	Annuity	Life Estate	Remainder	Age	Annuity	Life Estate	Remainder
0	15.6175	.93705	.06295	55	10.2960	.61776	.38224
1	16.0362	.96217	.03783	56	10.0777	.60466	.39534
2	16.0283	.96170	.03830	57	9.8552	.59131	.40869
3	16.0089	.96053	.03947	58	9.6297	.57778	.42222
4	15.9841	.95905	.04095	59	9.4028	.56417	.43583
5	15.9553	.95732	.04268	60	9.1753	.55052	.44948
6	15.9233	.95540	.04460	61	8.9478	.53687	.46313
7	15.8885	.95331	.04669	62	8.7202	.52321	.47679
8	15.8508	.95105	.04895	63	8.4924	.50954	.49046
9	15.8101	.94861	.05139	64	8.2642	.49585	.50415
10	15.7663	.94598	.05402	65	8.0353	.48212	.51788
11	15.7194	.94316	.05684	66	7.8060	.46836	.53164
12	15.6698	.94019	.05981	67	7.5763	.45458	.54542
13	15.6180	.93708	.06292	68	7.3462	.44077	.55923
14	15.5651	.93391	.06609	69	7.1149	.42689	.57311
15	15.5115	.93069	.06931	70	6.8823	.41294	.58706
16	15.4576	.92746	.07254	71	6.6481	.39889	.60111
17	15.4031	.92419	.07581	72	6.4123	.38474	.61526
18	15.3481	.92089	.07911	73	6.1752	.37051	.62949
19	15.2918	.91751	.08249	74	5.9373	.35624	.64376
20	15.2339	.91403	.08597	75	5.6990	.34194	.65806
21	15.1744	.91046	.08954	76	5.4602	.32761	.67239
22	15.1130	.90678	.09328	77	5.2211	.31327	.68673
23	15.0487	.90292	.09702	78	4.9825	.29895	.70105
24	14.9807	.89884	.10116	79	4.7469	.28481	.71519
25	14.9075	.89445	.10555	80	4.5164	.27098	.72902
26	14.8287	.88972	.11028	81	4.2955	.25773	.74227
27	14.7442	.88465	.11535	82	4.0879	.24527	.75473
28	14.6542	.87925	.12075	83	3.8924	.23354	.76646
29	14.5588	.87353	.12647	84	3.7029	.22217	.77783
30	14.4584	.86750	.13250	85	3.5117	.21070	.78930
31	14.3528	.86117	.13883	86	3.3259	.19955	.80045
32	14.2418	.85451	.14549	87	3.1450	.18820	.81130
33	14.1254	.84752	.15248	88	2.9703	.17872	.82178
34	14.0034	.84020	.15980	89	2.8052	.16831	.83169
35	13.8758	.83255	.16745	90	2.6536	.15922	.84078
36	13.7425	.82455	.17545	91	2.5162	.15097	.84903
37	13.6036	.81622	.18378	92	2.3917	.14350	.85650
38	13.4591	.80755	.19245	93	2.2801	.13681	.86319
39	13.3090	.79854	.20146	94	2.1802	.13081	.86919
40	13.1538	.78923	.21077	95	2.0891	.12535	.87465
41	12.9934	.77960	.22040	96	1.0997	.11998	.88002
42	12.8279	.76967	.23033	97	1.9145	.11487	.88513
43	12.6574	.75944	.24056	98	1.8331	.10999	.89001
44	12.4819	.74891	.25109	99	1.7554	.10532	.89468
45	12.3013	.73808	.26192	100	1.6812	.10087	.89913
46	12.1158	.72695	.27305	101	1.6101	.09661	.90339
47	11.9253	.71552	.28448	102	1.5416	.09250	.90750
48	11.7308	.70385	.29615	103	1.4744	.08846	.91154
49	11.5330	.69198	.30802	104	1.4065	.08439	.91561
50	11.3329	.67997	.32003	105	1.3334	.08000	.92000
51	11.1308	.66785	.33215	106	1.2452	.07471	.92529
52	10.9267	.65560	.34440	107	1.1196	.06718	.93282
53	10.7200	.64320	.35680	108	.9043	.05426	.94574
54	10.5100	.63060	.36940	109	.4717	.02830	.97170

Single life female, 6% showing the present worth of an
annuity, a life interest and a remainder interest

Age	Annuity	Life Estate	Remainder	Age	Annuity	Life Estate	Remainder
0	15.8972	0.95383	0.04617	55	11.6432	.69859	.30141
1	16.2284	.97370	.02630	56	11.4353	.68612	.31388
2	16.2287	.97372	.02628	57	11.2200	.67320	.32680
3	16.2180	.97308	.02692	58	10.9980	.65988	.34012
4	16.2029	.97217	.20783	59	10.7703	.64622	.35378
5	16.1850	.97110	.02890	60	10.5376	.63226	.36774
6	16.1648	.96989	.03011	61	10.3005	.61803	.38197
7	16.1421	.96853	.03147	62	10.0587	.60352	.39648
8	16.1172	.96703	.03297	63	9.8118	.58871	.41129
9	16.0901	.96541	.03459	64	9.5592	.57355	.42645
10	16.0608	.96365	.03635	65	9.3005	.55803	.44197
11	16.0293	.96176	.03824	66	9.0352	.54211	.45789
12	15.9958	.95975	.04025	67	8.7639	.52583	.47417
13	15.9607	.95764	.04236	68	8.4874	.50924	.49076
14	15.9239	.95543	.04457	69	8.2068	.49241	.50759
15	15.8856	.95314	.04686	70	7.9234	.47540	.52460
16	15.8460	.95076	.04924	71	7.6371	.45823	.54177
17	15.8048	.94829	.05171	72	7.3480	.44088	.55912
18	15.7620	.94572	.05428	73	7.0568	.42341	.57659
19	15.7172	.94303	.05697	74	6.7645	.40587	.59413
20	15.6701	.94021	.05979	75	6.4721	.38833	.61167
21	15.6207	.93724	.06276	76	6.1788	.37073	.62927
22	15.5687	.93412	.06588	77	5.8845	.35307	.64693
23	15.5141	.93085	.06915	78	5.5910	.33546	.66454
24	15.4565	.92739	.07261	79	5.3018	.31811	.68189
25	15.3959	.92375	.07625	80	5.0195	.30117	.69883
26	15.3322	.91993	.08007	81	4.7482	.28489	.71511
27	15.2652	.91591	.08409	82	4.4892	.26935	.73065
28	15.1946	.91168	.08832	83	4.2398	.25439	.74561
29	15.1208	.90725	.09275	84	3.9927	.23956	.76044
30	15.0432	.90259	.09741	85	3.7401	.22441	.77559
31	14.9622	.89773	.10227	86	3.5016	.21010	.78990
32	14.8775	.89265	.10735	87	3.2790	.19674	.80326
33	14.7888	.88733	.11267	88	3.0719	.18431	.81569
34	14.6960	.88176	.11824	89	2.8808	.17285	.82715
35	14.5989	.87593	.12407	90	2.7068	.16241	.83759
36	14.4975	.86985	.13015	91	2.5502	.15301	.84699
37	14.3915	.86349	.13651	92	2.4116	.14470	.85530
38	14.2811	.85687	.14313	93	2.2901	.13741	.86259
39	14.1663	.84998	.15002	94	2.1839	.13103	.86897
40	14.0468	.84281	.15719	95	2.0891	.12535	.87465
41	13.9227	.83536	.16464	96	1.9997	.11998	.88002
42	13.7940	.82764	.17236	97	1.9145	.11487	.88513
43	13.6604	.81962	.18038	98	1.8331	.10999	.89001
44	13.5219	.81131	.18869	99	1.7554	.10532	.89468
45	13.3781	.80269	.19731				
46	13.2290	.79374	.20626	100	1.6812	.10087	.89913
47	13.0746	.78448	.21552	101	1.6101	.09661	.90339
48	12.9147	.77488	.22512	102	1.5416	.09250	.90750
49	12.7496	.76498	.23502	103	1.4744	.08846	.91154
				104	1.4065	.08439	.91561
50	12.5793	.75476	.24524	105	1.3334	.08000	.92000
51	12.4039	.74423	.25577	106	1.2452	.07471	.92529
52	12.2232	.73339	.26661	107	1.1196	.06718	.93282
53	12.0367	.72220	.27780	108	.9043	.05426	.94574
54	11.8436	.71062	.28938	109	.4717	.02830	.97170

A Valuation of Term for Years or Remainder Interest Following
Term for Years (Table B) for Gifts Made on or After January 1, 1971

Table B

The present worth at 6% of an annuity for a term certain, an income
interest for a term certain and a remainder interest postponed for a
term certain

Number of Years	Annuity	Term Certain	Remainder	Number of Years	Annuity	Term Certain	Remainder
1	0.9434	0.056604	0.943396	31	13.9291	.835745	.164255
2	1.8334	.110004	.889996	32	14.0840	.845043	.154957
3	2.6730	.160381	.839619	33	14.2302	.853814	.146186
4	3.4651	.207906	.792094	34	14.3681	.862088	.137912
5	4.2124	.252742	.747258	35	14.4982	.869895	.130105
6	4.9173	.295309	.704961	36	14.6210	.877259	.122741
7	5.5824	.334943	.665057	37	14.7368	.884207	.115793
8	6.2098	.372588	.627412	38	14.8460	.890761	.109239
9	6.8017	.408102	.591898	39	14.9491	.896944	.103056
10	7.3601	.441605	.558395	40	15.0463	.902778	.097222
11	7.8869	.473212	.526788	41	15.1380	.908281	.091719
12	8.3838	.503031	.496969	42	15.2245	.913473	.086527
13	8.8527	.531161	.468839	43	15.3062	.918370	.081630
14	9.2950	.557699	.442301	44	15.3832	.922991	.077009
15	9.7122	.582735	.417265	45	15.4558	.927350	.072650
16	10.1059	.606354	.393646	46	15.5244	.931462	.068538
17	10.4773	.628636	.371364	47	15.5890	.935342	.064658
18	10.8276	.649656	.350344	48	15.6500	.939002	.060998
19	11.1581	.669487	.330513	49	15.7076	.942454	.057546
20	11.4699	.688195	.311805	50	15.7619	.945712	.054288
21	11.7641	.705845	.294155	51	15.8131	.948785	.051215
22	12.0416	.722495	.277505	52	15.8614	.951684	.048316
23	12.3034	.738203	.261797	53	15.9070	.954418	.045582
24	12.5504	.753021	.246979	54	15.9500	.956999	.043001
25	12.7834	.767001	.232999	55	15.9905	.959433	.040567
26	13.0032	.780190	.219810	56	16.0288	.961729	.038271
27	13.2105	.792632	.207368	57	16.0649	.963895	.036105
28	13.4062	.804370	.195630	58	16.0990	.965939	.034061
29	13.5907	.815443	.184557	59	16.1311	.967867	.032133
30	13.7648	.825890	.174110	60	16.1614	.969686	.030314

The following group of tables give rule-of-thumb costs of various types of annuities and the necessary figures for computing the tax-free and taxable portions of annuity payments.

SINGLE PREMIUM DEFERRED ANNUITY

The following table shows how much of an annuity you get for a single premium paid at an age earlier than the age when the annuity is to begin.

Monthly Life Income Per $1,000 of Single Premium

Age at Issue		Age When Annuity is Elected							
		M 55 or F 60		M 60 or F 65		M 65 or F 70		MALE 70	
Male	Female	Cash Refund	120 Mos. Certain	Cash Refund	120 Mos. Certain	Cash Refund	120 Mos. Certain	Cash Refund	120 Mos. Certain
30	35	8.10	8.96	10.06	11.33	12.62	14.39	16.04	18.32
31	36	7.91	8.75	9.81	11.05	12.32	14.05	15.65	17.88
32	37	7.71	8.53	9.57	10.78	12.02	13.70	15.27	17.44
33	38	7.52	8.32	9.34	10.52	11.72	13.37	14.90	17.02
34	39	7.34	8.12	9.11	10.26	11.44	13.04	14.53	16.60
35	40	7.16	7.92	8.89	10.01	11.16	12.72	14.18	16.19
36	41	6.98	7.73	8.67	9.77	10.89	12.42	13.84	15.80
37	42	6.81	7.54	8.46	9.53	10.62	12.11	13.50	15.41
38	43	6.65	7.36	8.26	9.30	10.36	11.82	13.17	15.04
39	44	6.49	7.18	8.05	9.07	10.11	11.53	12.85	14.67
40	45	6.33	7.00	7.86	8.85	9.86	11.25	12.53	14.31
41	46	6.16	6.82	7.66	8.63	9.62	10.98	12.23	13.97
42	47	5.99	6.63	7.48	8.42	9.39	10.70	11.93	13.62
43	48	5.83	6.45	7.30	8.22	9.16	10.45	11.64	13.29
44	49	5.68	6.28	7.12	8.01	8.93	10.19	11.36	12.97
45	50	5.52	6.11	6.94	7.82	8.72	9.94	11.08	12.65
46	51	5.36	5.93	6.76	7.61	8.50	9.70	10.81	12.35
47	52	5.21	5.75	6.57	7.40	8.30	9.46	10.54	12.04
48	53	5.06	5.59	6.40	7.21	8.09	9.23	10.29	11.75
49	54	4.91	5.43	6.23	7.01	7.89	9.00	10.04	11.46
50	55	4.77	5.27	6.06	6.83	7.71	8.79	9.79	11.18
51	56	4.62	5.12	5.89	6.63	7.50	8.55	9.55	10.91
52	57	4.48	4.96	5.71	6.44	7.29	8.32	9.32	10.64
53	58	4.35	4.81	5.55	6.25	7.10	8.10	9.09	10.39
54	59	4.22	4.67	5.39	6.07	6.91	7.88	8.87	10.13
55	60			5.23	5.89	6.72	7.67	8.66	9.88
56	61			5.07	5.71	6.53	7.45	8.43	9.62
57	62			4.92	5.54	6.34	7.23	8.19	9.36
58	63			4.77	5.37	6.16	7.02	7.98	9.11
59	64			4.63	5.21	5.98	6.82	7.76	8.86
60	65					5.80	6.62	7.55	8.63
61						5.63	6.42	7.34	8.38
62						5.45	6.22	7.12	8.13
63						5.29	6.04	6.92	7.90
64						5.13	5.85	6.71	7.67
65								6.52	7.44

ANNUAL PREMIUM DEFERRED ANNUITY

The following table shows how much of an annuity you get beginning at a deferred date for annual premiums beginning at the ages indicated.

Monthly Life Income per $100 of Annual Premium

Age When Annuity is Elected

AGE AT ISSUE	MALE 55 Cash Re-fund	MALE 55 120 Mos. Certain	MALE 60 Cash Re-fund	MALE 60 120 Mos. Certain	MALE 65 Cash Re-fund	MALE 65 120 Mos. Certain	MALE 70 Cash Re-fund	MALE 70 120 Mos. Certain	FEMALE 55 Cash Re-fund	FEMALE 55 120 Mos. Certain	FEMALE 60 Cash Re-fund	FEMALE 60 120 Mos. Certain	FEMALE 65 Cash Re-fund	FEMALE 65 120 Mos. Certain	FEMALE 70 Cash Re-fund	FEMALE 70 120 Mos. Certain
35	10.45	11.56	15.40	17.35	22.03	25.12	31.03	35.43	9.60	10.45	14.04	15.53	19.85	22.36	27.62	31.50
36	9.79	10.83	14.59	16.43	21.01	23.96	29.74	33.96	9.00	9.79	13.30	14.71	18.94	21.33	26.48	30.20
37	9.15	10.12	13.79	15.54	20.02	22.83	28.48	32.52	8.41	9.15	12.57	13.91	18.05	20.33	25.35	28.92
38	8.53	9.43	13.02	14.66	19.05	21.73	27.25	31.12	7.84	8.53	11.87	13.13	17.17	19.34	24.26	27.67
39	7.91	8.75	12.26	13.81	18.10	20.65	26.05	29.75	7.27	7.91	11.18	12.36	16.32	18.38	23.19	26.45
40	7.31	8.09	11.52	12.97	17.18	19.59	24.88	28.41	6.72	7.31	10.50	11.62	15.48	17.44	22.14	25.26
41	6.75	7.46	10.83	12.19	16.31	18.60	23.79	27.16	6.20	6.75	9.87	10.92	14.70	16.56	21.18	24.15
42	6.19	6.85	10.15	11.43	15.46	17.63	22.72	25.95	5.69	6.19	9.25	10.23	13.94	15.70	20.23	23.07
43	5.65	6.25	9.48	10.67	14.64	16.69	21.67	24.75	5.19	5.65	8.64	9.56	13.19	14.86	19.29	22.00
44	5.11	5.66	8.82	9.94	13.82	15.76	20.65	23.58	4.70	5.11	8.04	8.89	12.45	14.03	18.38	20.96
45	4.59	5.08	8.18	9.21	13.02	14.85	19.64	22.43	4.22	4.59	7.46	8.25	11.73	13.21	17.49	19.94
46	4.06	4.49	7.52	8.47	12.19	13.90	18.59	21.23	3.73	4.06	6.85	7.58	10.99	12.37	16.55	18.87
47	3.54	3.91	6.87	7.74	11.38	12.98	17.56	20.05	3.25	3.54	6.26	6.93	10.26	11.56	15.63	17.83
48	3.03	3.35	6.25	7.04	10.59	12.08	16.56	18.91	2.78	3.03	5.69	6.30	9.55	10.75	14.74	16.81
49	2.54	2.81	5.63	6.35	9.82	11.20	15.58	17.79	2.33	2.54	5.13	5.68	8.85	9.97	13.87	15.82
50	2.06	2.28	5.03	5.67	9.07	10.35	14.62	16.70	1.89	2.06	4.59	5.08	8.18	9.21	13.02	14.85
51	1.61	1.78	4.45	5.01	8.34	9.51	13.69	15.64	1.48	1.61	4.06	4.49	7.52	8.47	12.19	13.90
52	1.16	1.29	3.88	4.37	7.63	8.70	12.79	14.60	1.07	1.16	3.54	3.91	6.87	7.74	11.38	12.98
53	.74	.81	3.32	3.75	6.93	7.90	11.90	13.59	.68	.74	3.03	3.35	6.25	7.04	10.59	12.08
54	.32	.35	2.78	3.14	6.25	7.13	11.04	12.60	.29	.32	2.54	2.81	5.63	6.35	9.82	11.20
55			2.26	2.54	5.59	6.37	10.20	11.64			2.06	2.28	5.03	5.67	9.08	10.35
56			1.77	1.99	4.94	5.64	9.38	10.71			1.61	1.78	4.46	5.02	8.35	9.52
57			1.29	1.46	4.32	4.92	8.58	9.80			1.18	1.30	3.89	4.38	7.64	8.72
58			.83	.94	3.71	4.23	7.81	8.92			.76	.84	3.34	3.77	6.95	7.93
59			.38	.43	3.11	3.55	7.05	8.05			.35	.38	2.81	3.16	6.28	7.16
60					2.53	2.89	6.31	7.21					2.28	2.57	5.62	6.41
61					2.01	2.30	5.66	6.46					1.81	2.04	5.04	5.75
62					1.49	1.70	4.97	5.67					1.34	1.51	4.42	5.04
63					.97	1.11	4.31	4.92					.87	.98	3.84	4.38
64					.44	.51	3.62	4.14					.40	.45	3.23	3.68
65							2.96	3.38							2.63	3.00

SINGLE PREMIUM STRAIGHT LIFE IMMEDIATE ANNUITIES

The following table gives the single premium cost of an immediate straight life annuity. In addition to acting as a guide for such premium costs, it is valuable in computing gain or loss on an exchange of property for a private annuity. It is also useful in computing the amount of a deductible contribution where a gift is made to a charity in exchange for a life annuity.

	Male Lives				Female Lives			
Age Last Birth-day	Price of Annuity of		Annuity Purchased By $1,000		Price of Annuity of		Annuity Purchased By $1,000	
	$100 Ann.	$10 Monthly	Ann. Pay-ment	Mo. Pay-ment	$100 Ann.	$10 Monthly	Ann. Pay-ment	Mo. Pay ment
35	2438.00	2983.80	41.02	3.35	2616.60	3198.12	38.22	3.13
36	2405.30	2944.56	41.57	3.40	2588.40	3164.28	38.63	3.16
37	2371.70	2904.24	42.16	3.44	2559.50	3129.60	39.07	3.20
38	2337.40	2863.08	42.78	3.49	2529.90	3094.08	39.53	3.23
39	2302.30	2820.96	43.43	3.54	2499.50	3057.60	40.01	3.27
40	2266.40	2777.88	44.12	3.60	2468.40	3020.28	40.51	3.31
41	2229.60	2733.72	44.85	3.66	2436.60	2982.12	41.04	3.35
42	2191.90	2688.48	45.62	3.72	2404.00	2943.00	41.60	3.40
43	2153.50	2642.40	46.44	3.78	2370.60	2902.92	42.18	3.44
44	2114.50	2595.60	47.29	3.85	2336.60	2862.12	42.80	3.49
45	2075.20	2548.44	48.19	3.92	2301.70	2820.24	43.45	3.55
46	2035.50	2500.80	49.13	4.00	2266.10	2777.52	44.13	3.60
47	1995.10	2452.32	50.12	4.08	2229.70	2733.84	44.85	3.66
48	1954.40	2403.48	51.17	4.16	2192.60	2689.32	45.61	3.72
49	1913.40	2354.28	52.26	4.25	2154.70	2643.84	46.41	3.78
50	1872.40	2305.08	53.41	4.34	2116.10	2597.52	47.26	3.85
51	1831.30	2255.76	54.61	4.43	2076.70	2550.24	48.15	3.92
52	1789.90	2206.08	55.87	4.53	2036.60	2502.12	49.10	4.00
53	1748.40	2156.28	57.20	4.64	1995.70	2453.04	50.11	4.08
54	1706.80	2106.36	58.59	4.75	1954.10	2403.12	51.17	4.16
55	1665.00	2056.20	60.06	4.86	1911.80	2352.36	52.31	4.25
56	1622.90	2005.68	61.62	4.99	1868.60	2300.52	53.52	4.35
57	1580.50	1954.80	63.27	5.12	1824.40	2247.48	54.81	4.45
58	1538.10	1903.92	65.02	5.25	1779.60	2193.72	56.19	4.56
59	1495.90	1853.28	66.85	5.40	1734.40	2139.48	57.66	4.67
60	1454.30	1803.36	68.76	5.55	1689.30	2085.36	59.20	4.80
61	1413.30	1754.16	70.76	5.70	1644.10	2031.12	60.82	4.92
62	1372.80	1705.56	72.84	5.86	1598.50	1976.40	62.56	5.06
63	1332.60	1657.32	75.04	6.03	1552.80	1921.56	64.40	5.20
64	1292.70	1609.44	77.36	6.21	1507.00	1866.60	66.36	5.36
65	1253.00	1561.80	79.81	6.40	1461.40	1811.88	68.43	5.52
66	1213.70	1514.64	82.39	6.60	1415.90	1757.28	70.63	5.69
67	1174.80	1467.96	85.12	6.81	1370.60	1702.92	72.96	5.87
68	1136.10	1421.52	88.02	7.03	1325.20	1648.44	75.46	6.07
69	1097.40	1375.08	91.12	7.27	1279.70	1593.84	78.14	6.27
70	1058.50	1328.40	94.47	7.53	1234.40	1539.24	81.02	6.50
71	1018.50	1280.40	98.18	7.81	1187.80	1483.56	84.19	6.74
72	977.70	1231.44	102.28	8.12	1140.70	1427.04	87.67	7.01
73	937.10	1182.72	106.71	8.46	1093.80	1370.76	91.42	7.30
74	898.10	1135.92	111.35	8.80	1048.30	1316.16	95.39	7.60
75	861.80	1092.36	116.04	9.15	1005.20	1264.44	99.48	7.91
76	828.80	1052.76	120.66	9.50	964.90	1216.08	103.64	8.22
77	798.40	1016.28	125.25	9.84	926.70	1170.24	107.91	8.55
78	769.60	981.72	129.94	10.19	890.00	1126.20	112.36	8.88
79	741.50	948.00	134.86	10.55	854.40	1083.48	117.04	9.23
80	713.30	914.16	140.19	10.94	819.40	1041.48	122.04	9.60
81	685.50	880.80	145.88	11.35	785.30	1000.56	127.34	9.99
82	658.70	848.64	151.81	11.78	752.40	961.08	132.91	10.40
83	632.10	816.72	158.20	12.24	720.20	922.44	138.85	10.84
84	604.70	783.84	165.37	12.76	688.20	884.04	145.31	11.31
85	575.60	748.92	173.73	13.35	655.90	845.28	152.46	11.83

Only part of each annuity payment received is taxed. The fraction formed by the cost of the annuity over the expected return determines the portion of each annuity payment that is tax free. The following tables are to be used in determining the expected return in various situations. These are tables issued by the Treasury.

Expected Return Per $1 Annual Payment For Single Life Annuity (Government Table 1)

Example of use of this table:

Find exempt portion of annuity of $100 per month for single male annuitant Annuitant is 65. Contract cost $14,000.

$$\frac{\text{Cost of contract (\$14,000)}}{\text{Annual payments (\$1200) X multiple from table (15)}} - \frac{14}{18} \text{ X } \$100 = \$77.78$$

Ages		Expected Return Per $1 Annual Payment	Ages		Expected Return Per $1 Annual Payment	Ages		Expected Return Per $1 Annual Payment
Male	Female		Male	Female		Male	Female	
16	21	55.8	41	46	33.0	66	71	14.4
17	22	54.9	42	47	32.1	67	72	13.8
18	23	53.9	43	48	31.2	68	73	13.2
19	24	53.0	44	49	30.4	69	74	12.6
20	25	52.1	45	50	29.6	70	75	12.1
21	26	51.1	46	51	28.7	71	76	11.6
22	27	50.2	47	52	27.9	72	77	11.0
23	28	49.3	48	53	27.1	73	78	10.5
24	29	48.3	49	54	26.3	74	79	10.1
25	30	47.4	50	55	25.5	75	80	9.6
26	31	46.5	51	56	24.7	76	81	9.1
27	32	45.6	52	57	24.0	77	82	8.7
28	33	44.6	53	58	23.2	78	83	8.3
29	34	43.7	54	59	22.4	79	84	7.8
30	35	42.8	55	60	21.7	80	85	7.5
31	36	41.9	56	61	21.0	81	86	7.1
32	37	41.0	57	62	20.3	82	87	6.7
33	38	40.0	58	63	19.6	83	88	6.3
34	39	39.1	59	64	18.9	84	89	6.0
35	40	38.2	60	65	18.2	85	90	5.7
36	41	37.3	61	66	17.5	86	91	5.4
37	42	36.5	62	67	16.9	87	92	5.1
38	43	35.6	63	68	16.2	88	93	4.8
39	44	34.7	64	69	15.6	89	94	4.5
40	45	33.8	65	70	15.0	90	95	4.2

If annuity payments are other than monthly or if first annuity payment is earlier than regular period for payment thereafter, the figures in the table must be adjusted. Add or subtract as follows:

If the number of whole months from the annuity starting date to the first payment date is	0-1	2	3	4	5	6	7	8	9	10	11	12
And payments under the contract are to be made:												
Annually	+.5	+.4	+.3	+.2	+.1	0	0	-.1	-.2	-.3	-.4	-.5
Semi-annually	+.2	+.1	0	0	-.1	-.2						
Quarterly	+.1	0	-.1									

Where wife is same age or older than husband use table on next page.

Example of use of this table:

Find exempt portion of annuity of $100 per month for a married couple. Husband is 67; wife is 62. Contract cost $21,000.

$$\frac{\text{Cost of contract (\$21,000)}}{\text{Annual payment (\$1200) X multiple from table (23)}} = \frac{210}{276} \text{ X } 100 = \$76.09$$

Note: See next page for use of Table II where variable annuity pays lesser amount to specified survivor. For adjustment for early or other than monthly payment see Table I.

Age of Husband	Wife Younger by							
	1 yr.	2 yr.	3 yr.	4 yr.	5 yr.	6 yr.	7 yr.	8 yr.
45	39.9	40.5	41.1	41.7	42.3	--	--	--
46	38.9	39.5	40.1	40.7	41.4	42.0	--	--
47	38.0	38.6	39.2	39.8	40.4	41.1	41.8	--
48	37.1	37.7	38.3	38.9	39.5	40.2	40.8	41.5
49	36.2	36.8	37.3	38.0	38.6	39.2	39.9	40.6
50	35.3	35.8	36.4	37.0	37.7	38.3	39.0	39.6
51	34.4	34.9	35.5	36.1	36.7	37.4	38.0	38.7
52	33.5	34.0	34.6	35.2	35.8	36.5	37.1	37.8
53	32.6	33.1	33.7	34.3	34.9	35.6	36.2	36.9
54	31.7	32.2	32.8	33.4	34.0	34.7	35.3	36.0
55	30.8	31.4	31.9	32.5	33.1	33.8	34.4	35.1
56	29.9	30.5	31.1	31.6	32.2	32.9	33.5	34.2
57	29.1	29.6	30.2	30.8	31.4	32.0	32.6	33.3
58	28.2	28.8	29.3	29.9	30.5	31.1	31.7	32.4
59	27.4	27.9	28.5	29.0	29.6	30.2	30.9	31.5
60	26.5	27.1	27.6	28.2	28.8	29.4	30.0	30.6
61	25.7	26.2	26.8	27.3	27.9	28.5	29.1	29.8
62	24.9	25.4	25.9	26.5	27.1	27.7	28.3	28.9
63	24.1	24.6	25.1	25.7	26.2	26.8	27.4	28.1
64	23.3	23.8	24.3	24.9	25.4	26.0	26.6	27.2
65	22.5	23.0	23.5	24.1	24.6	25.2	25.8	26.4
66	21.7	22.2	22.7	23.3	23.8	24.4	25.0	25.6
67	21.0	21.4	21.9	22.5	23.0	23.6	24.1	24.7
68	20.2	20.7	21.2	21.7	22.2	22.8	23.4	23.9
69	19.5	19.9	20.4	20.9	21.5	22.0	22.6	23.2
70	18.7	19.2	19.7	20.2	20.7	21.2	21.8	22.4
71	18.0	18.5	19.0	19.5	20.0	20.5	21.0	21.6
72	17.3	17.8	18.2	18.7	19.2	19.8	20.3	20.9
73	16.7	17.1	17.5	18.0	18.5	19.0	19.6	20.1
74	16.0	16.4	16.9	17.3	17.8	18.3	18.8	19.4
75	15.3	15.7	16.2	16.6	17.1	17.6	18.1	18.7
76	14.7	15.1	15.5	16.0	16.4	16.9	17.4	18.0
77	14.1	14.5	14.9	15.3	15.8	16.3	16.7	17.3
78	13.5	13.8	14.3	14.7	15.1	15.6	16.1	16.6
79	12.9	13.2	13.6	14.1	14.5	15.0	15.4	15.9
80	12.3	12.7	13.0	13.5	13.9	14.3	14.8	15.3

Expected Return on Joint and Surviror Annuity
--Wife Younger--Different Amount After
First Death (Government Table IIA)

Where wife is same age or older than husband use table on page 71.

Example of use of this table:

Find exclusion ratio of joint and survivor contract of $100 per month so long as both husband and wife live and $50 per month after death of one. Husband is 70; wife is 67. Cost of contract is $13,500.

Multiple from Table II on page 67 for husband 70, wife 3 years younger.....................................	19.7
Multiple from Table below....................................	9.3
Difference...	10.4
Portion of expected return (reduced payment) 10.4 x $600.......	$ 6,240
Portion of expected return (full payment) 9.3 x $1,200.........	$ 11,160
Expected Return...	$ 17,400

$$\text{Exclusion Ratio} = \frac{13,500 \text{ (cost of contract)}}{17,400 \text{ (expected return)}}$$

Note: See Table I for early or other than monthly payment.

Age of Husband	Wife Younger by							
	1 yr.	2 yr.	3 yr.	4 yr.	5 yr.	6 yr.	7 yr.	8 yr.
45	24.4	24.7	25.0	25.2	25.5	--	--	--
46	23.6	23.9	24.2	24.4	24.7	24.9	--	--
47	22.9	23.1	23.4	23.7	23.9	24.2	24.4	---
48	22.1	22.4	22.7	22.9	23.2	23.4	23.6	23.8
49	21.4	21.6	21.9	22.2	22.4	22.6	22.9	23.1
50	20.6	20.9	21.2	21.4	21.7	21.9	22.1	22.3
51	19.9	20.2	20.5	20.7	20.9	21.2	21.4	21.6
52	19.2	19.5	19.8	20.0	20.2	20.4	20.7	20.9
53	18.5	18.8	19.1	19.3	19.5	19.7	19.9	20.1
54	17.9	18.1	18.4	18.6	18.8	19.0	19.2	19.4
55	17.2	17.5	17.7	17.9	18.1	18.4	18.6	18.7
56	16.6	16.8	17.0	17.3	17.5	17.7	17.9	18.1
57	15.9	16.2	16.4	16.6	16.8	17.0	17.2	17.4
58	15.3	15.5	15.8	16.0	16.2	16.4	16.6	16.7
59	14.7	14.9	15.1	15.3	15.5	15.7	15.9	16.1
60	14.1	14.3	14.5	14.7	14.9	15.1	15.3	15.5
61	13.5	13.7	13.9	14.1	14.3	14.5	14.7	14.9
62	12.9	13.2	13.4	13.6	13.7	13.9	14.1	14.3
63	12.4	12.6	12.8	13.0	13.2	13.3	13.5	13.7
64	11.8	12.0	12.2	12.4	12.6	12.8	12.9	13.1
65	11.3	11.5	11.7	11.9	12.1	12.2	12.4	12.5
66	10.8	11.0	11.2	11.4	11.5	11.7	11.9	12.0
67	10.3	10.5	10.7	10.9	11.0	11.2	11.3	11.5
68	9.8	10.0	10.2	10.4	10.5	10.7	10.8	11.0
69	9.4	9.6	9.7	9.9	10.0	10.2	10.3	10.5
70	8.9	9.1	9.3	9.4	9.6	9.7	9.8	10.0
71	8.5	8.7	8.8	9.0	9.1	9.3	9.4	9.5
72	8.1	8.2	8.4	8.5	8.7	8.8	8.9	9.1
73	7.7	7.8	8.0	8.1	8.2	8.4	8.5	8.6
74	7.3	7.4	7.6	7.7	7.8	8.0	8.1	8.2
75	6.9	7.0	7.2	7.3	7.4	7.6	7.7	7.8
76	6.5	6.7	6.8	6.9	7.1	7.2	7.3	7.4
77	6.2	6.3	6.4	6.6	6.7	6.8	6.9	7.0
78	5.9	6.0	6.1	6.2	6.3	6.4	6.5	6.6
79	5.5	5.7	5.8	5.9	6.0	6.1	6.2	6.3
80	5.2	5.3	5.5	5.6	5.7	5.8	5.9	6.0

Cost of Contract With Refund or Payment
Certain Feature (Government Table III)

Example of use of this table:

Find cost of contract of $100 per month to husband, age 65. Purchase price is $21,053 and refund of purchase price guaranteed.

Purchase price....................................		$21,053
Annual payment	$ 1,200	
Years guaranteed ($21,053 refund ÷ $1,200 annual payment)...................................	17.5	
Rounded to nearest year...........................	18	
% in table at age 65 for 18 years.................	30%	
Value of refund: 30% of..........................	$21,053	6,316
Cost of Contract...................................		**$14,737**

Note: See Table I for early or other than monthly payment.

Age		Years Guaranteed											
Male	Female	5	8	10	12	15	18	20	22	25	28	30	35
40	45	1%	2%	3%	3%	4%	6%	7%	8%	9%	11%	13%	17%
41	46	1	2	3	3	5	6	7	8	10	12	14	18
42	47	1	2	3	4	5	6	8	9	11	13	15	19
43	48	1	2	3	4	5	7	8	9	12	14	16	21
44	49	1	3	3	4	6	7	9	10	12	15	17	22
45	50	2	3	4	5	6	8	9	11	13	16	18	23
46	51	2	3	4	5	7	9	10	12	14	17	19	25
47	52	2	3	4	5	7	9	11	12	15	18	20	26
48	53	2	3	5	6	8	10	12	13	16	19	22	28
49	54	2	4	5	6	8	11	12	14	17	21	23	29
50	55	2	4	5	7	9	11	13	15	18	22	24	31
51	56	3	4	6	7	9	12	14	16	20	23	26	32
52	57	3	5	6	8	10	13	15	17	21	25	27	34
53	58	3	5	7	8	11	14	16	19	22	26	29	38
54	59	3	5	7	9	12	15	17	20	24	28	31	38
55	60	3	6	8	9	13	16	18	21	25	29	32	39
56	61	4	6	8	10	13	17	20	22	27	31	34	41
57	62	4	7	9	11	14	18	21	24	28	33	36	43
58	63	4	7	9	12	15	19	22	25	30	34	37	45
59	64	5	8	10	12	16	21	24	27	31	36	39	47
60	65	5	8	11	13	18	22	25	28	33	38	41	48
61	66	5	9	12	14	19	23	27	30	35	40	43	50
62	67	6	10	12	15	20	25	28	32	37	42	45	52
63	68	6	10	13	16	21	26	30	33	39	44	47	54
64	69	7	11	14	17	23	28	32	35	41	46	49	55
65	70	7	12	15	19	24	30	33	37	42	47	50	57
66	71	8	13	16	20	26	31	35	39	44	49	52	59
67	72	8	14	17	21	27	33	37	41	46	51	54	61
68	73	9	14	18	23	29	35	39	43	48	53	56	62
69	74	9	16	20	24	30	37	41	45	50	55	58	64
70	75	10	17	21	26	32	39	43	47	52	57	60	65
71	76	11	18	22	27	34	41	45	49	54	59	61	67
72	77	12	19	24	29	36	43	47	51	56	60	63	68
73	78	12	20	25	30	38	45	49	53	58	62	65	70
74	79	13	22	27	32	40	47	51	55	60	64	66	71
75	80	14	23	29	34	42	49	53	57	62	66	68	72

PLANNING ESTATE ADMINISTRATION

The following group of tables are useful in planning the administration of an estate and in meeting technical requirements of estate law in the drawing and reviewing of wills and trusts.

FUNERAL AND ADMINISTRATION COSTS

The estate planner invariably considers the impact of estate taxes in computing shrinkage and in determining the amount of cash, insurance and liquid assets which should be available to the estate. While the impact of combined funeral and administration costs may not generally be as great, especially in larger estates, it should not be neglected. Payment of these costs are, with few exceptions, as sure as taxes, and the necessity for cash to meet them could make inroads into a thin controlling business interest or necessitate the sale of property which was intended to be held.

Included in the administration category are executors', attorneys', accountants' and appraisers' fees; court costs and miscellaneous items such as travelling and storage expenses, publication fees, title search fees, etc.

The table which follows is based upon a recent U.S. Treasury report on Fiduciary, Gift, and Estate Tax Returns Filed. Actual projections for any particular estate can, of course, not be presumed from this table. They will vary from case to case, depending upon the nature of the estate property, its intended distribution pattern, and place of probate and location of the property, as well as other factors.

Gross Estate	% Claimed for Funeral and Administration Expenses
$ 60,000 under 70,000	5.1
70,000 under 80,000	5.0
80,000 under 90,000	4.7
90,000 under 100,000	4.6
100,000 under 120,000	4.5
120,000 under 150,000	4.4
150,000 under 200,000	4.4
200,000 under 300,000	4.5
300,000 under 500,000	4.4
500,000 under 1,000,000	4.0
1,000,000 under 2,000,000	3.9
2,000,000 under 3,000,000	3.6
3,000,000 under 5,000,000	3.9
5,000,000 under 10,000,000	3.8
10,000,000 under 20,000,000	3.4

EXECUTORS' COMMISSIONS

Most states have a statutory schedule of fees for executors. Some merely call for reasonable fees, the reasonableness to be determined by the courts. In a number of states, fees for testamentary trustees are the same as those allowed to executors. Some states provide for a distinct statutory fee for trustees, but most provide for reasonable fees to be determined by the court, more often than not based in large measure upon trust receipts—with 5% annually being a fairly reasonable national average. In the case of both executors and testamentary trustees, additional reasonable fees may usually be charged for extraordinary services.

Note that the general rule is that there is nothing to prevent the testator from specifying the executor's commission right in the will (or even directing that there shall be no commissions). Then it's up to the executor to accept or refuse appointment under those terms.

The table that follows relates exclusively to compensation of executors and administrators, and is based both upon statutory fee allowances and the usual fees which are charged by corporate executors where a statutory rate does not apply. As to the latter, there are sometimes variations in different areas of the same state.*

Alabama

Not more than 2-1/2% of receipts and disbursements.

Alaska

First $1,000—7%
Next $1,000—5%
Next $2,000—4%
All above $4,000—2%

Arizona

First $1,000—7%
Next $9,000—5%
All above $10,000—4%

Arkansas

First $1,000—Not more than 10%
Next $4,000—5%
All above $5,000—3%

California

First $1,000—7%
Next $9,000—4%
Next $40,000—3%
Next $100,000—2%
Next $350,000—1-1/2%
All above $500,000—1%

Colorado

First $25,000—6%
Next $75,000—4%
All above $100,000—3%

Connecticut

No statutory fee schedule or minimums. The following schedule has been suggested as reasonable:
First $10,000—5%
Next $40,000—3%
Next $200,000—2-1/2%
Next $750,000—2%
Next $1,000,000—1-1/2%
All above $2,000,000—1%
Minimum fee—$200.

Delaware

No statutory fee schedule or minimums. Fees are determined by the Register of Wills. Some typical percentage fees allowed on total gross estates are as follows:
Less than $1,000—$100
$10,000-20,000—$800 + 5% over
$10,000
$40,000-60,000—$2,150 + 3-1/2%
over $40,000
$100,000-125,000—4.0% gross estate
$200,000-250,000—3.2% gross estate
$350,000-400,000—2.8% gross estate
$500,000 or over—2.5% gross estate

District of Columbia

Not under 1% nor more than 10% of inventory.

Florida

Reasonable fees

*1976 figures.
American College of Probate Counsel, 10964 West Pico Blvd., Los Angeles, Calif.

Georgia

2-1/2% of receipts and disbursements.

Hawaii

On receipts, 7% of first $5,000—all above $5,000, 5%.
On principal:
  First $1,000—5%
  Next $9,000—4%
  Next $10,000—3%
  All above $20,000—2%

Idaho

First $1,000—5%
Next $9,000—4%
All above $10,000—3%

Illinois

No statutory fee schedule or minimums. The following is an example of customary rate:
  First $25,000—5%
  Next $25,000—3-1/2%-4%
  Next $50,000—3%-3-1/2%
  Next $150,000—2-1/2%-3%
  Next $750,000—2%-2-1/2%
  All above $1,000,000—1-1/2%-2%

Indiana

No statutory fee schedule or minimums. The following is an example of customary rates for a corporate fiduciary:
  First $25,000—5%
  Next $25,000—4%
  Next $50,000—3%
  Next $650,000—2%

Iowa

First $1,000—not more than 6%
Next $4,000—4%
All above $5,000—2%

Kansas

No statutory fee schedule or minimums. The following is an example of customary rates:
  First $10,000—5%
  Next $15,000—4%
  Next $25,000—3%
  Next $50,000—2%
  All above $100,000—1%

Kentucky

Not more than 5% of income and 5% of personal estate.

Louisiana

Fee is 2-1/2% of the inventory of the estate—it may be increased by the court upon showing that usual commission is inadequate.

Maine

Not more than 5% of personal estate with rate being reduced as a matter of practice in larger estates.

Maryland

First $20,000—Not more than 10%
All above $20,000—Not more than 4%.

Massachusetts

No statutory fee schedule or minimums. The following is an example of customary rates: 2-1/2%-3% of personal estate up to $500,000 and 1% of balance.

Michigan

First $1,000—5%
Next $4,000—2-1/2%
All above $5,000—2%

Minnesota

No statutory fee schedule or minimums. The following is an example of customary rates for a corporate fiduciary:
  First $50,000—4%
  Next $50,000—3%
  Next $100,000—2-1/2%

Mississippi

Not more than 7% on amount of estate administered.

Missouri

First $5,000—5%
Next $20,000—4%
Next $75,000—3%
Next $300,000—2-3/4%
Next $600,000—2-1/2%
All above $1,000,000—2%

Montana

Not to exceed:
  First $40,000—3%
  All above $40,000—2%

Nebraska

First $1,000—5%
Next $4,000—2-1/2%
All above $5,000—2%

Nevada

First $1,000—6%
Next $4,000—4%
All above $5,000—2%

New Hampshire

Reasonable compensation.

New Jersey

On income, 6%. On corpus not
exceeding $100,000—5%.
On excess over $100,000, the
percentage, not in excess of 5%,
in discretion of the Court. Usual
rates—5% of first $100,000 and
5% of excess.

New Mexico

First $3,000—10%
All above $3,000—5%
For cash, U.S. Savings Bonds, or
life insurance proceeds, the
compensation is 5% on the first
$5,000 and 1% on everything above
that figure.

New York

First $25,000—4%
Next $125,000—3-1/2%
Next $150,000—3%
All above
  $300,000—2%

North Carolina

Not more than 5% of receipts and
disbursements.

North Dakota

First $1,000—5%
Next $5,000—3%
Next $44,000—2%
All above $50,000, within the
discretion of the Court, but not
above 2%.

Ohio

First $1,000—6%
Next $4,000—4%
All above $5,000—2%

Oklahoma

First $1,000—5%
Next $4,000—4%
All above $5,000—2-1/2%

Oregon

First $1,000—7%
Next $9,000—4%
Next $40,000—3%
All above $50,000—2%

Pennsylvania

Practice is:
  5% principal + income—small estate
  3% principal + income—large estate

Rhode Island

Statute provides for just compensation.
An example of customary charges
follows:
  3% to 3-1/2% of principal value,
  depending on complexity of estate.

South Carolina

Not more than 2-1/2% on receipts
and disbursements.

South Dakota

First $1,000—5%
Next $4,000—4%
All above $5,000—2-1/2%

Tennessee

No statutory fee schedule or
minimums. The following is an
example of suggested reasonable
rates:
  First $20,000—5%
  Next $80,000—4%
  Next $200,000—3%
  All above $200,000—2%

Texas

Not more than 5% of the value of the
administered estate. If compensation
unreasonably low, court may allow
reasonable compensation.

Utah

First $1,000—5%
Next $4,000—4%
Next $5,000—3%
Next $40,000—2%
Next $50,000—1-1/2%
All above $100,000—1%

Vermont

Statute provides $4 for each day's
attendance on business. Probate court
may allow further compensation.

Virginia

No statutory fee schedule or
minimums. The following is an
example of suggested reasonable
fees:
On principal:
  First $50,000—5%
  Next $50,000—4%

Washington

Statute provides for reasonable compensation minimum.
The following is an example of reasonable fees:
  First $5,000—5%
  Next $5,000—4%
  Next $10,000—3-1/2%
  Next $180,000—3%

West Virginia

Statute provides for reasonable compensation "in the form of a commission on receipts or otherwise." Example of customary rate is 5% on receipts.

Wisconsin

2% inventory value of property.

Wyoming

First $1,000—10%
Next $4,000—5%
Next $15,000—3%
All above $20,000—2%

USING TREASURY BONDS TO PAY ESTATE TAXES

Many estate owners enable their executors to take advantage of a peculiar feature of certain U.S. Treasury Bonds. Most of these bonds can be purchased at a discount from their par value. Yet, assuming they are still selling below par at the time of the decedent's death, they can nevertheless be turned in at par for the purpose of paying federal estate tax. Even a purchase in anticipation of death will permit the estate to get the benefit of the discount. It doesn't matter how long the decedent has held the bonds, so long as they were owned by him and formed a part of his estate at the time of his death.

Since these bonds form a part of the decedent's estate, the question arises as to how they are to be valued in the estate. The 2nd Circuit has ruled that to the extent the bonds can be used at par to pay estate taxes, whether or not they are so applied, they are to be valued at least at par in the gross estate (*Bankers Trust Co.*, 284 F.2d 537, 1960; *Fried*, 445 F.2d 979, 1970). The Tax Reform Act of 1976 has reduced, but not eliminated, the estate tax advantage inherent in such bonds when bought at a discount from par, by enacting the carryover basis rules. On redemption of the bonds, the Executor will incur a capital gain tax on the difference between par value and carryover basis (including the fresh start rules, if held on 12/31/76).

**Treasury Bonds Which Can Be Redeemed at Par
to Pay Federal Estate Taxes***

Series

4-1/4s, May 1975-78
3-1/4s, June 1978-83
4s,   Feb. 1980
3-1/2s, Nov. 1980
3-1/4s, May 1985
4-1/4s, Aug. 1987-92
4s,   Feb. 1988-93
4-1/8s, May 1989-94
3-1/2s, Feb. 1990
3s,   Feb. 1995
3-1/2s, Nov. 1998

*The market prices of these bonds can usually be found in many daily newspapers under the heading "Government Securities."

NUMBER OF WITNESSES REQUIRED FOR A WILL

It is usually provided by statute that a will be signed in the presence of witnesses, or that the will and signature be subsequently shown to the witnesses, who then sign as such. The following table shows the number of witnesses required by each state statute. Presented immediately below the table are a few comments on other witnessing requirements as they vary from state to state.

Alabama (2)	Illinois (2)	Montana (2)	Rhode Island (2)
Alaska (2)	Indiana (2)	Nebraska (2)	South Carolina (3)
Arizona (2)	Iowa (2)	Nevada (2)	South Dakota (2)
Arkansas (2)	Kansas (2)	New Hampshire (3)	Tennessee (2)
California (2)	Kentucky (2)	New Jersey (2)	Texas (2)
Colorado (2)	Louisiana (2)	New Mexico (2)	Utah (2)
Connecticut (2)	Maine (3)	New York (2)	Vermont (3)
Delaware (2)	Maryland (2)	North Carolina (2)	Virginia (2)
Dist. of Columbia (2)	Massachusetts (3)	North Dakota (2)	Washington (2)
Florida (2)	Michigan (2)	Ohio (2)	West Virginia (2)
Georgia (2)	Minnesota (2)	Oklahoma (2)	Wisconsin (2)
Hawaii (2)	Mississippi (2)	Oregon (2)	Wyoming (2)
Idaho (2)	Missouri (2)	Pennsylvania (0)	

Notes

A. As a practical matter, it is a good idea to have a will witnessed by at least 3 persons.

B. In most states, the following procedure is adhered to: the witnesses must sign in the presence of the testator, but not necessarily in the presence of each other; the testator must either sign in the presence of the witnesses before they sign or acknowledge his signature to them before they sign; (*Pennsylvania* does not require subscribing witnesses at the time of the will's execution, merely that the witnesses attest to the testator's signature; this attestation can even be after the testator's death.)

C. In the following states, the above procedure is adhered to except that the witnesses must sign in the presence of each other; *Colorado* (will still be valid where witness signed before testator); *Florida, Illinois, Montana, New Jersey, New Mexico* (witnesses must be present at time of execution), *Rhode Island, South Carolina, Tennessee, Utah* (testator must sign in presence of witnesses), *Vermont, Virginia, West Virginia* and *Wisconsin.*

D. *Louisiana* witnesses of a mystic will sign an already sealed instrument without seeing the signature when handed them by the testator. Prior to signing as witnesses, they must hear testator declare that the paper is his will; then the notary in whose presence the declaration is made shall draw up a subscription form on the paper or on the envelope holding same, which subscription is then signed by the testator, the notary and the witnesses. Louisiana also has provisions for other types of wills, some of which require from 3 to 7 witnesses. Also, a will is valid which is executed in the following manner: testator signs each separate sheet in the presence of 2 witnesses and notary all three of whom then sign at the end in his presence and in the presence of each other.

WHEN MARRIAGE, DIVORCE, OR BIRTH OF A CHILD CAN
CAUSE REVOCATION OR MODIFICATION OF A WILL

In many cases, a properly drawn will continues to be perfectly valid in its entirety even though the testator subsequently married, became divorced, or had a child. In other cases, statutory law or the decided cases, cause certain wills to be revoked (totally or partially) or to be modified on the occurrence of one or more of these three events.

To give you a working guide as to what you must do to avoid revocation or modification (if you want to avoid those consequences) or when you must revise a will because it would otherwise be revoked or modified, the following table, based on both statutes and case law, outlines the effect of marriage, divorce, and birth of a child on a previously drawn will in each of our states. (As to marriage, the table deals with the automatic effect of the law, not with provisions which may allow a surviving spouse to elect against a will.)

State laws for the following tables should be checked for recent changes enacted by state legislation.

MARRIAGE

Revokes Will

Alabama (women only)	Kentucky	South Carolina
Alaska	Massachusetts[3]	(woman's will);
Arizona[1]	Minnesota	man's will[8]
California[2]	Montana[1,6]	South Dakota[1]
Colorado[3]	Nevada[2]	Utah (man's will[1])
Connecticut[4]	North Carolina[7]	Washington[1]
Delaware[5]	North Dakota[1]	West Virginia[4]
Georgia[3]	Oklahoma (woman's	Wisconsin[1,3]
Hawaii (women only)	will); man's will[1]	
Idaho (woman's will);	Oregon[1]	
man's will[1]	Rhode Island[3]	

[1] If spouse survives and will has no provision for such contingency and no provision is made in marriage contract.

[2] Only as to surviving spouse, if will makes no provision for such contingency and no provision is made in marriage contract.

[3] Unless made in contemplation of marriage.

[4] Unless it provides for this contingency.

[5] Unless it contains provisions for spouse or spouse is otherwise provided for.

[6] Unless will provides to contrary.

[7] Unless surviving spouse elects to dissent without entire will being revoked.

[8] Unless in contemplation of marriage and wife or children of marriage survive.

Modifies Will to Give Spouse Intestate Share

Florida	New York[9]	Pennsylvania[10]

[9] Unless provision made for surviving spouse by antenuptial agreement. Statute applies only to wills executed before 9/1/30. But revisers' notes indicate that similar rights should apply as to later wills.

[10] Unless will grants larger share.

Has No Effect

Arkansas	Maryland	Ohio
District of Columbia	Michigan	Tennessee
Illinois	Mississippi	Texas
Indiana	Missouri	Utah (woman's will)
Iowa	Nebraska	Vermont
Kansas	New Hampshire	Virginia
Louisiana	New Jersey	Wisconsin
Maine	New Mexico	Wyoming

DIVORCE

Revokes Part of Will Making Provision for Spouse

Alabama	Kansas	Oakland
Alaska	Kentucky	Oregon
Arkansas	Michigan[11]	Pennsylvania
Colorado	Minnesota[11]	South Carolina
Connecticut	Missouri	Tennessee[11]
Florida	Nebraska[11]	Texas
Hawaii	Nevada	Virginia
Illinois	New Mexico	Washington
Indiana	New York[12]	Wisconsin
Iowa	North Carolina	Wyoming[11]

[11] When coupled with property settlement.
[12] Unless will expressly provides otherwise.

Revokes Will

Georgia[13]

[13] Unless made in contemplation of divorce.

Has No Effect

Arizona	Maryland	Ohio
California	Massachusetts	Rhode Island
Delaware	Mississippi	South Dakota
District of Columbia	Montana	Utah
Idaho	New Hampshire	Vermont
Louisiana	New Jersey[14]	West Virginia
Maine	North Dakota	

[14] Unless will makes it clear that bequest to spouse will be effective only if marriage still exists at the testator's death.

BIRTH OF CHILD

Revokes Will

California[15]	Kentucky[21]	North Dakota[19]
Connecticut[16]	Louisiana[16]	Oklahoma[19]
District of Columbia[20]	Maryland[18]	South Dakota[19]
Georgia[17]	Michigan[20]	Texas[23]
Hawaii[18]	Mississippi[21]	Utah[19]
Idaho[19]	Montana[19]	
Kansas[20]	New Jersey[22]	

[15] As to surviving child, where both marriage and birth are subsequent events, and contingency not provided in the will or by settlement.
[16] Unless the contingency is covered in the will.
[17] Unless made in contemplation of birth of child.
[18] Where both marriage and birth are subsequent events and will make no provision for these contingencies.
[19] Where both marriage and birth are subsequent events (and either spouse or

child survives) and no settlement has been made by will or otherwise. (In North Dakota, Oklahoma and South Dakota, only if child survives.)

[20] Where both marriage and birth are subsequent events.

[21] If no child was living when will made which does not provide for contingency, subject to being reinstated if child dies a minor, unmarried and without issue.

[22] Where no child living when will made and contingency not provided for in will.

[23] If no child was living when will made which does not provide for contingency, subject to being reinstated if child dies within one year of testator. (Has no effect if surviving spouse is named as principal beneficiary.)

Modifies or Partially Revokes Will Which Does Not Provide for this Contingency and Gives Child Intestate Share

Alabama	Massachusetts[24]	Oklahoma [24,25]
Alaska	Michigan	Oregon[24,25]
Arizona	Minnesota[24]	Pennsylvania[30]
Arkansas	Mississippi[29]	Rhode Island
California[24]	Missouri[26]	South Carolina
Colorado	Montana[24,25]	South Dakota[24,25]
Delaware[24]	Nebraska	Tennessee[24]
Florida[25]	Nevada[25]	Texas[29,31]
Idaho[24]	New Hampshire	Utah
Illinois	New Jersey[29]	Vermont
Indiana[26]	New Mexico	Washington
Iowa[24]	New York[24]	West Virginia[32,29,27]
Kentucky[24,27]	North Carolina	Wisconsin
Maine[25]	North Dakota[24]	
Maryland[28]	Ohio[24]	

[24] Unless child otherwise provided for.

[25] Unless child has received equivalent of intestate share by advancement. (In Maine, omission is obviously intentional and does not result from mistake.)

[26] Has no effect on children living when will made leaving everything to spouse.

[27] Unexpended share reverts to will beneficiaries if child dies while a minor, unmarried, and without issue.

[28] If will provides for children living when will made.

[29] If children living when will made, unless child otherwise provided for.

[30] Out of share not passing to surviving spouse.

[31] Has no effect if will leaves substantially everything to surviving spouse.

[32] If no child living when will made.

Has No Effect

Virginia	Wyoming[33]

[33] Apparently, birth of a child subsequent to will would not have any effect.

INDEX

*All index references are to paragraph (¶) numbers.